MICROHISTORIES OF COMPOSITION

MICROHISTORIES OF COMPOSITION

Edited by
BRUCE McCOMISKEY

UTAH STATE UNIVERSITY PRESS
Logan

© 2016 by the University Press of Colorado

Published by Utah State University Press
An imprint of University Press of Colorado
5589 Arapahoe Avenue, Suite 206C
Boulder, Colorado 80303

All rights reserved
Manufactured in the United States of America

 The University Press of Colorado is a proud member of
The Association of American University Presses.

The University Press of Colorado is a cooperative publishing enterprise supported,
in part, by Adams State University, Colorado State University, Fort Lewis College,
Metropolitan State University of Denver, Regis University, University of Colorado,
University of Northern Colorado, Utah State University, and Western State Colorado
University.

The paper used in this publication meets the minimum requirements of the American
National Standard for Information Sciences—Permanence of Paper for Printed Library
Materials. ANSI Z39.48-1992

ISBN: 978-1-60732-404-1 (paperback)
ISBN: 978-1-60732-405-8 (ebook)

Library of Congress Cataloging-in-Publication Data

Microhistories of composition / edited by Bruce McComiskey.
    pages cm
  ISBN 978-1-60732-404-1 (paperback) — ISBN 978-1-60732-405-8 (ebook)
1. Microhistory. 2. Historiography. I. McComiskey, Bruce, 1963–
  D16.138.M53 2016
  907.2—dc23

                           2015012845

For my teachers and mentors,
who taught me the importance of history,
especially . . .

Jim Berlin
Janice Lauer
Jan Neuleib
Ed Schiappa

CONTENTS

MICROHISTORIES OF COMPOSITION

INTRODUCTION

Bruce McComiskey

Once a year, every summer, I clean out my office at work, filing documents and memos that have been stacking up for months, reshelving books thrown lazily in haphazard piles, shredding and discarding old papers and exams. I do not relish this annual task, and by the time I get to my filing cabinet, I am always tired and bored enough to limit my work to the bare necessities. Every year, toward the end of this long and unpleasant day, I saw that red accordion folder in the back of my bottom filing-cabinet drawer, and every year I just left it there, completely unaware of its contents but convinced that if I had once placed it in that location, then that's where it must belong. So there it stayed for maybe thirty years.[1] But one recent summer, May or June 2013, was different. I decided to begin this distasteful annual task with my filing cabinet because space was becoming increasingly limited, and I needed to vet its contents more carefully than I had done in the past. And there was that red accordion folder, this time unavoidable. I pulled it from the drawer, unwound the latch, and lifted the flap, revealing some very old papers. As I slid the papers from their hiding place, I quickly realized what they were: this folder contained every essay I had written during my undergraduate degree at Illinois State University, including six handwritten essays from my fall 1982 section of English 101.

The identity of the person who wrote those compositions (as we called them) in 1982 was not even close to the identity of the person who was staring at them, somewhat bemused, a third of a century later. Back then, I was an eighteen-year-old physical-education major (it's a long story) enrolled in a slate of required general-education courses, but now I'm a teacher and a scholar whose specialized discipline is composition studies. Although I have never done any significant archival research, there I was, sitting in my office, staring at my own personal archive, and I had written its entire contents. To say the least, I became curious, having genuinely forgotten nearly all of this experience, so I started reflecting and reading.

DOI: 10.7330/9781607324058.c000

COMPOSITION, 1982

Since printed histories of composition studies covering the 1960s through the 1980s were far more present to my conscious mind than the actual events of 1982, I began my personal archival journey with one main question: what was going in rhetoric and composition at that time? Thinking back to all the disciplinary histories I have read through the years, four things in particular came to mind about composition studies from the early 1970s through the early 1980s: the emergence of PhD programs in the field; the transition from modes to rhetorical genres; the shift from product-centered pedagogies to process pedagogies; and the turn from individualist to social epistemologies.

Histories of composition studies reveal that the 1970s and 1980s were deeply fertile decades for the field since a number of significant changes were taking hold. Janice M. Lauer explains that several forces converged throughout the 1970s to professionalize rhetoric and composition as a full-fledged academic discipline, including the establishment of sixteen PhD programs, each producing college teachers trained in classical and modern rhetorics (Lauer 2003, 14–15). In 1987, David W. Chapman and Gary Tate identified no fewer than fifty-three doctoral programs in rhetoric and composition (Chapman and Tate 1987). Robert J. Connors (1981) writes about the rise of the modes of discourse in the nineteenth century and their fall and abandonment during the 1960s, replaced by pedagogies rooted in linguistics and rhetoric. Lad Tobin (1994) locates the birth of the writing process movement in the 1960s and 1970s with the work of Donald Murray, Janet Emig, Peter Elbow, James Moffett, and Ken Macrorie, and in 1982 Maxine Hairston described a complete paradigm shift in composition studies from product-centered pedagogies to process-centered pedagogies (Hairston 1982). In *Rhetoric and Reality*, James A. Berlin explains that the categories of composition pedagogies he describes there were no longer "as descriptive" after 1975 since even individualist pedagogies had shifted their grounding principles in the direction of social epistemologies (Berlin 1987, 183–89). By the early 1980s, then, graduate programs in rhetoric and composition were producing a new class of English professors interested in researching and teaching writing, not literature; the modes of discourse had fallen into disrepute and were supplanted by rhetorical genres; product-centered pedagogies had been replaced by process-centered pedagogies that emphasized students' own writing, not anthologies of model essays; and writing was increasingly being theorized and taught as a social act.

After reflecting on these transformations in composition studies during the late 1970s and early 1980s, I felt ready to approach the essays I had written during my own first semester in college, fall 1982. I decided to read the essays chronologically, arranging them by the dates listed in each heading. My teacher, S. G. McNamara, had written her name in red near the heading of my first essay, indicating that this was a required element in headings for her class. McNamara was a PhD candidate at the University of Illinois specializing in eighteenth-century British literature, if I remember correctly. Though not trained in rhetoric and composition, McNamara was a great teacher. She was invested in her students' development as writers, and she was partly responsible for my initial interest in the craft of writing, though my commitment to the discipline of rhetoric and composition would come a little bit later.[2]

As I flipped through the pages of my first composition, I noticed right away that it was clearly a narration. Before I could finish reading this essay, I had to know—was I looking at a stack of EDNAs, as Sharon Crowley (1990) might call them? *EDNA* is Crowley's acronym for the modes: exposition, description, narration, and argument. I saw no descriptive essay, which was strange, though my narration included a lot of concrete details covering all five senses, so perhaps those two modes were combined. But certainly, following that initial narration (incorporating description), exposition and argument were well represented. The next four essays were expositions (definition, classification/analysis, comparison/contrast, and cause/effect), and the last essay was an argumentative/persuasive research paper with a long formal outline stapled to the front. One of McNamara's comments at the end of this research paper refers to my note cards, so I must have used that method as a way to record bibliographic information and quotations from sources.

The textbook we used, *The Writer's Rhetoric and Handbook* (McMahan and Day 1980), first edition, published in 1980, was written by Elizabeth McMahan, Illinois State University's (then) director of composition, and Susan Day, who was an instructor of English at ISU. I know the title and edition of the textbook because in my cause/effect essay I cited a line from Bob Dylan's "Subterranean Homesick Blues," which was printed in the text and thus listed in my works cited. McMahan and Day were both literature specialists, and many of the examples of style and structure in the textbook are excerpts from works of American poetry and fiction. Just curious, I typed Elizabeth McMahan's name into the catalog database of the library at my current institution, the University of Alabama at Birmingham. To my utter surprise, there is actually a copy of the first edition of *The Writer's Rhetoric and Handbook* on the shelves. This textbook begins in an almost enlightened way with a brief discussion of rhetoric, including sections on invention, audience, purpose, tone, and formality; however, all of these sections put together occupy less than ten pages of the first chapter. Chapter 2, "Peerless Paragraphs," moves straight into relentlessly formalist patterns of development, such as narrative, process, definition, classification and analysis, comparison and contrast, and cause and effect. Chapter 3, "Writing Effective Sentences," emphasizes coordination and subordination, periodic and cumulative sentences, and concision. In Chapter 4, "Writing Strong Essays," students find that what is good for a paragraph is also good for an essay since the sections in this chapter also break down into patterns of development, including narrative, process, definition, classification and analysis, comparison and contrast, cause and effect, and persuasion and argument (which, interestingly, are considered practically synonymous). Chapter 4, I presume, is where all the essay assignments came from.

Class periods, I remember, often included discussions of essays that demonstrated the modal structure we were writing at the time. I know there was an anthology required for the class, but I could not say what it was, and there is no evidence of its identity in any of my compositions. I assume, then, that these essays were not meant to generate ideas for our own writing but were simply meant to be structural models: that is, we were expected to strip the content and mimic the format. We also wrote a lot in class, which makes sense. Scholars who were developing writing-process pedagogies during the 1970s encouraged teachers to let students compose during class, providing opportunities for teachers to intervene directly in students' writing processes. However, McNamara, perhaps unsure of how to handle the pedagogical downtime, usually graded our essays while we wrote, though she was happy to answer any questions we might have had. The day before our final essays were due, we brought rough drafts to class for peer-review sessions. I do not remember being prompted to say anything in particular about each draft, and I am certain we did not submit our drafts or our peer-review comments with our final compositions. Most likely, only a few students actually benefitted from this kind of undirected peer review, for which we were not held accountable in any way. McNamara's teaching methods (determined in part, at least, by the common departmental syllabus McMahan had designed) were generally formalist, and there was nothing social about them. Class discussions served formalist ends and did not construct a community of writers. Students wrote "together" in class, but only as individuals sitting in the same room. Peer review generated comments like "good job" or "great introduction," and after completing our reviews, the comments went into our folders never to be looked at again. We exchanged writing, of course, but this exchange had little effect (social or otherwise) on the compositions we produced. The only collaborative tasks students completed in the class were exercises from the book, and our goal was merely to generate correct answers, not to negotiate complex ideas.

So my experience in English 101, fall 1982, can be summarized like this: the class was led by a graduate student in literature, who taught composition as a means to a different end (though I had the sense that McNamara liked what she was doing); the textbook emphasized modal structures and divided essays into paragraphs, paragraphs into sentences, and sentences into grammatical units, ending with a list of 1,500 commonly misspelled words; students were taught "the writing process," but it was not emphasized in the curriculum, amounting to writing in class and peer-review workshops that were not valued or assessed; we were individual composition students, sitting together while writing in class but not creating a community of writers or engaging each other in the social play of ideas.

As I reflected on all of these memories flooding my mind, I was struck most of all by the fact that my own experience in first-year composition did not coincide with any of the best-known histories of the discipline. Based purely on my understanding of the narratives of composition history, I would have dated the compositions in that red accordion folder to the 1950s or 1960s, but certainly not to the 1980s. So were the historical narratives I had studied so closely wrong about composition studies in the 1970s and early 1980s? Or was there something more interesting going on (more interesting than simple negation or evidence to the contrary)? Were the essays in my own personal archive clues to a more complicated history of composition than I had previously perceived? And if so, why had I been unable to perceive this complexity?

My understanding of composition history (acquired from long hours spent reading Berlin, Crowley, Connors, Fulkerson, and others) created in me what Kenneth Burke calls a "trained incapacity," or "that state of affairs whereby one's abilities can function as blindnesses" (Burke 1954, 7). Burke explains that when a certain structure of knowledge that served our purposes in the past limits our ability to understand evolving and emerging situations, then these structures of knowledge "become an incapacity" (10). According to Burke, people often continue to act (ineffectively) according to these incapacities because "the very authority of their earlier ways interferes with the adoption of new ones" and because it is "difficult for them to perceive the nature of the reorientation required" (23). My trained incapacity was the belief that real historical writing had to be the composition of abstract narratives that tell coherent stories based on credible evidence, and my reliance on the legitimating function these stories served made any alternative difficult for me to perceive. However, as I encountered puzzling concrete experiences and contradictory evidence in my own personal archive, I was forced to reassess my assumptions regarding what history is, what historical narratives do, and how historical evidence should be marshaled in the service of an argument. I began to wonder, where are all the people in these histories of composition studies? I do not mean people like Ann E. Berthoff or Edward P. J. Corbett or Janet Emig or Fred Newton Scott or Sondra Perl. Their names are produced (or, more likely, reproduced) in every narrative. I mean people like S. G. McNamara, and me, her student at Illinois State University in 1982. Where were we? Has real teaching been abstracted out of our narratives of composition history? Have teachers and students been erased by the drive for temporal progression and narrative coherence? Has each individual classroom been obliterated by the abstraction *pedagogy*?

The established narratives of composition history served an important function during the 1980s and 1990s, transforming a little-respected course into a full-fledged academic discipline that rejected past formalisms in favor of complex social epistemologies. However, by the turn of the twenty-first century, the stale terminology of these older histories no longer represented the realities of the discipline, as specialization both fragmented rhetoric and composition into a variety of subdisciplines and also provided its specialists opportunities to develop complex knowledge not possible in the previous century.

REVISIONARY HISTORIES IN COMPOSITION STUDIES

As I have indicated, the grand narratives of composition history published during the 1980s and 1990s served important social and academic functions without which composition studies may not have evolved into a full-fledged discipline. During the 1970s, our colleagues in English departments equated rhetoric and composition, the emerging discipline, with English 101, the class. But histories like Berlin's (1984, 1987), Faigley's (1992), and Miller's (1991) taught us and our colleagues that our academic foundations were grounded on critical inquiry into epistemology, ideology, and discourse, not the uncritical requirement of modes, five-paragraph themes, and grammar drills. Throughout the 1970s and 1980s, the actual practice of teaching college composition varied widely from institution to institution and from classroom to classroom, causing some of our colleagues in English departments to view rhetoric and composition as an incoherent collection of menial tasks based on whatever textbook happened to have been written and required by the director of composition. But histories like Connors's (1997) and Crowley's (1990, 1998) and Richard Fulkerson's (1990) taught us and our colleagues that our classroom practices were becoming increasingly coherent due to the depth of their intellectual foundations and the rejection of their collective nemesis, "current-traditional" rhetoric. Throughout the 1970s, the writing-process movement established individualist epistemologies as the dominant force in the development of new composition pedagogies, resulting in the brief reign of expressivism and cognitivism, which caused many of our colleagues in English departments to wonder if we were unaware of the linguistic and social turns in the discourses of the human sciences. But histories like Berlin's (1987), Crowley's (1998), and Faigley's (1992) taught us and our colleagues the value for rhetoric of a social orientation toward language and epistemology, culminating in the mantra *rhetoric is (social) epistemic.* Yes, these narratives abstracted, erased, and obliterated, but they also constructed a discipline. I might not be writing this introduction today if they had not done the work of narrating composition into its present disciplinary status during the formative decades at the end of the twentieth century.

More recent histories of composition studies, however, have consciously revised these earlier histories, both extending and challenging the knowledge constructed through the grand narratives of disciplinary evolution composed during the 1980s and 1990s. These extensions and challenges have taken a number of different forms, yet in every case they are critical of grand historical abstractions, and they rely heavily on archival sources that reflect local knowledge, not abstract trends. Shortly before the turn of the twenty-first century, scholars in the field had already begun to recover marginalized voices from the archives of composition, historicize traditionally ignored subjects like assessment and technology, and limit the periods and locations within which historical forces are investigated. These efforts were not exactly microhistories of composition since microhistory implies the integration of several related methods and attitudes toward the past, but their importance in the development of a more complete sense of composition history has certainly heralded a need to move in that direction.

Dissatisfied with traditional histories of composition studies that base their evidence for historical progression on white male scholars teaching at elite or flagship institutions with predominately white male student bodies, a number of recent composition researchers have turned to alternative sources of evidence for real-life accounts of writing and teaching in populations not often considered due to the processes of narrative abstraction. In *Traces of a Stream: Literacy and Social Change among African American Women*, for example, Jacqueline Jones Royster (2000) uses archival research and multidisciplinary sources to recover and articulate the literate acts of noted nineteenth-century African American women. As Royster explains, although she herself knows "quite well that African American women have actively and consistently participated over the years in public discourses and in literate arenas," the unfortunate fact is that these women have been systematically denied "the lines of accreditation, the rights of agency, and the rights to an authority to make knowledge and to claim expertise" (3). Since the means of accreditation and rights to construct social knowledge are often the first criteria historians use in their selection of legitimate sources about past events, African American women's literate acts have generally been ignored in histories of rhetoric and writing. In *Liberating Language: Sites of Rhetorical Education in Nineteenth-Century Black America*, Shirley Wilson Logan (2008) turns her critical focus toward literacy education and the ways in which writing and speaking were taught and learned by African Americans throughout the nineteenth century and especially after the Civil War in religious institutions, literary societies, and the black press. These institutions are not considered legitimate sites of rhetorical education by traditional historians, and thus the education that has taken place in these marginal locations is not included in standard histories of rhetoric and composition. Like Royster before her, Logan's aim is to tell a story traditional historiography cannot tell.

Continuing this drive to reveal untold stories of rhetoric and writing, in her 2008 book *Refiguring Rhetorical Education: Women Teaching African American, Native American, and Chicano/a Students, 1865–1911*, Jessica Enoch (2008) explains that the traditional histories of rhetorical education and writing instruction focusing on the late nineteenth century and early twentieth century emphasize the cultural, theoretical, and pedagogical principles promoted by white men teaching in elite schools preparing white male students for leadership positions in dominant social institutions. However, this narrative is incomplete if we take these teachers as representations of "rhetorical history" and "writing instruction" at that time, as if there were neither women teaching nor nonwhite students learning. Enoch explores the pedagogical theories and practices of five women (Lydia Maria Child, Zitkala-Ša, Jovita Idar, Marta Peña, and Leonor Villegas de Magnón) who taught writing and rhetoric to traditionally disfranchised students, including African Americans, Native

Americans, and Mexican Americans, negotiating their traditional gender identities as purveyors of white male cultural values and subverting their traditional pedagogical tasks of preparing students for leadership roles in white male society. In her book *To Know Her Own History: Writing at the Woman's College, 1943–1963*, Kelly Ritter (2012) draws extensively from archival research to trace the intersections of rhetoric, composition, and creative writing at the Woman's College, which would later become the University of North Carolina, Greensboro. Through her archival research, the method most commonly used in the local-history movement, Ritter uncovered rich resources relating to women's rhetorical education, an aspect of composition's past neglected by the traditional histories written by Berlin, Connors, and Faigley, for example. Again, these early historians were not wrong in their descriptions of white male writing instruction during the middle decades of the twentieth century; they were wrong in their presumption that women did not play a significant role in the history of writing instruction at that time. In 2008, David Gold published *Rhetoric at the Margins: Revising the History of Writing Instruction in American Colleges, 1873–1947*. Gold's (2008) archival approach to recovering marginalized voices in the history of composition breathes new life into tired narratives. Gold pushes beyond the epistemological and ideological problematics that structured early historical narratives and uses archival research to closely examine rhetoric and composition at a private black college, a public women's university, and a rural normal college. While epistemological and ideological frameworks may describe the elite teachers and institutions that dominate traditional histories, they do not represent the more public and critical rhetorics and writing pedagogies developed in black colleges, normal colleges, and women's universities.

Several books, published mostly within the last decade, examine single themes that had been neglected in histories of composition. James Inman's (2004) *Computers and Writing*, for example, is a history of what he calls the "cyborg era," from 1960 through 2004, the year the book was published. Inman does not situate computers and writing within composition history, and he does not cite a single standard narrative. There is no reason he should. Computers and composition generally developed independent of the epistemological and ideological categories (and the debates surrounding them) that dominated the works of Berlin, Connors, Crowley, Fulkerson, and Faigley. Thus, Inman focuses instead on the technologies emerging after 1960 and the scholars exploring the intersections of these technologies with writing. In his book *Remixing Composition: A History of Multimodal Writing Pedagogy*, Jason Palmeri

(2012) calls direct attention to the fact that historians (such as Berlin, Crowley, Ede, Harris, and Miller) have generally ignored "the crucial role of multimodality and new media within the development of composition as a field" (6). Palmeri's approach is different from Inman's, though. Rather than writing a history of multimodal composition completely independent of composition history, Palmeri argues instead that composition history has always contended with multimodal technologies—it just hasn't been self-critically aware that this is what it was doing. Norbert Elliot's (2005) *On a Scale: A Social History of Writing Assessment in America* traces the history of writing assessment from the late nineteenth century through 2004, the year before the book was published, only occasionally invoking narratives of composition history. These accounts of neglected themes in the history of composition tend not to contradict traditional histories; instead, they either ignore traditional histories altogether, articulating an independent narrative of their own, or they supplement traditional histories with richer treatments of important subjects that the drive toward narrative abstraction had prevented.

One of the most straightforward means of limiting the scope of abstract narrative history is to limit the years of coverage, describing a few years in rich detail rather than a few decades in generalized abstraction. Several of the works already discussed limit the time of analysis to a shorter period than was common in earlier histories of the discipline: Enoch's history covers forth-six years, Inman's covers forty-four years, Palmeri's covers twenty-two years, and Ritter's covers only twenty years. But other recent histories limit time periods even further. In his 2011 book, *From Form to Meaning: Freshman Composition and the Long Sixties, 1957–1974*, David Fleming examines the University of Wisconsin-Madison's first-year writing program during that seventeen-year period that was so formative in composition history. Fleming explains that very few of those formative principles made their way into the writing classrooms at UW-Madison. However, one memo that surfaced during a local-history project Fleming directed in a research-methods course at UW-Madison provided an account of a meeting in which the TAs who taught English 101 got into a disagreement (that may have ended in a verbal altercation) with the director of composition and the chair of English over the nature of the course and the methods for teaching it. As Fleming's students delved deeper into the UW-Madison archives of composition, they discovered that some interesting things were going on, interesting things nowhere represented in the standard histories of composition studies. Fleming writes,

In the UW Freshman English program, the most important development during these years [1957–1974] was the rise of a short-lived but potent pedagogy, simultaneously critical and humanist, developed almost entirely by English graduate student teaching assistants working by and among themselves, and reflective of (but not reducible to) the new world created by the war in Vietnam, the civil rights movement, the struggle for ethnic studies programs, and the other political, cultural, and ideological transformations of the time. . . .

It was a pedagogy that promoted relevance as the key criterion for selecting and evaluating educational materials and tasks, that advocated a radical decentering of classroom authority away from the teacher, that used "emergent" curricula responsive to the day-by-day life of the course and the growing human beings involved in it, and that rejected conventional grading as the ultimate assessment of student work.

It was a pedagogy that was also profoundly unacceptable to the tenured faculty in the English department at the time, who were unwilling either to relinquish control over the freshman course or to take an active interest in it. (Fleming 2011, 24)

For Fleming, a standard story or representative history of composition cannot possibly account for the real richness of writing instruction at UW-Madison or any other institution, for that matter. When history writers narrativize periods beyond the scope of several years, they abstract the importance and meaning out of real-life events. In their 2007 book *1977: A Cultural Moment in Composition*, Brent Henze, Jack Selzer, and Wendy Sharer take temporal limitation to a new level, focusing on just one year in culture, English studies, and rhetoric and composition, particularly as they played out in the composition program at Penn State University. With their critical focus trained on a single year, it is no surprise that Henze, Selzer, and Sharer discovered more contradictions than consistencies, and their limited scope allows them to forego the drive to construct coherent abstractions leading to a consistent narrative. Henze, Selzer, and Sharer (2007) write, "Some of the stories we heard and the historical traces we uncovered were contradictory, and the interpretations of events in the department varied widely. . . . Rather than tidying these disparate, filtered, and embedded traces of the past into a unified story of progress that would make Penn State's current program seem like the culmination of a steady, always admirable, and self-reflective path of progress, we have tried to retain the messy traces of these conflicts within our narrative and to highlight how very unpredictable and contingent writing program development can be" (viii). Such historical writing, which represents conflicts and contingencies, simply cannot appear in a work that covers eighty-five years of an entire discipline, as Berlin's *Rhetoric and Reality* does. The limited temporal scope of

Henze, Selzer, and Sharer's *1977: A Cultural Moment in Composition* allows them to represent a certain richness and complexity that more abstract histories simply cannot represent.[3]

What all of these recent revisionary histories represent is a challenge to traditional history's criteria of selection for what gets told in historical narratives and what gets left on the floor of the archive: women, African Americans, Latina/o Americans, Native Americans, assessment, multimodal composition, computers and writing, critical pedagogies in the time of current-traditional dominance, and the conflicts of composition in 1977 at Penn State University. All of these revisionary histories seek to represent the unrepresented, to describe the neglected in our present historical knowledge. However, these revisionary histories are also individually incomplete. In their drive toward understanding local practices, some employ just one or two means to limit the scope of historical analysis, and others neglect the larger contexts that construct and constrain the discipline. In "Remapping Revisionist Historiography," Gold suggests that "future historiographic research will increasingly seek to locate pedagogical practices within their wider spheres of historical development, better understand the interplay between local and global patterns, and acknowledge the mixed up goals and hybrid forms that most often mark classroom practices" (Gold 2012, 22). One historiographical approach that leads firmly toward this future research, Gold explains, is microhistory, which does "not merely describe a local scene, but use[s] the local to illuminate larger historical questions" (26). The value of microhistory as an extension of existing revisionary histories of composition is that it brings together a full collection of related methodologies, all of which together reduce the scale of historical analysis and increase the complexity of our current historical knowledge.

MICROHISTORY

Microhistory emerged during the 1970s among a small group of Italian Marxist historians who had grown increasingly dissatisfied with the state of academic history, including the hegemonic grand narratives of social history and the anecdotal descriptions of cultural history. According to Giovanni Levi, both abstract social history and decontextualized cultural history had simplified the historian's task unnecessarily, and microhistory emerged "from the necessity of reappropriating a full complexity of analysis, abandoning therefore schematic and general interpretations in order to identify the real origins of forms of behavior, choice, and solidarity" (Levi 2012, 123). Social history assumes that relatively unified social forces determine individual actions, and cultural history assumes that individuals act according to their own free will; but microhistory assumes every act is conditioned by multiple forces at varying levels, some imposed socially (by institutions) and others emerging personally (from desires), all in a complex dialectic. The intention of these early microhistorians was to negotiate a methodological middle ground, emphasizing the concrete details characteristic of cultural history but also placing those concrete details back into the larger contexts of social history. These early Italian microhistorians emphasized contextualized lived experience over lifeless abstractions and isolated events, recovered marginalized tactics as responses to hegemonic strategies, and began their historical work with evidence in the archives, subsequently building their arguments out toward larger contexts.

Many of the most salient characteristics of social history were established during the nineteenth century when history was seeking legitimation as an academic discipline in Europe (and, later, in the United States), and these characteristics continue to legitimate the academic study and practice of history and historiography even today. According to Georg G. Iggers, "Central to the process of professionalization was the firm belief in the scientific status of history" (Iggers 1997, 2). Social history, as a scientific discipline, would produce objective knowledge about the past, which progresses through inherently diachronic processes driven by structures of causality. It is the social historian's task, then, to write objective accounts of these "great historical forces" (Iggers 1997, 32), tracing each particular cause and its necessary effect until a coherent narrative emerges. Levi explains that "macro-interpretations strive for linearity, coherence, continuity, and certainty—even in a biography—and aim to convey an impression of completeness in the data presented, or at least of an authoritative, coherent, and all-inclusive authorial point of view" (Levi 2012, 129) The *telos* of social history is a general narrative of Western progress (toward modernization or rationalization), and each new historical work strives to cover more and more of that general narrative through processes of abstraction and quantification, using credible sources and actual events as examples that illustrate conceptual claims. Edward Muir calls this constant drive toward greater abstraction "the giantification of historical scale, which has crushed all individuals to insignificance under the weight of vast impersonal structures and forces" (Muir 1991, xxi). The evolution of powerful computers throughout the latter half of the twentieth century led practitioners of social history deeper into methods of quantification and statistical abstraction. Even some Marxist historians by the mid-twentieth century considered themselves positivist social historians, arguing that historical studies was an objective science whose primary subject was the dialectical progression of broad economic forces, and abstract quantification served their interests very well.

Throughout the late 1960s and 1970s, an increasing number of historians began to challenge the settled practices of social history, arguing that abstract and coherent grand narratives did not represent the daily activities or special contexts of marginalized populations, which are inherently concrete and complex. Iggers (1997) argues that cultural history was primarily a response to the postmodern turn in historical studies (and in the social and human sciences generally) that refuted the possibility of objective knowledge and its legitimation through grand narratives. In *The Postmodern Condition*, Jean-François Lyotard defines postmodernism as "incredulity toward metanarratives" (Lyotard 1984, xxiv), resulting in a relativistic emphasis on little stories (*petit récits*) in paralogical competition. Based on this rejection of the legitimating functions of metanarratives, cultural historians relate only constricted stories outside of any larger temporal or social context. Further, Lyotard explains, related to this incredulity toward metanarratives is the postmodern loss of faith in the truth of representation and the objectivity of knowledge. If representation is always political and knowledge is always situated (if not subjective), then historical accounts become more like literary narratives than scientific treatises. Thus, in direct opposition to the modernist failings of social history, postmodern cultural historians wrote detailed descriptions of minute (thus often marginalized) historical objects and events without reference to larger historical contexts.

During the mid-1970s, four Italian Marxist historians, Carlo Ginzburg, Giovanni Levi, Edoardo Grendi, and Carlo Poni, began to develop what we now know as *microhistory*, believing that both positivist social history and relativist cultural history had reached points of theoretical and practical exhaustion. Social history's constant drive toward abstraction and quantification had drained the very life out of history, seeking concrete examples only as support for conceptual claims about linear temporal progression, and its desire to tell coherent stories that transcend contradiction destined these narratives to recount only hegemonic (thus unified but only partial) perspectives on the past. Cultural history's constant drive toward detailed thick description had turned its interests away from larger historical questions, suggesting that any attempt to contextualize their findings results in fiction, not science, and the drive to represent the internal complexity of cultures overstates their independence from sources of social power. Although microhistory emerged out of a dissatisfaction with the abstract narratives of social history and the insular descriptions of cultural history, it is best to understand microhistory as a negotiation of social history and cultural history. According to István M. Szijártó, "Microhistory is able to apply the approaches of both social and cultural history: to grasp the meanings of the latter and provide the explanations of the former and, within the frames of a very circumscribed investigation, show the historical actors' experiences, how they saw their lives and what meanings they attributed to the things that happened to them on one hand and on the other give explanations with references to historical structures, long-lived mentalities and global processes using retrospective analysis, all of which were absent from the actors' own horizons of interpretation" (Magnússon and Szijártó 2013, 75). In other words, microhistory uses microscopic analysis and progressive contextualization to answer what Szijártó calls "great historical questions" (Magnússon and Szijártó 2013, 6, 53).[4]

Microhistory is neither solely abstract, like social history, nor solely concrete, like cultural history. Instead, microhistory's dialectical negotiation of these two positions results in a methodology that is multiscopic, equally valuing and dialectically employing both abstract narrative and concrete description in the service of historical arguments. Iggers explains, "There is no reason why a history dealing with broad social transformations and one centering on individual existences cannot coexist and supplement each other. It should be the task of the historian to explore the connections between these two levels of experience" (Iggers 1997, 104). And Ginzburg and Poni explain, "Microhistorical analysis therefore has two fronts. On one side, by moving on a reduced scale, it permits in many cases a reconstitution of 'real life' unthinkable in other kinds of historiography. On the other side, it proposes to investigate the invisible structures within which that lived experience is articulated" (Ginzburg and Poni 1991, 4). But for Ginzburg, the simple copresence of multiple scopes of analysis is not sufficient. Instead, "The specific aim of this kind of historical research should be . . . the reconstruction of the *relationship* (about which we know so little) between individual lives and the contexts in which they unfold" (Ginzburg 1994, 301). The goal, in other words, is not multiscopic copresence but the dialectical and analytical integration of multiple layers of scope in any historical interpretation. This dialectical analysis is especially critical in historical studies of individuals since "any individual has a different set of relationships which determine his or her reactions to, and choices with regard to, the normative structure" (Levi 2001, 101). For this reason, contextualized biography is one of the standard genres in microhistorical scholarship.[5]

So the microhistorical method of changing the scale is a historio-graphic, methodological principle, but it is also predicated on the belief that social actors act on different levels as well, that these scales are actu-ally embedded in phenomena, and that if we perceive only one scale, we perceive only a small portion of any total phenomenon. Risto Alapuro explains that "Microhistorians' contextualization work implies that all historical actors take part in processes and belong in contexts whose levels vary from local to global" (Alapuro 2012, 140). The scale that is changed in microhistorical analysis, in other words, is not just a theo-retical or methodological construct, it is also an aspect of real acts and their contexts. Szijártó explains that "social actors appear in different contexts, micro- and macro-, at the same time" (Magnússon and Szijártó 2013, 31). Thus, according to Bernard Lepitit, changing the scale in microhistory helps historians identify "those systems of context that form the framework of social action" (quoted in Magnússon and Szijártó 2013, 31). These levels are thus present in the experience of everyday life, with actors sometimes performing highly personal and individual acts and other times participating in highly overdetermined and insti-tutionalized acts. To understand only personal acts through cultural history or only overdetermined acts through social history results in an incomplete understanding of historical action generally. Since microhis-tory moves dialectically among all levels of experience, its analyses are more complete.

Engaging in multiscopic analysis not only enables historians to describe more of the contexts that contain (construct or constrain) his-torical actions, but it also generates more complex historical knowledge. By alternating the scales of historical investigation, new insights emerge that are invisible to the authors of both social histories and cultural his-tories. In "On Microhistory," Levi explains, "Phenomena previously con-sidered to be sufficiently described and understood assume completely new meanings by altering the scale of observation. It is then possible to use these results to draw far wider generalizations although the ini-tial observations were made within relatively narrow dimensions and as experiments rather than examples" (Levi 2001, 102). Microhistorians believe that by shifting back and forth among scopic levels (or levels of abstraction), or by beginning with microscopic analysis and spinning its effects out toward larger contexts, new knowledge is gained, deeper than any knowledge gained through analysis at one level (as in social history or cultural history alone). As Kathleen Blee points out, "Microhistorians accrue significant explanatory power by moving between attention to the particular and the wider context, between the small details of social life and the large context, between the micro level and the macro levels of society, and between time periods" (Blee 2008, 41). When all levels of abstraction are combined into a single analysis, all levels of knowledge are revealed, creating a more complete historical picture than either social history or cultural history alone can paint.

The scale of analysis in social history and cultural history has not only methodological implications but political implications as well. The subjects of social history are powerful individuals (politicians, rulers) and hegemonic institutions (empires, monarchies) since these are the forces that push history along on its grand temporal path. The subjects of cultural history are marginalized people (peasants, criminals) and popular culture (family, entertainment, work) since these are the constituents of immediate experience. Microhistory seeks neither the "normal" (hegemonic strategies) alone nor the "exceptional" (marginalized tactics) alone; microhistory, instead, seeks the exceptional normal (or the normal exception). The exceptional normal is a particular case in history that is exceptional from the perspective of social history but may reveal a hidden normal from the perspective of cultural history. John Brewer explains that the exceptional normal is "an event or practice that, viewed in the context of modern 'scientific' enquiry, seems exotic, remarkable, or marginal, but that, when properly investigated, that is, placed or coded in its proper context, reveals its own logic and order" (Brewer 2010, 97–98). The point of microhistory is not to narrate the normal or describe the exceptional but to interpret their relationship, shedding light on the normal and lending more than anecdotal significance to the exceptional. According to Muir, "Since rebels, heretics, and criminals are the most likely candidates from the lower or nonliterate classes to leave sufficient traces to become the subjects of microhistories, their behavior is, by definition, exceptional" (Muir 1991, xiv). However, "certain kinds of transgressions against authority constitute normal behavior for those on the social periphery, . . . those illegal or socially proscribed actions that were normal for those who had no other means of redress. Some transgressors, therefore, might be exceptions to the norms defined by political or ecclesiastical authorities but would be perfectly representative of their own social milieu" (xiv). The case of the exceptional normal can be extended from historical individuals and their actions to historical documents as well. Muir writes, "If documents generated by the forces of authority systematically distort the social reality of the subaltern classes, then the exceptional document, especially one that records the exact words of a lower-class witness or defendant, could be much more revealing than a multitude of stereotypical sources" (Muir 1991, xvi; see also Ginzburg and Poni 1991, 8). Seeking the exceptional normal, which reveals the intersections between social systems and cultural activities, is a central starting point in microhistorical methodology.

When the exceptional normal is a historical person, as it so often is, this person is understood by microhistorians to have contextualized agency, or a certain ability to act according to the exigencies of personal desires, though this ability is not comprehensive and some exigencies may be conditioned. Levi explains that in microhistory, "all social action is seen to be the result of an individual's constant negotiation, manipulation, choices, and decisions in the face of a normative reality which, though pervasive, nevertheless offers many possibilities for personal interpretations and freedoms" (Levi 2001, 98–99). And Muir writes, microhistory seeks to understand "individuals making choices and developing strategies within the constraints of their own time and place" (Muir 1991, viii). In other words, in microhistory the acts of the exceptional normal reflect a dialectical interaction of individual free will (the sole focus of cultural history) and social conditioning (the sole focus of social history). Levi explains that microhistory is "the study of events or persons in context, that is to say, within the complex interplay of free choice and constraint where individuals and groups perform in the interstices of the contradictory pluralities of the normative systems that govern them" (Levi 2012, 126). The social formations that grand narratives unify through abstraction are actually messy and contradictory in local practice, leaving individuals to negotiate these contradictions based, at least in part, on personal motives. Further, Szijártó explains that microhistorians "point to the fact that structures—at a given moment those unalterable conditions that limit the historical actors' freedom of action—are to a large extent the product of individual decisions that point to the responsibility of the actor" (Magnússon and Szijártó 2013, 69). Since social structures are formed through collections of individual decisions, and since individual decisions are actually responses to contradictions in social contexts, then a deep understanding of individuals' actions and motives, especially of those who resist social structures, reveals complex dynamics that neither abstract social history nor descriptive cultural history can reveal.

By shifting the scope of analysis from abstract or concrete to multiscopic, and in seeking the exceptional normal with contextualized agency, microhistorians also must shift their attitude toward the sources they use as evidence in the service of historical arguments. In social history, good sources are objective and legitimate, relating actual events as they happened. Any kind of subjectivity is grounds to disregard a source as biased. These sources are also arranged in serial progression, mirroring and thus supporting the temporal progression of the grand narrative. However, social history's source material "has primarily been concerned with the upper classes and their ideological, political, or economic actions" (Myrdal 2012, 156) since these are the actions (and their representative sources) that drive social history. In cultural history, good sources are salient, reflecting the unique perspective of an individual or an isolated culture and its inhabitants. Any kind of pretense toward objectivity is grounds to disregard a source as manipulative. However, cultural history's source material is uncommon, often discarded as irrelevant and a waste of archival space. In both of these cases, sources are chosen because they illustrate a priori assumptions about events under analysis: if they support grand-narrative abstractions, they are objective; if they support an isolated cultural zeitgeist, they are salient. For microhistorians, sources are not objective or biased, salient or manipulative; all sources are rhetorical, and source plurality is the goal. As Marjatta Rahikainen and Susanna Fellman explain, the microhistorical practice of "combin[ing] different kinds of source materials" is "more fruitful than repeated re-interpretations of the same contemporary texts" (Rahikainen and Fellman 2012, 22) and results in what Richard D. Brown calls a more "contextual, three-dimensional, analytic narrative" (Brown 2003, 18). Incorporating a plurality of sources not only gives a better total picture of the object or event in question, but since each source is part of a particular context (legal, familial, etc.), this plurality of sources also reveals "systems of contexts of the observed particular case" (Szijártó in Magnússon and Szijártó 2013, 44).[6] For microhistorians, sources are not either objective or biased since "no source is innocent" (Rahikainen and Fellman 2012, 26). Instead, all sources interpret events (for certain audiences and specific purposes), and the historian's task is to collect a variety of interpretations from which a full and complex understanding might emerge. The search for a plurality of sources often begins in the archives, following a trail of clues, and this investigative methodology requires a new orientation toward sources, an orientation Ginzburg (1989) calls the "evidential paradigm" and Matti Peltonen (2001) calls the "method of clues."

In "Clues: Roots of an Evidential Paradigm," one of the central methodological chapters from *Clues, Myths, and the Historical Method*, Ginzburg describes the "silent emergence of an epistemological model" during the latter half of the nineteenth century, and he calls this epistemological model the "evidential paradigm" (Ginzburg 1989, 96). This paradigm was shaped by the work of three intellectuals from the 1870s through the 1890s: Giovanni Morelli, an art historian; Arthur Conan Doyle, or, more specifically, his character Sherlock Holmes, a detective; and Sigmund Freud, the founder of psychoanalysis. These three historical figures shifted the focus of analysis within their respective fields from obvious signs to trivial details, inaugurating "a method of interpretation based on discarded information, on marginal data, considered in some way significant" (101). Conceptual analysis yields abstract knowledge, but, Ginzburg explains, for Morelli, Holmes, and Freud, "infinitesimal traces permit the comprehension of a deeper, otherwise unattainable reality" (101). Ginzburg traces the roots of this new evidential paradigm all the way back to the earliest human hunters and gatherers as an acquired "attitude oriented towards the analysis of specific cases which could be reconstructed only through traces, symptoms, and clues" (104). This ancient "semiotic" paradigm, however, was "suppressed by the prestigious (and socially higher) model of knowledge developed by Plato" (105). More recently, and specifically in history (although it is true of other disciplines as well), this evidential paradigm has been suppressed by scientific positivism despite the fact that history is a "highly qualitative" discipline and "historical knowledge is indirect, presumptive, conjectural" (106). According to Ginzburg, the evidential paradigm was resuscitated during the late nineteenth century by Morelli, Doyle, and Freud, and it is currently being reinvigorated by the practitioners of microhistory.

Matti Peltonen (2001) describes the "method of clues" as a historical practice associated with the new evidential paradigm described by Ginzburg. Social historians frame their grand narratives using temporal generalizations and broad social categories often derived from prior narratives, and they seek evidence that supports their conclusions. According to Peltonen, however, microhistorians use the method of clues by "starting an investigation from something that does not quite fit, something odd that needs to be explained. This particular event or phenomenon is taken as a sign of a larger, but hidden or unknown, structure" (Peltonen 2001, 349). In other words, microhistorians do not apply generalizations to evidence; they apply the lessons of evidence, sought as clues to something hidden, in the construction of new generalizations. For Peltonen, the method of clues is specifically multiscopic: "Take for instance the concept of the clue as a micro-macro relation. On the one hand a clue is something that does not quite fit in with its immediate surroundings, something that seems odd or out of place. It is in certain respects discontinuous with its environment. On the other hand a clue leads thought to somewhere else, reveals connections, exposes some secret or crime. So there is continuity, too, which is equally important" (357). Rather than taking credible or salient sources at their word (as in social and cultural history), microhistorians interpret "insignificant and marginal, unconsciously or routinely performed actions *as clues*" (Peltonen 2012, 45; my emphasis).

Multiscopic analysis, the evidential paradigm, and the method of clues all assume a dialectical movement among grand narratives and little stories, among social elites and cultural subalterns. Thus, microhistorians recognize, as Richard Maddox points out, that "hegemonic processes are Janus-faced. One dimension of hegemony centers on the direct political and ideological struggles of specific groups, parties, classes, and alliances to win and maintain leadership and control over the general direction of social life. . . . However, far less attention has been given to the second dimension of hegemonic processes. This dimension consists of the more diffuse, indirect, and illusive cultural politics that permeate the conduct of everyday life and shape commonsense understandings of what is valuable, desirable, and practical in particular circumstances" (Maddox 2008, 18). Microhistory reclaims this second dimension of hegemonic processes by viewing everyday life and commonsense understandings through a microscopic lens and then placing these understandings back into the context of power and authority. According to Muir, "Understanding what behaviors and ideas were beyond the pale [of established social norms] might also help to describe better the characteristics of the dominant group that defined what was considered normal" (Muir 1991, xiv), and "our understanding of official institutions can be redefined through microhistorical studies of persons who were subject to their influence" (xvi). Microhistories thus "show in particular how the behavior of marginal persons can be used to clarify the nature of authority" (xv). Historians can only understand the evolution of hegemonic power if they understand how hegemony has evolved in direct response to resistance and to what microhistorians call the *exceptional normal.*

One final characteristic of microhistory is the self-conscious presentation in the narrative itself of methodological assumptions and difficulties in the evidence. Levi (2001) explains that one of the central characteristics of published microhistory is "incorporating into the main body of the narrative the procedures of research itself, the documentary limitations, techniques of persuasion and interpretive constructions. This method clearly breaks with the traditional assertive, authoritarian form of discourse adopted by historians who present reality as objective.

In microhistory, in contrast, the researcher's point of view becomes an intrinsic part of the account. The research process is explicitly described and the limitations of documentary evidence, the formulation of hypotheses and the lines of thought followed are no longer hidden away from the eyes of the uninitiated" (Levi 2001, 110; also see Levi 2012, 124–25). Methodological self-consciousness places microhistorians in dialogue with the historical sources they interpret, not in a position of power over them, and it places the audience of the historical text in dialogue with the past.

Microhistories of Composition

The authors in this edited collection apply the theories and methods of microhistory to composition studies not as if microhistory has emerged out of a vacuum but as an extension and complication of existing revisionary histories, collecting their disparate methodologies into a more coherent and more powerful historical practice. The early histories of composition treated the discipline as if it were a unified body of knowledge and practices that evolved almost predictably in dialectical response to broad historical and social pressures, and social history is the genre of choice for describing such abstract progression toward teleological ends. However, composition, as both a body of knowledge and a collection of practices, has never been unified or predictable, and the historical and social pressures that motivate its evolution are always both local and global, both individual and social. Thus, among choices of historiographic methodologies, microhistory is ideally suited for the complexities of a discipline like composition, which emerged and developed in local sites yet also shows signs of more general social and historical influences.

Microhistory, as I have argued, explores the dialectical interaction of social (grand) history and cultural (local) history, enabling historians to examine uncommon sites, objects, and agents of historical significance overlooked by social history and restricted to local effects by cultural history. Uncommon sites might include a Canadian conference in 1979 and a school of expression in the late nineteenth century; uncommon objects might include archival materials, such as annual reports, broken and redirected URLs, federal-grant applications, and teaching materials; uncommon agents might include forgotten or misunderstood scholars. Microhistory's proclivity for the margins, the exceptions, the uncommon (but always viewed within larger contexts) makes it an ideal methodology for exploring composition's other histories, the histories not included in grand narratives, such as composition's struggle with labor issues, its difficult relationship with literary studies, and its presence in a variety of educational institutions (community colleges, normal schools, HBCUs, women's universities, and, of course, huge land-grant universities, some of which have PhD programs in rhetoric and composition or one of its bourgeoning areas of specialization). Microhistory, more than any other historiographic approach, can account for the dialectical interaction of local and general historical forces in the formation and development of composition studies in all of its myriad varieties and contexts, as each individual chapter in this edited collection illustrates in its own way.

I have not divided the chapters into distinct sections because all the authors apply methods from a common historiographical approach, microhistory. However, the book is structured to flow across crucial themes with a certain coherence. Chapters 1 (Mendenhall) and 2 (Phelps), for example, challenge common assumptions in disciplinary origin narratives, suggesting that the watershed years 1963 and 1979 have been misunderstood. Chapters 3 (Ritter) and 4 (Eyman and Ball) continue the theme of disciplinarity, yet they shift focus from watershed years to salient texts, challenging the hegemony of published (print) journal articles in our understanding of composition's past. The next two chapters, 5 (Bordelon) and 6 (Zebroski), broaden their emphasis from years and texts to certain salient categories that drive grand-narrative histories of composition, including expressionism and grammar instruction, illustrating that archival research and a limited scope of analysis reveal complexity masked by narrative abstraction. Chapters 7 (Stock), 8 (Lerner), and 9 (Gold) also emphasize archival research, yet they shift their purpose from the critique of grand narratives to the recovery of little-known figures in composition history, theorizing along the way the reasons for their marginalization. The final two chapters, 10 (Gogan) and 11 (Craig, Davis, Martorana, Mehler, Mitchell, Ricks, Zawilski, and Yancey), retain a biographical emphasis, but they shift their purpose from recovering marginalized figures to reinterpreting central individuals, reframing their work by placing them into institutional and historical contexts available only through archival research and oral history. The remaining pages of this introduction provide detailed summaries of each chapter.

In Chapter 1, "'At a Hinge of History': Rereading Disciplinary Origins in Composition," Annie S. Mendenhall explains that 1963 represents a watershed moment in composition history, partly because of certain publications from that year that legitimated composition as an academic discipline. In *The Uses of the University,* Clark Kerr identifies 1963 as a "hinge of history" in university education, a bond between a historical frame and a door that opens to a new future. According to Mendenhall, two 1963 publications in composition studies—Richard Braddock, Richard Lloyd-Jones, and Lowell Schoer's *Research in Written Composition* (*RWC*) and Albert R. Kitzhaber's *Themes, Theories, and Therapy: The Teaching of Writing in College* (*TTT*)—also represent a hinge of history for the discipline, but the hinge Mendenhall describes is different from the hinge described in composition's best-known histories. For scholars such as Berlin, Connors, and North, *RWC* and *TTT* represent the first conscious attempts to shift composition's devotion to formalist or haphazard practice (current-traditional rhetoric, lore, etc.) toward a new interest in empirical research, thus initiating composition's rise to disciplinary status. Mendenhall, however, uses methods of microhistory to demonstrate that the authors of these 1963 texts were not concerned with a forward-looking attempt at disciplinary formation but instead with a backward-looking attempt to secure research funding from federal and private granting agencies and connect, in the process, with existing American cultural values. They were responding, in other words, more to the federal government's National Defense Education Act and NCTE's response, the National Interest, than they were to any perceived exigency to transform composition into a discipline. In the process of narrative abstraction in search of disciplinary origins, the contexts (the textual environment and personal motives) of real historical actors are replaced with the contexts (progress, development, democratization, rationalization) of historical writing. Using the microhistorical concern for reduced scale of analysis, and drawing from articles written by Lloyd-Jones and Kitzhaber after 1963, Mendenhall recovers (recontextualizes) the textual ecologies and personal motives that surrounded the production of *RWC* and *TTT,* identifying these watershed texts as rather mundane responses to funding exigencies, including the federal privileging of science and technology during the Cold War and the Space Race.

In Chapter 2, "The 1979 Ottawa Conference and Its Inscriptions: Recovering a Canadian Moment in American Rhetoric and Composition," Louise Wetherbee Phelps examines three conference proceedings volumes (*Reinventing the Rhetorical Tradition, Teaching/Writing/Learning,* and *Learning to Write: First Language/Second Language*) as inscriptions of the 1979 Ottawa Conference. This conference and its inscriptions represent a watershed moment in rhetoric and composition's development as a discipline, yet their character as multidisciplinary and multinational has been largely ignored in the historical grand narratives of composition studies, which tend to identify the field as a phenomenon unique to the United States. Phelps describes Ottawa 1979 as an "interaction ritual" in which knowledge is generated through sincere conversation, face-to-face engagement, dynamic interaction, social networking, emotional investment, diverse viewpoints, and creative conflict. Academic conferences are prototypical interaction rituals, and Ottawa 1979 was a critical context for generating knowledge about writing studies and forming rhetoric and composition into a discipline. In particular, the three volumes of conference proceedings edited by Aviva Freedman, Ian Pringle, and (for *Learning to Write*) Janice Yalden define rhetoric and composition as an intellectual discipline in its own right, with characteristic theories and practices, yet they also describe it as international in its reach. Freedman, Pringle, and Yalden, as Canadians (not from the United States), were "outliers" in the very discipline they helped to create, and the three conference proceedings they edited represent the exceptional normal: normal because they were familiar with the American phenomenon of rhetoric and composition; exceptional because they were not situated in the national context where rhetoric and composition was taking hold. Phelps draws from microhistorical methodologies to examine Ottawa 1979 and its inscriptions as a lost Canadian moment in North American rhetoric and composition.

In Chapter 3, "Journal Editors in the Archives: Reportage as Microhistory," Kelly Ritter argues that historical work on unusual source materials such as journal editors' annual reports can provide insights into the evolution of composition studies not available in published journals. Journal editors are often what microhistorians call "outliers," not average citizens of the rhetoric and composition community, and emphasizing the limited scope (or "minor episodes," as microhistorians call them) of the annual reports written by these outliers can both challenge and reinforce claims in established grand narratives of the field. Ritter draws from her own experience as the editor of *College English* to explore how the annual reports of past editors of both *College English* and *College Composition and Communication* (from 1954 to 1979) address issues that promoted and hindered the evolution of composition studies as a disciplinary formation. These reports comment directly and in highly personal ways on themes such as disciplinary identity in relation to literature and composition, revealing, for example, that insiders viewed the two journals not as competitors but as a cooperative team concerned with the equal development of English studies and composition studies. This insight counters narratives that assume *College English* favored literature and was either disinterested in or resistant to scholarship in composition. The editors' annual reports also reveal a concern for the work of editors who meant well but also had to deal with more submissions from scholars in a developing discipline than they were equipped to handle. Ritter's close attention to a limited time period and a single, usually ignored source of evidence represents microhistory's desire to make historical knowledge more complex.

In Chapter 4, "History of a Broken Thing: The Multijournal Special Issue on Electronic Publication," Douglas Eyman and Cheryl E. Ball direct their microscopic attention toward a special issue on electronic publishing, copublished simultaneously in 2002 by five different online journals: *Kairos, Enculturation, Academic.Writing, The Writing Instructor,* and *CCC Online.* This multijournal special issue was designed to both theorize and exemplify the power of electronic publishing; however, its very status as online discourse caused certain problems that were, at the time, unforeseeable. Eyman and Ball point out, for example, that among these five online journals, only *Kairos* has published consistently since the special issue went live, and *CCC Online* (at least its 2002 iteration) is not only inactive now but was also never archived, making at least one article in the special issue extremely difficult to access. Only two of the twelve articles published in the special issue are still available at their original URLs. However, despite its status as "a broken thing," the multijournal special issue on electronic publishing tapped into some of the key themes in digital publishing that were pressing at the time and resonate even today, including hypertext/theory, archiving/history, issues/challenges, pedagogy, and tenure/review. Eyman and Ball's microhistorical examination of this ground-breaking special issue that became a broken thing leads not to despair but to lessons learned and new best practices. With attention to three forms of infrastructure (scholarly, social, and technical), existing online journals and future online publishing venues will avoid the problems that plagued the 2002 multijournal special issue by insuring their accessibility, usability, and sustainability.

In Chapter 5, "Tracing Clues: 'Bodily Pedagogies,' the 'Action of the Mind,' and Women's Rhetorical Education at the School of Expression," Suzanne Bordelon uses methods of microhistory to recover expression and elocution from their present historical disparagement. Using the method of clues, Bordelon seeks the unsettled over the established, the strange over the familiar, the unexplained over the known, and in the process discovers an approach to expression that integrates mind, body, and voice into a unified pedagogy with precedents in ancient sophistic rhetorical education. Anna Baright Curry and Samuel Silas Curry, founders and directors of the School of Expression in Boston during the late nineteenth and early twentieth centuries, are described as "normal exceptions" in Bordelon's analysis, as exceptions to the dominant historical narratives that actually represent a different kind of norm among competing, though forgotten, voices in rhetorical history. Bordelon explains that the Currys emphasized not the mechanical movements and scripted vocalizations of what we now understand as expression and elocution, but instead they emphasized bodily movement and vocal representations as effects of emotion and intellect, necessitating their simultaneous and dialectical development. Thus, in addition to poetic recitation and oratorical performance, students at the Curry School of Expression learned gymnastics and pantomime, invoking similarities between this bodily pedagogy and the rhetorical education of the Sophists in ancient Greek gymnasia.

In Chapter 6, "Teaching Grammar to Improve Student Writing? Revisiting the Bateman-Zidonis Studies," James T. Zebroski employs microhistory's method of clues and conjectural (or evidential) paradigm to shift the scale of analysis from sweeping generalizations about grammar instruction to a specific examination of the Bateman-Zidonis projects conducted and described from 1959 to 1973. The earliest commentaries on Bateman and Zidonis's work limit their influence to sentence combining, and later discussions categorize their work with others who argued that teaching grammar improves student writing. However, Bateman and Zidonis's work is actually complex and defies simplistic categories (sentence combining, grammar instruction). These simplistic interpretations of Bateman and Zidonis resulted, Zebroski argues, first from an incomplete reliance on only one document in the Bateman-Zidonis corpus (their abridged 1966 NCTE report) and second from the narrative drive to abstract complex scholarship into coherent narratives of development (from grammar to style, for example). Zebroski reinterprets Bateman and Zidonis's work by revisiting their published scholarship, most of which has been completely ignored by modern historians, and by working to complete, as much as possible, a Bateman-Zidonis archive, filled with unpublished (or recently archived) research reports, grant applications, in-house manuscripts, and conference presentations. Zebroski follows a series of clues throughout this archival material, letting the plurality of evidence tell a new story, one in which Bateman and Zidonis had no interest in sentence combining and little interest in structural grammar or its teaching. Zebroski finds evolving interests throughout the Bateman-Zidonis projects, with later, more mature

documents (circa 1970) advocating instruction in the new transformational linguistics (not structural grammar) as a means for students and
teachers alike to inquire into the structures and functions of language.
It was through this mutual inquiry into language that Bateman and
Zidonis would find improvement in their students' writing, especially at
the sentence level. Thus, by shifting the scale of analysis from a history of
grammar in writing instruction toward a microscopic analysis of a plurality of sources in the emerging Bateman-Zidonis archive, Zebroski finds
linguistic complexity and methodological inquiry, not structural grammar and drill-and-kill exercises.

In Chapter 7, "Who Was Warren Taylor? A Microhistorical Footnote
to James A. Berlin's *Rhetoric and Reality*," David Stock argues that the
early histories of rhetoric and composition served important legitimating functions but also acquired subsequent normative effects that limited the terms of historical analysis to outmoded concepts and limited
subjects. In Particular, Stock argues that Berlin's *Rhetoric and Reality* was
itself the product of a specific historical moment in which rhetoric and
composition was being recovered as a discipline through its connection with social epistemologies and democratic politics. In this context,
Berlin praises Warren Taylor's 1938 essay "Rhetoric in a Democracy" as
an important early appeal to composition as a form of public (not private or formulaic) discourse. Berlin attributes some of Taylor's progressive political (thus rhetorical) views to his location, the University of
Wisconsin-Madison, which was a bastion of liberal politics at the time.
However, Stock points out, Warren Taylor never taught at the University
of Wisconsin-Madison; Warner Taylor, whose 1929 *A National Survey of
Conditions in Freshman English* is often cited in composition histories,
did. This simple misattribution in Berlin's text led Stock to write a brief
footnote about it in his dissertation, but a different focus forced him
to leave it behind. Stock's chapter in this volume is the development of
that footnote into a microhistorical recovery of Warren Taylor's evolving understanding of the roles of rhetoric, composition, literature,
and humanism in a liberal education that emphasizes participation
in democracy. Employing a microhistorical reduced scale of analysis,
Stock focuses on Warren Taylor's complete life and work as they evolved
and changed over time, viewing Taylor as an individual with historical
agency. Through archival research at Oberlin College, where Warren
Taylor taught for most of his career, Stock finds that Taylor valued
rhetoric and composition as a pedagogical means to prepare students
for participation in a democratic society; however, over the course of
his career, Taylor's interest in rhetoric faded and his commitment to

literature and the humanities emerged. Toward the middle and end of his career, Warren Taylor had stopped teaching composition, instead devoting his time to developing and teaching two advanced seminars, The Humanistic Tradition and The Twentieth Century. These courses, which included religion, literature, and philosophy, among other themes, prepared students for the critical thinking and complex writing they would need to participate in democratic life. Stock's microhistorical recovery of Warren Taylor's evolving view of composition, rhetoric, literature, and humanism adds complexity to Berlin's account of rhetoric's intersections with liberal education during the early and middle decades of the twentieth century.

In Chapter 8, "Remembering Roger Garrison: Composition Studies and the Star-Making Machine," Neal Lerner argues that the name-tag game we often play at conferences (look at the face, look at the name tag, look back at the face) is symptomatic of a larger historical process of remembering and forgetting. During the early writing-process movement, especially in writing center and one-on-one conferencing scholarship, Garrison's work was often cited, and he was considered among the major players of the time, which also included Peter Elbow, Janet Emig, and Donald Murray. However, as composition constructed its historical genealogies throughout the 1980s and 1990s, only those scholars who had institutional credibility seem to have been remembered. Murray, Elbow, and Emig all taught at well-recognized institutions, while Garrison spent his career at little-known Westbrook College in Portland, Maine. After about 1984, when composition studies began to examine its disciplinary history with some vigor, Murray, Elbow, and Emig were frequently referenced by, for example, Berlin, Connors, Crowley, Maureen Daly Goggin, and North. But Garrison had been forgotten, never cited once by any of these historians, a victim of the star-making process and composition's historical drive toward disciplinary legitimation. However, Lerner's microhistorical analysis of Garrison's work on conferencing and the writing process reveals that he was a normal exception, an individual who was not remembered in grand historical narratives but who was otherwise representative of teachers whose classrooms were filled with students writing and rewriting, editing and discussing. Thus, Garrison's work and legacy are worth remembering because he represents the norm, the teachers who work in undergraduate classrooms consulting with students on their writing and making a difference.

In Chapter 9, "Elizabeth Ervin and the Challenge of Civic Engagement: A Composition Teacher's Struggle to Make Writing Matter," David Gold analyzes the evolution of Elizabeth Ervin's published works related to public literacy and civic engagement. Grand narratives of rhetoric and composition tend to characterize certain influential scholars as if their ideas were conceptually static, having little space or time in the process of historical abstraction to consider personal and professional change over time. However, Gold's microhistorical reduction of scale enables him to consider the complex evolution of Ervin's thought over time regarding the role of civic engagement in her own writing classrooms. Covering the full extent of Ervin's publishing career, just a brief nineteen years (cut short by illness), Gold traces Ervin's development from her early enthusiasm for teaching civic engagement, through her own self-critical evaluation of those early successes and failures, and finally to her later attenuation of the promise of civic engagement in public-writing pedagogy. Gold's reduction of the scale of historical analysis also enables him to understand Ervin as a historical actor with agency, not the material effect of inexorable social forces. The evolution of Ervin's thinking and teaching over time, however short, illustrates that the force of her will, in both scholarship and teaching, derived not from surfing the tide but from making waves. Ervin's own historical agency emerged from self-critical examinations of her own practice and the resulting work her students produced. As a work of microhistory, Gold's analysis of Ervin's published career reveals nuances that would be lost in the process of grand-narrative abstraction.

In Chapter 10, "Going Public with Ken Macrorie," Brian Gogan reduces the scale of his inquiry to an individual whose complex scholarship and teaching has been simplified to an abstract category in the most influential grand narratives of the field. Ken Macrorie most often appears in these narratives as the poster child for expressivist rhetorics and pedagogies, but, Gogan points out, much of Macrorie's public rhetoric is ignored in the interest of coherence. Microhistorians seek historical sources known as *outliers*, sources that tend to get ignored by writers of grand narratives because they are messy, inconsistent, and difficult to reconcile with established stories. Since microhistorians seek outliers, their narratives are often centered less around the story of composition and more around the journey of discovery. Gogan writes about his encounter with one of Macrorie's early essays, "Spitting on the Campus Newspaper," and how this essay did not seem to fit in with, for example, Berlin's history of the expressivist movement and Macrorie's central role in it. Tracing evidence in the archives at Western Michigan University, where Macrorie taught throughout the 1960s and 1970s, Gogan finds evidence of a Macrorie who was dedicated not to radical individualism but to going public, especially with his students. Throughout the archival documents studied by Gogan (annual reports, unpublished lectures, and letters to administrators) there is clear evidence that Macrorie encouraged his writing students to publish their essays in the student newspaper and in magazines and that he taught courses about public language. Macrorie's relationship to public and personal writing was, in other words, complex, not simple, and complexity is difficult to represent in grand narratives of composition.

In Chapter 11, "Against the Rhetoric and Composition Grain: A Microhistorical View," Jacob Craig, Matthew Davis, Christine Martorana, Josh Mehler, Kendra Mitchell, Anthony N. Ricks, Bret Zawilski, and Kathleen Blake Yancey argue that the experience of individuals in rhetoric and composition is often different from the ethos represented in their published work, and the best way to recover such experience is through oral history. These authors conducted an interview with Charles Bazerman, focusing on his entry into and development within the discipline of rhetoric and composition. They discovered that while there were clear historical pressures influencing his perceptions of the field in its infancy, Bazerman was also free to resist and reject certain normative functions that came along with emerging disciplinarity. For the authors of this chapter, Bazerman is a normal exception who operated within normative structures yet retained individual agency, ultimately influencing composition through his exceptional beliefs and practices. In particular, Bazerman resisted the individualism developing in certain communities in the 1960s, turning toward social theory for his grounding in writing instruction. When open admissions came to the CUNY system where he was teaching, Bazerman turned away from the pedagogical emphasis of Mina Shaughnessy, for example, and advocated research into writing per se and attention to writing at all academic levels. This interest in writing research led him eventually to rhetoric; however, while other influential scholars were looking to classical rhetoric, Bazerman saw greater potential in the works of more recent rhetoricians like Adam Smith and Joseph Priestly, pragmatists like John Dewey, and linguists like Lev Vygotsky. Bazerman's interest in rhetoric and in writing research at all academic levels led him inevitably toward an early commitment to writing across the curriculum (WAC), but Bazerman favored a model of WAC in which composition teachers were not experts disseminating knowledge of academic writing but co-researchers with students into the possibilities and constraints of disciplinary communication. Bazerman, according to the authors of this chapter, is a normal exception, a teacher and scholar who was aware of some of the normative aspects of the emerging discipline of composition studies, accommodating some of these aspects and rejecting others, acting as an individual historical agent in social context.

Throughout the pages of this collection, the authors all engage in the dialectical processes of microhistory, integrating cultural history's interest in isolated acts, events, and people with social history's interest in broader contexts for social action. In so doing, we have tried to illuminate new aspects of composition's history that have been previously masked by the discipline's early drive toward abstract narrative histories, and we have also tried to illustrate a relatively new methodology on the scene of rhetorical historiography, opening it up to further use and development. Microhistory, we believe, has the potential to make composition history more complex, and we look forward to future microhistories of composition.[7]

Notes

1. Though my filing cabinets changed occasionally as I moved around, the placement of this folder always remained constant.

2. In the fall of 1983, I became a tutor in the university writing center, administered at the time by Janice Neuleib, who asked all of her tutors to read one short article or chapter about composition pedagogy for each of our weekly staff meetings. It was during this semester that I became hopelessly hooked on rhetoric and composition (the discipline, not just the craft of writing) and changed my major from physical education to English education.

3. There are, of course, other ways to limit the scope of historical analysis, thereby increasing the complexity of its results. In Patricia Lambert Stock's (2012) edited collection *Composition's Roots in English Education*, the contributing authors explore the little-known early development of composition in schools of education, not departments of English. In L'Eplattenier and Mastrangelo's (2004) edited collection *Historical Studies of Writing Program Administration: Individuals, Communities, and the Formation of a Discipline*, contributors examine the lives and careers of early WPAs whose work was ignored in histories of the discipline. In Donahue and Flesher Moon's (2007) edited collection *Local Histories: Reading the Archives of Composition*, the contributing authors explore archival methodologies as alternatives to traditional historiographic methods that result in incomplete understandings of composition's past. And in Massey and Gebhardt's (2011) edited collection *The Changing of Knowledge in Composition: Contemporary Perspectives*, contributors reexamine the historical and contemporary importance of Stephen North's (1987) *The Making of Knowledge in Composition*. These texts, like the others discussed in this section on revisionary histories in composition studies, reduce the scope of analysis by limiting the subject under study.

4. *Context* is a key term throughout most microhistory theory, yet its meaning and application are contested. For example, Magnússon and Szijártó (2013) articulate their own differences of opinion throughout *What Is Microhistory?* with Szijártó arguing that microhistory must consider larger historical contexts if it is to distinguish its method and purpose from cultural history and Magnússon arguing that microhisto-

ry is most effective when it maintains exclusive attention to the microscopic level of analysis. Further, even among microhistorians who agree that microscopic analyses gain power when they are placed back into larger historical contexts, the nature of those contexts is also contested. Levi (2001, 2012) argues that microhistory should begin with microscopic analyses and then refer those analyses back to abstract historical narratives, supplementing them and making them more complex. But Ginzburg (1980) argues that contexts should not exist prior to analysis and should be constructed from available evidence, building a context for individual acts, for example, by tracing clues in the archives until a social context emerges. I see no reason to take sides in the debate between Levi and Ginzburg since both senses of context are useful, and the one a historian prefers ought to be determined by the object of analysis. However, I do disagree with Magnússon, siding instead with Szijártó's claim that the distinction and value of microhistory is in its dialectical analysis of the relationship between microscopic objects and their broader contexts.

5. Linda Gordon (2008) explains that "in a simple sense, biography is always microhistory, inasmuch as individuals are the 'micro' in relation to the 'macro' themes of social and political history" (145).

6. Brown agrees, explaining that "because the microhistorian narrows the scope and shrinks the scale of his or her research, she or he can justify the time spent pursuing such stray facts so as to link data found in census records, vital records, town meeting and selectmen's records, tax records, probate records, land registries, court documents, diaries, letters, as well as printed sources—newspapers, pamphlets, book subscription lists, local histories, and individual biographies. Through these linkages, one comes to understand, however subjectively, the multiple contexts in which people made their decisions and acted out their lives. One recognizes that behavior rests on more than one or two planes selected from among the usual suspects—class, race, gender, economic interest, religious or ethnic identity" (Brown 2003, 18–19).

7. I would like to thank Suzanne Bordelon, David Gold, Neal Lerner, Annie Mendenhall, Louise Wetherbee Phelps, David Stock, and James Zebroski for providing helpful advice on an earlier draft of this introduction. I am also grateful for a productive WebEx conversation with Phelps's students from her summer 2014 graduate seminar, The Past Is the Future—Laurie Stankavich, Sherie Mungo, Aubrey Mishou, Corwin Baden, Sara Brandt, Danielle Huff, Jennifer Hitchcock, Kelly Cutchin, Michelle Maples, and Nathaniel Cloyd—which included, among other things, a discussion of an early draft of this text.

References

Alapuro, Risto. 2012. "Revisiting Microhistory from the Perspective of Comparisons." In *Historical Knowledge: In Quest of Theory, Method, and Evidence*, edited by Susanna Fellman and Marjatta Rahikainen, 133–54. Newcastle upon Tyne: Cambridge Scholars.

Berlin, James A. 1984. *Writing Instruction in Nineteenth-Century American Colleges*. Carbondale: Southern Illinois University Press.

Berlin, James A. 1987. *Rhetoric and Reality: Writing Instruction in American Colleges, 1900–1985*. Carbondale: Southern Illinois University Press.

Blee, Kathleen. 2008. "The Hidden Weight of the Past: A Microhistory of a Failed Social Movement Group." In *Small Worlds: Method, Meaning, and Narrative in Microhistory*, edited by James F. Brooks, Christopher R.N. DeCorse, and John Walton, 37–52. Santa Fe, NM: School for Advanced Research.

Brewer, John. 2010. "Microhistory and the Histories of Everyday Life." *Cultural and Social History* 7 (1): 87–109. http://dx.doi.org/10.2752/147800410X477359.

Brown, Richard D. 2003. "Microhistory and the Post-Modern Challenge." *Journal of the Early Republic* 23 (1): 1–20. http://dx.doi.org/10.2307/3124983.

Burke, Kenneth. 1954. *Permanence and Change: An Anatomy of Purpose.* Berkeley: University of California Press.

Chapman, David W., and Gary Tate. 1987. "A Survey of Doctoral Programs in Rhetoric and Composition." *Rhetoric Review* 5 (2): 124–86. http://dx.doi.org/10.1080 /07350198709359143.

Connors, Robert J. 1981. "The Rise and Fall of the Modes of Discourse." *College Composition and Communication* 32 (4): 444–55. http://dx.doi.org/10.2307/356607.

Connors, Robert J. 1997. *Composition-Rhetoric: Backgrounds, Theory, and Pedagogy.* Pittsburgh, PA: University of Pittsburgh Press.

Crowley, Sharon. 1990. *The Methodical Memory: Invention in Current-Traditional Rhetoric.* Carbondale: Southern Illinois University Press.

Crowley, Sharon. 1998. *Composition in the University: Historical and Polemical Essays.* Pittsburgh, PA: University of Pittsburgh Press.

Donahue, Patricia, and Gretchen Flesher Moon, eds. 2007. *Local Histories: Reading the Archives of Composition.* Pittsburgh, PA: University of Pittsburgh Press.

Elliot, Norbert. 2005. *On a Scale: A Social History of Writing Assessment in America.* New York: Peter Lang.

Enoch, Jessica. 2008. *Refiguring Rhetorical Education: Women Teaching African American, Native American, and Chicano/a Students, 1965–1911.* Carbondale: Southern Illinois University Press.

Faigley, Lester. 1992. *Fragments of Rationality: Postmodernity and the Subject of Composition.* Pittsburgh, PA: University of Pittsburgh Press.

Fleming, David. 2011. *From Form to Meaning: Freshman Composition and the Long Sixties, 1957–1974.* Pittsburgh, PA: University of Pittsburgh Press.

Fulkerson, Richard. 1990. "Composition Theory in the Eighties: Axiological Consensus and Paradigmatic Diversity." *College Composition and Communication* 41 (4): 409–29. http://dx.doi.org/10.2307/357931.

Ginzburg, Carlo. 1980. *The Cheese and the Worms: The Cosmos of a Sixteenth-Century Miller.* Translated by John Tedeschi and Anne E. Tedeschi. Baltimore, MD: Johns Hopkins University Press.

Ginzburg, Carlo. 1989. *Clues, Myths, and the Historical Method.* Translated by John Tedeschi and Anne E. Tedeschi. Baltimore, MD: Johns Hopkins University Press.

Ginzburg, Carlo. 1994. "Checking the Evidence: The Judge and the Historian." In *Questions of Evidence: Proof, Practice, and Persuasion across the Disciplines,* edited by James Chandler, Arnold I. Davidson, and Harry Harootunian, 291–303. Chicago, IL: University of Chicago Press.

Ginzburg, Carlo, and Carlo Poni. 1991. "The Name and the Game: Unequal Exchange and the Historiographic Marketplace." In *Microhistory and the Lost Peoples of Europe,* edited by Edward Muir and Guido Ruggiero, 1–10. Translated by Eren Branch. Baltimore, MA: Johns Hopkins University Press.

Gold, David. 2008. *Rhetoric at the Margins: Revising the History of Writing Instruction in American Colleges, 1873–1947.* Carbondale: Southern Illinois University Press.

Gold, David. 2012. "Remapping Revisionist Historiography." *College Composition and Communication* 64 (1): 15–34.

Gordon, Linda. 2008. "Biography as Microhistory, Photography as Microhistory." In *Small Worlds: Method, Meaning, and Narrative in Microhistory,* edited by James F. Brooks, Christopher R.N. DeCorse, and John Walton, 145–71. Santa Fe, NM: School for Advanced Research.

Hairston, Maxine. 1982. "The Winds of Change: Thomas Kuhn and the Revolution in the Teaching of Writing." *College Composition and Communication* 33 (1): 76–88. http:// dx.doi.org/10.2307/357846.

Henze, Brent, Jack Selzer, and Wendy Sharer. 2007. *1977: A Cultural Moment in Composition.* West Lafayette, IN: Parlor.

Iggers, Georg G. 1997. *Historiography in the Twentieth Century: From Scientific Objectivity to the Postmodern Challenge.* Middletown, CT: Wesleyan University Press.

Inman, James A. 2004. *Computers and Writing: The Cyborg Era.* Mahwah, NJ: Lawrence Erlbaum.

L'Eplattenier, Barbara, and Lisa Mastrangelo, eds. 2004. *Historical Studies of Writing Program Administration: Individuals, Communities, and the Formation of a Discipline.* West Lafayette, IN: Parlor.

Lauer, Janice M. 2003. "The Spaciousness of Rhetoric." In *Beyond Postprocess and Postmodernism: Essays on the Spaciousness of Rhetoric,* edited by Theresa Enos and Keith D. Miller, 3–21. Mahwah, NJ: Lawrence Erlbaum.

Levi, Giovanni. 2001. "On Microhistory." In *New Perspectives on Historical Writing.* 2nd ed. Edited by Peter Burke, 97–119. University Park: Pennsylvania State University Press.

Levi, Giovanni. 2012. "Microhistory and the Recovery of Complexity." In *Historical Knowledge: In Quest of Theory, Method, and Evidence,* edited by Susanna Fellman and Marjatta Rahikainen, 121–32. Newcastle upon Tyne: Cambridge Scholars.

Logan, Shirley Wilson. 2008. *Liberating Language: Sites of Rhetorical Education in Nineteenth-Century Black America.* Carbondale: Southern Illinois University Press.

Lyotard, Jean-François. 1984. *The Postmodern Condition: A Report on Knowledge.* Translated by Geoff Bennington and Brian Massumi. Minneapolis: University of Minnesota Press.

Maddox, Richard. 2008. "Lived Hegemonies and Biographical Fragments: Microsteps toward a Counterhistory of the Spanish Transitions from Dictatorship to Democracy." In *Small Worlds: Method, Meaning, and Narrative in Microhistory,* edited by James F. Brooks, Christopher R.N. DeCorse, and John Walton, 15–35. Santa Fe, NM: School for Advanced Research.

Magnússon, Sigurður Gylfi, and István M. Szijártó. 2013. *What Is Microhistory? Theory and Practice.* London: Routledge.

Massey, Lance, and Richard C. Gebhardt, eds. 2011. *The Changing of Knowledge in Composition: Contemporary Perspectives.* Logan: Utah State University Press.

McMahan, Elizabeth, and Susan Day. 1980. *The Writer's Rhetoric and Handbook.* New York: McGraw-Hill.

Miller, Susan. 1991. *Textual Carnivals: The Politics of Composition.* Carbondale: Southern Illinois University Press.

Muir, Edward. 1991. "Introduction: Observing Trifles." In *Microhistory and the Lost Peoples of Europe,* edited by Edward Muir and Guido Ruggiero, vii–xxviii. Translated by Eren Branch. Baltimore, MA: Johns Hopkins University Press.

Myrdal, Janken. 2012. "Source Pluralism as a Method of Historical Research." In *Historical Knowledge: In Quest of Theory, Method, and Evidence,* edited by Susanna Fellman and Marjatta Rahikainen, 155–89. Newcastle upon Tyne: Cambridge Scholars.

North, Stephen. 1987. *The Making of Knowledge in Composition: Portrait of an Emerging Field.* Upper Montclair, NJ: Boynton/Cook.

Palmeri, Jason. 2012. *Remixing Composition: A History of Multimodal Writing Pedagogy.* Carbondale: Southern Illinois University Press.

Peltonen, Matti. 2001. "Clues, Margins, and Monads: The Micro-Macro Link in Historical Research." *History and Theory* 40 (3): 347–59. http://dx.doi.org/10.1111/0018-2656 .00172.

Peltonen, Matti. 2012. "The Method of Clues and History Theory." In *Historical Knowledge: In Quest of Theory, Method, and Evidence,* edited by Susanna Fellman and Marjatta Rahikainen, 45–76. Newcastle upon Tyne: Cambridge Scholars.

Rahikainen, Marjatta, and Susanna Fellman. 2012. "On Historical Writing and Evidence." In *Historical Knowledge: In Quest of Theory, Method, and Evidence,* edited by Susanna Fellman and Marjatta Rahikainen, 5–44. Newcastle upon Tyne: Cambridge Scholars.

Ritter, Kelly. 2012. *To Know Her Own History: Writing at the Woman's College, 1943–1963.* Pittsburgh, PA: University of Pittsburgh Press.

Royster, Jacqueline Jones. 2000. *Traces of a Stream: Literacy and Social Change Among African American Women.* Pittsburgh, PA: University of Pittsburgh Press.

Stock, Patricia Lambert, ed. 2012. *Composition's Roots in English Education.* Portsmouth, NH: Boynton/Cook.

Tobin, Lad. 1994. "Introduction: How the Writing Process Was Born—And Other Conversion Narratives." In *Taking Stock: The Writing Process Movement in the 90s,* edited by Lad Tobin and Thomas Newkirk, 1–14. Portsmouth, NH: Heinemann.

1

"AT A HINGE OF HISTORY" IN 1963
Rereading Disciplinary Origins in Composition

Annie S. Mendenhall

Universities in America are at a hinge of history: while connected with their past, they are swinging in another direction.
— Clark Kerr, The Uses of the University

In 1963, University of California president Clark Kerr delivered a series of lectures at Harvard on the state of the American university, published as *The Uses of the University.* In that now famous work, Kerr argued that American universities had become integral to national welfare and economic success—"a prime instrument of national purpose" (Kerr 2001, 66). Kerr employs a synecdoche—the hinge—to describe this shift as a doorway to a new era, evoking grand acts of entrance and transition. In doing so, he mirrors the way composition historians have talked about disciplinary origins. Take, for example, Stephen M. North, who, in *The Making of Knowledge in Composition,* pinpoints "the birth of modern Composition, capital C, to 1963. And what marks its emergence as a nascent academic field more than anything else is this need to replace practice as the field's dominant mode of inquiry" (North 1987, 15). Emergence and replacement function like Kerr's hinge, separating (but not severing) modern composition from its lore-based past. The parallels in Kerr's and North's arguments invite us to revisit the structure of historical narratives of composition and to reread how we use markers, moments, and objects to define historical transitions.

North and other early composition historians share another commonality with Kerr: the belief that the 1960s was a transformative decade. According to many historical narratives of the field, the increasing visibility of composition research in the 1960s—and in 1963 in particular—forged new legitimacy for composition. Robert J. Connors argues that during the years between 1960 and 1965, "the efforts of . . . new theorists changed the face of the field forever" (Connors 1997, 205),

DOI: 10.7330/9781607324058.c001

creating the modern discipline of composition studies. Connors singles out the 1963 Conference on College Composition and Communication (CCCC) as "qualitatively changed from earlier conferences" (206). The year 1963 is also cited anecdotally by scholars, including, for example, David Smit, who calls it "the year the profession came of age" (Smit 2004, 2), and Louise Wetherbee Phelps (2010, 124) in her "Composition Studies" entry in the *Encyclopedia of Rhetoric and Composition*. For many historians, key publications in 1963 catalyzed this disciplinary emergence—specifically Richard Braddock, Richard Lloyd-Jones, and Lowell Schoer's *Research in Written Composition* (*RWC*) and Albert R. Kitzhaber's *Themes, Theories, and Therapy: The Teaching of Writing in College* (*TTT*). For example, James A. Berlin's (1987, 135) *Rhetoric and Reality* calls *RWC* a sign that composition was "confident of its value and its future [as a] discipline." North refers to *RWC* as "the charter of modern Composition" (North 1987, 17) and calls *TTT* "the first book-length study of college writing" (North 1987, 14). Both *RWC* and *TTT*, self-described "reports," called for scholarly attention to writing, and historians have considered them formative texts that authorized research in the field.

Reflecting on the impact of *RWC*, Lloyd-Jones has noted that historians viewed its publication as "a watershed for separating the old order in composition studies from the new," although the authors "considered [them]selves as doing routine status summaries of conventional empirical research as a basis for identifying sound practice" (Lloyd-Jones 2006, 18). The disconnect between the motives of researchers like Lloyd-Jones and the interpretation of historians invites a reexamination of 1963 in light of new historiographies that disrupt the idea of fixed disciplinary origins. Microhistory serves as a useful analytical stance for this project because it changes the scale of analysis from entire decades or centuries to moments and individuals. More important, microhistory attempts to account for the complexity of historical contexts by maintaining "sensitivity to the language of and the categorization made by the actors themselves" (Alapuro 2012, 141). As Simona Cerutti explains, microhistory strives to avoid "the anachronisms arising from 'received historical common sense'" and instead seeks "to construct 'relevant' contexts of analysis rather than sticking to preconceived ideas of what was relevant" (Cerutti 2004, 21). In this collection, chapters by David Stock and Brian Gogan employ a similar approach to reconstructing individual figures' contexts erased by Berlin's historical taxonomy. Here I am interested in how contexts can be erased or flattened when historians construct timelines, which, as Louise Wetherbee Phelps's study of the 1979 Ottawa Conference demonstrates, involves a seemingly arbitrary but politically, institutionally, and individually significant process of selecting (and simultaneously ignoring) a particular year as a watershed. As the quotes by Kerr and Lloyd-Jones suggest, contemporaries of 1963 saw that year as both a transformative era and a period of routine academic work. These individuals' assessments invite us to look back for a different history of 1963—a history not motivated by the desire to find an origin point but by a curiosity about what was seen as both significant and mundane about composition work at that time.

In this essay, I revisit composition's disciplinary origin narratives through an analysis of *TTT* and *RWC*—texts frequently cited but rarely analyzed in detail. What makes these texts compelling for a microhistorical analysis is the way they have functioned as markers of an interest in disciplinary research with little attention to the sponsorship and aims of that research. They have been used as signposts in macronarratives, but the texts themselves provide valuable information about individual scholars and research projects. When I began this project, I wanted to know how composition research operated at the time and whether Kitzhaber and Braddock, Lloyd-Jones, and Schoer saw themselves as participating in a disciplinary movement. What were their goals? Who sponsored their research? How were these texts published and distributed? To answer these questions, I examine what Sigurður Gylfi Magnússon and István M. Szijártó refer to as the "textual environment," in other words, a text's paratext, sponsorship, and discursive connections to other contemporary texts (Magnússon and Szijártó 2013, 135). Attention to the textual environment (and what it suggests about actors' institutional relationships and perspective on their own work) is part of what microhistorians refer to as *contextualization*. Identified by Magnússon and Szijártó as one of microhistories' key commitments, contextualization is especially valuable for scholars trained in rhetoric who already possess a rich set of tools for analyzing texts and attending to the rhetorical and situated ways individuals and groups use language. Adapting microhistory to a rhetorical approach, I reread the field's research turn in 1963 as a response to a national investment in education research rather than a concerted disciplinary movement. As I show, these prominent research reports emerged as part of a larger push in American culture and politics to fund education research promising to improve the stature of the nation's citizens during an era when the government and public were increasingly concerned with America's global reputation.

In constructing the textual environment of *TTT* and *RWC*, I understand context as "networks, ties of alliances and solidarities, and the mutual dependence between individual behavior and institutional relations" (Alapuro 2012, 139). To analyze the relationship between individuals and institutions, my approach to contextualization employs what Risto Alapuro calls "critical distance" to draw some connections people may not have known or articulated in 1963 (142). I see this critical distance as inescapable and necessary. Because our understanding of historical context is always mediated through texts, we can never completely reconstruct context from the perspective of individuals who lived it. But the point of contextualization is not to construct a complete account of history; rather, this approach seeks to bring texture to grand narratives of the past by studying "events or persons in context, that is to say, within the complex interplay of free choice and constraint where individuals and groups perform in the interstices of the contradictory pluralities of the normative systems that govern them" (Levi 2012, 126). The work of contextualization proves particularly useful for rereading disciplinary history because disciplines function as normative systems impacted by a web of individuals, organizations, and governing bodies. Given their complexity, the application of a broad concept like *discipline* or *disciplinary origin* to the past always simplifies and obscures the motives of individuals and differences across fields of knowledge.

To contextualize the work of Kitzhaber and Braddock, Lloyd-Jones, and Schoer, I begin by discussing how English responded to the National Defense Education Act of 1958 (NDEA) with the publication of *The National Interest and the Teaching of English* in 1961 (Squire et al.). This earlier document frames my analysis of research efforts in composition by showing how English appropriated the discourses of scientific research to argue for funding and to call public attention to the need to improve writing instruction at all levels. Such efforts benefited from the hope that education in English, like science and math, could contribute to national advancement during the Space Race era. Both *RWC* and *TTT* employed this discourse to construct a research agenda for composition, but in different ways. Even as *RWC* and *TTT* differed in approach, each text also presented ambivalent visions of writing as a field of study and teaching subject. These texts were written during a time when several invested parties with differing motives wanted a better definition for English and for composition as a key component of English. Rather than showing a concerted movement toward disciplinarity, a history of 1963 demonstrates that early research efforts in composition raised questions we still grapple with today—questions about composition's lack of clear definition, its complicity with the assumptions of literacy crises, and its ambivalent relationship to English studies.

SEEING THE FRAME: THE CONTEXT FOR COMPOSITION RESEARCH

So many of the hopes and fears of the American people are now related to our educational system and particularly to our universities—the hope for longer life, for getting into outer space, for a higher standard of living; our fears of Russian or Chinese supremacy, of the bomb and annihilation, of individual loss of purpose in the changing world. For all these reasons and others, the university has become a prime instrument of national purpose. This is new.

—Clark Kerr, The Uses of the University

What made composition research gain recognition in the 1960s? Or, put differently, what made historians look to the studies of the 1960s as a marker of interest in composition research? A brief glance through the archives of *College English, English Journal,* or *CCC* reveals that composition research existed prior to 1963. In fact, *RWC* contains no original research on writing but instead catalogs five hundred prior studies of written composition. For North, a desire to replace lore seems to be the significant difference. For Berlin, it's an aura of confidence. For Connors, it's a qualitative feeling of change. *RWC* and *TTT* tell a different story, a story beginning with national funding sources that made book-length academic publications possible.

In the 1960s, research became an increasingly predominant function of university work, entangling that work with federal and corporate sponsorship in new ways. The influence of nationalistic and entrepreneurial discourse contributed to the sense that the university was now what Kerr (2001, 5) calls a "multiversity" driven by different and often competing interests. According to data cited by Kerr, economist Fritz Machlup claimed in 1962 that 29 percent of the gross national product (GNP) came from the knowledge economy, which was growing at twice the rate of the rest of the economy (Kerr 2001, 66). Yet the research boom did not benefit all areas of the university equally. Federal funding of university research in 1961, for example, largely went toward three areas: defense (40 percent), science and technology (20 percent), and health (37 percent) (Kerr 2001, 41). Funding for English projects was comparatively small but was substantial if the project could contribute to public education. A 1964 call for proposals posted in the *ADE Bulletin* by the Cooperative Research division of the US Office of Education (which funded *RWC*) noted that funds of $11 million were available for teaching-related research in English and indicated as much as $17 million might be available the next year (Fisher 1964, 2).[1]

The prevalence of federal funding for research was in large part due to the NDEA of 1958. As Wayne J. Urban shows in *More Than Science and*

Sputnik: The National Defense Education Act of 1958, the NDEA catalyzed a period of unprecedented federal investment in higher education by capitalizing on media hype over the Soviet launch of the Sputnik satellite in 1957, which became "a story of educational deficiency for the American public by the media" (Urban 2010, 116). Urban argues that the Eisenhower administration was skeptical about the media's portrayal of American deficiency in science and technological advancement but passed the NDEA as a temporary measure to reassure the American public (80–81). However, the NDEA became a major achievement for politicians and educators seeking to expand federal funding to education.[2] After it passed, the National Council of Teachers of English (NCTE) sought NDEA funding by publishing *The National Interest,* which led to the development of the Project English curriculum research centers and increased the availability of federal money for general and applied research studies.[3]

The National Interest served an important role in positioning composition's work as having tangible effects on the improvement of the nation and its citizens. As others have noted, the extension of the NDEA to English disproportionately impacted composition over literature because it emphasized literacy skills and teaching methods, two areas seen as directly applicable to national welfare (Gallagher 2002, 113). But the NDEA, and NCTE's response to it, also set the precedent for how composition research would be framed in this era. The NDEA argued that national security depended on "the mental resources and technical skills of its young men and women" and "the mastery of modern techniques developed from complex scientific principles" (NDEA 1958, 2). NCTE's arguments hinged on the claim that English could use scientific methods to conduct research and improve curricula, establishing an explicit parallel to the STEM disciplines. *The National Interest* aligned the problems of science and math education with English but highlighted the difference in the public's view of those problems: "In English the disparity between what specialists and research scholars know and what the school teaches is even greater than it was in science, but no dramatic orbiting of a linguistic satellite draws public attention to this disparity" (Squire et al. 1961, 75). This claim invokes the Space Race to imply a "disparity" not simply between research and teaching but also between the literacy skills of other countries and of the United States; just as the United States was surpassed in the creation of satellite technology, so too it had been surpassed in its citizens' literacy skills. This analogy allowed NCTE to transfer the exigency for funding from STEM to English.

Underpinning *The National Interest*'s appeal for literacy education was a concern about the global perception of the United States. Students needed English to navigate increasingly global economic and political interactions in a "world . . . where East meets West in almost daily encounter, when travelers and businessmen represent our culture and our values no less than do our statesmen and military personnel—in a world in which the profile of the 'Ugly American' is all too vividly etched" (Squire et al. 1961, 17). The focus on the East was no coincidence. American-studies scholar Christina Klein argues that in the Cold War era, orientalism played a role in mobilizing support for education: "Middlebrow intellectuals often presented the Cold War as something that ordinary Americans could take part in, as a set of activities in which they could invest their emotional and intellectual energy. . . . Middlebrow culture brought these alliances [with non-Communist parts of Asia] to life by translating them into personal terms and imbuing them with sentiment, so that they became emotionally rich relationships that Americans could inhabit imaginatively in their everyday lives" (Klein 2003, 7–8). In this context, Americans needed English to preserve their "heritage"—framed as the "myth and folklore of lumbering, pioneering, and railroading"—and convey it to a racialized Other through the "vehicle" of "language and literature" (Squire et al. 1961, 16). The text argued for a central place for English in helping "Americans everywhere fully understand their heritage and see themselves not only as bearers of aid, technology, and materialism but also of ideas, of human dignity and freedom—ideas articulated with such vision by Jefferson, Lincoln, Emerson, Thoreau, and Whitman" (17). In other words, the appeal to support literacy education was an affective appeal to the economic and cultural values of American liberalism.

The irony of *The National Interest*'s construction of English as the creator of good citizens and the preserver of national heritage is that the document also bemoaned the lack of definition for English. English had "lost clear definition" and "been burdened with an increase in miscellaneous duties and responsibilities" (Squire et al. 1961, 26). The writers lamented that because "English is the subject in which virtually all students are enrolled, it has frequently seemed natural to school administrators to consign to English teachers many special responsibilities" (26). They proposed limiting English to language, literature, and composition (26) and outlined numerous research projects for the future (3–12). However, by simultaneously rejecting and reinforcing a vision of English as an all-encompassing humanistic endeavor, the document undercut its own argument that English needed to be clearly demarcated and defined—something texts like *TTT* and *RWC* grappled with, as I discuss below.

Furthermore, private sponsors of English outside the profession also invoked grand rhetoric about the possibility of English to improve humanity and America. A salient example is a 1961 article, "Projecting the Image of America," in the December issue of *College Composition and Communication* (CCC) by George V. Allen, director of the Tobacco Institute and former director of the US Information Agency. Allen assured readers that composition played a vital role in conveying America's image to the world. He explained that citizens and political forces needed to "organize the world in a somewhat more sensible basis than we have been able to manage so far" (Allen 1961, 203). In order to do so, the world needed "more wide-spread communication among people" (203). He assured composition teachers they were "making perhaps the most important contribution of all by seeing to it that Americans communicate intelligibly" (203). Allen's argument parallels *The National Interest*'s rhetoric of using communication to improve global relationships with the aim of allowing America to "organize the world." This idea was repeated in various instantiations by private sponsors, particularly the funding powerhouses of the era—the Carnegie, Ford, and Rockefeller foundations (known as the Big Three). As Edward H. Berman argues in *The Influence of the Carnegie, Ford, and Rockefeller Foundations on American Foreign Policy: The Ideology of Philanthropy*, "The Carnegie, Ford, and Rockefeller foundations have consistently supported the major aims of United States foreign policy while simultaneously helping to construct an intellectual framework supportive of that policy's major tenets. . . . Indeed, many of these individuals regularly moved back and forth between corporate headquarters, foundation offices, and State or Defense department positions" (Berman 1983, 5). Berman's analysis shows how the advancement of American liberalism and economic and foreign policy became entangled with university research. With research funding coming primarily from the government or foundations, English had to be framed as a national problem, and its research had to ameliorate that problem within the ideological boundaries of its sponsors.

OPENING THE DOOR: COMPOSITION RESEARCH IN 1963

The books in this series have resulted from studies made under grants from the Carnegie Corporation of New York. . . . The Corporation . . . has a continuing interest in the improvement of American education. It financed the studies in this series to provide

facts and recommendations which would be useful to all those who
make or influence the decisions which shape American educational poli-
cies and institutions.

—Publisher's colophon, *Themes,*
Theories, and Therapy (Kitzhaber 1963)

First instructed to complete the manuscript in six to eight months, the
ad hoc committee soon realized that a review of "all" the research on
composition was a prodigious undertaking which would necessitate a
much longer period of preparation. Consequently, as it began its task,
the chairman of the committee applied to the Office of Education, U.S.
Department of Health, Education, and Welfare, for a Cooperative
Research Program grant. A grant was awarded in the amount of
$13,345, supplemented by an allocation of $4,397 from the University
of Iowa.

—Braddock, Lloyd-Jones, and Schoer, *Research*
in Written Composition (1963)

The publication of *TTT* and *RWC* followed closely on the heels of *The National Interest* and NDEA, and both texts show the rhetoric of national concern for education taken up in productive but often contradictory ways. Kitzhaber's project was funded by the Carnegie Corporation, which valued efforts to strengthen American public education. According to Kitzhaber (1963, ix), the project proposal was submitted originally in fall 1958 by a committee of Dartmouth faculty concerned about the poor literacy skills of otherwise excellent college students. These "young men" at Dartmouth were "handicapped by the inability to write with correctness and precision" and they needed "training . . . to become liberally educated men" (Kitzhaber 1963, ix)—a description of students that resonates with the perception of American education as deficient. Kitzhaber observed that college English teachers were so concerned with "improving American secondary education in the missile age" (8) that they overlooked the responsibility of college teachers—at all levels and in all disciplines—in improving students' writing (Kitzhaber 1963, 10). These introductory comments in *TTT* exemplify the contradictory arguments about writing in *TTT*—writing was both a complex "skill" for which all teachers at all levels were responsible and a discipline in correctness necessary so students could overcome the individual "handicap" of illiteracy and participate in liberal society.

The focus on liberal aims for education carries throughout Kitzhaber's text, particularly in the underlying argument that good writing conveys intelligence—a quality emphasized in *The National Interest* and elsewhere as critical to improving the reputation of America globally. Kitzhaber argued further that haphazard writing pedagogy reflected badly on America: "Teaching young people to write well has always proved so frustratingly difficult and the methods used so time-consuming and laborious for teacher and student alike, that to many people in this country the problem has seemed to be a kind of standing affront to the American reputation for efficiency" (Kitzhaber 1963, 73). In addition, Kitzhaber viewed students' literacy deficiencies as a reflection of individual intelligence, arguing, "Careless and imprecise use of language betrays a careless and imprecise intelligence" (152). Conversely, "a clear, correct, and responsible use of language is a principle hallmark of an educated man" (151). Like *The National Interest's* focus on "businessmen," Kitzhaber emphasized the impact of education for men. In fact, he dismissed female students early in his text by suggesting, "Many girls frankly want only a college-educated husband because of his greater earning power, and they plan to remain students just long enough to get one, then quit to go work or have babies" (1). The focus on men reinforces the assumption that communication skills served primarily public rather than personal or domestic ends.

Because he linked writing to intelligence, Kitzhaber struggled to articulate whether composition was a content discipline or skill. He spoke optimistically of the post-Sputnik curriculum reform as a "rationaliz[ation]" of the curriculum that would "bring [teaching] into line with current knowledge as has been done so successfully in the teaching of science and mathematics and foreign languages" (Kitzhaber 1963, 98). At the same time, Kitzhaber argued adamantly and repeatedly that "composition is not a body of knowledge; instead it is a highly complex skill" (92). Despite this argument, he critiqued curriculum reform that focused on pedagogical methods: "With the encouragement of several of the big foundations, an increasing number of English teachers in schools and colleges are now busily involved with 'team teaching,' 'lay readers,' closed-circuit television, overhead projectors, 'resource teachers,' 'teacher aides,' etc., in the hopes of 'scoring a major breakthrough'" (75). He dismissed research on experimental pedagogy as fads with little potential, but he remained silent about an appropriate research agenda for composition.

Kitzhaber concluded with ambivalent remarks about writing knowledge and curricula. He analyzed survey data and syllabi from across the nation and student writing at Dartmouth to determine the consistency and efficacy of first-year composition courses. Although disturbed by the lack of consistency across institutions, Kitzhaber nevertheless ended with the assertion, "There are many ways to teach composition, and nearly all appear to succeed from time to time" (Kitzhaber 1963, 131). This remark seems to derive from his study of student writing at Dartmouth, where, as he found in his error analysis of student essays, student writing improved despite the course focus on literature (72). Yet he maintained that the courses were not writing courses and not "the best way" to teach writing (72). Kitzhaber advocated a few recommendations for composition, including teaching expository writing and providing rhetorical instruction, but he did not propose a larger disciplinary agenda or dictate how to teach the course. Thomas P. Miller criticizes him for this silence, writing that Kitzhaber's "lack of a unifying conceptual vision for composition studies undercut varied aspects of English studies, as is evident in Kitzhaber's recommendations that improving the course depended upon changing teacher assignments and training, broadening graduate and undergraduate writing curricula, and reassessing the general teaching of reading and writing" (Miller 2011, 188). By making ambivalent remarks about pedagogy, Kitzhaber implied the main concerns of composition were organizational and administrative problems rather than research or content problems—a tension still evident in debates about first-year composition today. Kitzhaber's vision for composition in some ways resisted the aims of his research sponsors, both explicitly, in his critique of pedagogical methods promising quick fixes, and implicitly, in his refusal to argue definitively about composition's content or to affirm that writing could be taught in a single course. Yet in other ways he capitulated by highlighting American students' literacy deficiencies and by suggesting correct writing reflected intelligence in a way that reaffirmed rather than dismissed public concerns about America's reputation.

This struggle to define productive research and effective teaching in composition also appeared in *RWC*, but *RWC* presented composition's primary problem as a dearth of research, not a lack of pedagogical consistency. This conclusion makes sense given that Braddock, Lloyd-Jones, and Schoer's research emerged from work done for an ad hoc NCTE Committee on the State of Knowledge about Composition and it received funding from public sources—a Cooperative Research Grant from the Office of Education and additional funds from the University of Iowa. Demonstrating to the federal government the dire lack of research on composition was the goal of NCTE's *The National Interest*, and *RWC* made a similar claim supported by extensive research. As Braddock, Lloyd-Jones, and Schoer stated in their introduction, NCTE requested the study out of concern over "the nature of public pronouncements about how writing should be taught—the sound and the wild seem to share space equally in the press" (Braddock, Lloyd-Jones, and Schoer 1963, 1). By highlighting the media's concern with literacy, *RWC* employed the same rhetoric that made the NDEA so successful, using research as a response to media outcry about deficiency.

Projecting objectivity, *RWC* referenced the "missile age" context less overtly than *TTT*, but like Kitzhaber and NCTE, Braddock, Lloyd-Jones, and Schoer defined the report's exigency by contrasting the state of knowledge in composition to the state of knowledge in the sciences. Research in composition, they noted, "has not frequently been conducted with the knowledge and care that one associates with the physical sciences" (Braddock, Lloyd-Jones, and Schoer 1963, 5). *RWC* argued current composition research "may be compared to chemical research as it emerged from the period of alchemy: some terms are being defined usefully, a number of procedures are being refined, but the field as a whole is laced with dreams, prejudices, and makeshift operations" (5). After establishing a disparity between the state of knowledge in composition versus the sciences, *RWC* then defined good research in written composition within a paradigm that upheld "'scientific methods,' like controlled experimentation," and "textual analysis," like error frequency counts (1); it limited valid studies to "written composition, and, more particularly, to studies in which some actual writing was involved" (Braddock, Lloyd-Jones, and Schoer 1963, 1). At first glance, *RWC* does seem to position composition research against pedagogical lore by setting up the alchemy/chemistry divide. However, *RWC* in fact singled out the poor research methods of previous scholars as alchemy—out of over five hundred studies, the authors find only five to recommend. In context, *RWC*'s legacy seems to be not a dismissal of pedagogy but rather a desire to raise standards in composition research to a level at which it could compete with the sciences, hinting at the larger concern that the sciences dominated the market for research funding.

To improve composition research, Braddock, Lloyd-Jones, and Schoer provided guidelines for projects—defining variables to consider in writing experiments, explaining how to set up experimental and control groups, providing guidelines for reporting results, and reminding readers that color graphs "become meaningless in the black and white medium [of microfilm]" (Braddock, Lloyd-Jones, and Schoer 1963, 28). Of course, *RWC*'s recommendations were useful and likely much desired at the time by those who felt lost in a new research paradigm. This desire is evident in, for example, Taylor Culbert's *CCC* article, "Methodology in Research in Composition," which described the literary training of the "would-be researcher in composition" as a major obstacle in conducting fundable research (Culbert 1961, 39). However, Braddock, Lloyd-Jones, and Schoer omitted humanistic methods from consideration as research, placing them outside the realm of valid projects that deserved funding. Out of the five hundred studies included in their bibliography—from *Dissertation Abstracts*, *Psychological Abstracts*, and *Review of Educational Research*—their report pulled very little research from English, or even *CCC*. The final five studies they proposed as exemplars for future research were selected on the basis of maintaining a "controlled experiment" and researcher objectivity (Braddock, Lloyd-Jones, and Schoer 1963, 56).

RWC's attitude about humanistic research is more explicit when referencing Kitzhaber's *TTT*. Although Kitzhaber is listed twice in the acknowledgments for his help with the project, *TTT* is excluded from *RWC*'s list of valid research studies for "hav[ing] a different approach to truth than the scientific studies which fall within the purview of this report. As a colleague put it, Kitzhaber's book uses a kind of 'informed intuition' with its 'controls' rooted in the author's accumulated experience" (Braddock, Lloyd-Jones, and Schoer 1963, 38). Braddock, Lloyd-Jones, and Schoer defined Kitzhaber's research within the vocabulary of scientific research—it had analytical tools (intuition) and controls (experience)—but they did so in a way that implicitly invalidated Kitzhaber's work. *RWC* ignored Kitzhaber's concerns about the administration and representation of first-year composition and its transinstitutional identity and instead focused on the act of writing, as is evident in their questions for researchers, including "How does a writer generate sentences?" and "Of what does skill in writing really consist?" (Braddock, Lloyd-Jones, and Schoer 1963, 52–53).

In their recommendations, the authors of *RWC* argued that good writing research should observe people writing, describe experimental procedures, use appropriate statistics for analyzing data, control the variables in an experiment, and maintain researcher objectivity (Braddock, Lloyd-Jones, and Schoer 1963, 55–56). This statement of best practices, however, was based on the assumption that scientific methods could transfer to the kinds of knowledge investigated by composition research. In fact, Braddock, Lloyd-Jones, and Schoer begin chapter 2 by dismissing the remarks of a colleague who questioned the possibility of controlling variables in writing studies. The colleague argued, "It is something close to mockery to organize these structures as though we were conducting a controlled experiment" (5). Braddock, Lloyd-Jones, and Schoer responded by suggesting that this obstacle could be overcome by using the "knowledge and care that one associates with the physical sciences"

(Braddock, Lloyd-Jones, and Schoer 1963, 5). The problem was not that appropriate research needed to be rethought and reworked for composition but rather that composition simply needed to be treated like a science in order for knowledge to be discovered. In subsequent decades, this kind of contention, reiterated by writing researchers working from a cognitive psychology stance, would spark intense debate about composition's relationship to English and to rhetoric.

Key publications from the 1960s reveal that, at best, discourses connecting research and disciplinarity in composition were indistinct and based largely on an attempt to respond appropriately to ideas about research shaped by funding sources and cultural attitudes about literacy and intelligence. Furthermore, composition's place within English was in the process of negotiation as researchers articulated standards for research that represented very different assumptions about knowledge and as they attempted to define writing in a way that made it relevant to research sponsors. Such arguments over composition's research fueled ongoing debates over skills, course content, research methods, and the administrative organization of first-year composition. As such, texts like *RWC* and *TTT* are better understood not as disciplinary markers but as highly visible participants in a discourse that shaped how we talk about writing and composition's knowledge today.

LOOKING FORWARD, LOOKING BACK: USING
RETROSPECTIVE TO COMPLICATE HISTORY

> *All research is implicitly political. . . . The researcher has power, but the general public, the educational establishment, and the departments of English by virtue of their powers and preconceptions and policies have the ability to start or stop sensible research projects. Political control is often not in the grasp of the actual researcher.*
>   —Richard Lloyd-Jones (1977), "The Politics
>   of Research into the Teaching of Composition"

To this point, I have been arguing that we must read composition research in the 1960s as part of a larger social scene set by NCTE's funding efforts more than as composition's disciplinary desires. Yet, in making this argument, I do not mean to portray power as a simple, unidirectional force that sways unsuspecting researchers. As Magnússon and Szijártó (2013, 123) remind microhistorians, contextualization should emphasize the inevitable paradoxes and inconsistencies of individual actors in institutional contexts. This focus on the complexity of individuals prevents contextualization from becoming a tautological enterprise in which a scholar uses context to interpret a text and the text to define the context (Magnússon and Szijártó 2013, 40). Historical actors operate in variable contexts that can be interpreted in different ways by historians. Here I read later publications by Kitzhaber and Lloyd-Jones to reframe my analysis, demonstrating these authors' awareness of the shaping power of the context in which they worked. Kitzhaber's and Lloyd-Jones's later writings suggest that composition scholars have historically been adept at navigating the political landscape to garner attention for writing research. Although the assumptions and ends of such research were not always productive, as I argue above, and contributed at times to the field's complicity with problematic claims about writing, they nevertheless present an important awareness of the way multiple constituencies shape knowledge.

Four years after the publication of *TTT*, Kitzhaber reflected on the aftermath of *The National Interest* and the Project English curriculum research centers. In "The Government and English Teaching: A Retrospective View," Kitzhaber analyzed the emergence of English research as "an outgrowth of the Cold War," tracing it explicitly to America's "reflex action to the stimulus provided by Russian scientific achievements" (Kitzhaber 1967, 135). Applauding NCTE and the Modern Language Association's (MLA) concern over the public reputation of the profession, Kitzhaber argued that these organizations responded adeptly to what they saw as a "dangerous imbalance in American education" favoring STEM subjects over the humanities and social sciences (1967, 134–35). Kitzhaber noted that *The National Interest* "shocked" a wide audience outside of English and paved the way for NCTE and MLA to testify before Congress about the need for funding English research (136). Kitzhaber described the testimony before Congress as a rhetorical negotiation of Congress's expectations, and with characteristic good humor he told of one member of Congress who "was especially anxious to be assured that none of the money the Commissioner [of Education] was requesting for English would be used to 'teach novels and poems,' an activity which, it was clear, the Congressman thought insane, possibly un-American" (136–37). The Commissioner, Sterling McMurrin, a former philosophy professor, responded euphemistically that funds would be used to teach reading, "in effect . . . bootleg[ging] literature into the curriculum" (Kitzhaber 1967, 137). Furthermore, Kitzhaber maintained a nuanced position on the aftermath of Project English's curriculum research, arguing that it had not yielded definition and rigor in English analogous to the sciences; instead, researchers supported the idea that English study was "not without its practical applications but not to be summed up or justified by these alone" (Kitzhaber 1967, 139). He argued that Project English had created "a defensible structure and sequence for English," stressing that English needed to be able to defend its work to the public (Kitzhaber 1967, 140).

Demonstrating a similar acuity about composition research, Lloyd-Jones described the complexity of negotiating public and other expectations in the "The Politics of Research into the Teaching of Composition" (1977). Research, he suggested, "potentially threatens the *status quo*. Even if its results confirm our present thoughts, research weakens the opposition and thus alters the balance of power in a society" (Lloyd-Jones 1977, 218). Lloyd-Jones elaborated by explaining that widespread concern about the teaching of writing (however misguided) presented composition with opportunity to engage the public, which "when aroused . . . overrides the inertia of institutions" (218). He argued that the public needed to understand the work and time commitment involved in reading student writing, the kinds of expertise necessary for teaching writing, and the struggles students experience writing about intellectually challenging material (220). The problem for composition researchers, as he saw it, was that composition had to appeal to so many audiences—the public, institutions, and departments of English—and "few want to support research into topics which most people imagine are thoroughly explored" (220). In other words, Lloyd-Jones saw opportunity for composition to precipitate real change, but he acknowledged that opportunity presented a double bind—public interest in writing also meant, as he put it, that "political control is often not in the grasp of the actual researcher" (218).

In composition, we are aware of the importance of framing our work differently for different audiences. The work of Kitzhaber, Lloyd-Jones, and the other authors of *RWC* suggest that this awareness has long been part of the work of composition, even before scholars were concerned with the composition's distinct disciplinary identity. While a history of 1963 uncovers a deep-seated ambivalence about the nature of composition in the discourse of research, it nevertheless also shows that ambivalence was often understood by scholars as part of the rhetorical work of conducting research with the potential to effect change in curricula and the public. Certainly, some historians may continue to use 1963 as an origin date for the field, but any markers of origin were never simply a fixed event or an intentional beginning. Historical texts can always be reinterpreted, reimagined, through prior and subsequent discourses that give new meaning to a scene of action.

SEEING OUR FRAME: MICROHISTORY IN COMPOSITION

By revising our understanding of 1963, this project questions macronar-ratives correlating disciplinarity in composition with the appearance of research. Such histories, I argue, are not necessarily wrong; however, they reify research as a product of a concerted effort to establish the dis-cipline when, in fact, research only appears as such in hindsight. At the same time, hindsight is our only vantage point as historians, and chang-ing the scope of our project does not necessarily mean we escape cat-egories or assumptions shaped by macrohistory. Indeed, a total rejection of grand narratives is not the point of microhistory, which seeks balance between the desire to destroy grand narratives and the desire to reaf-firm them (Magnússon and Szijártó 2013, 116). As John Walton, James F. Brooks, and Christopher R.N. DeCorse write, "*Micro* and *macro* are comparative terms that have meaning only in relation to one another" (Walton, Brooks, and DeCorse 2008, 6). Using the macro and micro to inform each other, microhistory reframes categories by illuminating a small object of study—a year, individual, or text—and providing insight that changes our understanding of events, places, work, or disciplines. Changing the scope of analysis makes space for disruptions and contra-dictions that do not necessarily present tidy conclusions about the past. This is valuable work because it allows us to examine history and the writing of history simultaneously.

As Giovanni Levi argues, microhistory should not simply focus on objects or individuals, nor should it uphold grand narratives; rather, he argues, "what the historian can and should generalize are questions" (Levi 2012, 127). A microhistory of 1963 provides us with compelling questions about composition research and its relationship to hegemonic political and economic forces: When has composition sought to distance itself from those forces and when has it sought alliance with them? How have we acknowledged the role of different sponsors outside composi-tion or even the academy in bolstering our work? How have individuals or projects sought to resist simplistic assumptions about literacy and writ-ing? When (and why) have those assumptions been accepted or unchal-lenged in order to further particular goals? These kinds of questions can be generalized and asked about several moments and persons in com-position's history, or even about our individual histories and contexts, as the contributions here by Kelly Ritter and James T. Zebroski illustrate. If microhistory teaches us nothing else, we see from Kitzhaber's and Braddock, Lloyd-Jones, and Schoer's work how scholars and teachers work with and in institutional constraints created by local and global contexts. That lesson can help us construct more contextually nuanced histories. It should also make us more aware of the significance of small moments in our own careers, how we are always, to borrow Kerr's image, connected to the past while moving in different directions.

Notes

1. To put this in perspective, Kerr (2001, 40) notes that in 1960 the federal government contributed $1.5 billion to education.
2. Urban (2010, 203) is cautious, however, about the way the Sputnik story translated into educational reform, noting that the ten titles of the NDEA introduced a funding system based primarily on fostering naturally gifted students rather than addressing issues of equity. Urban also notes that researchers used the opportunity of Sputnik to question public education and to argue for educational reform, circumventing the input of educators at the primary and secondary levels (170). Thus, the NDEA had a mixed legacy both in terms of its support of public education and its support of progressive education.
3. See Margaret M. Strain (2005) for an analysis of the congressional hearings in which NCTE and Sterling McMurrin attempted to argue for NDEA and Project English funding. Strain explains that Project English was a separate but related attempt to garner funding for English research modeled after the National Science Foundation, but *The National Interest* served as evidence for the congressional hearings for Project English and NDEA funding (525).

References

Alapuro, Risto. 2012. "Revisiting Microhistory from the Perspective of Comparisons." In *Historical Knowledge: In Quest of Theory, Method, and Evidence*, edited by Susanna Fellman and Marjatta Rahikainen, 133–54. Newcastle upon Tyne: Cambridge Scholars.

Allen, George V. 1961. "Projecting the Image of America: A Problem in Communication." *College Composition and Communication* 12 (4): 197–203. http://dx.doi.org/10.2307/354189.

Berlin, James. 1987. *Rhetoric and Reality: Writing Instruction in American Colleges, 1880–1985*. Carbondale: Southern Illinois University Press.

Berman, Edward H. 1983. *The Influence of the Carnegie, Ford, and Rockefeller Foundations on American Foreign Policy: The Ideology of Philanthropy*. Albany: SUNY Press.

Braddock, Richard, Richard Lloyd-Jones, and Lowell Schoer. 1963. *Research in Written Composition*. Champaign, IL: National Council of Teachers of English.

Cerutti, Simona. 2004. "Microhistory: Social Relations versus Cultural Models?" In *Between Sociology and History: Essays on Microhistory, Collective Action, and Nation Building*, edited by Anna-Maija Castrén, Markku Lonkila, and Matti Peltonen, 17–40. Helsinki: Suomalaisen Kirjallisuuden Seura.

Connors, Robert J. 1997. *Composition-Rhetoric: Backgrounds, Theory, and Pedagogy*. Pittsburgh, PA: University of Pittsburgh Press.

Culbert, Taylor. 1961. "Methodology in Research in Composition." *College Composition and Communication* 12 (1): 39–42. http://dx.doi.org/10.2307/354310.

Fisher, John H. 1964. "News Notes from John H. Fisher." *ADE Bulletin* 1:2. http://dx.doi.org/10.1632/ade.1.2a.

Gallagher, Chris. 2002. *Radical Departures: Composition and Progressive Pedagogy*. Urbana, IL: NCTE.

Kerr, Clark. 2001. *The Uses of the University*. 5th ed. Cambridge, MA: Harvard University Press.

Kitzhaber, Albert R. 1963. *Themes, Theories, and Therapy: The Teaching of Writing in College*. New York: McGraw-Hill.

Kitzhaber, Albert R. 1967. "The Government and English Teaching: A Retrospective View." *College Composition and Communication* 18 (3): 135–41. http://dx.doi.org /10.2307/355685.

Klein, Christina. 2003. *Cold War Orientalism: Asia in the Middlebrow Imagination: 1945–1961*. Berkeley: University of California Press.

Levi, Giovanni. 2012. "Microhistory and the Recovery of Complexity." In *Historical Knowledge: In Quest of Theory, Method, and Evidence*, edited by Susanna Fellman and Marjatta Rahikainen, 121–32. Newcastle upon Tyne: Cambridge Scholars.

Lloyd-Jones, Richard. 1977. "The Politics of Research into the Teaching of Composition." *College Composition and Communication* 28 (3): 218–22. http://dx.doi.org/10.2307 /357202.

Lloyd-Jones, Richard. 2006. "A View from the Center." In *Views from the Center: The CCCC Chairs' Addresses, 1977–2005*, edited by Duane Roen, 45–53. Boston, MA: Bedford/St. Martins.

Magnússon, Sigurður Gylfi, and István M. Szijártó. 2013. *What Is Microhistory? Theory and Practice*. London: Routledge.

Miller, Thomas P. 2011. *The Evolution of College English: Literacy Studies from the Puritans to the Postmoderns*. Pittsburgh, PA: University of Pittsburgh Press.

National Defense Education Act of 1958. Pub. L. No. 85–864. 72 *U.S. Statutes at Large* 1580.

North, Stephen M. 1987. *The Making of Knowledge in Composition: Portrait of an Emerging Field*. Portsmouth, NH: Boynton/Cook.

Phelps, Louise Wetherbee. 2010. "Composition Studies." In *Encyclopedia of Rhetoric and Composition: Communication from Ancient Times to the Information Age*, ed. Theresa Enos, 2nd ed. 123–33. New York: Routledge.

Smit, David. 2004. *The End of Composition Studies*. Carbondale: Southern Illinois University Press.

Squire, James R., Harold B. Allen, George H. Henry, J. N. Hook, Albert H. Marckwardt, Richard A. Meade, Josesph Mersand, Eugene E. Slaughter, George Winchester Stone Jr., and Ruth G. Strickland. 1961. *The National Interest and the Teaching of English: A Report on the Status of the Profession*. Champaign, IL: NCTE.

Strain, Margaret M. 2005. "In Defense of a Nation: The National Defense Education Act, Project English, and the Origins of Empirical Research in Composition." *JAC* 25 (3): 513–42.

Urban, Wayne J. 2010. *More Than Science and Sputnik: The National Defense Education Act of 1958*. Tuscaloosa: University of Alabama Press.

Walton, John, James F. Brooks, and Christopher R.N. DeCorse. 2008. Introduction to *Small Worlds: Method, Meaning, and Narrative in Microhistory*, edited by James F. Brooks, Christopher R.N. DeCorse, and John Walton, 3–12. Santa Fe, NM: School for Advanced Social Research.

2

THE 1979 OTTAWA CONFERENCE AND ITS INSCRIPTIONS
Recovering a Canadian Moment in American Rhetoric and Composition

Louise Wetherbee Phelps

In May 1979, Aviva Freedman and Ian Pringle hosted an international conference on "Learning to Write" at Carleton University in Ottawa, Canada, featuring a concentrated assemblage of eminent scholars as speakers and respondents. Those present sensed immediately that they were part of a momentous and historic event. Janet Emig, who delivered her famous "Tacit Tradition" speech at the conference, remembered it later as "the single most electric professional meeting I ever participated in" (Emig 1983, n.p.). Many delegates saw it as the rightful successor to the landmark Dartmouth Conference of 1966, and when Anthony Adams, the closing speaker, suggested it might even eclipse Dartmouth as the most important conference ever held on English education, "there was a general murmur of assent" (Oster 1979, 24).

Freedman and Pringle (1980) acknowledged and honored this heritage, but as editors of *Reinventing the Rhetorical Tradition*, one volume of papers from the conference, they consequentially shifted its context, recasting the meaning and significance of the event in terms of the disciplinary study of writing rather than the teaching of English. Freedman spoke of the 1979 conference later as corroborating "the reality of a new, or should I say renewed, discipline: writing research or rhetoric or composition theory" (Maguire 1995, 83).[1] The primary theme of *Reinventing* is a coming-of-age story in which the conference is both the occasion and the means for writing studies to emerge on the scene as a full-fledged, intellectually compelling, and already international discipline. This is not the whole story, though, because the two other publications from the conference focused on layers of its meanings that more fully engage the broad concerns of internationalized English and

DOI: 10.7330/9781607324058.c002

language-arts education. But it is this bold claim of disciplinary maturation and international scope, made at such an early date, that should have assured Ottawa 1979 a place in the origin stories of modern writing studies.[2] Certainly the high caliber of its scholarship left its trace: many of the published conference papers became classics of American rhetoric and composition.[3]

Yet, inexplicably, the Ottawa Conference has vanished from disciplinary memory and is rarely even noted in histories of the period, much less recognized as a seminal moment. Only recently has James Zebroski remedied this oversight in his revisionist account of English education's role in early composition, where he dramatically declares that "the 1979 Ottawa conference is one site where the discipline was born" (Zebroski 2012, 42). Zebroski credits Freedman and Pringle (especially in *Reinventing*) with being "among the very first to call composition and rhetoric a discipline" and to appreciate its multiple roots and traditions (44–45).

This discrepancy between contemporaneous judgment and historical memory is just the kind of anomaly that calls for microhistorical inquiry (Ginzburg, Tedeschi, and Tedeschi 1993, 33; Peltonen 2001, 349). In this essay, I follow Zebroski's lead and work to recover the 1979 Ottawa conference from the mists of history as a Canadian moment in American rhetoric and composition. Like most such events, this conference was captured—or, as I will say, inscribed—for contemporaries and for history primarily through its published accounts and products, in this case three volumes of conference proceedings edited by its organizers. I will focus my inquiry sharply on these volumes because the relationship of the conference to its public inscriptions lies at the heart of my study as a microhistory.[4] By embodying and disseminating the conference-as-event beyond the circle of those who directly experienced it, these texts permit us—using the method of clues (Ginzburg and Davin 1980)—to gaze *through* the inscriptions at the conference itself as a consequential enactment and lived experience of the field at a particular moment in time. In this instance we see it through the fresh eyes of Canadians, who were both learning about the field and participating in its development. At the same time, these edited volumes constitute purposeful texts by which authors and editors, as responsible historical actors (Magnusson and Szijarto 2013, 69), carry out important rhetorical, hermeneutical, scholarly, and pedagogical actions. By elucidating that relationship as it unfolds in the singular case of Ottawa 1979, this microhistory can point beyond its unique particularities to suggest how such events and publications serve to develop and sustain a discipline and its scholars.

This study draws on a range of microhistorical strategies, viewing microhistory in Levi's terms as "a series of practices and methods rather than a theory" (Levi 2012, 126). They include the microscale of description (Levi 2001, 99–102); attention to outliers (Magnusson and Szijarto 2013, 152) and the "exceptional normal" (attributed to Edoardo Grendi 1977); the conjectural model of clues or signs (Ginzburg and Davin 1980); contextualization (Magnusson and Szijarto 2013, 74–76); and generalization to questions, not answers (Levi 2012, 127). Conceptually, it relies on the notion of a fractal relationship between selected cases and a larger whole in which historians' contextual knowledge allows them to recognize patterns that crystallize more general understandings, especially from the exceptional or obscure case (Magnusson and Szijarto 2013, 64–65, 75). These methods also embody an ethic of historical practice that honors individuals' agency, an ethic I share with many microhistorians, including those represented in this volume.

OTTAWA 1979: THE CONFERENCE AND ITS CONTEXTS

The Event

The professional conference called "Learning to Write," sponsored by the Canadian Council of Teachers of English (CCTE) as its annual meeting, was held May 8–11, 1979, at Carleton University in Ottawa, Canada.[5] Professor John Oster, a Canadian delegate who provided impressions of the conference for a CCTE journal, wrote vividly of the spring setting: "Ottawa was beautiful, with clear blue skies, freshly burgeoning foliage, bright tulips bordering the canal and rivers, and grass so green it appeared freshly painted for our arrival" (Oster 1979, 23–24). Twelve-hundred-fifty delegates—many more than expected—registered for the conference and were housed on two campuses and in local hotels. Popular sessions were crowded to capacity, and discussions spilled over onto the campus and into local bars afterwards. The international mix of the delegates represented five continents, but the great majority was Anglo-American, from Canada, the United States, Great Britain (the UK), and Australia.[6]

The Ottawa 1979 conference had a general program in English and language arts ("all levels" of education), which ran from Tuesday through Saturday and a specialized program in ESL ("Anglais, French Immersion, E.S.L."), which ran concurrently on Friday and Saturday. Freedman and Pringle were general program chairs, and Janice Yalden was responsible for the ESL program. At the time, Pringle was an associate professor of English and linguistics at Carleton, and Freedman was director of writing tutorial services at the university. Yalden chaired Carleton's Department of Linguistics and directed its ESL program.

Since the two parts of the conference each had its own printed program, it is possible to distinguish them in terms of both speakers and session types. English and language arts had 156 speakers and respondents sprinkled densely throughout the program like stars in a galaxy of multidisciplinary talent. The ESL program had another forty-seven speakers and workshop leaders, with Henry (H.G.) Widdowson, a prominent British scholar in applied linguistics and English-language teaching, as the keynote speaker. Together, the disciplines represented included—at least—education (English education, language arts), rhetoric, composition, linguistics, grammar, applied linguistics, cognitive psychology, ESL, and communication.[7]

The two conferences organized time differently. The English and language arts program was studded with featured presentations: opening and closing addresses, keynotes, and invited speeches. Distinguished respondents, often featured speakers themselves, assured that debates continued across sessions. Following an "Opening Day" of general interest, Wednesday through Saturday were devoted (though not exclusively) to particular educational sectors and interests: "Sentence-Combining Day," "Secondary Day," "Elementary Day," and "E.S.L. Day." This concern for the needs of different constituencies was echoed in the variations in session format, designed to enable different forms of learning and participation: besides the addresses, sessions included panels, seminars, practical workshops, sector or special-interest luncheons (like the "Post-Secondary Luncheon," with Canadian linguist H. A. Gleason as guest speaker), and meetings of special-interest groups (e.g., Canadian Community College Teachers). Some sessions were invitational, although Oster remarks that at least one, on teaching writing to nonmatriculated students, "immediately developed into a large panel discussion . . . limited only by size of the theatre in which it was held" (Oster 1979, 27).

Rather than a day-to-day schedule, the ESL program provides abstracts for the presentations, organized under three categories: research papers, public lectures, and workshops, with date and time attached. These are preceded by a program summary that maps out activities by day and hour, including besides concurrent sessions the keynote by Widdowson and an ESL lunch speaker (Richard Yorkey). There is little overlap between the two programs.

Many of the distinctive features of the conference programming, including its concurrent programs, mix of session types and focus, and segues from research or theory to practice (in and between sessions) found expression in the three postconference volumes, each with its own content and audience. In *Reinventing the Rhetorical Tradition,* editors Freedman and Pringle (1980) selected presentations from the English and language arts program for an audience of scholars in writing. It was published for CCTE in the United States by L and S Books (a bootstrap operation run out of an American English department). This press was then one of the few ways to publish a scholarly book in American rhetoric and composition, and for that reason *Reinventing* quickly entered the discourse of the field. Pringle and Freedman (1981) edited the next volume, *Teaching/Writing/Learning,* for classroom teachers. Published directly by CCTE, it sought to "cast into written form what happened" in the practical workshops distributed throughout the conference (O'Hara 1981, iii). Yalden joined Freedman and Pringle to edit the third conference proceedings, *Learning to Write: First Language/Second Language* (Freedman, Pringle, and Yalden 1983). This book, which draws on both programs (only two pieces overlap with *Reinventing*), was published for CCTE in London (and New York) by Longman in a series on applied linguistics and language study. As its title and publication venue suggest, it is oriented to a more international (especially British) audience, situates writing studies in disciplines of language study rather than in (American) composition and rhetoric, emphasizes language learning over a broader range of ages and levels, and links first-language and second-language learning and pedagogies through research on writing.

To unfold the potential meanings of the Ottawa conference and its inscriptions, I next reinsert them into broader historical contexts, retrospectively understood (Levi 2001; Magnusson and Szijarto 2013, 65; Phillips 2004).

1979 and Thereabout

In 2003, Martin Nystrand and John Duffy prefaced an edited volume on new directions in writing studies by asserting that "the leading edge of research on writing, reading, and literacy . . . is defined by its intersection with sociocultural, historical, political, disciplinary, institutional, and everyday contexts" (Nystrand and Duffy 2003a, viii). Their own historical overview begins with the provocative premise that "ideas take hold because some receptive context valorizes them" (xviii). While that receptive context includes ideas (extradisciplinary sources and influences), these are insufficient to explain the rapid development of composition in the late 1960s and 1970s: it is necessary to examine

the sociocultural contexts and events that "provided the critical cata-
lyst . . . [and] helped set agendas of change and define issues in the
particular forms they took" (xviii). A number of other scholars develop
this connection in historical accounts of the period (Ede 2004; Faigley
1992; Goggin 2000; Zebroski 2012; see also Applebee 1974, 184–243).[8]

Briefly, here is the picture these scholars draw of the events and
sociohistorical forces that shaped the "receptive context" for the rise of
(American) composition and rhetoric throughout the 1970s.[9] Maureen
Daly Goggin describes how in the 1960s and early 1970s a "confluence
of social, political, ethical, and economic upheavals . . . [including] the
civil rights movement; the women's movement; political assassinations
of President John F. Kennedy [1965], Martin Luther King [1968], and
Robert Kennedy [1968]; and the Vietnam War and the draft . . . radically
realigned the social and cultural matrix in the United States and . . . had
an enormous impact on education" (Goggin 2000, 75). Students were
radicalized and campuses saw widespread protests and disruptions.
Composition was not immune to this countercultural activism and,
indeed, was deeply engaged with it (Faigley 1992, 48–79; Parks 2013;
Zebroski 2012, 30)

At the same time, however, under a "liberal consensus" that prevailed throughout most of the 1960s, the federal government generously funded the War on Poverty and all levels of education, including the Economic Opportunity Act in 1964 and the Elementary and
Secondary Act and Higher Education Act in 1965 (Faigley 1992, 51).[10]
By the late 1960s, community colleges were opening at a rate of one a
week (Nystrand and Duffy 2003a, xix). A huge expansion was underway
in higher education: postsecondary enrollment grew to 3.6 million in
1959–60; exceeded 8 million by 1969–70; and soared above 11.5 million
in 1979–80 (Faigley 1999, 27–28).

As these contexts began to shift in the next decade, with the United
States' departure from Vietnam, Watergate and President Nixon's res-
ignation, the rise of oil prices with gas rationing, and a stock-market
decline (Faigley 1992, 62), anxieties rose about education, fueled by
conservative critics like John Simon and Edwin Newman. In 1974, NAEP
issued a report on the decline of writing abilities, and, with *Newsweek*'s
publication of "Why Johnny Can't Write" in 1975, the literacy crisis was
born. Ironically, the perceived literacy crisis and cries of "back to basics,"
in tandem with postsecondary expansion, open admissions, demo-
graphic changes, increased ethnic diversity, and the 1960s-based emphasis on student-centered education, constituted a highly receptive climate
for composition to thrive. Writing teachers and administrators were

needed for the influx of students, which meant jobs (unavailable to literature graduates), and federal and foundation money flowed liberally to support writing-related professional development for teachers as well as research on writing. Lisa Ede defines the climate as more than simply "receptive": "Specific material *interventions* . . . enabled the field to—in a remarkably compressed period of time—improve its professional and disciplinary status" (Ede 2004, 50; italics mine). Ede (2004, 54–60), and Goggin (2000, 75–111) in her chapter "Sowing the Seeds, 1965–1980," detail the copious menu of funded and unfunded professional-development opportunities, which were especially attractive—and necessary—to scholars educated in literature who wanted to retool in composition.[11]

The year 1979 has never been identified as particularly crucial in the annals of composition history, but these contextualizations and scholars' narratives (e.g., D'Angelo 1999) tend to lead toward and away from it, treating it tacitly as a watershed that divides (and joins) the decade of sowing the seeds from the decade of harvesting their fruits. The Ottawa conference, falling precisely at that moment of transition becomes identified with the watershed. Or, more precisely, if viewed broadly as a process, it crosses the watershed: it was proposed in 1977, planned and prepared between then and 1980, and inscribed over the next several years. Shifting the metaphor, we might say that the Ottawa conference rode and crested the rising wave of the 1970s while the publications from it (1980, 1981, 1983) flowed away into the new era.

A lot happened "around 1979," to echo David Bartholomae's (1993) afterword to *Pre/Text: The First Decade* in which he assembles bits and pieces of history "around 1980" as context for the founding of *Pre/Text* that year: articles published and books advertised, seven postdoctoral seminars one might attend, the scene at 4Cs, and so on. I can add one scrap to his collage: Ottawa 1979 was one scene where Victor Vitanza and others from Richard Young's NEH seminar at Carnegie-Mellon plotted to start the journal.[12] *Pre/Text* was one of six new journals in rhetoric and composition founded between the Ottawa conference and its last published inscription in 1983 (Goggin 2000, 36). Over that time span, doctoral programs sprang up in sudden profusion. Of thirty-eight programs listed in Chapman and Tate's (1987, 128) earliest survey of doctoral programs in rhetoric, half were founded during that period: a startling ten in 1979–80, and nine more by 1983.

Also in 1979, I completed my own self-designed interdisciplinary PhD in composition and rhetoric. When I found a job at the University of Southern California (teaching in one of the earliest doctoral programs in the field), I joined an emerging cohort of tenure-line faculty who, together with the pioneering scholars who inspired them, formed the critical mass necessary to "legitimate [composition's] situation in the academy—if it could develop a strong disciplinary project" (Ede 2004, 61). Most of the new faculty were still postdoctoral "converts" or had cobbled together ad hoc studies in writing and rhetoric in the absence of full-scale graduate degrees, but their credible scholarly expertise and growing numbers finally made possible the collective creation in the United States of discipline-based doctoral education in the 1980s.

THE CONFERENCE AS INTERACTION RITUAL

Interaction Rituals as Scholarly Practice

The scholars I've been citing tie this receptive or catalytic context to a trajectory of professionalization that accelerated during the 1970s and reached a plateau around 1980, which ushered in a decade of consolidating and securing the gains that had been made in achieving an academic identity as a discipline (see Goggin 2000, 113–46). In her history, Ede draws attention to the relationships between "individual career building and the effort to establish composition's scholarly expertise in the academy in the 1970s and early 1980s" (Ede 2004, 51). Frank D'Angelo (1999, 2002) highlights this synchrony between autobiography and field, making the story of how he—and his cohort—invented themselves as writing scholars isomorphic with stages in the growth of the discipline. In his 1999 narrative, he traces their parallel trajectories from "initiation" through a "quest" stage to the triumphant emergence of an academic discipline of rhetoric and composition, which he places in 1978–1980. That success was manifest in a geometric increase in scholarly activity and social interaction: between 1978 and 1980, D'Angelo "participated in 22 conferences and symposiums, four workshops, and four colloquiums. . . . You could probably multiply the number of speaking engagements, colloquiums, seminars, and workshops by a hundred if you were to ask other scholars what they were doing at this time" (D'Angelo 1999, 277).

Ede challenges conventional histories of composition for focusing on "changes enacted at the level of theory" while neglecting "the *scholarly practices* that enabled various theories to gain ascendancy" (Ede 2004, 51; italics mine). I'm not sure she meant this phrase in exactly the sense I want to take it up, but the practices she goes on to describe (as "activities" and "opportunities") are overwhelmingly embodied experiences of intellectual exchange with other scholars (55–60). They are the face-to-face, interactive, deeply engaging professional events—seminars, institutes, conferences, workshops, and the like, ranging in length from a few days to a year—that D'Angelo (and Ede herself) attended.[13]

Ede perceptively highlights the importance of these face-to-face events—including appreciation of the Ottawa conference itself (Ede 2004, 57). But even she focuses on the achievement, dually, of scholarly careers for individuals and credibility and status in the academy for the discipline ("professionalization") rather than on the events themselves as embodiments and experiences of scholarly activity. That focus on professionalism attends to the pragmatic consequences of such events rather than what happens there, specifically as a phenomenon of scholarly practice.[14] This section directs attention to the Ottawa conference in just those terms: as enacting a recurrent pattern of embodied scholarly practice, which reveals its fractal relation to a system of intellectual activity (see Magnusson and Szijarto 2013, 63). To crystallize this pattern from the hints and glimpses offered by the inscriptions, I will need some conceptual tools.

D'Angelo's accounts express the nature of these events as recurrent encounters of small groups in emotionally stimulating exchanges (intense, involving, energizing) focused on ideas (D'Angelo 1999, 2002).[15] These are precisely the defining features of the "interaction rituals" (or IRs) Randall Collins (1998) deems essential to the motives and the intellectual work of disciplines.[16] They are also the qualities that Mary Catherine Bateson (1984) dramatizes in her memoir of her parents, Margaret Mead and Gregory Bateson, vividly evoking the lives of two generative scholars for whom conversation was the primary medium for making knowledge. In Collins's work, as in Bateson's, the face-to-face encounter is a sine qua non for successful intellectual communities. (The role of texts, to be discussed later, is derivative).

In naming the conference an *interaction ritual*, I am invoking Collins's (1998) grand theory of intellectual work as a function of social networks, whose structures and dynamics account for the life of ideas over time.[17] Although such networks have widening, concentric circles of participants, at their core are small, concentrated groups of leading scholars engaged directly with one another in developing ideas about common objects and concerns. These groups are organized into networks by their horizontal (peer) relationships and vertical (intergenerational) relations and by their alliances and oppositions.

Collins's (1998) analytical framework offers here a tightly woven network of concepts, with interaction ritual (IR) at the center, to specify the eventful nature of the Ottawa conference. Bateson (1984) complements his abstract description of IRs with her poetic representation of

conversation as scholarly thinking, epitomized by the scholarly conference.[18] What Collins and Bateson share is a profound understanding
of thinking as social and, specifically, as communication. For Collins,
"Ideas . . . are first of all communication, which is to say interaction
among bodily humans. . . . Ideas are formed in the process of communication between one thinker and another. . . . The communicative
process creates the thinkers as nodes of the process" (Collins 1998, 2).
Bateson's book recreates her parents' ideas and their lives as a tissue of
conversations, from the microcosm of the family to the formal venue of
the conferences they frequently arranged: "I had . . . spent my life in and
out and on the edge of conferences, formal and informal, treating them
as a normal mode of interaction—perhaps indeed as *the* normal mode of
interaction . . . I had grown up to believe that conferences are the way
to think" (Bateson 1984, 179). Both Collins and Bateson agree closely
on the processes, structures, and qualities of this communication. Both
emphasize small, generative groups who meet face to face—Collins's
"innovative core" (Collins 1998, 5) and Bateson's "evolution clusters,"
her mother's term for "groups of people among whom ideas develop
and within which the contributions of an outstanding mind resonate
and are amplified" (Bateson 1984, 198). Both stress emotion as an indispensable component of scholarly thinking-through-communication:
Collins, in his foundational concept of "emotional energy"; Bateson,
in her portrait of intense intellectual conversation as a passion akin to
lovemaking (199), infused with emotions like love, bewilderment, rage,
dismay, and illumination (180).

Relatedly, each conceives scholarship as stimulated by diversity of
viewpoint and energized by opposition among scholars, positions, and
movements. Conflicts are, Collins (1998, 1) writes, the indispensable
"energy source of intellectual life" and, as "lines of difference between
positions," "implicitly the most prized possessions of intellectuals" (6).
Although intellectual communities generate a huge volume or flow of
thoughts, ideas and rival positions must compete for the network's attention, and only a few can become the focus of creative conflict at a particular moment. Collins argues there is only room for three to six successful
"knots of argument" (38) to occupy niches simultaneously in the limited,
stratified attention space of a field. These constitute a structured "field of
forces within which individuals act and think"—stable until it is restruc-
tured in revolutionary moments (42). In contrast, Bateson emphasizes
the productive potential for argument as joint performance: as in dance
or jazz improvisation, enabling participants "to say something which no
one of them knew as they came in the door" (Bateson 1984, 178).

We can recognize scholarly events as interaction rituals by these defining qualities: an assembled group (two or more) whose members are copresent in time and space; participants' focus on a common object or action; and a shared mood or sentiment (Collins 1998, 22, 47). As prototypical scholarly IRs, conferences are unlikely to achieve unity on issues—just the opposite since the intellectual network is characterized by its oppositional structure. Rather, what unifies participants is their membership in the community of scholars: "The consciousness of the group's continuity itself as an activity of discourse" in a chain of IRs and their products (thoughts, symbols, discourses, and generations) that link past and future (Collins 1998, 28).

Functionally, IRs serve as engines of intellectual activity and creativity. By focusing collective attention and sentiment on particular objects or ideas, IRs infuse symbols (concepts, objects, images, texts, even scholars themselves) with emotional significance; the most meaningful become "sacred objects" for the network "that act as magnetic poles in intellectual thinking, that are the focus of the long and serious attention that is the activity of the intellectual world at its most intense" (Collins 1998, 41). Individuals store up these charged symbols as "cultural capital" (24), knowledge of the field Collins defines as a repertoire of "ideas and the sense of what to do with them" (71) or the ability to grasp the field as an evolving set of "fruitful tasks" and intellectual possibilities (28).

Like an electric battery, an IR event like a conference, through its social interactions, common focus, and mood, also "charges" up participants themselves—both speakers and audiences—not only with cultural capital but with "emotional energy" for conducting intellectual work (Collins 1998, 29–37). Emotional energy (differentially accessible to members of a network) encompasses motivation, enthusiasm, confidence, mental and physical strength for pursuing scholarly activity. But these charges fade with time, and scholars must constantly renew energy and cultural capital by forging their own personal IR chains in a "grid of encounters" from everyday meetings to the membership rituals of professional organizations (29). In the bigger picture, IRs are microsituations in a dynamic macrocontext of social interaction that links human bodies and minds (and, as we will see below, texts) into disciplinary networks through which ideas and emotional energy flow ceaselessly across time and space.

Realizing the Ottawa Conference as Interaction Ritual

For Collins and Bateson, conferences are prototypical sites for scholars to think and communicate, which is to say they are IRs by definition and intent. So it seems a truism to call the Ottawa conference an *interaction ritual* and redundant to exhaustively document its IR features. However, the organizers of Ottawa 1979 faced a unique and challenging set of circumstances in designing and orchestrating this conference as an IR. I want to define these challenges and show how the purposes and strategies they adopted resulted in a distinctive IR with heightened qualities and special functions. I'll explore these points further in the final section, which portrays the conference as an example of the microhistorical concept of the exceptional normal.

A useful reference point for this analysis is Collins's (1998) three identifying features of an IR as scholarly practice: the copresence of participants in space and time; a flow of ideas and debates around a common focus in a structured attention space; and feelings generated in the encounter (shared mood, "charge"). His theory expects most conference attendees to belong to an intellectual community already bound together socially by chains of communication events so their copresence and coordinated thinking at the conference will be felt as part of a continuity of both network (people) and dialogue (ideas). Such members would bring to the conference shared symbolic resources for communication and expectations about which topics, arguments, and figures would dominate discussion.

In other words, Collins assumes a discipline as the context for any particular IR to make it both intelligible and involving for members of the network. But that context is exactly what the organizers did not, and could not, assume about the eclectic mix of conference delegates. Without a specific context, the conference had to conjure up the discipline for them as a living practice. Broadly, the strategy adopted was to make the conference itself a microcosm of the discipline—its structure and dynamics to be evoked, experienced, in a sense even accomplished by the conference itself. (As we will see in the next section, this strategy was flipped in the inscriptions to use the conference as proof of the discipline.)

To understand both the necessity and the execution of this strategy, we must start with the participants. Of the 1,250 delegates, about 16 percent were speakers or workshop leaders in two streams of meetings, English and language arts (156) and ESL (47). They were layered in a hierarchy that reflects Collins's portrait of the intellectual network, with leading scholars, "stars," at the "hot center" (Collins 1998, 30) and others in widening circles of membership out to a periphery. In *Reinventing*, Freedman and Pringle (1980, 173, 176, 178) clearly identify this inner circle and its members' role at the conference and in the field: as "leading researchers and composition scholars," they were "at the vanguard," "at the forefront of the discipline," "operating out of a different intellectual matrix" from the outer circle of practitioners. Other layers included established scholars with different degrees of experience and eminence; novice scholars, including graduate students; and teachers from different levels of schooling. The periphery of the network was defined by "the outsider," as Freedman and Pringle noted about E. D. Hirsch (1977), a literary critic whose book *The Philosophy of Composition* was critiqued in his absence (Freedman and Pringle 1980, 176).[19]

On the surface, the participants in Ottawa 1979 may seem a typical conference mix, but they are different from Collins's model of IR participants in several striking ways. First, there was an enormous distance between the leading scholars and the most distant circle, the practitioners, many of whom (especially teachers from Canada) were complete newcomers to even the very idea of a discipline. In *Inkshed* (a Canadian newsletter), Phyllis Artiss wrote, Ottawa 1979 was "a turning point for me, as for a good many other teachers in this country. . . . Here I discovered that there were other teachers in English in this country who shared my commitment to teaching writing and were willing to actually talk about it in public! What was even more astonishing was to learn that there were lots of professors of English in universities (mostly in the U.S.) who wrote books and articles about teaching composition, got research grants to do this kind of work, and won awards for it" (Artiss 1991, 1).[20]

However, not even the speakers themselves, as a multidisciplinary, international group, came to the conference as members of a shared intellectual network or necessarily self-identified as writing scholars. In proposing a conference with a singular focus on writing, Freedman and Pringle "fantasize[d] . . . bringing together" the disparate and geographically scattered thinkers they saw as constituting a new, transnational discipline by their research on composing and writing development but who "seemed to be only dimly aware of each other's work" (Freedman 1995, 84).[21]

To make this nascent community come to life for delegates, the organizers had to envision it for themselves and then orchestrate the processes of a genuine IR.[22] To this task they brought complementary expertise, Freedman's in writing scholarship and Pringle's in linguistics (syntactic development). (Their vision included an ESL component, but that planning was delegated to Janice Yalden.) For a previous research project with Pringle, Freedman had developed a comprehensive reading knowledge of composition work in the 1970s; and in 1978 she attended Janice Lauer's two-week Rhetoric Seminar (then at the University of

Detroit), which provided her with a concentrated scholarly overview of American composition and rhetoric from representatives of its most current scholarship (Lauer 1998). That base was broadened by what each knew about lines of research on writing and writing development in international settings and in other disciplines.

Intuitively, Freedman and Pringle built the Ottawa 1979 IR around an inner core. To construct one, they first "approached a number of the real recognized stars in the field"; while Freedman was at Lauer's Rhetoric Seminar, she invited all the speakers there to the conference (five of eight accepted). They successfully used these "big players" like magnets to attract one another, some to meet for the first time. When I interviewed Freedman in December 2013, she told me the call for papers drew "huge numbers" of proposals, suggesting that already they had tapped into an incipient sense of a common enterprise: "You could really sense the discipline burgeoning, flourishing at that moment."

These charismatic figures, along with other major scholars speaking in concurrent sessions, became the key to the organizers' strategies for creating a shared focus of thought and sense of community among such mixed participants. They used the choices and arrangement of speakers on the program to map out the event as an attention space (a synecdoche for the attention space of the discipline), establishing focal points for the delegates' "micro-coordination" of thought and communication (Collins 1998, 23). This process was necessarily inductive; Freedman describes their reading the work of invited speakers along with hundreds of proposals to discover the shape of the "new psychic terrain" (Freedman 1995, 84).[23] They deployed the speakers throughout the program to articulate the objects and symbols—topics, concepts, issues, problems, arguments—that would order the intellectual space. The "stars" provided classic, eloquent statements that introduced these symbols (accessibly for novices), saturated them with social meaning and emotional significance, and initiated dialogue between opposing positions. The conference amped up the emotional energy that flowed to participants with the high density and quality of speakers distributed over each day (and adding their presence to other sessions); the generative sparks of conflict; and opportunities in the crowded spaces of small classrooms for social interaction among all levels of participants, continuing in "even more valuable, extended conversations over beer in the evenings and over lunch on those magically lovely days on the campus" (Freedman 1995, 84).

Both Pringle and Freedman came increasingly to appreciate the role agonistic conflict plays in energizing scholarly practice.[24] The speaker-respondent pairs were designed to dramatize differences around argument "knots," but there were also confrontations arising from the audience. In an e-mail message to me on February 17, 2014, Pringle described a "magic moment" early in the conference when British educator Tony Adams confronted cognitive psychologist Carl Bereiter "cogently and forthrightly," including the statement that "'we have already heard too much about cognitive psychology at this conference.'" Pringle continued: "It literally made the hair on the back of my neck stand on end, and the reaction in the audience as a whole was all a conference organizer could hope for in terms of setting the tone for the conference and starting discussion and debate which could and did continue throughout the rest of the conference."[25] Such conflicts hint at divisions with complex correlations to disciplinary orientation, level of education, and national identity: for example, Oster reports, "Basic British distrust of the North American obsession with models, classifications, and techniques was revealed by a number of British comments, in tones not suggesting reverence, about heuristics, tagmemics, and sentence-combining" (Oster 1979, 26). Referring to the deepest division at Ottawa—the "clash of paradigms" initiated by Emig's "Tacit Tradition" speech—Oster says "the sparks from these collisions certainly contributed to the liveliness of the conference and . . . to igniting new areas of thought and research for many participants" (26).

Through the inscriptions and other sources, in spite or because of these conflicts, we get a glimpse of the affect of the conference, which suggests its success in creating a high degree of energy, emotional investment, and sense of common purpose. The terms characterizing mood include "buoyant, exhilarated, confident" (Freedman and Pringle 1980, 176); "electric" (Emig 1995, 79); and "vibrancy" and "air of excitement" (Oster 1979, 24). In an e-mail message to me on February 7, 2014, James Reither described the conference as "enormously exciting and invigorating . . . an injection of energy into my sense that this was a field I could devote myself to."[26]

Freedman and Pringle have much to say about what these feelings signify in terms of the accomplishments of the conference as event. But their powerful claims take us from reconstructing the event as interaction ritual *through* the inscriptions to examining the inscriptions as texts performing their own acts and functions within a larger discourse.

CONFERENCE INSCRIPTIONS AS SCHOLARSHIP,
RHETORIC, HERMENEUTIC, AND PEDAGOGY

Collins's insistence on the primacy of face-to-face interaction for intel-lectual life doesn't prevent him from understanding the crucial role played by texts: "An intellectual IR is generally a situational embodiment of the texts which are the long-term life of the discipline. Lectures and texts are chained together: this is what makes the distinctiveness of the intellectual community" (Collins 1998, 27). Indeed, reading and writ-ing amount to virtual IRs, producing similar effects from participating vicariously in "coalitions in the mind" (36). Collins points out that intel-lectual communities depend for their sustainability on writing, more specifically on a text-distribution structure that allows ideas to cross time and space, transcending embodied occasions and persons: "Intellectual events in the present—lectures, debates, discussions—take place against an explicit backdrop of past texts, whether building upon them or cri-tiquing them" (27).

Conference proceedings, as inscriptions of actual IRs, play a special but unexamined role in these textual functions. In particular, they have attracted little notice from historians as artifacts that document—as a kind of "history of the present" (Ash 1999; Little 2009)—how scholarly practice was enacted face to face, from which we might trace the trajec-tory of intellectual movements, restructurings of the attention space, development of symbols and sacred objects, and other phenomena of disciplinary dynamics. But in their own time they have their own, variable discourse purposes and intended functions within disciplin-ary discourse. The three volumes of conference proceedings edited by Freedman, Pringle, and Yalden display the possibilities for a rich range of goals that such inscriptions might serve, of which four kinds stand out: *scholarly, hermeneutical, rhetorical,* and *pedagogical.*

To consider these, I will sharpen the focus in several respects. First, there are two layers of text in an edited volume, corresponding to the roles of authors and editors: (1) essays reproducing (or derived from) scholars' conference talks; and (2) the editorial writings and features of each volume. These purposes independently animate both levels, but I'll be concerned only with how they figure in the editorial work performed by the volumes, individually and collectively. Each volume, differentiated by audience, integrates these four purposes in different ratios. Given space limitations, I'll devote the most detailed attention to *Reinventing the Rhetorical Tradition* (Freedman and Pringle 1980).

This first volume, aimed at the emergent scholarly community, is key to grasping the editors' goals in producing inscriptions of the conference, so I will begin with their own statement of purpose: "No book can hope to give more than a hint of the excitement generated on the campus of Carleton University as the 1250 delegates to the conference listened to each other's presentations and then argued, challenged, discussed, explained, and argued further throughout the conference. . . . But if the impact of the conference on those who attended cannot be recreated, at least some of the most important of the presentations can be shared, through publication in book form, with those who did not attend" (Freedman and Pringle 1980, ix). The preface goes on to frame this particular volume as an expression of three strands "in the fabric of the conference," emphasizing how the papers "deal with the relationship of the rhetorical theories discussed at the conference (and their practical applications), to the rhetorical traditions which they are superseding" and to note that the epilogue provides "our own view of the larger context of these theories," that is, of the discipline. Two strands refer to concepts: tradition as it relates to the contemporary field and invention as a distinctive focus of scholarship on writing. The third is mood: the pervasive excitement that reflects delegates' discovery of their commonality in a scholarly enterprise. The editors then briefly place the essays in the book in relation to these themes of emergent disciplinarity and add another, "pedagogical implications of the new discipline" (xi). From this starting point, we can discern in *Reinventing* a complex integration of codependent scholarly, hermeneutic, and rhetorical purposes, acting both as subgoals and as means to accomplish a broader editorial function for the inscriptions (with a hint at how pedagogical purpose will become dominant in the second volume).

A fundamental goal of the inscriptions is to enlarge the circle of those who can participate vicariously in the conference and, therefore, the discipline. At the most basic level, that means providing directly— in inscribed talks or, in the case of *Teaching/Writing/Learning* (Pringle and Freedman 1981), translations of workshop events—the scholarly ideas and arguments that circulated at the conference. The editors perform a scholarly function in selecting material from the conference for inclusion, framing it, summarizing it, and synthesizing it (in all three volumes). However, in *Reinventing* they go well beyond this minimal editorial work, in part through the synecdochal relationship they set up between conference and discipline. The epilogue here, and collectively all the background materials written for workshops in *Teaching/Writing/Learning*, use the conference as a platform for painting a picture of the (evoked/imagined) field at that critical, watershed moment in 1979.

That portrait includes sketching (illustrating with figures, essays, and moments at the conference) the partitioned and hierarchical shape of its intellectual activity, its motifs, differences, and oppositions; characterizing the "mood of the profession . . . as it revealed itself at the conference" (Pringle and Freedman 1981, 176); historicizing the field's development; and projecting its future trajectory.

But this image of the discipline is not neutral, of course; it has a hermeneutical dimension and rhetorical force. In a comment posted to the blog *Understanding History* on August 2, 2009, Daniel Little's language defining a "history of the present" works surprisingly well to characterize the editors' work as hermeneutic: "This is an act of 'apperception'— taking many separate pieces of evidence and experience and forging them together into a unified representation" (Little 2009, 1). As contemporary observers of the conference, Freedman and Pringle sought to grasp, in Little's words, "what is occurring, over what terrain, by what actors, in response to what forces and motives," producing an "evidence-based integrative narrative of what the processes of the present *amount to*"—that is, what they mean (Little 2009, 2; italics mine). Broadly, the hermeneutical task in *Reinventing* was to *interpret what the conference meant for/about a discipline of writing,* not only in their present but in our future.

One way to observe this interpretive work is to look at the symbols Freedman and Pringle foregrounded in *Reinventing.* Tradition is a condensed symbol for a set of questions debated at the conference about the discipline: From what (competing) traditions has it drawn ideas and values? How relevant are those traditions today? Which is most "congenial" and productive for future development of the field? (Freedman and Pringle 1980, 178). The editors' historical review places the contemporary (1979–1980) field in relation to two past traditions: the "current-traditional" practice of teaching composition that has been repudiated (173) and the tradition of classical rhetoric, whose primacy is now challenged (most powerfully and controversially in Emig's "Tacit Tradition" speech) by "the contemporary intellectual matrix," whose genealogy includes twentieth-century thinkers about language as well as paradigms and research from fields like cognitive psychology and linguistics (178). By constructing historical relationships in this way, the epilogue largely ignores an alternate way of framing the past in terms of the broader realm of English or language-arts education, internationalized (in IR terms) by the Dartmouth Conference, in favor of the more explicitly disciplinary history of rhetoric and composition in the United States. (However, this alternate tradition reappears in the third volume, *Learning to Write* [Freedman, Pringle, and Yalden 1983].)

This clash of traditions, dramatized at the conference, presents Freedman and Pringle with the specter of a deep fracture in the field, even at its (re)birth as a discipline of writing studies. It threatens one of their major (rhetorical) claims, that the conference mood expresses commonality, signifying the emergent disciplinary network. They resolve this problem hermeneutically by using their second highlighted symbol, invention, as a mediating term. In the context of new research on composing, they cast the term as bridging the two traditions by reinterpreting the concept in light of modern research. This term is then resituated to characterize the new discipline itself as "reinventing" the rhetorical tradition so that "there is no great difficulty in reconciling" the rhetorical distant past with the modern tradition evoked by Emig (1980, 179). "Reinventing" is a "fundamentally eclectic" approach: "seeking out those theoretic statements most consistent with our shared assumptions and explicit formulations which might give shape to our intuitions and perhaps suggest further implications. But these insights and formulations have been reconceived from a modern perspective and set within a contemporary philosophical context" (179). Much of the epilogue is devoted to advocating this understanding of the discipline by showing how it applies to illustrative issues and concepts in the conference papers, often to the effect of reconciling positions many regarded as opposed or incompatible.

This position is grounded rhetorically, first, in an expanded definition of *commonality* and, second, in the treatment of *the discipline* itself as a symbol. For their rhetorical purposes at this moment in time/space, the editors needed to emphasize unity over "the issues that divide us" (the theme of the second Ottawa Conference, only six years later). The editors argue that commonality is not just a sentiment or spirit, though it is that. First, it is a shared, active relationship to the competing traditions—the ongoing activity of "reinventing" the one with the other. Second, they insist, despite its diversity, the intellectual network embraces a body of shared assumptions, specific concepts, beliefs, and values (named here and greatly detailed for practitioners in *Teaching/ Learning/Writing* [1981]). Among these are focusing on processes of composing and viewing texts as fundamentally social, not autonomous, "within a total rhetorical context which includes writer, audience, and world" (Emig 1980, 177).

Emerging from this conference, the most sacred object, saturated with social meaning, was the idea of the discipline itself, not as a status but as a transcendent scholarly practice. Freedman and Pringle are careful to place the discipline in a time stream that has both a past (traditions, IR chains) and a future of "tremendous ongoing activity: the sense of work in progress, of what remains to be done; the active involvement of so many researchers, theorists and pedagogues in charting the new territory" (Freedman and Pringle 1980, 184). Moreover, they powerfully assert the "immense importance" of the discipline insofar as composing/invention is an "essential human activity" of thinking, learning, and knowing (180).

A cascade of rhetorical claims, then, flows from the fundamental one of existence: there is now a discipline—a scholarly study with this object, nature, and scope, these qualities and premises, a network of participants both international and multidisciplinary. While I can't analyze the other two volumes in detail, I want to note briefly how each works within this hermeneutical-rhetorical framework and also modifies and extends it.

Teaching/Learning/Writing (Pringle and Freedman 1981) is an unusual effort to extend the conference event and its effects—the sense of community, the energy and intellectual capital generated by the conference—to include practitioners as an integral part of the discipline. Its method is to capture in writing the most quintessentially face-to-face component of the conference, its workshops: "to translate 'happenings' into pieces of transactional writing, a creative act akin to transforming a poem into a painting, a symphony into a drama" (O'Hara 1981, iii). But these translations become pedagogical and rhetorical through an extensive layer of contextualizing editorial material specific to each workshop, which persuasively explicates theory and research relevant to the practices embodied there. Unlike the relatively autonomous essays of the other volumes (as collections), this editorial material is used to make the book a cohesive reading experience through explicit linkages (backward and forward) to other workshops so it could function pedagogically as a kind of textbook (perhaps, one speculates, intended for use in professional-development settings for teachers). The editors are frank advocates for particular values and positions, but, more broadly, they seek to persuade teachers that scholarship in the new discipline can and should inform and guide their classroom goals and strategies. Thus, this volume embodies a position on theory-practice relationships, a fundamental division (and question about the nature of the field) that was muted in *Reinventing*'s drive to articulate the discipline as first and foremost an intellectual enterprise.

The final volume in the series represents the ESL strand of the conference, but not autonomously (as one might expect from its separate, parallel programming at Ottawa). Instead of that easy option, in *Learning to Write: First Language/Second Language*, Freedman, Pringle, and Yalden

(1983) use their selections and editorial writings (introductions to each of four parts) to put disciplinary studies of writing developed in the context of first-language learning in dialogue with the field of ESL, concerned with second-language learners.[27] Compared to *Reinventing*, the book, published in an applied linguistics and language study series, exposes readers more richly to British, Australian, and Canadian perspectives as well as multidisciplinary linguistic, cognitive, and developmental research on a wider spectrum of educational levels. The emphasis on commonality as defining a disciplinary community in *Reinventing* shifts in this volume, where differences are between two independent disciplines (although many familiar polarities cut across ESL and the new writing studies). The editors conduct a respectful examination of how different contexts—first-language versus second-language learner, or developmental levels from elementary to adult—explain and justify differences, intellectually, in the foci of scholars' attention, and pedagogically, in educational practice. From this base the editors suggest different modes of compatibility and complementarity with the hope of engaging the two fields in mutual learning.

The rhetorical purpose of putting composition and rhetoric into dialogue with ESL has the paradoxical hermeneutical effect of reframing a writing discipline as less autonomous. In *Reinventing*, the discipline is differentiated from a larger, nebulous (international) field of English education by its strong scholarly focus on writing. But the US base of this discipline (despite important contributions from scholars in English education) was limited by its overidentification with American "college" composition. This volume situates writing in the full developmental span, encompassing all levels of learning, and expands the geographical compass of its study and teaching. Although the editors never suggest a merger, the intellectual pressure of this dialogue reinserts writing scholarship into a broader, more diffuse intellectual enterprise—more frankly pedagogical than the discipline of *Reinventing*—and blurs some of its carefully drawn boundaries. Besides ESL, Candlin's preface argues that the issues discussed here (e.g., "The Use of Writing for Learning and Knowing") affect not just writing but "language learning and teaching as a whole, and one might add, the entire process of education" (Candlin 1983, ix).

THE MICROHISTORICAL VALUE OF OTTAWA 1979

It seems obvious, in theory if not in practice, that we should return to primary sources, not only to reconstruct the disciplinary past but to teach it to the next generation of scholars. Through this microhistory, we see the added value of studying these sources in their original context. Conferences and their editorial inscriptions offer a usefully circumscribed context for this purpose: to understand a particular historical crisis or change as enacted at a given moment in talk and text; as meaningful for a range of historical actors; and as interpreted and integrated by contemporaneous participant-observers writing "histories of the present." Microhistories are distinctive in incorporating both emic and etic perspectives. They foreground participants' own language expressing their "experiences, how they saw their lives and what meaning they attributed to the things that happened to them"; at the same time, relying on historians' contextual knowledge, microhistories "give explanations with references to historical structures, long-lived mentalities and global processes using a retrospective analysis, all of which were absent from the actors' own horizons of interpretation" (Magnusson and Szijarto 2013, 75). This principle signifies microhistorians' profound respect for historical actors not only as active agents "operating within the interstices of contradictory normative systems" (Levi 2001, 111) but also as reflective thinkers about those systems. Their own attempt to understand themselves historically "makes a claim on the future," as Eiss describes an object whose inscription "was a demand to be read not only by contemporaries but perhaps by others who might one day understand the events of that day as the beginning of a history that was yet to take place" (Eiss 2008, 74).[28]

What makes the case of the Ottawa conference doubly valuable is that it represents what microhistorians call the "exceptional normal" if we stretch that concept to its more general interpretation (Magnusson and Szijarto 2013, 19; see McComiskey, introduction, this volume). By describing the Ottawa conference through the template of Collins's "interaction ritual," I assimilate it to "normal" intellectual practices in academic disciplines. In fact, one of Freedman and Pringle's implicit premises in *Reinventing* is that these typical features and qualities of scholarship *signify* the disciplinarity of writing studies. But the inscriptions themselves bear witness to its singularity, first, as a historical moment: "To many who were present . . . it seemed that the conference served as a culmination of all that had been achieved in the study of rhetoric since the beginning of the recent resurgence of interest in the discipline . . . [and] provided a moment to pause and reflect on these developments" (Freedman and Pringle 1980, 173). Unspoken, but embodied in their own identities, is the additional uniqueness of the conference and its inscriptions as performing an early Canadian intervention in the discipline. So it is the chronotope that defines the event and its inscriptions together as exceptional: the nexus of time—the watershed moment of 1979; place—Carleton University, Ottawa, Canada; and agency—that of Canadian scholars whose participation in the discipline then troubles many unquestioned assumptions about that period of composition and rhetoric.

The context of 1979 created a watershed moment when certain things were possible. What difference did it make that it was Canadians who seized that moment?

In relation to the mainly US-based discipline of composition-rhetoric in 1979, Canadians who had taken up the discipline were outliers with an ambiguous and sometimes ambivalent identification with its American sources and viewpoints. Freedman and Pringle had Canadian-based contexts and experiences of writing instruction, but they had educated themselves in the scholarship of American rhetoric and composition through reading and (Freedman) face-to-face interactions with US scholars. If we think of rhetoric and composition then as becoming a community of practice, in Lave and Wenger's terms, these two scholars can be thought of as "legitimate peripheral participants"—newly engaged learners who had certain advantages in that role. One was the clear eyes and fresh perspectives of outsiders; another was that, as members of other (national and disciplinary) communities, they were in a position to articulate related communities (Lave and Wenger 1991, 36). As Lave and Wenger recognize, legitimate peripheral participation as a process of learning is a two-way street: in developing "knowledgeably skilled identities" through their participation, newcomers also transform the community of practice itself (55).

After preparing for and closely observing the conference, Freedman and Pringle (1980) were able, in *Reinventing*, to present a complex, nuanced historical overview of composition and rhetoric as it had developed, largely in the United States, and to interpret its value and importance in emic (insider) terms. As Canadians, however, they dramatically changed the concept of the emerging discipline by internationalizing it. To my knowledge, this was the first conference outside the United States to focus on writing as a disciplinary study; and, in the inscriptions, Freeman and Pringle were surely the first to proclaim it as not only a discipline but an international one. The template of the discipline in *Reinventing*, despite its debt to American work and perspectives, is already rhetorically presented as international, and in the third volume, *Learning to Write: First Language/Second Language* (1983), edited with Yalden, they more fully realize this ambition, although still limited in its global reach. As I pointed out, that volume foreshadows a much broader conception of the future of writing studies—to encompass studies of writers, language learners, and users of all ages; English across geographical and cultural boundaries; even writing in other languages—an interdiscipline with multiple roots, branches, and traditions only now finally taking shape.

Viewed through the microscope, Ottawa 1979 reminds us vividly of things we know—or thought we knew—heightened by the qualities of lived experience, like the intellectual pleasure scholars felt in talking and thinking together. The exceptional chronotope also defamiliarizes and revitalizes ideas, debates, and figures flattened and oversimplified by grand narratives that read them deductively through the lens of stereotypes and reductionist categories (Levi 2001, 114). Microhistory changes their sedimented meanings by recontextualizing them in the globalized community of the conference, a landscape populated by actors, ideas, and traditions unfamiliar to us as part of the discipline in that era, with consequences for how we view its American history (e.g., its roots in English education: see Stock 2012). "The micro-scale acts as a solvent on the alleged trajectory of macro-developments. Such a research agenda then links scale, possibility, agency, and the desire for a usable past" (Gregory 1999).[29]

This microhistory prompts a rethinking of Americanist histories of the discipline in light of an exceptional Canadian intervention at its watershed moment. But as an exceptional *normal*, it suggests that conferences and other interaction rituals are at the leading edge of scholarly practice, as important to disciplinary formation and advancement as journals, textbooks, and monographs. As fractals, they should not be treated as unique events (as we have Dartmouth 1966). Rather, we need to design fine-grained studies to trace ideas, scholars, and scholarly networks through IR chains and examine inscriptions of these events as historical artifacts and scholarly contributions. In making such investigations, we can test Collins's model of intellectual activity for its value and limitations when applied to the messy, complex, multirooted, and multibranching field we have become. Especially, we need to find out whether a hypothesis that may be historically true—that face-to-face interaction is essential to creative scholarly practice—holds up in a world transformed by digital technology, where IR events like conferences, seminars, even graduate programs can be experienced virtually, synchronously and asynchronously; inscribed, interpreted, and circulated by participants and observers as they happen; and extended in continuing interactions through multiple modes and media. Collins predicted that "the importance of personal connections will not decline in the future, no matter what overlay of new communications technology is invented"; he argued that no "dispersed and defocused structure of communication" can take the place of focused, face-to-face interaction (Collins 1998, 73). Will digitally mediated interactions and all their inscriptional capabilities replace or complement embodied ones to form and sustain peer and intergenerational networks and fulfill those social and intellectual functions that have enabled "coalitions of minds"? How can we study the rapid transformation of scholarly practices to foreground this question . . . and facilitate that possibility?

Appendix 2.1

MAJOR SPEAKERS AND RESPONDENTS AT THE OTTAWA CONFERENCE, CARLETON UNIVERSITY, 1979
General Program: English and Language Arts

Merron Chorny, University of Calgary, Canada

Lee Odell, SUNY Albany, USA. Respondent: Carl Bereiter, Ontario Institute for Studies in Education, Canada

Richard Young, Carnegie Mellon University, USA. Respondents: Janice Lauer, University of Detroit and Marygrove College, USA; Anthony Adams, Cambridge University, UK

James Squire, Ginn and Company, USA

James L. Kinneavy, University of Texas-Austin, USA. Respondents: Richard Larson, Herbert H. Lehman College, City University of New York, USA; Alan Coman, University of Toronto, Canada

Carl Bereiter, Ontario Institute for Studies in Education, Canada. Respondents: Elsa Bartlett, Rockefeller University, USA; Merron Chorny, University of Calgary, Canada

John Dixon, Bretton Hall College of Education, UK. Respondents: Janet Emig, Rutgers University, USA; Don Gutteridge, University of Western Ontario, Canada

W. Ross Winterowd, University of Southern California, USA. Respondents: Bruce Bennett, University of Western Australia, Australia; R. E. McConnell, University of British Columbia, UK

Donald Graves, University of New Hampshire, USA. Respondents: Bryant Fillion, Ontario Institute for Studies in Education, Canada; Nancy Martin, University of Surrey, UK

Marshall McLuhan, University of Toronto, Canada

Andrew Wilkinson, University of Exeter, UK. Respondents: Donald Graves,
    University of New Hampshire, USA; Peter Evans, Ontario Institute
    for Studies in Education, Canada

Janet Emig, Rutgers University, USA. Respondents: Murray F. Stewart,
    University of New Brunswick, Canada; H. A. Gleason Jr., University
    of Toronto, Canada

Elsa Bartlett, Rockefeller University, USA. Respondents: Andrew Wilkinson,
    University of Exeter, UK; Doris Etherington, Toronto, Canada

Randolph Quirk, University College, London, UK.

Edward P.J. Corbett, Ohio State University, USA. Respondents: Frank
    O'Hare, Ohio State University, USA; Michael Herrick, St. Mary's
    University, Canada

James Britton, University of London (Emeritus), UK

Anthony Adams, Cambridge University, UK

E.S.L. Program: Anglais, French Immersion,
English as a Second Language

Henry Widdowson, University of London, UK

Richard Yorkey, Concordia University, Canada

Notes

1.   Freedman and Pringle left open the naming of the new field. At that time, *composi-*
      tion or *composition studies* or *composition and rhetoric* were the most common designa-
      tions in the United States.

2.   Despite a consensus among historians on dating the modern rebirth of composi-
      tion in 1963 (see Harris 2012; Rice 2007), James Zebroski argues convincingly that
      composition and rhetoric didn't achieve full disciplinary status until the late 1970s,
      preceded by a decade or so of its development from informal collectives he calls
      "social formations" (Zebroski 2012, 28–29). (Goggin [2000] concurs in a time-
      line based on the history of scholarly journals.) "The Winds of Change," Maxine
      Hairston's (1982) famous proclamation of paradigm change in the teaching of
      writing (implicitly disciplinary), didn't appear until 1982, three years after Ottawa,
      while articles and books explicitly defining the discipline emerged later in the '80s
      (Brannon 1985; Lauer 1984; North 1987; Phelps 1986, 1988). But see Park (1979)
      for an early effort to discuss the potential disciplinarity in what he saw as a chaotic
      and ill-defined enterprise.

3.   Besides Emig's "The Tacit Tradition," other memorable essays in *Reinventing the*
      Rhetorical Tradition (Freedman and Pringle 1980) included James Kinneavy's "A
      Pluralistic Synthesis of Four Contemporary Models for Teaching Composition";
      Richard Young's "Arts, Crafts, Gifts and Knacks: Some Disharmonies in the New
      Rhetoric"; James Britton's "Shaping at the Point of Utterance"; and Ann Berthoff's
      "Learning the Uses of Chaos."

4.   Besides the three book publications from the conference, other sources that count
      as inscriptions for this inquiry include the conference's own artifacts (e.g., the print-
      ed program/s) and contemporaneous postconference reports. Some inscriptions

were not available for this project: neither the original CFP nor audiotapes of major speakers sold by the conference sponsor (Council of Canadian Teachers of English, then CCTE, now CCTELA). I limited other types of inquiry (for example, extensive interviewing of participants) as outside the bounds of the project but gathered supplementary information about the conference from sources like personal communications, retrospective interviews or commentary, and published histories. I myself am a potential source since I attended the conference as a graduate student and presented a paper based on the dissertation I was then writing. However, I will not be treating myself as a primary informant, although I have occasionally drawn on memories of the experience.

5.   The conference was originally titled "The Carleton Conference," but subsequent references are most commonly to the Ottawa Conference of 1979. The following description assembles historical facts of the conference event from multiple sources.

6.   In 1986, Freedman and Pringle collaborated on a second international conference, "The Issues That Divide Us," on the teaching of English worldwide. This one was sponsored by the International Federation of Teachers of English (IFTE) in a series established after Dartmouth 1966 to continue international meetings on English education (Watson 2013). Ottawa 1986 had much broader international representation than Ottawa 1979 because Pringle ensured that delegates were invited from every English-speaking country; in addition, a much greater effort was made to include teachers as well as scholars (Maguire 1995, 29–30; Pringle, e-mail, Feb. 15, 2014).

7.   All major speakers from both programs are listed in appendix 2.1.

8.   These scholars, like most other historians (e.g., Rosner, Boehm, and Journet 1999), assume the American provenance of the twentieth-century discipline as a unique phenomenon of US higher education. Accordingly, their surveys of sociocultural contexts (and the educational scene) are almost entirely US based. I don't have the space or expertise to expand them here to other countries. However, we will see later how Ottawa 1979 upends this assumption.

9.   Most of these scholars examine intellectual as well as material contexts for their receptive or catalytic influence on the "reinvention" of composition. I omit those here for two reasons: (1) the question of which intellectual contexts (traditions, sources, ideas, figures, seminal events) are pertinent is highly disputed, as more and more scholars write alternate histories of composition's roots and construe the discipline they produced accordingly, and (2) I don't want to anticipate or bias a reading of the conference and its inscriptions—as contemporaneous expressions and representations of the discipline—by imposing one or more of these lenses. For example, Nystrand and Duffy's (2003b) lens foregrounds the expansion of composition's contexts to encompass the "rhetoric of everyday life"; Faigley's (1992) explores the complex relations of composition to postmodern thought and culture.

10. Zebroski demonstrates how educational projects for the schools, like Project English curriculum study centers, deeply influenced rhetoric and composition, as did "the larger amounts of capital invested invisibly and directly in the education of working-class students," like the work-study program, tuition grants, Upward Bound, and SEEK (Zebroski 2012, 35).

11. Scholars' personal narratives provide insight into the role played by these activities in developing an intellectual community around the study of writing (see D'Angelo (1999), Lloyd-Jones (1994), Roen, Brown, and Enos (1999) and Williams (2002) on the role of institutes and projects).

12. I sat in on this conversation in Ottawa as an interested observer, having met the group as a visitor to Young's NEH seminar that spring.

13. Lloyd-Jones notes that "it is easy to overlook these programs that were essentially oral, and much of the exchange of ideas in this period has been oral or bureau-

cratic. Here the reports, ephemeral documents, memoirs, and other materials created at the same time offer symptoms of what was a messy, shifting, uneven series of personal encounters. At times connections seem to be quite accidental, results serendipitous. The early stages have less structure than a cocktail party conversation. Yet, the basic institute idea looms behind the most important devices for dissemination of new ideas about teaching composition and, I suspect, directly but less evidently behind much of its scholarship" (Lloyd-Jones 1994, 166).

14. There is an implicit argument in my contrast between professionalization and scholarly activity that has to do with what constitutes disciplinarity. In previous writing (Phelps 2014), I developed a distinction between a discipline, referring to an intellectual community and its work, and a field's academic identity, roughly, its ethos in the academy as a recognized discipline, coupled with the resources that both support and symbolize that status. The process of achieving and connecting the two is professionalization (cf. Collins's analysis of the three requisites for successful intellectual fields: "the intellectual network and its dynamics"; an "organizational base" like the university in the Western academy, providing material resources and status; and a receptive context in terms of political and economic forces (Collins 1998, 51, 622).

15. D'Angelo's (1999, 2002) narratives emphasize intellectual motives (to learn, explore, discover), and the sheer intellectual joy of conversation and debate with other scholars, over either pedagogical applications or professional status in the academy; he describes this period as an intellectual quest for an "object of study" (D'Angelo 2002). I take his narratives as representative of the experiences of the core group that met in these venues.

16. The term *interaction ritual* is adapted by Collins (1998) from Goffman (1967).

17. Collins (1998) developed his sociological theory of how intellectual communities work based on a global, comparative history of philosophy, but he intends its general application to disciplines as sites of scholarly thinking, including a pedagogical component (how it is taught and learned through intergenerational chains). He recognizes important variations from the philosophical archetype but lacks any account of the role in certain fields of relations between scholarly thought and activities like teaching, artistic expression, professional practice, or advocacy. The concepts in Collins's theory are embedded, richly elaborated, and interconnected. In pulling them selectively from that context, I necessarily simplify their definitions and relationships. But I've kept his vocabulary (often clunky to humanists' ears) as the most precise guide to those concepts.

18. Besides her memoir, Bateson invented a novelistic genre to represent the intellectual exchanges at one of her father's conferences, based on tape recordings (*Our Own Metaphor*, Bateson 1991). This conference distilled the essence of Collins's IRs, creating a dialogue among a very few eminent minds laser focused on a single problem. Bateson's parents orchestrated conferences deliberately to achieve a heightened quality of scholarly thought, in part through compressing the event in time and space. Bateson writes that the conference narratized in *Our Own Metaphor* can be seen as "a world in itself, sealed off in its own self-definition, as the participants are lifted out of their normal lives and backgrounds and forced into the effort of mutual adaptation. One is held in an envelope of time and inaccessibility, like the glass sides of an aquarium, as different kinds of mind work sometimes toward conflict and sometimes fall into a sort of dance or symmetry or counterpoint that leads to moments of revelation" (Bateson 1984, 181).

19. Collins describes five levels of stratification among scientists: stars, inner core, outer core, transients (occasional participants in scholarly conversation), and "audience and would-be recruits" (Collins 1998, 43). Arguably, in writing studies,

teachers fall into the last category as both readers who may use scholarship and also as potential scholars.

20. Inspired by the conference, Artiss went on to attend Janice Lauer's Rhetoric Seminar (by then at Purdue) and graduate school at the University of Texas-Austin.

21. In fact, the title "Learning to Write" cleverly finesses the gap between scholars and practitioners, between studying writing and teaching students, providing an inviting scope to contributions and easing accommodation of other potential divisions: disciplinary differences (e.g., composition/rhetoric versus English education), national differences (British versus American), levels of schooling, first- and second-language teaching, each associated with completely different IR chains.

22. Information about their backgrounds and planning activities is drawn from an interview I conducted with Aviva Freedman (December 2013) on behalf of Andrea Williams for her study of Canadian scholars (in progress); a 1990 interview of Freedman by Mary Maguire (1995); and personal communications with Freedman and Ian Pringle. Janice Lauer (personal communications) provided a list of Canadians who attended the seminar as well as a list of the 1978 speakers.

23. For comparison to the discipline today, as represented in the United States by the annual IR called Conference on College Composition and Communication, organizers issuing a call for proposals to the 2015 conference prestructured the attention space into fourteen areas, specified as over one hundred specialized topics. IRs that frame the discipline internationally (e.g., the writing-research-across-borders conferences now under the auspices of the International Society for the Advancement of Writing Research), still lack that fine grain of prestructure, with attention spaces more inductively constructed from invitations and proposals.

24. For Freedman's nuanced position on this issue, see her 1990 interview in Maguire (1995, 91–92). The interviews in this book (which put six international women scholars, including Janet Emig, in dialogue with the interviewer, Mary Maguire, and one another) frequently reference the 1979 and 1986 Ottawa conferences. In that context, Freedman and other scholars, notably Emig, discuss agonistic argument and its role in scholarly conferences and disciplines.

25. In a February 15, 2014, e-mail message, Pringle told me the memory of this moment deeply influenced the way he and Freedman designed the program for the 1986 conference, "The Issues That Divide Us," as a set of strands with "some kind of exposition of differing positions by two major figures in the strand."

26. Reither went on to become founding editor of the *Inkshed* newsletter, a primary force in developing a Canadian disciplinary community for writing studies in its early years.

27. The table of contents is divided into "The writing process: three orientations"; "The development of writing abilities"; "Text and discourse"; and "Implications for teaching." In the preface, Candlin describes each part as patterned by three themes: a comprehensive review of writing research and pedagogy; "a characteristic applied linguistic interplay between research and practice"; and the broader implications of writing issues for language education (Candlin 1983, ix).

28. The inscribed object was a crude carving of a gun, left by insurgents in a hacienda in the Yucatan in May 1913, after an uprising (Eiss 2008).

29. Gregory was referencing the research agenda of microhistorians like Wolfgang Kaschuba, who argue for relating microphenomena to macrohistorical processes, in his review comparing Italian microhistorical approaches with the German "history of everyday life."

References

Applebee, Arthur. 1974. *Tradition and Reform in the Teaching of English*. Urbana, IL: NCTE.

Artiss, Phyllis. 1991. "AC(C)UTE Revisited." *Inkshed* 10 (2): 1–2.

Ash, Timothy Garton. 1999. *Introduction to History of the Present: Essays, Sketches and Dispatches from Europe in the 1990s*. London: Penguin.

Bartholomae, David. 1993. "Around 1980." In *Pre/Text: The First Decade*, edited by Victor Vitanza, 287–98. Pittsburgh, PA: University of Pittsburgh Press.

Bateson, Mary Catherine. 1984. *With a Daughter's Eye: A Memoir of Margaret Mead and Gregory Bateson*. New York: Washington Square.

Bateson, Mary Catherine. (1972) 1991. *Our Own Metaphor: A Personal Account of a Conference on the Effects of Conscious Purpose on Human Adaptation*. Washington, DC: Smithsonian Institution.

Brannon, Lil. 1985. "Toward a Theory of Composition." In *Perspectives on Research and Scholarship in Composition*, edited by Ben W. McClellan and Timothy R. Donovan, 6–25. New York: MLA.

Candlin, Christopher. 1983. Preface to *Learning to Write: First Language/Second Language: Selected Papers from the 1979 CCTE Conference, Ottawa, Canada*, edited by Aviva Freedman, Ian Pringle, and Janice Yalden, ix–xii. London: Longman.

Chapman, David W., and Gary Tate. 1987. "A Survey of Doctoral Programs in Rhetoric and Composition." *Rhetoric Review* 5 (2): 124–86. http://dx.doi.org/10.1080/07350198709359143.

Collins, Randall. 1998. *The Sociology of Philosophies: A Global Theory of Intellectual Change*. Cambridge, MA: Belknap.

D'Angelo, Frank J. 1999. "Professing Rhetoric and Composition: A Personal Odyssey." In *History, Reflection, and Narrative: The Professionalization of Composition, 1963–1983*, edited by Mary Rosner, Beth Boehm, and Debra Journet, 269–81. Stamford, CT: Ablex.

D'Angelo, Frank J. 2002. "Looking for an Object of Study in the 1970s." In *Visions and Re-Visions: Continuity and Change in Rhetoric and Composition*, edited by James Williams, 49–68. Carbondale: Southern Illinois University Press.

Ede, Lisa. 2004. *Situating Composition: Composition Studies and the Politics of Location*. Carbondale: Southern Illinois University Press.

Eiss, Paul K. 2008. "To Write Liberation: Time, History, and Hope in Ucatan." In *Small Worlds: Method, Meaning and Narrative in Microhistory*, edited by James F. Brooks, Christopher R.N. DeCorse, and John Walton, 53–76. Santa Fe: School for Advanced Research.

Emig, Janet. 1980. "The Tacit Tradition: The Inevitability of a Multi-Disciplinary Approach to Writing Research." In *Reinventing the Rhetorical Tradition*, edited by Aviva Freedman and Ian Pringle, 9–17. Conway, AR: L & S Books (CCTE).

Emig, Janet. 1983. Preface to *The Web of Meaning: Essays on Writing, Teaching, Learning, and Thinking*, edited by Dixie Goswami and Maureen Butler. Upper Montclair, NJ: Boynton/Cook.

Emig, Janet. (1986) 1995. "Scanning the U.S Scene." In *Dialogue in a Major Key: Women Scholars Speak*, edited by Mary H. Maguire, 62–77. Urbana, IL: NCTE.

Faigley, Lester. 1992. *Fragments of Rationality: Postmodernity and the Subject of Composition*. Pittsburgh, PA: University of Pittsburgh Press.

Faigley, Lester. 1999. "Veterans' Stories on the Porch." In *History, Reflection, and Narrative: The Professionalization of Composition, 1963–1983*, edited by Mary Rosner, Beth Boehm, and Debra Journet, 23–37. Stamford, CT: Ablex.

Freedman, Aviva. (1990) 1995. "Reinventing the Discipline—Reinventing Ourselves." In *Dialogue in a Major Key: Women Scholars Speak*, edited by Mary H. Maguire, 83–100. Urbana, IL: NCTE.

Freedman, Aviva, and Ian Pringle, eds. 1980. *Reinventing the Rhetorical Tradition.* Conway, AR: L & S Books (CCTE).

Freedman, Aviva, Ian Pringle, and Janice Yalden, eds. 1983. *Learning to Write: First Language/Second Language: Selected Papers from the 1979 CCTE Conference, Ottawa, Canada.* London: Longman.

Ginzburg, Carlo, and Anna Davin. 1980. "Morelli, Freud and Sherlock Holmes: Clues and Scientific Method." *History Workshop* 9 (1): 5–36. http://dx.doi.org/10.1093/hwj/9.1.5.

Ginzburg, Carlo, John Tedeschi, and Anne C. Tedeschi. 1993. "Microhistory: Two or Three Things That I Know about It." *Critical Inquiry* 20 (1): 10–35. http://dx.doi.org/10.1086/448699.

Goffman, Erving. 1967. *Interaction Ritual.* New York: Doubleday.

Goggin, Maureen Daly. 2000. *Authoring a Discipline: Scholarly Journals and the Post-World War II Emergence of Rhetoric and Composition.* Mahwah, NJ: Erlbaum.

Gregory, Brad S. 1999. "Is Small Beautiful? Microhistory and the History of Everyday Life." *History and Theory* 38 (1): 100–10. http://dx.doi.org/10.1111/0018-2656.791999079.

Grendi, Edoardo. 1977. "Micro-analisi e storia sociale." *Quaderni Storici* 35 (August): 506–20.

Hairston, Maxine. 1982. "The Winds of Change: Thomas Kuhn and the Revolution in the Teaching of Writing." *College Composition and Communication* 33 (1): 76–88. http://dx.doi.org/10.2307/357846.

Harris, Joseph. 2012. *A Teaching Subject: Composition Since 1966.* New ed. Logan: Utah State University Press.

Hirsch, E. D. Jr. 1977. *The Philosophy of Composition.* Chicago, IL: University of Chicago Press.

Lauer, Janice M. 1984. "Composition Studies: Dappled Discipline." *Rhetoric Review* 3 (1): 20–29. http://dx.doi.org/10.1080/07350198409359074.

Lauer, Janice M. 1998. "Disciplinary Formation: The Summer Rhetoric Seminar." *JAC* 18 (2): 503–8.

Lave, Jean, and Etienne Wenger. 1991. *Situated Learning: Legitimate Peripheral Participation.* Cambridge: Cambridge University Press. http://dx.doi.org/10.1017/CBO9780511815355.

Levi, Giovanni. 2001. "On Microhistory." In *New Perspectives on Historical Writing.* 2nd ed. Edited by Peter Burke, 97–119 University Park: Pennsylvania State University Press.

Levi, Giovanni. 2012. "Microhistory and the Recovery of Complexity." In *Historical Knowledge: In Quest of Theory, Method, and Evidence,* edited by Susanna Fellman and Marjatta Rahikaninen, 121–32. Newcastle upon Tyne: Cambridge Scholars.

Little, Daniel. 2009. "History of the Present." *Understanding Society* (blog), August 2, 2009, http://understandingsociety.blogspot.com/2009/08/historyofthepresent.html.

Lloyd-Jones, Richard. 1994. "On Institutes and Projects." In *Composition in Context: Essays in Honor of Donald C. Stewart,* edited by W. Ross Winterowd and Vincent Gillespie, 152–66. Carbondale: Southern Illinois University Press.

Magnusson, Sigurtur Gylfi, and Istvan M. Szijarto. 2013. *What Is Microhistory? Theory and Practice.* London: Routledge.

Maguire, Mary H., ed. 1995. *Dialogue in a Major Key: Women Scholars Speak.* Urbana, IL: NCTE.

North, Stephen M. 1987. *The Making of Knowledge in Composition: Portrait of an Emerging Field.* Upper Montclair, NJ: Boynton/Cook.

Nystrand, Martin, and John Duffy. 2003a. "The Sociocultural Context for the New Discourse about Writing." In *Towards a Rhetoric of Everyday Life: New Directions in Research on Writing, Text, and Discourse,* edited by Martin Nystrand and John Duffy, xv–xxxiv. Madison: University of Wisconsin Press.

Nystrand, Martin, and John Duffy, eds. 2003b. *Towards a Rhetoric of Everyday Life: New Directions in Research on Writing, Text, and Discourse.* Madison: University of Wisconsin Press.

O'Hara, J. Martin. 1981. Preface to *Teaching Writing Learning,* edited by Aviva Freedman and Ian Pringle, iii. Ottawa: CCTE.

Oster, John. 1979. "Tulips, Tagmemics, and the Ghost of Dartmouth." *English Quarterly* 12 (1): 23–32.

Park, Douglas B. 1979. "Theories and Expectations: On Conceiving Composition and Rhetoric as a Discipline." *College English* 41 (1): 47–56. http://dx.doi.org/10.2307/376359.

Parks, Stephen. (2000) 2013. *Class Politics: The Movement for the Students' Right to Their Own Language.* 2nd ed. Anderson, SC: Parlor.

Peltonen, Matti. 2001. "Clues, Margins, and Monads: The Micro-Macro Link in Historical Research." *History and Theory* 40 (3): 347–59. http://dx.doi.org/10.1111/0018-2656.00172.

Phelps, Louise Wetherbee. 1986. "The Domain of Composition." *Rhetoric Review* 4 (2): 182–95. http://dx.doi.org/10.1080/07350198609359122.

Phelps, Louise Wetherbee. 1988. *Composition as a Human Science: Contributions to the Self-Understanding of a Discipline.* New York: Oxford University Press.

Phelps, Louise Wetherbee. 2014. "The Historical Formation of Academic Identities: Rhetoric and Composition, Discourse and Writing." *Canadian Journal for Studies in Discourse and Writing* 25 (1): 3–23.

Phillips, Mark Salber. 2004. "Distance and Historical Representation." *History Workshop Journal* 57 (1): 123–41. http://dx.doi.org/10.1093/hwj/57.1.123.

Pringle, Ian, and Aviva Freedman, eds. 1981. *Teaching Writing Learning.* Ottawa: CCTE.

Rice, Jeff. 2007. *The Rhetoric of Cool: Composition Studies and New Media.* Carbondale: Southern Illinois University Press.

Roen, Duane, Stuart C. Brown, and Theresa Enos, eds. 1999. *Living Rhetoric and Composition: Stories of the Discipline.* Mahwah, NJ: Erlbaum.

Rosner, Mary, Beth Boehm, and Debra Journet, eds. 1999. *History, Reflection, and Narrative: The Professionalization of Composition, 1963–1983.* Stamford, CT: Ablex.

Stock, Patricia L., ed. 2012. *Composition's Roots in English Education.* Portsmouth, NH: Heinemann.

Watson, Ken. 2013. *A Brief History of IFTE—1966 to 1992.* NCTE Connected Community. http://ncte.connectedcommunity.org/ifte/history.

Williams, James D., ed. 2002. *Visions and Re-Visions: Continuity and Change in Rhetoric and Composition.* Carbondale: Southern Illinois University Press.

Zebroski, James. 2012. "Hidden from History; English Education and the Multiple Origins of Contemporary Composition Studies, 1960–2000." In *Composition's Roots in English Education,* edited by Patricia L. Stock, 26–50. Portsmouth, NH: Heinemann.

3

JOURNAL EDITORS IN THE ARCHIVES
Reportage as Microhistory

Kelly Ritter

Journal editing brings together perfectly the big three in the academy: scholarship, service, and teaching. When it works well, it's a pedagogical act, clearly grounded in professional expertise, focused on two things: constructing the conversation in the field and nurturing the creativity and careers of our colleagues. In other words, it's like hosting the very best ongoing party: inviting guests who will scintillate and sparkle, introducing new colleagues to old friends, celebrating and promoting the best in the field—and also doing the setup beforehand and the cleanup after.

—"Coda: Tales from the Editorial Life" 2009

Attempts have been made to add spice to these issues by sometimes presenting lead articles far afield from the themes of the issues. But novelty is difficult to sustain. It may be that some issues of College English look as though they have been published before. The editor is constantly casting about means to shock the constituency into action without sacrificing soundness and solidity. Suggestions, however wild, are welcome.

—James E. Miller Jr., 1963 College
English Annual Report

I would like to think CCC is a professional journal that gets read, not filed.

—William Irmscher, 1971 College Composition and
Communication Annual Report

At the time of this writing, I am the editor of *College English* (*CE*), the flagship journal of the college section of the National Council of Teachers of English (NCTE). Being a journal editor is integral to my larger professional identity as a scholar of rhetoric and composition studies, even as I am not completely beholden to it: I pursue my own research and scholarship corresponding to my intellectual interests, which are confidently

DOI: 10.7330/9781607324058.c003

my own and not necessarily the journal's. On the other hand, the words I produce *are* inextricably tied to my identity as editor if I consider what it might mean for not just utterances (print or otherwise), but also *persons*, to be archived. At some point, as has been the case with the editors who preceded me, I will be "read" as not just a scholar of this or that (in my case, primarily local historiographies of writing) but also the gatekeeper—to paraphrase Robert J. Connors's noted observation in his 1984 review of *CE* and *College Composition and Communication* (*CCC*)—of scholarship that is or is not like my own and of a journal that stands both separate from and always beside me.[1]

Realistically, editors are memorialized as a public presence forever linked to their corresponding journals because what they say and do, in a digital age, is imminently traceable. My editorials, my comments on authors' work, my public statements about the journal, my conversations about the act of editing, my choices about what does or does not get published, even my comments on social media related to *being* an editor—all of these are theoretically traceable, recorded, remembered. As an editor, I help create issues of the journal that will be stored in electronic databases and in print—the physical archives of publication. But also as editor, I am archiving *myself* and being archived *upon*, with every external reading of my identity theoretically linked to how that identity might go toward defining what scholarship becomes a published part of the field.

I foreground my own identity in this way to clarify how my study—the reportage of journal editors in the archives as a microhistorical view of composition studies—bears upon recognition of my implication in this very microhistory and the archiving of my past fellow editors of both *CE* and *CCC*. As the above comparative epigraphs attempt to show, what is and can be said in the greater public about journal editing in comparison with what can and does get reported in the more private logs of editors' reports to governing organizations reveals a complex, historiographic view of both the enterprise of scholarly editing and the field in which that editing takes place. It also reveals how important individually archived voices standing beside their journals are in this historiographic, longitudinal consideration. In this chapter, I explore the archived annual journal editors' reports from *CE* and *CCC*, which were published in the NCTE Annual Reports to officers and executive committee members each November from 1954 to 1979. In doing so, I argue that these editors' reports serve as one microhistory of our field that differs from other public accounting of or reflections on editorial work. In the aggregate, these reports are a tracing emblematic of larger concerns and problems in composition studies in its formative years, particularly its identity issues relevant to promoting the field's scholarly work while still staying true to its core pedagogical imperatives.

I rely for my analysis on a few established definitions of microhistory and microhistorical work. According to Sigurður Gylfi Magnusson, microhistorians "tend to focus on *outliers* rather than looking for the *average* individual. . . . [T]hey scrutinize those individuals who did not follow the paths of their average fellow countryman" (Magnússon 2006). One might, in fact, see editors as outliers given the distinct subgrouping of scholars they come to be as veterans of a war only few have fought, if we accept battle metaphors for the beleaguered nature of editorial work, or as isolated journeys only few travelers have taken, if we prefer a more romantic conception of the job. Hans Renders and Binne de Hann (2011) posit their definition of microhistory in terms of grand narratives—a familiar concept to composition studies historians like myself and many others in this collection who research "local" histories of writing. Renders and de Hann ask, "What is the meaning of a grand historical narrative in relation to a real life, painting, or village? . . . Microhistorians proceed with this problem by using the term 'normal exception.' This concept means from the perspective of mainstream history many individuals are regarded as obscure and strange" (Renders and de Hann 2011, 4).

We might regard editors as "normal exceptions" to the typical figures in grand narratives—well-known scholars, teachers, program administrators, or even academic institutions themselves. They are often *larger* than life, characterizing multitudes below and beside them in order to explain how writing "gets taught" or how composition functions within English departments or other superstructures that also appear in parallel historical narratives. Grand narratives become our dominant origin stories, often masculine by nature—a quality also evident in the gendering of editors and editorial work during this twenty-five year period I examine—overriding those whose words and actions are less regarded or even silenced in field formations.

To counterbalance these grand perspectives, Brad S. Gregory notes that microhistory is characterized by "relentless scrutiny of a specific encounter or a seemingly minor 'episode' in order to illuminate aspects of a past society and culture that resist disclosure through more conventional historical methods" (Gregory 1999, 102). Arguably, journal editors' reports—especially archived, private ones—are minor "episodes" that can do this kind of illumination, providing relatively unknown information that may explain widely known occurrences or movements in the field. Reports themselves are episodic, chronicling a time in the journal's production that, when read backward into the historical moment, arguably means more than when the report was actually filed. While once a temporal accounting—a reckoning, even—now the report is an artifact of a field's time and place, further illuminated by our own readerly mediation of these reports in the context of what we now know about the historical happenings taking place around them.

These archived reports, written for a conscripted audience (NCTE officers and the Executive Committee) were by definition an emerging genre authored by persons new to it (and to the work of editing) who became increasingly aware of the genre's core features and purposes across the long trajectory of the reporting itself. We can understand the intellectual growth of composition studies *as* a field through its relationship with the journals charged to represent that very growth to the academy at large. In comparing the reports filed by *CE* editors with the reports filed by *CCC* editors, we can witness both the personal positions these editors brought to the job as well as the values and stances the field accepted, rejected, and amended during its critical twenty-five-year (early) history.

The reading of these reports, while open to anyone interested in archival research and knowledgeable about composition studies, is best undertaken, I would contend, by someone in my position: a current (or past) journal editor who can read *into and on* these reports with a modicum of insider knowledge and field experience. This reportage I re-present is in the aggregate familiar to me in its tones and valences, sometimes painfully so. As Mark Salber Phillips argues in relation to microhistorical work, "What we sometimes call the 'perspective of history' is surely a much more variable and complex construction than we like to pretend, and one that would be worth thinking about in a more serious, systematic, and (above all) historical fashion" (Phillips 2004, 124). This is because "historical accounts not only function at a received distance from events; they also reconstruct and reshape that distance in a variety of ways that bear upon every aspect of our view of the past" (125). It is that reconstruction and reshaping I hope to accomplish in examining these reports as microhistory.

WHO TELLS MY STORY? ILLUSIONS OF DISTANCE

This insider position I hold as analyst of these archival reports, I would want readers to know, is not only what I consider an analytical and positional asset. It also renders exceedingly difficult distinctions between my undertaking of this work as a *biographer* of the editors through

their annual reports and as a *microhistorian* of those reports as a coun-
ter- or micronarrative of our field's rise to status in academia, particularly if I consider Jill Lepore's (2001) salient distinctions between these
two genres and the investigative stance required to produce them. As
Lepore (2001, 132) argues, to say that "microhistorians study ordinary
people while biographers study extraordinary people does not get us
very far" because some microhistories examine "famous" people and
some biographies are of "humble folk" (Lepore 2001, 139). Indeed,
depending upon one's own position in the field, a journal editor might
be "famous" or "extraordinary" or might become so during a career.
But editors might also be "humble folk" if we consider them as behind-
the-scenes, Oz-like characters who assemble the greatness of others with
little regard for their own critical role in that assemblage. Further still,
when one is an editor—and often a senior scholar—one's colleagues-in-
kind are increasingly going to *be* journal editors due to the nature of the
work and the necessary security (tenure, senior status) required to do it
with some measure of confidence and authority.

But something else in Lepore's distinction catches my own positional
eye, which is how she interrogates the relationship microhistorians have
with their subjects versus the same relationship biographers have with
theirs. Lepore (2001, 139) concludes, "In telling a person's life story,
many biographers identify (and confess their identification) with their
subjects. Microhistorians, meanwhile, identify with a particular *contemporary* of their subjects, in particular, with a person who was in a position to investigate or judge the subject. Because of this, microhistorians
are far more likely to become characters in their own books, or, more
commonly, to use the detective/judge figure as a loosely disguised version of themselves, a kind of historian's double" (Lepore 2001, 139).
Lepore calls the distance microhistorians maintain from their subject(s)
an "illusion of distance," which enables microhistorians to celebrate
the very figure *of* the microhistorian as a "careful, assiduous, insightful, usually brilliant character who tracks down and evaluates evidence
with astonishing, even breathtaking skill" (Lepore 2001, 141). I will
freely admit that I see my research into journal editors' annual reports
as neither brilliant nor breathtaking; additionally, I maintain no illusion of distance. I am wrapped up in the histories of these editors as if
their work was my own because in many ways, it is. So does that mean
my examination of these reports is not really microhistory but is actually
some diffused version of *biography?*

Lepore offers four propositions that distinguish biography from
microhistory. These are, in sum, (1) biography emphasizes an individual's

contribution to history, whereas microhistory emphasizes an individual life—even if seemingly insignificant—as "allegory" for a larger culture; (2) biographers want to profile and "recapitulate" a person's life story, whereas microhistorians "solve small mysteries about a person's life as a means to exploring the culture; (3) biographers worry over intimacy with subjects (or being a "crazed stalker rather than a faithful husband" [134]) and then betraying them, but microhistorians "tend to betray people who have left abundant records in order to resurrect those who did not"; and (4) as stated above, a microhistorian may be "a character in his own book" where as a biographer's "alter ego" serves as the subject of the biography at hand (Lepore 2001, 141). But overall, microhistory will "always draw the writer's, and the reader's, attention away from the subject and toward the culture" (142).

So when I parse out Lepore's distinctions more fully, in this taxonomical manner, I can argue for the reportage of journal editors—and my role in bringing that reportage to a wider swathe of readers than originally intended—as microhistory. This is because in the end, editor's reports are *not about the editors*, even as what editors view as their role in shepherding the journal to publication necessarily affects how that report gets written, and to an extent, what it contains. While this may seem like a contrary statement to the claims I made above about my own positionality, I stand behind it. What I argue is that these reports are, in fact, a means of exploring the culture, with the culture being the rise of composition studies as a scholarly field. Further, they are in many senses allegorical in that they parallel the changes we see in both the role of "gatekeeping" in composition studies from the mid-1950s through the end of the 1970s and in the microcosms of scholarship that would make up that field *as* a field.

THESE THINGS ARE NOT LIKE THE OTHERS: PUBLIC VERSUS ARCHIVAL EDITORIAL UTTERANCES

The trajectory of these journal editors' reports is emblematic of an untapped, linear perspective on our field as a whole, one that brings to bear both large-scale studies of journals, primarily Maureen Daly Goggin's (2000) important book *Authoring a Discipline*, as well as smaller-scale individual or collective narratives of editorial life. But critically, the work of these reports is very different from these other more familiar narratives of editing, many of which respond to a public curiosity about how journals "work" and, important to note, how new scholars can enter the conversation in these journals so necessary to sustaining their professional careers.

There is an abundance of archival evidence of the general, ahistorical labors of journal editors; these documents are the editorial columns that open many issues of journals in both rhetoric and composition studies and in other fields. A subset of these editorials is the farewell essay, or the final editorial a journal editors lodge before their terms expire. One example is the opening passage from Marilyn Cooper's final issue of *CCC* in December 2004: "Writing this column for the last issue of *CCC* under my editorship I feel both regret and relief. Relief because editing a journal like *CCC* with substantial numbers of submissions is like teaching a writing class in which students offer new essays or revisions full of wonderful ideas every day and eagerly await your comments—an ideal writing class, perhaps, if it didn't last five years with no breaks. And regret for the same reasons: all those new ideas, intriguing citations, thoughtful analyses I got to read all the time. And regret, too, for the end of my work with all the wonderful people who helped put the issues together" (Cooper 2004, 197).[2]

While Cooper's editorial, and others like it, performs in a particular, expected way (thanking those who helped make the journal a success, chronicling the changes made and/or opportunities lost, reflecting on the work of editing per se), it is a *public* performance. An entire study could be made of such editorials, which are available as their own kind of microhistorical record of a role within our profession that, as William Irmscher notes in his 1973 annual report for *CCC*, is "a rare professional opportunity accessible to only a few men and women" (Annual Reports of Officers and Committees 1946–79, Boxes 1–2: p. 29). But editorials are still made for public consumption and function as epideictic rhetoric—a ceremonial performance for readers, who expect the editor to preside over the journal and make declarative—and gracious, sometimes verging on benevolent—statements about it and the work required to produce it, month after month, year after year. These editorials do not require archival tools to seek out nor a sympathetic positionality to understand and interpret fully.

There also exists the larger public accounting of what editorial work is, constructed and reconstructed of pastiche, as it is a genre that circles back and reiterates past points of advice and reflection without an intentional, accumulative sense of organizing those data points or narratives referentially. Such statements make up a loosely defined genre that explains—especially to newer members of the profession—what it means to edit a journal and/or how the specific decisions get made within a particular publication (rate of acceptances, quality of scholarship sought, common mistakes made by and advice to prospective authors). Much of this accounting takes place, as Jana Argersinger and Michael Cornett (2009) have also noted, at conferences or other gatherings in which editors talk about how to get published—a particularly popular type of conference session in an increasingly poor job market. But as Argersinger and Cornett lament in their introduction to the symposium on editing in *Profession 2009*, there is still a notable lack of editors' public sharing of their "hopes, ambitions, experiences, ideals" (Argersinger and Cornett 2009, 106).

As Melissa Ianetta (2014) has further and more recently argued in "Dull Duty and Discretionary Power: Looking for the Editor in Writing Studies," while some (scant) attention has been paid to the role of journals and the stock duties of editorial work within those journals, composition studies has yet to make fully visible the work of journal editing, nor has it made a concerted effort to highlight the intellectual labor this work entails against other labor undertaken by faculty (and graduate-student assistant editors, an even more invisible grouping, as Ianetta notes). She observes, in relation to Goggin's (1997) "Composing a Discipline: The Role of Scholarly Journals in the Disciplinary Emergence of Rhetoric and Composition since 1950," that its

> emphasis on the "artifacts" (i.e., journals) rather than individuals (i.e., editors) effaces this agent's role and activities. To be clear, marking this distinction is not offered as a criticism of Goggin's study. Because its purpose was to "trace some of the attributes of the post-WWII emergence of rhetoric and composition as a discipline" via its journals, her work was well served by this emphasis. But, the conflation of the editor and the journal nevertheless serves to further obscure the range of editorial activities and ideals, leaving few traces of precedent to aid future editors. And, as the paucity of scholarship in this area suggests, such a role is already obscure to the point of invisibility. (Ianetta 2014, 162)

It is this invisibility that I argue the annual editors' reports, as microhistory evincing a narrative field arc, might overcome, concomitant with a new perspective on how the role of the individual as aligned with the institution can help to clarify the growth (and stumblings and recoveries) of our field.

What we get in print and in person from editors is more often than not less than revealing and relatively detached from larger field trends that might track back onto specific editorial actions. Such statements achieve more affectual goals in their utterances but ultimately may tell us little about the relationship between editors and our field at large. One example of this is Beth Luey's 2009 *Profession* piece within the Argersinger and Cornett symposium in which she puts forward the perils and realities of editing a journal: "If the journal receives more submissions than it can publish, the editor must decide not only that an article is worthy but also that it is the best of the submissions on the subject. It is the editor who decides what 'best' means, because the decision will be quite different if it means 'most interesting,' 'best written,' 'most unusual,' 'most controversial,' 'most authoritative,' or something else altogether. What we read and rely on rests on such judgments. Editors also decide what we won't get to read, the work that is not good enough. And again, 'not good enough' can mean many different things" (115).

Such advice, it seems to me, while useful in sum, has become a commonplace by now, at least in a field as pragmatically oriented as composition studies, presented as public rehearsal of familiar tropes related to editorial work. There are the caveats, the hedging, the generalizations—because editorial work is, ultimately, *situationally specific*. No such narrative really comes close to tracking actual experience or identifying why a particular editorial action affected the field or was affected by it. What is *less* known but more valuable are the unfiltered, personalized editorial reports that are part of a real rhetorical situation that necessitates their production. The reports perform a variety of duties at once but always in relation to the report that has come before—often explicitly so. They are dialogic, both chronologically *and* logically; they speak forward and backward into other reports, modifying and overriding genre conventions as they modify and override past editorial stances and initiatives in the content of the journals they are reporting on. They are, in mundane terms, an account of the organization of the journal's work over the past year. But they are also more affectively the personal accounts of editors' (perceived) successes and failures—what these editors had hoped to accomplish *in that moment* and what they were able to augment or change. In addition, the reports are the accounting of actions to a body holding the editors accountable—the "bosses," if you will, to whom editors working within a scholarly organization must ultimately report.

Critically, these reports are commentaries *on* the role of editing, and on the positionality of the editors themselves, in a field still finding its intellectual and institutional way. Readers of these reports often bear witness to frustration, exclamation, and commiseration within editorial reportage and across series of editors' commentaries. As rhetoric, they are less ceremonial than deliberative, even forensic in nature. And as a genre, they develop their own distinct qualities *as* they proceed, with early reports evincing little recognition of what should or can be reported to the officers and later reports illustrating quite the opposite—a heightened self-awareness of genre (including audience and purpose), one that matches the increased confidence and solidifying identity of the field itself. In short, I see these editors' reports as indeed allegorical in sum to the historical trajectory of the field of rhetoric and composition, in—to nod to Hayden White—the content of their form. In the next section, I will examine some specific moments from the reports in relation to what I see as two historical "identity crises" in composition studies in order to illustrate how this allegory plays out.

IN THE ARCHIVES: COMPOSITION STUDIES AS/ AND EDITORIAL MICRONARRATIVES

A word first about my methods, which were quite straightforward, not necessarily by choice: in the NCTE archives, housed on the campus of the University of Illinois, there are two boxes of Annual Reports of Officers and Committees. These reports begin in 1939 and end in 1979, but editors' reports for *CCC* and *CE* do not begin until the mid-1950s. While *CE* began publishing in 1939 as a newly created college-level publication stemming from *English Journal,* and *CCC* began in 1950 as a sixteen-page leaflet that would eventually grow to a full-fledged journal, neither publication reported on its annual work until after W. Wilbur Hatfield sold *CE* to NCTE in 1954 and the reports of the two journals began to subsequently appear side by side in annual reports.[3]

So, while my archival work here is limited by what has been archived, ending my study in 1979 also allows for a nice stopping point for the editorship of *CE* (Donald J. Gray's first report as editor) and *CCC* (Edward P.J. Corbett's last report).[4] More important, this twenty-five-year period that these editors' reports encompass also allows a view into several movements or moments that would come to characterize the rise of rhetoric and composition as an intellectual and scholarly discipline just before its graduate-level programs exploded on the scene—an event that in itself may be a method for defining a discipline. These include the communications movement, the creativity movement, the rise of expressivism, and, later, cognitivist approaches. This era also encompasses the controversial elimination of basic writing courses at various institutions postwar, the historical field marker of 1963 (the subject of Annie Mendenhall's contribution to this collection), the Dartmouth seminar, Students' Right to Their Own Language, CUNY's open admissions, and the emergence of many other independent and organizationally sponsored journals that would come to enrich the field.

Surveying these reports requires a further methodological choice on my part. Do I analyze each year separately or look at arcs across multiple years? The latter tells me more about this archival collection as a microhistory and takes the personal focus (somewhat) off the editors themselves. It also allows me to take note of general trends in reporting across years as well as where reporting trends were discontinued or revised as the publications became more mature and the editors more invested in their own methods of reportage. These variances between reporting years are, in a way, a detriment to the historiographer, as certain stock content (e.g., statistics on types of manuscripts submitted versus those accepted) gives us important historical information about contributors' scholarship, information unavailable in any other location. When that content chooses not to be reported in favor of more impressionistic or personalized observations about the work of the journal that year, we lose the continuum of data. On the other hand, the choice *to* discontinue or disregard statistical reporting tells us something about the perspective of the editor on the journal itself and on the field as a whole. In other words, if the type of work being submitted is less important than the quality and scope of its intellectual contributions, we see through these editors' eyes a new valuation of the journal *as* a microcosm of an established field rather than just the journal as an aggregator of "what's out there" to be submitted for consideration. These valuations are evident as components of two crises—first, of disciplinarity boundaries and, second, of responsibilities of/for representation.

Identity Crisis #1: Whose Journal Is on First? Or, We Are (Not) PMLA

Goggin (2000) devotes twenty-six pages of *Authoring a Discipline* to a discussion of the founding and growth of *CCC* in relation to the emergence of the CCCC. Comparatively, she only spends slightly over two pages discussing *CE*. Her subhead for this discussion, "Limited and Limiting Intellectual Space: *College English*," seeks to characterize the paucity of composition and rhetoric coverage (and editorial interest) in the journal as one reason *CCC* was such a professional necessity for the field. While I do not dispute this general claim, an examination of the comparative editorial reports indicates less clear-cut contrasts—at least as characterized by the editors themselves—between the two journals than a blurring of the concept of English as a field that also wanted, postwar, to pay real attention to *teaching* as part of its scholarly production and professional concern. Certainly *CE* privileged literary scholarship in its pages, but its mission trajectory as articulated by its various editors between 1954 and 1979 also indicates that with *CCC* in existence, *CE*'s identity was both further conscripted and more capacious in terms of identifying what English teaching meant—and to whom—and how that would compete with and run parallel to the concerns of *CC*. I would argue that this quasicompetition—one I admittedly still feel as *CE* editor whenever I receive manuscripts on rhetoric and composition—is one emblematic of the excitement and confusion felt within composition studies as a whole during these early years. As most—if not all—of its scholars were emerging from programs in literary study, questions abounded. What is the relationship between literature and composition? What are our professional concerns? What *is* our profession now? How do we write about it, and where does that writing go?

Thus, the first striking thread that emerges from an archival reading of these editors' reports is the core differences between *CE* and *CCC* as journals—and how they did and did not (and do and do not, still) bear a clear relationship to one another, despite being flagship journals of the college section and the college conference, respectively. *CE* began as a journal framed for generalists in English studies, primarily focusing its attention on literary scholarship to the point that submissions focused on composition or writing (in this era, specifically first-year writing and/or "remedial" composition) were initially shuttled to the editor(s) of *CCC*. Goggin notes this in her comprehensive history of the journals in *Authoring* (Goggin 2000, 41), but it is also referenced implicitly in editor Frederick Gwynn's 1958 annual report of *CE*, which notes that there is a "comparatively small number of articles on teaching composition ow[ing] to natural respect for the staple of *CCC*" (Annual Reports, A15). This slightly uneasy agreement between the two journals, designed to get *CCC* off the ground and establish it as the go-to site for scholarship on composition teaching, manifests itself in a growing dissatisfaction on *CE* editors' parts with the balance of submissions coming into the journal, particularly those classified by the editors as "pedagogical."

As the editors' reports for *CE* progress chronologically, we see open discussion of, and sometimes dissatisfaction over, the balance of scholarship received, especially as relevant to other perceived competitor (literary studies) journals outside NCTE. For example, in his 1957 annual report, Gwynn notes an astounding *592* manuscripts were received in the previous year, with 169 of those accepted. He comments, "Like *PMLA* and other professional journals, we are receiving such good submissions these days that we can take only the outstanding ones" (Annual Reports, A12). Of those 169 manuscripts published at the time of the report, 7 were on drama, 25 on fiction, 9 on poetry, and 3 on criticism; in the broad category of "teaching," 15 were on composition, 9 on literature, 20 on language, and 37 on "general" (A12). In addition, the journal began in this year to run "almost every month" (and recall that at this time, *CE* ran eight issues a year compared to the six it publishes now) a "long article surveying textbooks in various fields—composition, communications, poetry, drama, essay, short story, etc." (A14). In the 1958 report, Gwynn comments that the statistics on manuscripts published in categories similar to those found in the 1957 report "deserve some interpretation and comment" (A15). He then notes that the "professional articles were probably the most significant of the year" and that it is "highly significant that only two of the 22 items on fiction concentrated on writers not in the twentieth century" (A15–16). By 1959, Gwynn was reconstructing the journal around special issues, such as "Earlier British Masterworks" in October and, notably in the following February, "Composition/Communication/Linguistics" (A15; A17), the first structuring of either *CE* or *CCC* with this eye toward groupings.

So while Goggin remarks that Gwynn, in particular, favored literary-centered scholarship (as compared to later editor James E. Miller Jr., for example) and that "English Studies had become virtually synonymous with literary studies" by the 1950s (Goggin 2000, 42), in tracing the arc of the filed editors' reports, I note more tension over coverage and territory than might be gleaned from either Goggin's comprehensive look at *CE* versus *CCC* or than might be in evidence in the journal's actual pages. This tension seems emblematic of an organization championing a field literally splitting off from its origins—as composition is filed as both a "teaching" category within English, for *CE* indexing purposes in the reports, and as a subject of its own standing in *CCC* reports. How would *CE* continue to distinguish itself in a time when English was slowly becoming more than literature but when NCTE had already created a separate journal (and conference) for nonliterary work? Further, what does *nonliterary* really mean?

The desire for *CE* to include more scholarship *not* literary in nature—particularly items discussing broadly professional concerns—becomes overt in later editors' reports. Editor Miller, in 1960, was the first to write an editorial *policy* for the journal—the same year he lamented "there are many, many items on contemporary literature and on fiction and too few on other periods and forms" (Annual Reports, A20). His policy on "Round Table Articles," which Goggin (2000, 42) describes as his way to "relegate" composition scholarship to the margins, instead reads in this overall arc of reports as an *explicit* call for manuscripts on composition (specifically composition pedagogy) whereas other *CE* editors had failed to call this subject area out at all—in consort with the primacy of *CCC* as a publication venue. My reading is further supported by Miller's 1964 report, wherein he admits that while there were eighty "pedagogical" articles as compared with fifty-nine in the previous year, characterized in his report as a "welcome swing of the pendulum," the "decision as to whether an article is critical or pedagogical (or both) is purely arbitrary" (Annual Reports, A22). On the one hand, he openly appreciates more articles on pedagogy in relation to (literary) criticism; on the other hand, the lines dividing pedagogy and criticism were rapidly blurring—matching the evolving scholarship of not only composition studies but also literary studies and what was being submitted to *CE* as a venue for that scholarship.[5]

Even more radical a departure than Miller's—and true to his own politics—were the editors' reports by Richard Ohmann, whose agenda for the journal is abundantly clear in his annual notes. Here, for example, is one extended comment from his first report in 1967.

> My intention was to feature articles (of almost any length) on the concepts of criticism, the theory of literature, the state of the profession, curriculum, pedagogy, and the like and to exclude explications and critical studies of single works. . . . All these changes have been difficult to manage, to no one's surprise. At first the contributors failed to note the new policy, and considerably more than half of the articles submitted were explications and specific critical studies. . . . However, the main editorial problem continues to be a shortage of good articles of the sort I want. (Annual Reports, A24)

As Ohmann's editorial arc progresses (and in this era, he serves the longest, at eleven consecutive years), he continues to identify and reidentify the purpose and scope of *CE* as both distinct from *CCC* and in relation to it. In 1969, Ohmann reports that the "drift of the journal, following the interests of contributors, has been towards cultural criticism and inquiry into the basic premises of the profession" (A25). In 1970, he notes that the journal continues to "reflect current interests and controversies in the profession" and that two of the areas *CE* has "set out to cover" have also been represented in "an excellent new journal, *New Literary History*" (A33). Still, Ohmann laments that even though *CE* "offers better and more useful reading than most journals, it has not found the best ways to help debate and effect the great changes needed in the teaching of English in colleges" (A33). In his statement regarding quality and, important to note, *influence*, one can hear echoes of Miller's 1961 declaration that "*College English* is more widely read than other professional journals" (A32) and Cecil B. Williams's 1961 statement in his *CCC* report that it "has grown into a professional journal of considerable stature. . . . Its healthy growth will continue and probably accelerate" (A34).

We might compare this arc of observations to Irmscher's *CCC* report in 1970, in which he declares that the journal "tries constantly to help teachers of undergraduate college students reevaluate the premises on which they operate and to provide them with viable resources in order to encourage better teaching" (Annual Reports, A33). In 1971, Irmscher continues his declarations of intent—and the journal's intrinsic value— by observing that "from my own experience . . . the journal seems to be more vital than it has ever been. [It] attracts more and more substantive and imaginative articles from both beginning and established writers, advertising continues to increase, and reader-interest in the journal seems to remain high. I would like to think *CCC* is a professional journal that gets read, not filed" (29). Irmscher's possible mission statement of the journal across 1970–1971 reads, comparatively, as solidly positive and progressive—as a location for the growth of a field increasing in strength and numbers. As Ohmann draws parallels between other literary journals, he also (perhaps defensively) claims superiority over those other possible competing venues at the same time that he doubts whether *CE*'s representation is meaningful. In 1965, earlier in his editorship and earlier in the history of composition studies and its scholarship, Irmscher himself was both more and less positive, remarking that the "growing sophistication of the conference [CCCC]" was reflected in the journal but also that he was "not yet persuaded" that the journal's reputation was "solid" (A26). In 1968, he comments that "new books on rhetoric and the teaching of writing consistently make reference to articles that have appeared in the journal" (A27), and by 1969 he reports that the journal is being indexed in two compendiums of journals on English education (A26), a telling identity marker in itself.

As the purpose and scope of *CCC* became more and more clear, in other words, the purpose and scope of *CE* became less so, or at least less exclusively *literary* and aspirational toward heavy-hitting journals such as *PMLA*—reflecting, I believe, a similar trend in composition studies during this same period. The uneasy relationship between literature and composition, professional and theoretical, resided in *CE*. The offshoot progression of composition studies *qua* composition studies was more freely and vibrantly taken up in *CCC*. But both journals continued to be published—one not consuming the other, and neither laying complete and total claim to the scholarship of writing and the teaching of writing— and both flourishing in terms of submissions, with Ohmann remarking for *CE* in 1973 that "we have gradually expanded the magazine without really intending to" (Annual Reports, 29) and Corbett noting in his 1975 *CCC* report that he received "an average of three [manuscripts] a day" (26). Indeed, the numbers for submissions are astounding in these reports, where they are noted, indicating a rush to define the discipline (in the case of *CCC*) and redefine the enterprise of *teaching* English (in the case of *CE*) through scholarly publication. The reported numbers of submissions for years in which the *CE* editors lodged them in reports are as follows: 225 manuscripts in 1959, 592 in 1957, 500 (estimated) in 1960, 772 in 1969, and 600 (estimated) in 1979.[6] In 1977, Ohmann did not report a number of submissions but claimed that the total manuscripts equaled "five feet, three inches and 180 pounds" (23).

Irmscher's 1972 report is perhaps the best summary of the declarative difference that *CCC* aims to articulate against and beside *CE*. Appended only by raw numbers related to publication data (publication of forty articles, three poems, and twenty-one reviews), the sum total of Irmscher's full report this year consists of these remarks, which turn more pointedly toward the still-shifting territory of the field itself: "As editor of *CCC*, I have conscientiously attempted to keep its pages an open vehicle for the publication of fresh and viable ideas about composition, language, and communication, and for the expression of counterviews, both radical and conservative. I have excluded what I consider *ad hominem* attacks, but I have not attempted to suppress dissenting views in the interest of a unified front. We are not a unified organization in our views, and I maintain that, if the journal of the organization is to represent its membership so that it is a journal that is read by various members, it must also reflect their diverse approaches and views" (Annual Reports, 29–30). Irmscher's declaration is much more reader defined than Ken Macrorie's earlier editorial statement about *CCC* in 1964. In his report, Macrorie characterizes the purpose and scope of the journal as one that

> bring[s] to its subscribers the new and leading ideas in the field and also present[s] practical classroom strategies and programs. I perceive more clearly than ever before that every committed English teacher wants to find a new way to accomplish that seemingly impossible job of creating good freshman writers and every teacher thinks he has the answer. I think the journal must keep its pages open to the possibility of an answer or answers. But I am more convinced than ever that a formula approach will not do the job—whether it be from new grammar, semantics, the new rhetoric, tagmemics, or whatever. I feel that English teachers over the years and through the grades and high school and college have cramped the life and language in their students, pushed them toward phony pedantic and abstract writing and squeezed the juice out of them by saying wrong, wrong, wrong. English teachers are the Great Discouragers. (A23–24)

Compare this declaration of war on current-traditional schooling during a year in which *CCC* would focus an entire issue on the creative arts and composition, with Gwynn's restatement of the editorial mission of *CE* in 1955, which he notes Hatfield established: "(1) To be representative, to 'give voice to teachers in all sorts of schools and in all sections of the country' as 'a clearing-house of opinions, experience, and investigation'; (2) To be 'progressive' (the adjective has taken on equivocal connotations since 1912): 'We do not wish to root, tear up, and overthrow, but we are eager to move steadily forward'; (3) To aim 'at a high standard of excellence in style and topography'" (A11). In 1978, over twenty years after Gwynn's report, Ohmann observes that "the last year of my editorship went as expected: more debate about 'basics,' dialects, invention, reader-centered criticism and teaching, and other topics that are engaging our contributors and (I hope) our readers. . . . One generalization: Articles submitted (and those accepted) increasingly reflect the crises of money and confidence that have come upon our profession. I hope *CE* has made some contribution to clear thought about those crises" (25).

One can see in Gwynn's report the explicit desire to continue tradition—a tradition rooted in a journal for *secondary*-school teachers; in Ohmann's report, the contrasting tone is one of slight defiance and forward looking to new territories (of scholarship, of membership). The desire to speak *with* as well as *for* readerly constituencies is common across both journal editors' reports, but for Gwynn, and for subsequent editors of *CE*, the ability to look forward into *new* territory becomes less and less clear as the definition of English becomes more and more intertwined with composition and rhetoric and teaching as a *profession*—a particular cause of Ohmann's later editorship.[7] As is clear from other portions of these archived editors' reports, these questions of territory and community bled into more day-to-day concerns about *coverage* and *workload*—namely, how editors handled the weight of their jobs, who would do reviewing for them, particularly of new books, and how that reviewing would come to characterize the journals as storehouses of the latest scholarly trends. This is the identity crisis—the growing pain, as it were—that I turn to next.

Identity Crisis #2: Who Speaks for Composition (and Who Referees It?)

While coming from macro issues in disciplinary identity down to micro issues of workload for editors and reviewers may seem less than noteworthy, I argue that the responsibility for circulation of knowledge in composition studies—especially as it evolved so rapidly within the paradigms of a new field—bore significant weight on the editors of *CCC* and *CE* during these earlier years of their publication history. When *CE* existed on its own for over a decade as the college-level journal for NCTE, serving only as a sister publication to *English Journal*, scholarship on literature and the profession was both less plentiful *and* reviews of this scholarship were spread more evenly across other like-minded literary journals. But with *CCC* emerging as both a new space for review of books—including all this new work on composition and teaching writing—*and* as a counterpart to *CE* as a college-level publication, the stress on both publications regarding what would be reviewed, with what expedience, and how those reviews would be handled internally was real and omnipresent. This stress led to new ways of thinking about external reviewers versus editorial boards versus reviews editors—an important evolutionary moment for both journals and for the discipline if we note that concerted peer review is one critical marker of identity that moves a nascent community of like-minded scholars into "field" status.

The earliest indication of problems with handling the general influx of manuscript submissions comes in the 1956 *CE* report filed by Gwynn.[8] Gwynn first notes that his own approach to responding to authors has already evolved, even this early in his editorship. He reports that "with a return to a full-time teaching schedule plus two new courses to give, we have had to abandon the practice of rejecting MSS with a personal letter of reasons and suggestions, and have returned to a gentle form letter in the manner of the former editor" (Annual Reports, A16). Related to this time problem, Gwynn characterizes himself as a "part-time editor, with a full-time teaching job and a full-time wife and children" who cannot "read enough material every month to fill more than two pages with good items. We hope to enlist the aid of some colleagues soon to give fuller coverage to new professional notions" (A16). In F. E. Bowman's 1957 *CCC* report, he expresses hope that the $500 annual honorarium for editing will continue while also noting that "maximum demand for reviews has by no means been reached and members of the Editorial Board have been somewhat burdened with reviewing" (A14). Indeed, workload was an explicit issue for many editors; in 1964, Macrorie states that he must resign his position as editor "in order to free myself to do more of my own writing" (A23), further characterizing his editorial policy as including the tedious work of "edit[ing] out (with prior approval of authors) much of the normal and expected pedantic language from articles I have accepted," noting that "I have tried to print articles that were alive, and I think I succeeded in large measure" (A23).

What is clear from Gwynn's and Bowman's reports, and is supported by subsequent editors' reports for both journals, is that the early history of *CE* and *CCC* was very much a one-man operation, with editors neither as well compensated as they might be now (in terms of institutional support, if not honoraria—a nominal yearly sum NCTE journal editors do still receive) nor prepared for the flood of scholarship the field was beginning to produce. In 1959, Bowman—who was serving as interim editor of *CCC* for one year while Williams was on a Fulbright—notes that both the conference and the journal "are meeting the obligation to stimulate professional discussion and to provide younger members with means for gaining recognition" (Annual Reports, A15). But he also expresses concern over *representing* all of that work, especially in a newly created department called, aptly, "Some of the Year's Work." Bowman remarks that "no means, not even a committee, has been found to accomplish the voracious reading done by Editor George Wykoff, who began the department. . . . Informal agreement with the Editor of *College English* satisfactorily prevents duplication of notices of new and revised texts, but *CCC* has not completely defined its own policy for coping with the annual outpouring of such texts" (A16). In 1960, Williams reassumed the editorship from Bowman and reported that the "Some of the Year's Work" column had gone dormant and was "not revived" but that book reviews proper had increased "prodigiously, from thirteen to thirty-one this year" (A23); in 1961, he would report that reviews increased yet again, from thirty-one to fifty-three (A33). Williams goes on to say in the 1960 report that the "pressure for more reviews is continuing to mount" and that he is "levying on Editorial Board members and local colleagues" to do these reviews, offering them "no payment beyond a copy of a text which they might receive anyway, and the satisfaction which comes from seeing one's writing usefully in print" (A23).

In 1965, we see an important shift in perspective—moving from reviews as small, nagging burdens on the journal and its editor to reviews as representative of field promotion. *CCC*'s Irmscher first explicitly responds to the deluge of reviews as a marker of the field's growth in his 1965 report; he notes that he is "expanding the review section because it permits more and more people to write for the journal" and is also "allowing reviewers adequate space to do more than a snippet of summary on the theory that often many worthwhile observations are made in response to another person's work" (Annual Report, A26). This allows the number of distinct reviews to dwindle from the high number of fifty-three to twenty-nine in 1973, for example, but still with coverage of eighty-seven books in that year's total reviews (30). By 1976, Corbett notes that *CCC* was including alongside regular reviews a special May issue featuring Richard Larson's annotated bibliography of composition titles published in the previous year (24), a further indication that the journal was not only prioritizing reviews of scholarship but also *archiving itself* in the pages of the journal as a discipline. As the journal settled into its identity as a site for review of relevant and quality scholarship, it also began to better organize how that scholarship would be presented, especially in terms of workload; a scan of reports from editors of *CCC* in the 1970s notes far less anxiety over this facet of the journal as a now-accepted component of its core responsibilities.

Similarly, while *CCC* bore the burden of most composition-related reviews, and therefore its reports in the aggregate illustrate more struggles with accomplishing those reviews, editors of *CE* had review troubles as well. Editor Richard Ohmann in 1967 laments that "reviewers are slow to get in their copy once they have accepted an assignment." Secondary to his lack of time to do the "requisite soliciting, badgering, and pleading," he also comments that the book-review section needs its own editor "who can give the section more time than I can," thereby also highlighting the importance of this work to the journal in the tradition of Irmscher's declarations (Annual Reports, A24). In 1969, he would do this, appointing William B. Coley, chair of English at Wesleyan, as reviews editor (A25). Ohmann is also one of the first editors of *CE* to recognize in his reports his editorial assistant—Susan McAllester—whom he claims "has virtually been editor during periods of provostial frenzy at Wesleyan" (A24) and, in his 1969 report, says McAllester "makes it possible for *CE* to appear every now and then" (A25).[9]

In 1962, an interesting variation on editor workload, shared reporting, and reviews appears in Miller's annual *CE* report. He writes that in May, "a new section of *College English* was inaugurated—'Departmental Memo.' This should prove a useful and popular section of the magazine but will require cooperation from the busiest people in the profession—chairmen and directors" (Annual Reports, A28). In 1963, he assigned the editorial responsibilities for this section to Jerome W. Archer, a faculty member at Arizona State University, whom he declares will, with "all of us working in concert . . . attempt to keep readers abreast of new developments in the profession" (A34). What is interesting about Departmental Memo, and other features like it that came and went during these early years of *CE*, is that, first, it emphasized the profession and provided a creative means to review those developments (outside the book reviews that were being channeled to *CCC* fairly exclusively), and, second, it fulfilled the desire to make the editorial process *collaborative* in nature.

Of course, composition studies has always argued for attention to collaborative work in both the classroom and in its scholarship; collaboration is now essentially a trope in/of the field. But these reports seem to reveal that collaboration is twofold. On the one hand, it represents some true desire to bring in other voices to help characterize these flagship publications, which would in turn characterize the field. For example, Ohmann's 1978 report calls *CE* "a small editorial collective" (Annual Reports, 29); in 1957, Bowman's *CCC* report indicates a desire for the editorial board to meet each year at CCCC in order to take on "larger responsibility in shaping editorial policy" (A11). This spirit continues on to a great extent for editors whose work happens well after the era of these reports. On the other hand, a desperate need to *divide the labor*, which was clearly overwhelming and unlikely to abate as the field continued to grow, is also evident throughout these early reports. What editors variously called a "magazine" was anything, at this point, but light reading—or light work for those responsible for producing it.

Thinking about the culture of reviewing in relation to workload and representation puts a slightly different spin on the reading of these archival reports than I did in the previous section on disciplinary boundaries. In terms of thinking about composition as a discipline, one might read *CE* and *CCC* as competing, often literally, for space that would allow them to declare their stake in the fledgling discipline—*CCC* staking out primacy and *CE* scooping up what was left over. But reading the two journals' reports simultaneously in terms of a common *practical and intellectual problem*—namely, how to present all the good work of the discipline available but do so within reasonable work-life boundaries and the available time in the editors' and editorial boards' days—requires a different reading of the archives, one that puts the two journals together as a *team* of sorts. Every editor in some way laments the workload; some articulate it more explicitly than others. But what these reports evince as a common trajectory is the difficulty a new discipline has in determining what will get represented, and by whom, and what the ultimate responsibilities are of the given editor to select this or that book over another, to assign this or that review to a particular board member.

Further, one can see in several years of the *CCC* report a strange, but notable, concern: that the largest number of *states* as possible should be represented in the scholarship of the journal—in other words, geographic representation as something of significant importance. This, again, goes to who does and does not appear in the journal and how those appearances are determined. In his 1961 report, Williams is openly frustrated with the representation in the current volume year;

he remarks, "Articles came from 21 states, the District of Columbia, and Jamaica. . . . To the editor it seems odd that in a national organization fewer than half the 50 states would contribute articles to the official journal. Only four additional states are represented by book reviews" (Annual Reports, A33). Similarly, the various initiatives for special features in *CE* seek to parse out representation of members in other ways—such as Gray's 1979 creation of the "Opinion" feature (a feature that existed until my editorship began, so from 1979 to 2012), which was designed to "be a kind of Hyde Park Corner" where authors could "try out an idea in public" (33).

This constant concern with representation—often manifested through implicit or explicit *collaboration*—certainly seems emblematic of the field's growth, and its continuing concerns, as set apart from other disciplines in the humanities and elsewhere. It also complicates the popular notion, often held by newer scholars, that journals (or journal editors) operate independently of field concerns and/or larger collaborative bodies—that journal editors sometimes capriciously seek to define a field on their own, particularly in the case of flagship journals with high selectivity ratings. While composition studies is often viewed as a more organically grown field—for lack of a better term—than literary studies, these persuasive myths about the roles journal editors actually play, particularly as generalized tales residing outside specific rhetorical situations, carry on. They are, in fact, their own stories—ones the archives can go some distance toward disputing.

COMING TO CONCLUSIONS: WHAT'S A FIELD NARRATIVE?

The two traceable microhistorical concerns I label as allegories of composition's identity crises are but a sampling of ways these reports might be read. One could read the reports as purely financial histories, the costs of starting a discipline and of breaking it off from a "master" field (English studies) within an umbrella organization such as NCTE. This reading would emerge through noting the comments on the journals being "finally in the black" or "paying for" themselves, or through a continual tracing of the discussion of advertising pages across many years of reports; like book reviews and manuscript submissions, advertising space sold (and allotted) grows exponentially across the years of reports filed and is its own powerful economic history. One could also read these reports as *personal* identity crises on the part of the editors, all of whom are male and all of whom clearly make the journal a significant part of their personal and professional profile, whether positively or negatively.

The references to vacations, sabbaticals, leaves, fatigue, and family all provide a narrative of *work* both masculine in nature and at the same time familiar to me as a woman editor.

One could further read these reports as counternarratives to the grand narratives of both journals and individuals; for example, one of the most famous editors (as a scholar) in this bunch—Corbett—wrote and filed some of the most basic, uninformative reports of the era, whereas editors whose names are probably much less familiar, at least to nonhistorians (e.g., Gray and Bowman) write the most fascinating, detailed, and telling annual reports. Similarly, while *CCC* is typically seen as *the* field journal for composition studies, a reading of *CE* reports alone might illustrate just how much that journal really did—and I would argue, does—contribute to the field, as I've partially discussed in the above pages (and here, I remind readers of my implication as a current editor in this reading process and in these archives). Finally, one could read these reports in a larger context—within the full annual reports of the organization, including other journals' reports and officers' reports and additional annual business—and make yet further and different conclusions about how the reports do or do not reflect the more organizational, inward-focused issues frequently at work in the reports to the officers and executive committee as a whole.

Each of these ways of reading would, to my mind, be a reasonable and alternative take on microhistory, and any or all of these readings can and should be done in the future by others. Once a scholar privileges these "smaller" voices and occurrences, these less known utterances against the dominant, published, and public ones that make up our historiographic endeavors, it's fairly open season on what that means for telling *the* narrative of a field. More important, this narrative is—as I hope the examination of these reports might imply—a moving target, as the microscope goes down on a particular year or set of years that means more as part of the continuum, which itself is not yet complete, than as a distinct moment. Further, to examine the reports of these or any journal is never to examine them in archival isolation; they, too, are moving targets, absorbing and reflecting and responding to the real people of composition studies who make them possible. As Irmscher said in 1973, "An editor is nothing without manuscripts to read" (Annual Reports, 30).

But even more so, to close this chapter, and to sum up this concept better than I am able to do so in my own words, we should listen to the eloquent past editor of *CE*, Gray, and his extensive, reflective, and insightful 1979 first annual report as editor, in which he took a stand in saying that he would not allow the journal to be a "monthly chronicle of how we are all marking small adjustments to accommodate ourselves to less" (Annual Reports, 35); he also declared, perhaps, what a journal *means*, especially to us now, in the archives.

> I have noticed . . . a turn away from excitement about open and self-expressive modes of writing and teaching, and a turn toward more dogmatic and authoritarian styles of teaching. The result of all of that will be, probably is already, a journal whose contents are more guarded and predictable, whose tone is less exuberant, whose authors take fewer chances and display smaller expectations, than readers of *College English* in the late sixties and early seventies came to expect. But that is, I think, the state and tone of the profession right now—at least it is the tone of most of the submissions I read. If *College English* changes, then, it will be because we are changing, and the journal will be responsive to the ideas and tone of the most thoughtful of our colleagues in the profession. (32)

How, I ask readers as I close, are we changing? What will the next wave of microhistories tell us about ourselves and our publications between, say, now and twenty-five years from now? And what will be our collective response when these microhistories emerge? That is the reportage yet to come.

Notes

1. Connors's (1984) piece is a standout amongst the small quantity of scholarship on journal editing and journals as pillars of our field. But it is also a "review" piece that is a genre unto itself, I argue, and worthy of treatment not allowed in this chapter, secondary to space limitations. Here Connors provides a variety of historical and theoretical insights into the function of journals in the field, the differences between established and nascent publications, and the role of the editor—though on this point, he says remarkably little, with the exception of this notable passage, which Ianetta also draws upon in her "Dull and Discretionary Power."

    Editors of journals, especially major journals like *College Composition and Communication* and *College English*, act in their own persons as "gates," determining what sorts of scholarship will be accredited, deemed permissible. The selective perpetuation of new ideas that is carried on by these wielders of institutional power has an immense effect on what constitutes the body of knowledge defining the discipline itself. Editors are not, of course, completely free of constraint; they cannot publicly exclude work that has intrinsic or obvious claim to intellectual authority, nor can they easily exclude work by acknowledged scholars in the discipline. Within these limitations, however, editors can apply a huge discretionary power, which is one reason that institutional selection of a journal editor is taken much more seriously than the annual selection of officers. When an essay appears in a major field journal, it carries with it a weight of considerable authority. (352)

2. As others have noted, the work of editing in the two journals I profile here—*CE* and *CCC*—has been done significantly by men. Cooper was the first woman editor of *CCC*, and in the close of her farewell column, she makes mention of her successor, Deborah Holdstein, as her appointment means that Cooper "will no longer be the only woman editor of *CCC*" (Cooper 2004, 198). As of 2014, only three women have

served as editor of *CCC*: Cooper, Holdstein, and Kathleen Blake Yancey (who will be succeeded in 2015 by Jonathan Alexander). Coincidentally, only three women have served as editor of *CE*: Louise Z. Smith, Jeanne Gunner, and myself. At the time of this writing, my successor (to begin editorial work in 2017)—and that successor's gender—is unknown.

3. For a ceremonial accounting of Hatfield's life's work—which, notably, includes none of these specifics about his sale of *English Journal* and *CE* to NCTE, see Jean Copland's 1980 piece in *English Journal* titled "W. Wilbur Hatfield: Precursor of Present Composition Practices." It stands out as both containing no mention of *CE* as a journal (perhaps due to its publication venue) and as another type of retrospective on editing and editors available in small number in our field scholarship.

4. It may be helpful for readers to have a full accounting of the editors who served during this time period. This accounting is also noted in Goggin's (2000) *Authoring a Discipline*, page 211. Goggin's book contains many other charts and graphs related to these and other journals and their editors. Of particular interest may be her charts on pages 150–152, which detail the institution from which editors received their PhDs as well as their dissertation topics. Note that *CCC* editors turn over at the start of the year (with the February issue) whereas *CE* editors turn over near the end of the year (with the September issue); hence the difference in start and end points between the two journal editors' terms below.

    CCC
    1954–1955 George S. Wykoff
    1956–1958 Francis E. Bowman
    1959   Cecil B. Williams (as a one-year sabbatical replacement for
              Bowman, who was on a Fulbright)
    1959–1960 Francis E. Bowman
    1960–1961 Cecil B. Williams
    1962–1964 Ken Macrorie
    1965–1973 William F. Irmscher
    1974–1979 Edward P.J. Corbett

    College English
    1954–1955 W. Wilbur Hatfield
    1955–1960 Frederick L. Gwynn
    1960–1966 James E. Miller Jr.
    1966–1978 Richard Ohmann
    1978–1979 Donald J. Gray (actually served until 1985, but the rest of his term
              is outside my study)

5. Miller also remarks in his 1963 report that he would like to have "issues devoted to Linguistics or English Abroad—but the manuscripts do not exist" (Annual Reports, A34).

6. Whether intentional or unintentional, no annual *CCC* reports include any total numbers of manuscripts submitted, even as many indicate the broad types of works published (articles, reviews, and other features). *CE* editors report these figures sporadically, as I have noted, but it would be valuable to have comparative statistics from *CCC* editors to allow better illustration of the growth of the field as perceived by prospective contributors—and to compare it to the rate of submission growth at *CE*.

7. This is not even to mention the infamous "4th C," or communication. One explicit mention of communication is in the 1958 *CCC* report by Bowman, which notes that "the two areas of composition and communication, not always characterized by mutual regard, appear to have reached compatibility. Few of the articles [in this

past volume] could be described as distinctively communication and none of them are defensive" (Annual Reports, A14). A microhistory of that "4th C" as represented in archived journal materials is surely overdue.

8. It is in this same year—his first as editor—that NCTE sent out a survey to all *CE* readers regarding the journal. Gwynn reports that of the 520 replies (2,500 questionnaires were sent, presumably to the entire subscriber base), "60–80% of the respondents said that the departments of features of College English were just right, 2–17% expressed a disapproval of certain features, and 6–33% wanted more of certain features than they were getting" (Annual Reports, A15). While I do not know why these odd percentage ranges—slightly unscientific in nature—were reported as such, the presence of a survey to subscribers indicates both (1) a query regarding identity where the journal was concerned, as noted in my previous discussion and (2) a closer attention to the *community* of readers, which would be further reflected in considerations of book reviews and who would serve as reviewers for them, and for manuscripts.

9. Ohmann's recognition of McAllester—even as some readers might interpret her presence as the "woman behind the man"—is a far cry from earlier *CE* editors' mention of women employees. For example, while Hatfield did credit the ten-plus years of work by his female colleague assistant, Dr. LaTourette Stockwell, who "persistently work[ed] many hours that she d[id] not report" (Annual Reports, A11), Gwynn's notable mention of women behind the scenes comes in his 1958 report, in which he laments that "A series of sick, pregnant, or ethereal secretaries has caused occasional interruptions to continuity" (A17).

References

Annual Reports of Officers and Committees. 1946–79. Series number 15/70/2. Boxes 1–2. NCTE archives, University of Illinois Urbana-Champaign, Urbana, IL.

Argersinger, Jana, and Michael Cornett. 2009. "Everyone's Argus: The Journal Editor in the Academy." *Profession* 2009 (1): 105–11. http://dx.doi.org/10.1632/prof.2009 .2009.1.105.

"Coda: Tales from the Editorial Life." 2009. *Profession* 2009.175–79.

Connors, Robert J. 1984. "Journals in Composition Studies." *College English* 46 (4): 348–65. http://dx.doi.org/10.2307/376941.

Cooper, Marilyn. 2004. "From the Editor." *College Composition and Communication* 56 (2): 197–98.

Copland, Jean. 1980. "W. Wilbur Hatfield: Precursor of Present Composition Practices." *English Journal* 69 (8): 37–43. http://dx.doi.org/10.2307/816816.

Goggin, Maureen Daly. 1997. "Composing a Discipline: The Role of Scholarly Journals in the Disciplinary Emergence of Rhetoric and Composition since 1950." *Rhetoric Review* 15 (2): 322–48. http://dx.doi.org/10.1080/07350199709359222.

Goggin, Maureen Daly. 2000. *Authoring a Discipline: Scholarly Journals and the Post-World War II Emergence of Rhetoric and Composition.* Mahwah, NJ: Lawrence Erlbaum.

Gregory, Brad S. 1999. "*Is* Small Beautiful? Microhistory and the History of Everyday Life." *History and Theory* 38 (1): 100–10. http://dx.doi.org/10.1111/0018-2656 .791999079.

Ianetta, Melissa. 2014. "Dull and Discretionary Power: Looking for the Editor in Writing Studies." *College English* 77 (2): 157–66.

Lepore, Jill. 2001. "Historians Who Love Too Much: Reflections on Microhistory and Biography." *Journal of American History* 88 (1): 129–44. http://dx.doi.org/10.2307 /2674921.

Luey, Beth. 2009. "The Profession of Journal Editing." *Profession* 2009: 112–18. http://dx.doi.org/10.1632/prof.2009.2009.1.112.

Magnússon, Sigurður Gylfi. 2006. "What Is Microhistory?" *History News Network*, May 8. http://historynewsnetwork.org/.

Phillips, Mark Salber. 2004. "Distance and Historical Representation." *History Workshop Journal* 57 (1): 123–41. http://dx.doi.org/10.1093/hwj/57.1.123.

Renders, Hans, and Binne de Hann. 2011. "The Limits of Representativeness: Biography, Life Writing, and Microhistory." *Storia della Storiografia* 59–60 (1–2): 32–42.

4
HISTORY OF A BROKEN THING
The Multijournal Special Issue on Electronic Publication

Douglas Eyman and Cheryl E. Ball

It is the aim of microhistory to focus on individuals rather than groups and to seek accounts otherwise hidden or unavailable to traditional historiographic methods (Muir 1994, 619). Rather than focus on individuals, our project traces what might be seen as uncelebrated *texts*—academic work that has not been directly influential and has not been widely cited (if at all). Some of these texts were missing for several years and had to be recovered; at least one was literally erased. In the print archives of our field's scholarship, it is difficult, if not actually impossible, to disappear scholarly work, and because the majority of our scholarship is still produced and housed following a print paradigm, the particular challenges we recount here are certainly not a normal occurrence. But microhistory as method requires a focus on what Muir and Ruggiero (1991) identify as the "normal exception," wherein "a truly exceptional (and thus statistically infrequent) document can be much more revealing" (8) than a collection of standard documents that are in agreement; in this chapter we are interested not in the everyday successes of scholarly publication in the field but in an instructive, "exceptional" instance that helps us to "[identify] incoherence, discontinuity, contradictions and ruptures" (Boge 2001, 45) in the otherwise standardized view of the operations of journal publication as the main scholarly archive of our field.

Indeed, in this chapter, we are interested in the effects and consequences of instability and erasure that have plagued online publishing in the field of rhetoric and composition. One view of this instability and erasure can be seen in Jeremy Tirrell's (2009, 2012) visualizations of independent, online rhetoric and composition journals, which trace the staff and board members of eight of these journals through time and space, showing how journals move institutional homes across a decade (from 1998 to 2008). *Kairos*, for instance, moved its original operations

DOI: 10.7330/9781607324058.c004

from Lubbock, Texas, to Michigan, Illinois, and Virginia, where editors were subsequently located. Some of these journals both move *and* disappear from view for years at a time, such as when *Enculturation*'s then-sole editor, Byron Hawk, moved from Texas to Virginia to begin a new tenure-track job. We can see these moves (and hiatuses), and others, on Tirrell's maps, but those visualizations don't tell us *why* the moves or hiatuses happened. This is the stuff of journal-editor lore, and that's the view we want to unearth and concretize in this chapter—not the story of each of those eight journals, but the story of one multijournal special issue on digital publishing from 2002.

We begin with three scenarios.

1. An author's article is published in the online version of a reputable print journal with a long institutional history. The issue is part of a multijournal special issue on electronic publishing featuring five online journals. Several years later, without warning, the online version of this journal is disappeared from the institution's website and is seemingly wiped from institutional memory. There is no record the author's article ever existed, let alone that it was published.

2. A reader finds the perfect multijournal special issue on electronic publishing to use as a framework for one of her dissertation chapters on digital scholarship. She cites the work, but when reworking the chapter for publication two years later, she finds that not only are a majority of the dozen articles missing but that three of the five journals are completely offline, with one of those journals having been scrubbed from the web entirely.

3. An editor spearheads a special issue on electronic publishing, the first of its kind to bring five online journals together to produce a multijournal collaboration. Five years after its publication, that editor's journal is the only one still consistently publishing.

These scenarios are the ugly truth for what was meant to be one of rhetoric and composition's finer moments in digital history: the multijournal special issue on electronic publication, copublished in *Kairos, Enculturation, Academic.Writing, The Writing Instructor,* and (the first iteration of) *CCC Online* in the summer of 2002. Of those five journals, *Kairos* is the only journal that has published every year since it was founded (as of this writing in fall 2014). Every other journal in that issue has either stopped publishing temporarily, usually for several years, or has altogether ceased to exist (as in the case of *CCC Online*). (Of note, *Computers and Composition Online* did not publish from 2000 to 2004 as it transitioned editorial leadership from the University of Texas to Bowling Green State University, so it was not included in this special issue.)

Although the individual stories of what happened to these journals is beyond the scope of this microhistory, this essay will explore the repercussions of this multijournal special issue and the challenges posed by the fact that of the twelve webtexts published in that special issue, ten of those webtexts no longer exist at the URLs where they were originally published. The two webtexts still accessible at their original URLs are published in *Kairos*. Drawing on Patricia Galloway's (2011) approach to the microhistory of the personal computer, we see our own memories and experiences as one of the primary sources for our historiographic work; this approach dovetails with Giovanni Levi's (1991) assertion that microhistorians "do not study villages, they study in villages" (96)—that is, there is an element of ethnographic and even autoethnographic method to contemporary microhistory research. From our perspective as *Kairos* editors, we want to document this microhistory, this broken thing, as a way to help the field learn from our mistakes.

The multiple broken links and missing journals we examine in this chapter impinge on our field's ability to archive its own history, to stabilize it and call it a field full of scholarly productivity. Over the years, this history of a broken thing has taught us at *Kairos* many lessons about the sustainability (or lack thereof) of electronic publishing. This essay will outline those lessons by first providing a review of the webtexts published in that special issue, as they were thematically addressed to cover key concepts in digital publishing at the time. We scaffold this review with three types of infrastructural criteria paramount to consider when publishing digital scholarship: scholarly, social, and technical (see Eyman and Ball 2015). Technical infrastructure includes the hardware, software, networks, and coding practices and standards that make digital publishing possible. Scholarly infrastructure includes peer review, genre conventions, and citation practices that allow digital scholarship to be found and used. And social infrastructure includes both the labor and expertise of editors and the tools that allow digital works to be accessible to all kinds of readers. Using these infrastructures as a framework for looking back at this broken thing, we focus particularly on how the field has overlooked technical infrastructures as a priority in preserving its own scholarship and suggest a few best practices for maintaining this work in our field.

CONTEXT FOR THE SPECIAL ISSUE

In 2001, the debates about the value of digital publication were in full swing. Although both *Kairos* and *Enculturation* had been publishing for a number of years, forwarding examples of rigorous peer review and editorial quality in the publication of webtexts, the editors still had to regularly defend the scholarliness of the works we published. In conversations at the Conference on College Composition and Communication and at Computers and Writing, Byron Hawk and Doug Eyman came up with the idea of making these arguments for electronic publication more explicit, not just in one online journal but in and across all the major online publication venues of the time. Hawk's plan had initially been to produce a special issue of *Enculturation* that would focus on the issue, but Eyman suggested that the affordances of the network itself could help to make the argument for electronic publication more strongly by showing how scholarship across several online journals could be linked—it would be an argument forwarded not only by an individual journal but by a whole field as represented through multiple journals.

As noted in the various voices present in the introduction to the multijournal special issue (which are distinct rather than interwoven, perhaps an indication that even those of us who were making these arguments had still not fully conceptualized the possibility of web authoring as a truly collaborative enterprise), the question of whether to publish in electronic journals and how that work would "count" (particularly in terms of tenure and promotion) was a focal conversation both in our field and across academic disciplines. Even in 2001, the economic pressures on academic publishing (which continue to drive questions about the health and viability of the current model of university presses and corporate-controlled journals) were being decried and debated. It seemed that electronic publication, as a response to the exigence of financial challenges to traditional publishing models, would be a natural progression except that there were many voices pushing against innovation in publishing due to ideological commitment to print text as the only valid mode of expression in scholarly work (fields outside the arts have long understood that creative productions can themselves be scholarly endeavors). In his portion of the introduction to the special issue, David Blakesley et al. (2002) highlight the push against innovation that electronic journals were fighting.

> In English Departments across the country, I suspect there are those who have accepted unquestioningly the notion that "anyone can publish electronically" and who would rather evaluate a colleague's scholarship not on its merit, but on a vague or outdated hierarchical system that ranks the quality of the scholarship exclusively by a journal's medium or by name recognition. That attitude, I believe, is more rampant and thus more damaging in the humanities, where electronic publication has thrived, even

as its status as valuable scholarship has met with resistance. (Blakesley et al. 2002)

In his part of the introduction, Eyman also highlights the challenges inherent in developing new forms of writing scholarly argument that are embedded in larger cultures of production that have their own strongly rooted traditions and norms.

> Since its inception, *Kairos* has been criticized both for being too non-traditional and for being too traditional. The journal has always been engaged in a delicate balancing act: we want our authors to have their submissions recognized as valid peer-reviewed scholarship for purposes of tenure and promotion, and we want to make sure that we aren't simply replicating the kind of scholarship that could just as easily exist in a print journal. The tension between these two goals has led to several compromises, including the development of a production cycle that publishes "issues" rather than creating a space that is constantly growing, changing, and evolving over time. In a way, too, *Kairos* has served as an initial model upon which other groups have based new online journals to varying degrees, in some cases pushing *against* the compromises we have made. (Blakesley, et al. 2002)

Byron Hawk took on the role of lead editor on the larger project, one of the goals of which was to show a wide range of approaches to the question, what can digital scholarship be? As he notes in his section of the introduction, commenting on the relationship between argument and design,

> This particular multi-journal issue is one such experiment in form. I began this project as a special issue of *Enculturation*, but came to realize that such a topic lent itself to experimentation at the journal level, not just the article level (thanks in part to discussions with Doug Eyman of *Kairos*). Print technology does not lend itself to a journal issue that incorporates multiple journals. It is possible, but the articles would remain separated by space/time. The kind of space provided by the web makes a more integrated multi-journal issue possible. . . . What good is a new space if the avenues for communication, collaboration, and community are not followed? (Blakesley et al. 2002)

In each participant journal, at least one webtext looks like a more traditional, linear argument and one webtext utilizes the affordances of the medium (through hypertext, linking, multimedia, or interactive Flash interfaces). No one journal takes on the role of innovator at the expense of any other journal, and in that sense, the multijournal issue does succeed in the goal of representing new publication models while also addressing the challenges (both technical and social) that had driven the overall development of each journal's approach.

There was some wrangling over which pieces would appear in which journal. For instance, Mick Doherty and Michael Salvo (who were both founding editors of *Kairos*) initially hoped that their webtext, which was about *Kairos*, would appear in one of the other journals, as locating it within *Kairos* itself felt too self-referential; however, each journal took on a different theme, and it seemed most at home in the "histories of electronic publication" strand. But the final articulation of the multi-journal issue (at least, at the time of its publication) was a coherent set of webtexts that addressed the larger issues and arguments about electronic publication, and all of the editors were proud of the outcome. As Mike Palmquist noted in his section of the introduction, "As we move into publication, I'm pleased to be a part of this special issue not only because it provides a new means of advancing the debate about online publishing, but because of the quality of the articles included in the issue" (Blakesley et al. 2002).

KEY THEMES IN DIGITAL PUBLISHING

In the special issue, the articles were broken down in the following journals and according to the following themes, which mirrored the key themes in digital publishing in 2002 as much as they still do in 2016. In this chapter, we will refer to the issue as the *7.x* issue because that is how we decided to enumerate it in the volume-issue structure of *Kairos*. We wanted to acknowledge the year of publication with the volume but indicate that it was special in more than the regular special-issue-of-a-journal sense, so instead of a numerical issue number we chose *x* to represent the intersections of the five journals that cocreated the issue.

Each journal replicated the main table of contents within that journal's interface, although the order of webtexts was not the same across the journals—each one moved its publications to the top of the list. The original front pages of that issue are still available at their original URLs at *Enculturation* (http://www.enculturation.net/4_1/toc.html) and *Kairos* (http://kairos.technorhetoric.net/7.x/index.html); archival versions, while not at the original location, are still available at *Academic. Writing* (http://wac.colostate.edu/aw/articles/epub_special.htm) and *The Writing Instructor* (http://www.writinginstructor.org/). The version of *CCC Online* that participated was decommissioned and no longer exists (NCTE, the organization that published it, also declined to archive it). In addition to the table of contents, *Enculturation* also featured a "splash page" that announced the issue (http://www.enculturation.net/4_1/index.html). The Flash animation that opens the issue is representative of a moment in time in 2002 when Macromedia Flash (as it was still then owned by Macromedia and not Adobe) was one of the few tools for webtext writing that would easily allow authors to create animations and interactive texts, although the level of sophistication was constrained by the limitations of what that program could do then as well as by the authors' particular expertise with it. The table of contents for the issue included a series of introductions crafted by the journal editors ("Facing the Future of Electronic Publication") and links to the articles grouped under the following headings (each journal was responsible for the webtexts grouped under one of these key terms): "Hypertext/Theory" (*Enculturation*), "Archiving/History" (*Kairos*), "Issues/Challenges" (*The Writing Instructor*), "Pedagogy" (*Academic.Writing*), and "Tenure/Review" (*CCC Online*).

Hypertext/Theory

Enculturation published three webtexts related to hypertext theory—two feature-length pieces and one book review. In Collin Brooke's (2002) "Perspective: Notes Toward the Remediation of Style," he argues that the visual/spatial elements of hypertext and (more recently) multimedia encourage us to revalue the canon of style in terms of situatedness. And in "Responding in Kind: Down in the Body in the Undergraduate Poetry Course (Thoughts on Bakhtin, Hypertext, and Cheap Wigs)," Cynthia Nichols (2002) discusses using hypertext to teach poetry as a mode of published response in a way that helps students better understand the genre as utterance and argues that academic hypertexts can be revalued as dialogic. Finally, Byron Hawk (2002) reviewed Elizabeth Loizeaux and Neil Fraistat's collection *Reimagining Textuality: Textual Studies in the Late Age of Print*. In Hawk's review, he summarizes key concepts authors and editors writing and editing in a digital age must account for.

a. The book must be retrospectively understood as a technology in and of itself.

b. Textuality must be seen both linearly and nonlinearly in both print and electronic forms.

c. The primary text can retain its center or be decentered through ever-growing marginalia and linkage.

d. Indexes must be conceptualized in terms of searchability, accessibility, interactivity, and storage capacity (memory).

e. Texts exist in a new relation between hierarchy and complexity (the web often reinforces the former while attempting to deal with the latter).

f. In addition to visual and design elements, textuality and writing extends to the code and programming that goes behind the text, thus becoming a part of the text (which, as Fraistat and Loizeaux note, creates the possibility for an aesthetics "within the writing of the mediating code itself" [8]).

g. All of this cutting and pasting, grafting, transplanting, and recombining creates increasingly blurred lines among authors, editors, programmers, producers, consumers, users, and commentators/critics, not to mention the blurred lines of juridical, institutional, national, and economic interests. (Hawk 2002)

Substitute the word *webtext* for *book* in the first point and this list becomes not a summary of digital textual editing (in the literary-traditional sense) but a list that summarizes the current considerations for digital journal publishing, then and now. These are all arguments that we, as editors of *Kairos* and as scholars of digital rhetoric, must make daily for our authors and our own work. And the affordances of hypertextuality have made it possible for the specializations of digital rhetoric, digital media composition, digital writing studies, and other names and intersecting fields, such as postmodern literary studies, media studies, and electronic literature, to contribute new knowledge in writing studies.

Brooke's (2002) webtext, "Perspective: Notes Toward the Remediation of Style," is a fantastic example of hypertextual theory in action, as Brooke creates an exploratory webtext, designed not unlike a StorySpace-built hypertext but this time in Flash. The piece contains two primary reading paths (one linked from the word *remediation* in the title and the other linked from *style*), and within each path is a relatively linear navigation path wherein each node on the path contains a single word or phrase that signals, through its typeface formatting (usually bold and in a different color), that it is a hyperlink. What the reader of this chapter cannot appreciate from the screenshot in Figure 4.1 is Brooke's relatively judicious (for the time period) use of animation and sound effects to signal transitions between each content node. That the image of a Greek rhetorician spins out in 360-degree twirls perfectly performs what Bolter and Grusin (1999) dubbed the double logic of remediation: the *hypermediacy* of a spinning Aristotle upon a reader's click creates a sensory impact that overloads readers, forcing them to ask what the rhetorical point of such spinning might be, while the *immediacy* of that typical genre convention for this multimedia-authoring platform in 2002 reinforces Brooke's point regarding the dissolution of readers' microperceptions by forcing us to reexamine and recover what we've lost—a point that a large portion of his webtext goes on to explore.

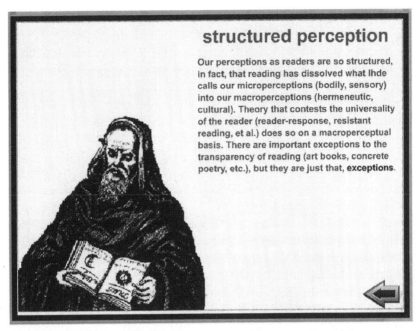

Figure 4.1. A screenshot from Brooke's (2002) "Perspective: Notes Toward the Remediation of Style," in which the word exceptions is in a different color to signal that it is clickable.

Hypertext theory affords us this work: both the recovery of micro-perceptions (in Brooke's terms, quoting Ihde 1993, 74) and the macro-perceptions of theory building. And while we could go on at length articulating this case, it's not really the point of *this* chapter. These ideas about hypertext theory were givens in digital writing studies in 2002, just as they are now. So what is perhaps more important to note here is *how* this knowledge is made in the special issue. In these two examples—Hawk's link-node, or "next" button, webtext and Brooke's Flash-based exploratory (but really rather linear) webtext—the questions we editors often find ourselves asking are thus: Which of these webtexts are easier to cite? Easier to quote? Easier for readers to understand? Is "easy" the metric we want to encourage? Is hypertext in *any* form easy? Is it supposed to be?

Brooke's (2002) work makes a clear and compelling argument, but the substance of it has not been taken up by other scholars or researchers. The lack of citation of this work may be due in part to questions of accessibility (you can't cut and paste text from the Flash container, and the lack of navigation elements makes it difficult to move around in the text without retracing one's path). In terms of scholarly infrastructure, *Enculturation* does at least provide a model citation on the entry page for each article. But as an artifact of digital publishing, this work aptly embodies the tension between dominant modes of scholarly reading and writing and the affordances of interactivity in earlier versions of Flash. Perhaps this is an example of trading innovation and experimentation for scholarly visibility and circulation.

Archiving/History

The portion of the multijournal issue that discussed the history and archivability of electronic publishing was found in *Kairos*. That section starts with George Pullman's (2002) descriptive title, "A Brief History and Technical Overview of the Current State of *JAC Online*, with a Few Observations about How the Internet Is Influencing (or Failing to Influence) Scholarship: Or, Who Says You Can't Find *JAC Online?*" In this piece, Pullman discusses the development of the (original) *JAC* website in terms of technical and theoretical concerns and the relationship between a print journal and its online archive. The *JAC* website was, as it is now (at a different location and under different leadership), an archive for the print journal. In "*Kairos*: Past, Present and Future(s)," Michael J. Salvo and Mick Doherty (2002) examine the development of *Kairos* in both theoretical and personal terms and speculate about the future of electronic publishing.

Concerns about accessibility and archivability are key issues for the technical infrastructures of digital publishing, but these issues are also connected to the requirements that scholarship be presented in stable venues both findable and usable. Pullman's (2002) article addresses the question of information architecture, which is a critical consideration for online journals and for the online interfaces that grant access to digitized print articles. Pullman notes that

> while creating clean and consistent HTML copies proved incredibly time-consuming, designing the information architecture proved surprisingly simple. I chose to use folders labeled to reflect the volume and issue numbers, with subdirectories called Articles, Reviews, and Reviews Reviewed. So, jac/1/Articles/1.htm refers to the first article in the first volume while jac/10/Articles/2.htm refers to the second article in the 10th volume. The obviousness of this structure makes it portable (whoever inherits the archive will be able to find their way around easily enough, and savvy browsers can easily figure out how to climb up and down the tree). (Pullman 2002)

This invocation of portability also highlights one of the issues that isn't applicable to print scholarship: because online journals reside on servers that may change ownership or require updates or repairs, it is likely that digital journals will at some time need to be moved from one server to another. For instance, *Kairos* has moved from its original server at Texas Tech to a server at Michigan State and recently shifted away from institutional hosting altogether and now uses a cloud-based virtual server from a reputable hosting company. *Enculturation* has also moved servers from its original location. Such moves mean that following best practices in terms of naming files and directories can prevent unwanted chaos when moving across servers (which may also mean changing base operating systems, which will impact, for instance, whether or not it is permissible to place spaces in filenames).

Salvo and Doherty's (2002) piece also focuses on the social infra-structures of online publishing, including the need for collaboration between webtext authors and designers (on both aesthetic and technical grounds) and in terms of the collaborative possibilities for peer review in digital networks of production. Their webtext also speaks to the tension between stability and experimentation that is a hallmark of online publishing. As Salvo notes,

> As I write this narrative, I am simultaneously embarrassed by some of the things I used to believe about the potential power of the World Wide Web and of hypertext, and amazed that *Kairos* continues to exist at all. It has indeed outlived the original occasion of its invention . . . (http://kairos .technorhetoric.net/7.x/kairos/salvo3.htm)
>
> *Kairos*, the journal, changes those who have worked on it and written for it. And there are also many histories of the journal that can be written from these individuals' many perspectives. I like to think (need to think?) it has changed the field. So while *Kairos* changes, kairos changes, and the people have themselves changed. This opportunity will not come again, but new opportunities will emerge and indeed, be created by others. (http://kairos.technorhetoric.net/7.x/kairos/salvo20.htm)

Issues/Challenges

The texts published in *The Writing Instructor* similarly take up questions of technical and scholarly infrastructure under the heading of "Issues/ Challenges." Both *The Writing Instructor* and *Enculturation* faced infrastructural challenges as they transitioned from collections of static HTML (the format still used by *Kairos*) to a content-management system that would assist with the editorial workflow (using Drupal in both cases).

In "eBooks: A Battle for Standards," Paul Cesarini (2002) details the battle over eBook standards taking place at the time of publication (which predates the Kindle and Apple iBook formats). Cesarini discusses the economic issues surrounding various platforms and the attempts to create reader/user-friendly texts via both hardware eBook readers and software applications. The article as a whole now reads like a microhistory of a moment in time when the idea of eBooks was being extolled in technology and education circles but the implementation was confounded by competing visions and a mix of proprietary standards. The messiness of the many attempts to develop eBooks highlights the importance of open standards and the value of restricting the works we publish to nonproprietary standards whenever possible. Long-term sustainability and archivability require knowledge of the appropriate standards and putting in place mechanisms for porting or upgrading works that become inaccessible as their formats are no longer supported.

The other two articles in *The Writing Instructor* both focus on the relationship between new digital publication practices and traditional scholarly apparatus: in "Writing and Publishing in the Boundaries: Academic Writing in/through the Virtual Age," Patricia Webb-Peterson (2002) develops a set of criteria for comparing online journals and print journals by examining their histories and cataloguing rhetorical differences in the texts/writing and in journal design using *Computers and Composition* (print) and *Kairos* (online) as comparative cases. Janice McIntire-Strasburg (2002), in "Modern Chivalry and the Case for Electronic Texts," argues for standards in the scholarly editing of online texts (specifically classics and out-of-print books/material) to ensure their usefulness for scholarship; she traces her own editorial decisions in the production of her online edition of *Modern Chivalry*, Hugh Henry Brackenridge's eighteenth-century novel, which has been made available through the Crossroads project, part of the University of Virginia's Electronic Text Center.

Pedagogy

The articles in the special multijournal issue published in *Academic. Writing* focus on how we teach and assess digital writing practices—and particularly how we may begin to teach online editing and publishing in advanced composition courses. The classroom focus combines the infrastructures of scholarly practices and social elements of digital production (the authors of this chapter would encourage the addition of technical infrastructure as well, but it is yet a rare occurrence for all three forms of infrastructure to be addressed in composition courses).

In "World Wide Words: A Rationale and Preliminary Report on a Publishing Project for an Advanced Writing Workshop," Peter Sands (2002) discusses an advanced composition course project that required students to send their writing to online publishing venues and the anxiety those student writers experienced. Several of the challenges facing the students are quite familiar to publishers of online journals—writing for online venues requires more time and time management than traditional class-based essay assignments; there aren't enough quality online publishing venues; and "even upper-division English and English Education majors in the class self-reported ignorance of publishing conventions." These students' experiences echo the concerns we hear from potential authors who experience their own anxieties about crafting scholarly work for online publication.

While Sands's (2002) article takes the form of a more traditional, linear work (also available as a PDF download), Carl Whithaus (2002) provides a more designed and linked webtext in "Think Different/ Think Differently: A Tale of Green Squiggly Lines, or Evaluating Student Writing in Computer-Mediated Environments." Whithaus argues that we should not construct elaborate systems of electronic writing assessment based on portfolio models without confronting the material conditions of students' new technological publishing environments.

The history of *Academic.Writing*, like the webtexts of this multijournal special issue, also foregrounds the scholarly and social infrastructures of digital publishing. In 2004, *Academic.Writing* completed a transition from a more loose affiliation of articles about communication across the curriculum to a full-fledged academic journal when it merged with *Language and Learning Across the Disciplines* (a more traditional print journal established in 1994) to form *Across the Disciplines*. This merger shifted the location of many of the original works published in *Academic.Writing*, thus breaking the links in the original multijournal issue's table of contents; that unintended consequence demonstrates the ways in which scholarly and social elements can impact technical infrastructures as much as changes to technical infrastructures (which may cause extended periods of nonpublication) can impact scholarly and social infrastructures.

Tenure/Review

While the articles in *Academic.Writing* moved, and those in *The Writing Instructor* and *Enculturation* were unavailable for an extended period of time, the final article in the issue, Steve Krause's (2002) "Where Do

I List This on My CV? Considering the Values of Self-Published Web Sites" vanished altogether as the first version of *CCC Online* ceased to exist. Ironically, the only journal in the collection whose infrastructure and backing were provided by a large institution (NCTE) was also the only journal that did not work diligently to produce accessible, archivable issues. Despite its experience with print journals, NCTE's approach broke all three forms of infrastructure—the technical (as it decommissioned the journal but did not archive the works published therein), the scholarly (by granting its imprimatur to what should have been a strong venue for digital publication in the discipline), and the social (by not following through with its obligations to its editors and authors).

The original article is now no longer available even at the author's site; there is a copy in the archive.org database, but that copy cannot be relied on as stable: if NCTE ever adds a robots.txt file requesting that the part of the site that had hosted the article not be indexed by search engines, it will be removed from archive.org as well (https://web.archive.org /web/20021021040043/http://www.ncte.org/ccc/www/2/54.1/krause _copy.html). This is a known problem with archive.org, which renders it unreliable for archival research purposes.

In 2007, *Kairos* published an updated version of Krause's article, including commentary on the fate of the original, which had disappeared in the intervening five years. For some time, a copy was available at the site of *CCCO*, which was a reenvisioning of *CCC Online* as a database of metadata about *CCC* (print) rather than as an electronic journal per se; that endeavor was abruptly abandoned by NCTE in 2008 as they attempted to create a new version of *CCC Online* as a digital journal. This new version begins with issue 1.1, effectively erasing the history of all prior versions, thus hitting the triple play of failure of the technical, scholarly, *and* social infrastructures. In the revised and updated version that appears in *Kairos*, Krause (2007) notes the importance of archiving for digital publishing (an issue to which fairly little attention had been paid prior to the disappearance of the original *CCC Online*).

> I think the experiences I and other disappeared writers had represent yet another example of why the future of all electronic publishing should involve co/self/simultaneous web publishing. This experience has taught me that in the future, I should make every effort to simultaneously publish in academic publications, be they electronic or print, *and* to self-publish my work and make it available via a web site I manage. (Krause 2007)

We conclude the thematic review of the 7.x issue by noting, again with irony, that Krause's webtext about the positionality and legitimacy of online publishing, which appeared in the tenure/review theme of the multijournal special issue, was no longer available for readers—including T&P reviewers—in its original, peer-reviewed publication venue.

FIXING BROKEN THINGS: INFRASTRUCTURES OF ELECTRONIC SCHOLARLY PUBLISHING

Although *Kairos* has published more consistently than the other journals that participated in the special issue, we have also had challenges with technical infrastructure. In the summer of 2014, a networking issue took *Kairos* offline for nearly a month. In the troubleshooting process, it became clear that we needed a new server and that we needed to have more direct control over the networking features. Technical infrastructure is in some ways both simpler (because there are known best practices) and more challenging for digital publishing in the humanities (because fewer journal editors have the technical expertise to run servers and networks). In our field in particular (where academics are highly mobile), the social and technical infrastructures interact as editors and publishers move from one institution to another, sometimes bringing their journals with them and sometimes leaving them behind.

We make knowledge and disseminate it in our field via books, edited collections, and journals (both print and digital). As the economics of publishing further erodes the capacity to produce and mail out new print texts, there is a gradual shift to more online venues: from the excellent library of rhetoric and composition books available for download from the WAC Clearinghouse (wac.colostate.edu), to online long-form "book" publishing produced by the Computers and Composition Digital Press (ccdigitalpress.org) and the University of Michigan's Sweetland series and new Digital Rhetoric series, to databases that provide access to the entire history of our key print journals, to the development of new electronic journals. As the landscape of knowledge production becomes increasingly a digital, networked endeavor, it is incumbent upon us to make sure our scholarship is consistently findable, usable, and sustainable. And, we argue, this attention to the infrastructures of electronic publication should begin to infuse general writing curricula as we prepare students for writing contexts that begin with "born digital" as a standard approach rather than an innovation only technorhetoricians may engage.

It may seem that one outcome of the narrative of the special multijournal issue may be that one should avoid publishing in digital venues because they may not be as stable as print journals. But many of the journals in this history, we are pleased to report, are once again publishing—and often are better positioned after changes in technical and social infrastructure: *Academic.Writing* is now *Across the Disciplines*, which has been publishing continuously since 2004; *Enculturation* returned after a several-year hiatus but is now once again in the forefront of digital publishing in our field (and recent technical updates have been put in place to keep the technical infrastructure on a sound footing); *The Writing Instructor* also returned after a hiatus and is also publishing regularly; and of course *Kairos* has, with a brief exception in the summer of 2014, always been available. Of the five original journals, only the original *CCC Online* is completely defunct. NCTE is once again trying to develop a new version, but that organization has not traditionally given much consideration to all the necessary forms of infrastructure needed to build a successful scholarly journal (and to our knowledge, it has never consulted those of us who have experience and expertise in this area).

So rather than argue against publishing in digital venues, we would rather encourage the development of new journals—but we also hope editors and publishers can learn from this microhistory and make conscious decisions about the three critical forms of infrastructure that support any scholarly enterprise. And to be clear, we aren't advocating that new journals replicate the approach of *Kairos*—indeed, the four remaining journals from the multijournal special issue represent a range of approaches, from the publication of more print-centric works to fully multimedia and from regular issue publication to ongoing, publish-as-works-are-ready models, among other considerations. And as the appearance of newer journals, like *Harlot of the Arts*, *Present Tense*, *Technoculture*, *Hybrid Pedagogy*, and *Literacy in Composition Studies*, bear out our contention that more online publishing venues will be forming, we hope to help our colleagues as they wrestle with the questions of best practices in editing and publishing.

And this is how we fix broken things: we encourage editors and publishers to carefully consider all three forms of infrastructure and to reach out to those of us who have histories and experiences we are happy to share. As most editors have a strong sense of the scholarly infrastructure (peer review, placement in appropriate directories and bibliographies, the apparatus authors need for tenure and promotion), and the social infrastructure will be specific to each journal's institutional context and mission, we end our chapter with a brief series of technical infrastructure recommendations based on our own history and reflections as editors of *Kairos*. It has been our experience that the rhetoric and composition field tends to overlook the technical as a core element of writing practices (partly rooted in the anticomputer movement in the 1980s), and we aim to correct that, at least in terms of digital scholarship and electronic publication.

ONLINE JOURNALS IN RHETORIC AND COMPOSITION: BEST PRACTICES

In a way, we are constantly performing microhistories of our own experiences and practices at *Kairos*—paying attention to and recording the training arc of our assistant editors and periodically looking back to interrogate our decisions about all our choices with regard to technical infrastructure, scholarly expectations, and the social capital that serves as the economic engine for our particular journal. While a full overview of what we have learned is far beyond the scope of this chapter, we provide here a series of best practices that address some of the key failings highlighted in the microhistory of the multijournal special issue.

These best practices focus on the technical infrastructure needed to support three key aspects of online publication: accessibility, usability, and sustainability. Accessibility must be supported in order to reach the widest possible audience. While originally shaped by a focus on users who rely on adaptive technologies, techniques that provide greater access benefit all users. And we have found that accessibility also includes consideration of the user's access to bandwidth and the constraints that come with limited access per se (our logs show visitors to *Kairos* from over 180 countries, many of whom are connected via slow modem connections or through cellphones). An accessible text is not necessarily a usable text (but addressing accessibility concerns does tend to increase usability). Usability includes navigational schema and the apparatus that helps the reader use the text. In some ways, usability intersects with scholarly infrastructure as we strive to make webtexts more easily used for research purposes by adding metadata, making sure the text is open to copying and remix, and providing ways to easily cite the works we publish. Usability also applies to the editorial functions; thus, some of the usability requirements listed below are intended to support the efficiency of the editorial workflow (which we have refined over the years based on encounters with badly organized and nonstandardly coded submissions). Finally, sustainability relates to maintaining a stable archive and provides a means for users to find past iterations in the event that a journal moves or changes its primary URL.

While the lists below are specific to *Kairos* (these are our actual requirements for authors of webtexts) and elaborate upon typical web-design guidelines promoted by the W3C, many of the elements are applicable to any online publication. Some of these best practices are supported (or subverted) by the use of content-management systems; we recommend that editors attempt to accommodate or code these practices into the CMS itself where possible.

Accessibility

Use alt attributes with every image and embedded media element to provide a clear and concise description of the image and improve accessibility; alt attributes should describe the image, and title tags should explain the rhetorical use of the image.

All submissions that include audio or video multimedia files must also include transcripts.

Screenshots that primarily contain text should not be placed as images in a webtext (transcribe the text and style it with CSS).

If using proprietary presentation software (e.g., Flash, Quicktime, .wav, PDFs, etc.), please provide alternate versions of your text as external XML and/or multimodal transcripts to increase readabilty and accessibility of your webtext. In addition, you may be asked to submit the editable version (.fla, .doc, .aup, etc.) for editing by the staff once a piece has been accepted for publication.

Use WAVE (http://wave.webaim.org/) to review your webtext for accessibility issues, including code requirements and design considerations such as making sure text elements are presented with sufficient background-foreground contrast.

Upon acceptance, any text files or transcripts (usually Word or PDF files) linked to the webtext must be supplied for archiving on our server.

Usability

All submissions require an HTML page (e.g., for a video or audio text, there must be an HTML page container for the media elements); this container also includes the metadata for the multimedia elements and for the work itself.

The home page for all webtexts should be index.html.

All HTML-based filenames and folders must be lowercase and include no spaces or nonweb characters.

All webpages should have titles that follow *Kairos*'s page-title conventions (e.g., Authorlastname, Short Webtext Title - PageTitle). See current issue for examples.

Double check to make sure all internal and external links work.

All images should reside in an /images/ folder (or /media/ folder, as appropriate).

HTML-based webtexts should demonstrate cross-browser compatibility (i.e., Internet Explorer 6+, Firefox 1.0+, Safari 1.0+, Opera 8+) and degrade gracefully when elements such as JavaScript are not enabled by a user's browser or when images/CSS fail to load.

Sustainability

We need to be able to archive everything we publish, so we cannot accept webtexts hosted on third-party sites (like WIX and Weebly).

We strongly encourage authors to use standard, nonproprietary formats (HTML 5, CSS, etc.) rather than Flash or other embedded proprietary media or template engines.

Upon acceptance, we will need copies of all embedded media files, and all third-party sites that host files must be shared with the journal in order to facilitate editing and archiving.

If you are currently editing an online journal, or plan to begin one in the future, we encourage you to carefully consider the lessons learned from this microhistory about the importance of addressing the technical, social, and scholarly infrastructures. We also welcome queries and would be happy to provide assistance and support to any new publishing venues in our field.

References

Blakesley, David, Douglas Eyman, Byron Hawk, Mike Palmquist, and Todd Taylor, eds. 2002. "Introduction: Facing the Future of Electronic Publishing." *Enculturation: A Journal of Rhetoric, Writing, and Culture* 4 (1). http://enculturation.net/4_1/intro/.

Boge, David M. 2001. *Narrative Methods for Organizational & Communication Research.* Sage Series in Management Research, edited by Richard Thorpe and Mark Easterby-Smith. London: SAGE.

Bolter, Jay David, and David Grusin. 1999. *Remediation: Understanding New Media.* Cambridge, MA: MIT Press.

Brooke, Collin. 2002. "Perspective: Notes Toward the Remediation of Style." *Enculturation: A Journal of Rhetoric, Writing, and Culture* 4 (1). http://enculturation.net/4_1/style.

Cesarini, Paul. 2002. "eBooks: A Battle for Standards." *The Writing Instructor* 2 (5). http://www.writinginstructor.org/cesarini-2002-08.

Eyman, Douglas, and Cheryl E. Ball. 2015. "Digital Humanities Scholarship and Electronic Publication." In *Rhetoric and the Digital Humanities*, edited by Jim Ridolfo and William Hart-Davidson, 65–79. Chicago: University of Chicago Press.

Galloway, Patricia. 2011. "Personal Computers, Microhistory, and Shared Authority: Documenting the Inventor-Early Adopter Dialectic." *IEEE Annals of the History of Computing* 33 (2): 60–74. http://dx.doi.org/10.1109/MAHC.2011.45.

Hawk, Byron. 2002. "Editing (Journals?) in the Late Age of Print." *Enculturation: A Journal of Rhetoric, Writing, and Culture* 4 (1). http://enculturation.net/4_1/hawk.

Ihde, Don. 1993. *Postphenomenology: Essays in the Postmodern Context.* Evanston, IL: Northwestern University Press.

Krause, Steve. 2002. "Where Do I List This on My CV? Considering the Value of Self-Published Websites." Wayback Machine. https://web.archive.org/web/20021021 040043/http://www.ncte.org/ccc/www/2/54.1/krause_copy.html.

Krause, Steve. 2007. "Where Do I List This on My CV? Considering the Value of Self-Published Websites-Version 2.0." *Kairos: A Journal of Rhetoric, Technology, and Pedagogy* 12 (1). http://kairos.technorhetoric.net/12.1/binder.html?topoi/krause/index.html.

Levi, Giovanni. 1991. "On Microhistory." In *New Perspectives on Historical Writing*, edited by Peter Burke, 93–113. Cambridge: Polity.

McIntire-Strasburg, Janice. 2002. "*Modern Chivalry* and the Case for Electronic Texts." *The Writing Instructor* 2 (5). http://www.writinginstructor.org/mcintire-strasburg-2002-08.

Muir, Edward. 1994. "Microhistory." In *Encyclopedia of Social History*, edited by Peter Stearns, 619–21. New York: Routledge.

Muir, Edward, and Guido Ruggiero. 1991. *Microhistory and the Lost Peoples of Europe.* Baltimore, MD: Johns Hopkins University Press.

Nichols, Cynthia. 2002. "Responding in Kind: Down in the Body in the Undergraduate Poetry Course (Thoughts on Bakhtin, Hypertext, and Cheap Wigs)." *Enculturation: A Journal of Rhetoric, Writing, and Culture* 4 (1). http://enculturation.net/4_1 /responding.

Pullman, George. 2002. "A Brief History and Technical Overview of the Current State of *JAC Online*, with a Few Observations about How the Internet Is Influencing (or Failing to Influence) Scholarship: Or, Who Says You Can't Find *JAC Online*?" *Kairos: A Journal of Rhetoric, Technology, and Pedagogy* 12 (1). http://kairos.technorhetoric.net /7.x/binder.html?jac/JAC-history.html.

Salvo, Michael, and Mick Doherty. 2002. "*Kairos*: Past, Present and Future(s)." *Kairos: A Journal of Rhetoric, Technology, and Pedagogy* 12 (1). http://kairos.technorhetoric.net /7.x/binder.html?kairos/title.htm.

Sands, Peter. 2002. "World Wide Words: A Rationale and Preliminary Report on a Publishing Project for an Advanced Writing Workshop." *Academic.Writing* 3. http:// wac.colostate.edu/aw/articles/sands_2002.htm.

Tirrell, Jeremy. 2009. *Mapping Digital Technology in Rhetoric and Composition History.* http://people.uncw.edu/tirrellj/mappingrc.

Tirrell, Jeremy. 2012. "A Geographical History of Online Rhetoric and Composition Journals." *Kairos: A Journal of Rhetoric, Technology, and Pedagogy* 16 (3). http://kairos .technorhetoric.net/16.3/topoi/tirrell/index.html.

Webb-Peterson, Patricia. 2002. "Writing and Publishing in the Boundaries: Academic Writing in/through the Virtual Age." *The Writing Instructor* 2 (5). http://www.writing instructor.org/Peterson-2002-08.

Whithaus, Carl. 2002. "Think Different/Think Differently: A Tale of Green Squiggly Lines, or Evaluating Student Writing in Computer-Mediated Environments." *Academic.Writing* 3. http://wac.colostate.edu/aw/articles/whithaus2002.

5

TRACING CLUES

"Bodily Pedagogies," the "Action of the Mind," and Women's Rhetorical Education at the School of Expression

Suzanne Bordelon

Never regard your exercises as merely physical. The expression "physical training" is a misnomer. All training is the action of the mind. . . . It is the emotion we feel more than the movement that accomplishes the results.
—S. S. Curry (1915a)

According to Matti Peltonen, a significant facet of the "new microhistory" supported by Giovanni Levi and Carlo Ginzburg is the "method of clues," which means starting an inquiry by examining "something that does not quite fit, something odd that needs to be explained. The peculiar event or phenomenon is taken as a sign of a larger, but hidden or unknown, structure" (Peltonen 2001, 349). The method is attributed to Ginzburg, who traces its beginnings to early human hunters and gatherers but who observes the emergence of what he calls a "semiotic" or "evidential paradigm" in the late nineteenth century in the parallel methods of Giovanni Morelli, who was an art historian; Sherlock Holmes, who was a fictional character created by Arthur Conan Doyle; and Sigmund Freud, who founded psychoanalysis. According to Ginzburg, "In all three cases tiny details provide the key to a deeper reality, inaccessible by other methods" (Ginzburg 1983, 87).

Ginzburg describes how Morelli, in distinguishing fakes from original paintings, did not focus on the main features of the work because imitators could easily replicate those aspects. Instead, he underscored the importance of "minor details, especially those least significant in the style typical of the painter's own school: earlobes, fingernails, shapes of fingers and toes" (Ginzburg 1983, 82). It was these details, which the imitator failed to recast in the terms of the master, that Morelli found most revealing. Ginzburg notes that both Morelli's and detective Holmes's

DOI: 10.7330/9781607324058.c005

method of solving questions related to the authorship of paintings or crimes typically involved tracing clues "unnoticed by others" (82). As Ginzburg observes, Sherlock Holmes's abilities to interpret "footprints, cigarette ash, and so on are countless and well known" (82). Likewise, in "The Moses of Michelangelo," Freud (1914) comments on Morelli's method, noting similarities to psychoanalysis, which also is "accustomed to divine secret and concealed things from despised or unnoticed features, from the rubbish-heap, as it were, of our observations" (quoted in Ginzburg 1983, 85).

In addition to the method of clues, the notion of the "normal exception" or "exceptional normal" is integral to microhistory, which often involves a focus on the marginal, "the outliers," and the "exceptions." These are individuals "who in one segment of society are considered obscure, strange, and even dangerous. They might be, in other circles, at the center of attention and fully accepted in their daily affairs" (Magnússon 2006, para. 3). Investigating the exception can help us to understand why they might be viewed as different from the norm but also allow us to appreciate the ways such cases or individuals may be "perfectly representative of their own social milieu" (Muir 1991, xiv). In other words, they can help us to grasp more fully aspects of the dominant norms as well as a "hidden reality, when the sources are silent about the lower social strata, or when they systemically distort their social reality" (Magnússon and Szijártó 2013, 19). When we apply the concept of the normal exception to conventional histories of the field of rhetoric, we can see the ways these narratives have largely overlooked or provided distorted depictions of elocution and expression in the eighteenth and nineteenth centuries. With a focus on discerning both the norm and the exception, questioning the anomalies of the past, and tracing often-unnoticed clues, I approached my research into a private school of expression founded in Boston in the late nineteenth century.

Traditionally, histories of speech have viewed elocution and schools of expression as "something odd," the square peg in the round hole of larger narratives on the rhetorical tradition. These narratives have labeled the elocutionary movement as "that strange phenomenon" (Howell 1954, 3), and the concepts of French acting and vocal instructor François Delsarte (1811–1871), whose ideas were highly influential to late nineteenth-century American audiences, as "all but unintelligible to the modern student, when they do not seem ludicrous" (Cohen 1994, 3). These histories have generally depicted elocution and expression of both the eighteenth and the nineteenth centuries as being limited to artificial gestures, an overabundance of emotions, and parroted readings of literature. However, they haven't investigated the ways these private schools integrated the teaching of the mind, voice, and body and the bodily pedagogies often integral to these schools, which trained both men and women but attracted a largely female student population.

Using a microhistorical approach, my analysis complicates this research gap by examining the School of Expression (now Curry College), founded originally in Boston in 1879 by Anna Baright Curry, who with Samuel Silas Curry directed the school from 1885 to 1921. Under the Currys' administration, the school had several famous patrons, including Alexander Graham Bell, Alexander Melville Bell, Charles W. Eliot, and William Dean Howells (Blanchard 1954, 626). According to Mary Margaret Robb, the school was "one of the most famous and most important of the professional schools" of its time (Robb 1968, 129).

Seeking the normal exception in elocution and expression, this analysis examines the Currys' organic approach to the training of the mind, voice, and body in the teaching of expression and the way they viewed these elements as dynamic, complex, integrated systems. This research reveals that such theories and practices were not merely "the stilted expression of emotion through learned (and practiced) bodily gestures and positions" (Brown 1996, 214) but were part of a comprehensive, integrated training program aimed at attuning the mind, body, and voice to achieve effective expression. This study problematizes more conventional understandings by demonstrating the ways the Currys' approach promoted rhetoric as an embodied practice.[1]

In "Bodily Pedagogies: Rhetoric, Athletics, and the Sophists' Three Rs," Debra Hawhee (2002) highlights such connections in the writings of Isocrates, who observed that the pedagogical practices of athletics and rhetoric were similar.[2] In the late nineteenth century, according to Katherine Adams Davis, there was a "revival of the Greek emphasis on physical culture" (Davis 1959, 6). As Davis explains, "To secure mental control over the body, the ancient Greeks had emphasized a rigorous program of gymnastics" (6). This stress on the significance of physical training and of gaining mental control over the body is evident in the curricula of numerous schools of expression during this period, including the School of Expression. Although the Curry approach was not geared specifically to the rhetorical training of men as was the sophistic approach, it featured this notion of expression as integrating the mind, voice, and body, which is evident in everything from the school's courses in gymnastics and pantomime to archival evidence, such as lecture notes and unpublished manuscripts. Further, the method demonstrates significant parallels to the early Sophists' bodily pedagogies, particularly the stress on rhythm and repetition through practice as well as a focus on reading the body. As Hawhee's argument demonstrates, physical exercise appeared integral to the early rhetorical tradition. A focus on the body as well as performance is apparent in the work of Kenneth Burke (1953),[3] and, more recently, to name just a few examples, in the work of African American scholars such as bell hooks (Conquergood 2006, 155); in the writing of composition and rhetoric scholars such as Selzer and Crowley (1999) and Andrea Lunsford (Fishman, Lunsford, McGregor, and Otuteye 2005); and in the work of feminist rhetorical scholars exploring "embodiments of the feminine in the rhetorical tradition" (Selzer 1999, 9). However, historians in the field have largely overlooked this emphasis, particularly the interconnection between physical and rhetorical training.

In "On Microhistory," Levi asserts that a central framing concept of such research "is the belief that microscopic observation will reveal factors previously unobserved" (Levi 2001, 101) and that "completely new meanings" can emerge by reducing the scale of observation (102). By examining various archival clues related to the bodily pedagogy of the School of Expression, this investigation hopes to address aspects "previously unobserved" in our broader macrohistories of the field. In so doing, it aims to suggest new ways of understanding these private schools, the complexity of expression, and the importance of body and emotion—not merely words—in the communicative process.

To illuminate the bodily pedagogy evident at the School of Expression, I first introduce some of the different clues I traced, the background on the Currys, and the main features of their approach. I then use Hawhee's (2002) article as an analytical frame to draw parallels between the Currys' approach and that of the early Sophists by examining their use of rhythm, repetition, and reading the body. In doing so, I wish to demonstrate how the Currys' approach (and by extension the approaches of other schools of expression) is significant not only in light of research on embodied pedagogy, but, more important, in its own right.

TRACING CLUES: UNPUBLISHED BOOKS AND BODILY TRAINING

I began my research on the School of Expression by visiting its small, rather inconspicuous archives located in the basement of the Levin Library at Curry College.[4] During that visit, I uncovered an abundance of materials about the school and important traces of the bodily pedagogy integral to its curriculum, including syllabi, lecture notes, and student notebooks. However, a significant lead came about rather serendipitously after I returned home and googled Anna Baright Curry on the Internet. I discovered that one of the Currys' great-granddaughters, MaryAnne Curry Shults, lives in Southern California close to my location in San Diego. Eventually, I was able to contact MaryAnne and to meet with her, and she graciously shared with me family pictures, letters, and other documents related to the Currys.[5] One letter in particular caught my attention. In a May 13, 1921, letter to her son Haskell Curry after the death of S. S. Curry, Anna Baright Curry offers suggestions related to the distribution of her husband's will, which was to be executed by Haskell Curry. She writes, "There is an enormous number of manuscripts which are in a more or less chaotic state. . . . You are left free to use your judgment as to which shall be finished with the aid of Secretaries, and I am sure you can do it well" (Baright Curry 1921, 2).

In her letter, Baright Curry also tells her son about new editions of books that are ready to publish and the need to renew the copyrights on existing texts. She notes that there is "a list of nearly 50 books that have been started, but many of these have never been finished" (Baright Curry 1921, 2). One that was started was a book on pantomime, which includes "a lot of manuscripts of Delsarte and Mackaye [*sic*], all of which should be credited to these authors" (2). I was intrigued by the amount of material Baright Curry mentions. It made me want to discover what had become of all those unpublished books. I also found her reference to the work of Delsarte and MacKaye somewhat odd, given that S. S. Curry (1891) in a chapter of *The Province of Expression* specifically critiques the methods of Delsarte in attempts to delineate differences between elocution and Curry's focus on expression. (A student of Delsarte's, James Steele MacKaye, was a key promoter of his ideas in America.) In her letter, Baright Curry also mentions her own work on pantomime and the broader significance of pantomime in preparing students physically, emotionally, and mentally for expression. Baright Curry's letter interested me because previous histories of the rhetorical tradition had largely overlooked the importance of pantomime to the expressive process, yet it seemed integral to those involved in elocution and expression.

After completing further research, I discovered a 1973 article by Paul H. Gray that briefly mentions S. S. Curry's bodily training program and what Gray viewed as the most "striking" aspect—"the overwhelming influence of Delsartism and more particularly Steele MacKaye" (326). A footnote in the article also cites an unpublished manuscript of S. S. Curry's, noting that it was in the Delsarte Collection at Louisiana State

University (LSU).[6] Here again was another connection between Delsarte and S. S. Curry. After contacting staff at LSU's Hill Memorial Library, I learned that a significant portion of S. S. Curry's manuscripts is in the Delsarte Collection. This material includes several of the book manuscripts Baright Curry had mentioned in her letter almost one hundred years earlier. Both seemingly insignificant yet important clues—Baright Curry's long-overlooked letter and Gray's footnote—sparked my interest and helped me to locate several of S. S. Curry's unpublished books.

S. S. Curry's materials are in the Delsarte Collection because he earlier had owned the collection before it was eventually donated to the LSU archives. In reviewing the library's administrative files on the Delsarte Collection, I discovered a letter from Martin Luther to Claude M. Wise, dated February 6, 1936, that discusses these papers. Delsarte's wife and daughter had previously given Steele MacKaye the collection, thought to be "the only manuscripts, notes, drawings, letters, outlines, lectures, etc." of Delsarte, and that MacKaye intended to translate and publish the materials (Delsarte Papers, Admin. Files, Accession Folder 3). However, after MacKaye's death in 1894, MacKaye's widow, Mary, gave the materials (and the notes and manuscripts of MacKaye on Delsarte) to S. S. Curry, who had been a student of MacKaye's. As Martin Luther, who was general manager of the Expression Company, the School of Expression's publishing company, explains, "Strangely enough, Dr. Curry emulated the procedure of Steele Mackaye [sic], for though he wrote and published 15 books of his own, he never completed the monumental task he set out upon, namely, to correlate and to unite into one workable plan the ideas of Delsarte, Steele Mackaye [sic], and his own" (Delsarte Papers, Admin. Files, Accession Folder 3). Although S. S. Curry and some other expressionists distanced themselves from elocutionists such as Delsarte, the connections, particularly in terms of bodily training, are highlighted in this study but clearly merit further investigation.

BACKGROUND ON THE CURRYS AND THE CURRY METHOD

In order to understand the Curry Method, it is helpful to know something about the couple and their education. Both Currys were academically trained in elocution and vocal expression and talented in their own right; S. S. Curry (1847–1921) prolifically published more than a dozen books on the topic, and Baright Curry (1854–1924) was a skilled dramatic reader. Although scholars have tended to ignore the contributions of Baright Curry, the School of Expression developed from the school she herself established in 1879. The Currys both graduated from the Boston University School of Oratory, studying under Lewis B. Monroe, dean of the school and "a pioneer credited with exerting power in changing the emphasis in oratory and declamation from outward form to inner cause" (Craigie 1925; Renshaw 1954, vii). An "indefatigable student" (Ruyter 1999, 24), S. S. Curry continued his education by investigating different systems of expression and gymnastics and studying with various instructors in the United States and in Europe (Curry 1915a, 8). Studying both expression and exercise gave him a "different" perspective. S. S. Curry writes, "I have discovered that the voice cannot be adequately trained without also improving the body; that the improvement of the voice can be doubly accelerated if the body is considered a factor" (Curry 1915a, 8). As will become evident, this integrated perspective was crucial to the Currys' approach.

While it trained both males and females as future clergy, actors, and teachers, the School of Expression highlighted the significance of oral reading and interpretation, which helps explain its attraction to female students, an attraction not limited to this school.[7] However, perhaps because of the hierarchical nature of traditional speech histories and the association of these schools with women, these private schools have tended to be overlooked. Expressionists such as the Currys, though, developed a pedagogy that we, today, would regard as promoting reflection, critical thinking, deep reading, and assimilation, not simply artificial gestures and memorization, as some historians might have us believe.[8] Stressing rigorous mental training and regular public performance, the school promoted physical and vocal self-confidence and control. During the late nineteenth century, women faced numerous constraints, from the tight-fitting corsets that limited their physical mobility, to the prominent medical notions of the period that proclaimed women's "intellectual and physiological inferiority," to "the still-powerful prohibitions on women who spoke in public" (Rudnick 1991, 69–70). The Currys' training pushed against this cultural backdrop by fostering self-reliance in the white middle-class women who made up the majority of the school's population during this time frame.

MIND, VOICE, AND BODY TRAINING

In "Bodily Pedagogies," Hawhee observes that for the Sophists, the gymnasium, the palaestra, served as a site for both athletic and rhetorical training. From studying this sharing of space, Hawhee surmises that the type of pedagogy used in gymnastics may have permeated and shaped the space of rhetorical training. She suggests that this parallel training is apparent in what she labels "the three Rs of sophistic pedagogy: rhythm, repetition, and response" (Hawhee 2002, 145). In the School of Expression, this commingling did not necessarily occur because of shared space but was theorized and practiced as part of the Curry Method, which stressed the integration of the mind, voice, and body. A central tenet was that speaking and gestures should be "spontaneous" and "natural," emerging from "the inside" instead of from "the stilted exercises imposed from 'the outside' by many of the teachers of 'elocution' of that time" (Mather 1970, 1–2). The Curry approach stressed that the mind, voice, and body should be trained simultaneously since they are interconnected; however, it put special emphasis on thinking and developing individuals and their "inner fullness" (Bacon n.d., 65).

In articles in *Expression: A Quarterly Review of Art, Literature, and Spoken Word*, published by the School of Expression, the Currys explain that thinking and feeling directly control the voice (Curry 1896b, 264); they believed, therefore, that the "development of a vigorous process of thinking, the development of attention" is "the foundation of all expression" (Curry 1895b, 102). Exercise, then, was viewed as a mental rather than a physical process. As S. S. Curry explains, "All training is the action of the mind. It may manifest itself in a physical direction, but training itself—the putting forth,—is mental. It is the emotion we feel more than the movement that accomplishes the results" (Curry 1915a, 45). Emphasizing the interrelation of the mind, voice, and body, the education program at the School of Expression ultimately was a character-development program stressing "right thinking and feeling" (Curry 1915a, 8). Because he viewed character formation as an indirect and unconscious process, S. S. Curry asserts that "true education is all-sided and consists ever in stimulating the faculties to spontaneous activity" (Curry 1891, 233). The aim of education, then, is not "merely to acquire knowledge" but to introduce the mind to objects that will spur unconscious activity and "the normal processes of growth" (233). The Currys believed this focus was necessary to develop the individual, particularly to cultivate feeling and imagination, which, as a former student clarifies, was "not merely the playful or fanciful kind, but the deeper literary and creative imagination discussed by Wordsworth, Coleridge, and Ruskin, all of whom were basic influences on Curry's thought" (Rahskopf 1968, 276).

S. S. Curry argued that speaking and singing teachers had been slow to make improvements to the voice because training procedures were "mechanical": "There has been no special study of the psychology of exercises, no effort to associate an exercise with an awakening of imagination with the conscious, the involuntary and spontaneous with voluntary conditions" (Curry 1910, 43). As S. S. Curry said in his 1890 lecture "Physical Training," this was the work he was attempting to complete, "the relation of physical training to the voice and the responsiveness of the body to emotion" (Delsarte Papers, Range 35, Box 12b, File 102, p. 116).

As Gray observes, although S. S. Curry did not publish a textbook specifically on the training of the body, "there is considerable evidence that physical training was a fundamental part of the Curry method" (Gray 1973, 326). In *Mind and Voice: Principles and Methods in Vocal Training*, S. S. Curry writes in a footnote that further discussion of training procedures is available in "the author's book 'Principles of Training'" (Curry 1910, 47).[9] Although this book was never published, a draft version is among S. S. Curry's personal papers, as is a draft of a book on pantomime, which meant much more than simply gesture to the Currys. Martin Luther's 1936 letter to Wise states that pantomime, in fact, is "rendering the body sensitive to the point of revealing in mirror-like fashion the emotions and conceptions which motivate and activate the being" (Delsarte Papers, Admin. Files, Accession Folder 3). Likewise, in 1915, S. S. Curry published a small book, *How to Add Ten Years to Your Life and Double Its Satisfaction*, which includes an exercise program but which has received little if any attention from scholars. Course materials, lecture notes, articles, and other manuscripts also provide an understanding of how the Currys integrated the training of the body into their approach. Further, in 1934, Eliza Josephine Harwood, a former Curry student and instructor, coauthored *How to Train Your Body*.[10] In the preface to the revised edition, Harwood acknowledges her debt to the Currys, stating that her book "is an epitome of the principles upon which the author constructed the system of body training for The (Curry) School of Expression, Boston, at the instance [*sic*] of its founders, Dr. S. S. Curry and Anna Baright Curry, some forty years ago" (Harwood and Wagner 1934, XVII). When these varied sources or textual clues are considered, we gain a deeper understanding of the school's approach to training the body.

Hawhee suggests that for the Sophists, the distinctive aspect of physical and of rhetorical training "does not lie in material learned, but rather inheres in a learned *manner*, a kind of habit-production based on movement" (Hawhee 2002, 145). This notion of "habit-production," particularly the development of right habits, was vital to the Curry approach because they viewed education as the development of character, with the training of the voice being integral to the process. In *The Smile*, another of his books that has received little scholarly attention,

S. S. Curry specifically attributes this connection to classical rhetorical education: "To the ancients, especially the Romans, the development of oratory was one of the highest phases of education, and Cicero has said, 'Oratory is a good man speaking well'" (Curry 1915b, 11). However, he laments that few understand how expression and action connect to character development: "Possibly no subject in the world is so frequently misunderstood as man's own simplest modes of expression, such as the mobility of his face, the simplest movements of his body—their nature, their cause and importance in the development of his character" (Curry 1915b, 14). Considering individuals as complex organisms, the Curry approach focused specifically on the relationship between expressive action and character formation.

BODILY RHYTHMS: POETRY AND THE "LIVING VOICE"

For the Sophists, the development of a "learned *manner*" began with rhythm, which Hawhee discusses in terms of the *aulos*, an ancient reed instrument that established the beat or rhythm for gymnastic exercises (Hawhee 2002, 145). Hawhee suggests that given the penetrating noise of the *aulos*, "it is also likely that music flowed into the recitations and sophistic lectures, producing an awareness of—indeed, facilitating—the rhythmic, tonic quality of speeches" (146). Rhythm in the form of music is significant because it promotes habit formation and the molding of character. Drawing on Aristotle, Hawhee observes that "music differs from other mimetic arts in that it more powerfully conveys *ethos*" (146). This notion is echoed in the works of Damon, Aristotle, and Plato, who all comment on the power of music to affect the character and the soul. More specifically, Aristotle and Plato, according to Hawhee, saw "music as an almost mystical mode of provoking particular dispositions" (147). Thus, they highlighted the transformational potential of music and urged its use—albeit with care—in education. Besides its potential in shaping the soul, rhythm linked to bodily motion "enables a *forgetting* of directives" (148–49). As Hawhee explains, rhythm helps make knowledge of fundamentals more a bodily than a conscious process, which allows for habituation.

Rhythm was also fundamental to the Curry Method, which is described not so much as music but as energy and its rhythmical action in nature. In *Mind and Voice*, S. S. Curry describes natural rhythmic action in terms of the body: "Force always acts rhythmically in nature. There seems to be an alternation between that which is strong and that which is weak. The heart beats in rhythm; man breathes rhythmically; all thinking is rhythmic. Hence, all expression must be also rhythmic" (Curry 1910, 317). This focus on nature and developing methods based on the processes of nature was integral to the Curry Method. The passage also suggests the close relationship between rhythm and the body in the approach.

In *Mind and Voice*, the discussion of rhythm focuses on poetry since the embodied rendering of poetry and literature was vital to the School of Expression and a large part of the school's appeal to women. Further, the Currys viewed poetry as one of the highest forms of imaginative expression. S. S. Curry distinguishes between "natural rhythm," which is "found in breathing as in sleep, the beating of the heart, the peristaltic action of the stomach, and all vital actions" (Curry 1910, 319) and "mechanical expressions of rhythm," often apparent in meter and song (319). However, meter does have a "natural basis" (319). When a poem is well crafted—not dominated by mechanical metric rules—"its rhythm is part of the inevitable manifestation of the feeling or spirit" (320). Thus, S. S. Curry asserts, "No cultivated person should fail to appreciate the true nature of metre" (321). Further, mastery of meter can foster "rhythmic agility of the voice" and "articulation" (321). In addition, it can assist in understanding form, which "cannot be indicated in print" (321). As S. S. Curry explains, "[Form] is part of vocal expression, and can be indicated only through the living voice" (321). Meter and form need to be studied orally as embodied expression rather than silently as mere text. Meter also must be considered in terms of natural, rather than mechanical, rhythm. In the Curry approach natural rhythm was fundamental to well-written poetry, and the embodied rendering of such poetry through "the living voice," therefore, was vital in grasping meter and form.

S. S. Curry's notion of rhythm and its bodily connection to form and, by extension, imagination anticipates those of Kenneth Burke in *Counter-Statement*: "A rhythm is a promise which the poet makes to the reader—and in proportion as the reader comes to rely upon this promise, he falls into a state of general surrender which makes him more likely to accept without resistance the rest of the poet's material. . . . The varied rhythms of prose also have their 'motor' analogies. . . . We mean that in all rhythmic experiences one's 'muscular imagination' is touched" (Burke 1953, 140–41). Burke doesn't underscore the necessity of reading poetry aloud to comprehend fully its effects as does S. S. Curry. However, he does seem to understand rhythm and form in prose in a similar way, as an experience that touches the emotions and the sensitivity of the body to these emotions. Similar to the Sophists, the Curry approach viewed rhythm, more specifically poetry, as working directly on the individual, not so much through the soul but through the "inevitable manifestation of the feeling or spirit" (Curry 1910, 320). In other words, the method viewed knowledge of natural rhythm and poetry as potentially transformative to the individual.

PRACTICE OF FUNDAMENTAL ACTIONS TO STIMULATE CREATIVITY

In addition to stressing rhythm, Hawhee underscores the significance of repetition and response for both rhetorical and physical training in ancient Greece. As Hawhee explains, Isocrates used the term *epimeleias* to characterize both athletic and rhetorical training. The word "encapsulates several dimensions of an intense engagement: 'diligent attention,' 'care,' and even, in plural form, 'pains.' . . . Its root, *meletê*, means 'practice,' 'exercise,' and, when used in terms of rhetorical training, often means declamation" (Hawhee 2002, 149). It is through concentrated and repeated practice that one gains the self-discipline "to make oneself capable of training" (151). Thus, education comes through the routine of *meletê*, "a belief in the transformative work of practice" (151). As Hawhee suggests, Isocrates saw these "twin arts"—rhetorical and athletic training—as essential for males in learning to be productive citizens (quoted in Hawhee 2002, 151).

Not only did practice enable one to gain the discipline to train and to become an effective citizen, but it also was integral to learning response. As Hawhee observes, drawing on the words of Isocrates, students were to unite through practice the *schêmata* "in order that they may grasp them more firmly . . . and bring their [notions] [*doxais*] in closer touch with the occasions [*tôn kairôn*] for applying them" (quoted in Hawhee 2002, 151). In this passage, Hawhee underscores that the significant connection between rhetorical and physical training for Isocrates "is precisely the link between *schêmata*—forms of movement acquired through repetitive habituation—and their use in response to particular situations" (151–52). Thus, as Hawhee states, students learned how to recognize *kairos* through "repeated encounters with difference: different opponents, different subject matter, different times and places" (152).

This notion of physical training and practice as being central to expression was integral to the School of Expression's curriculum. S. S. Curry understood the relation of eloquence to liberty and citizenry, declaring that "a free people must be a race of speakers" (Curry 1907, 3). However, the approach also aimed at stimulating spontaneity and creativity. Training of the body typically began "with relaxation and the development of good posture and poise in standing, walking, and sitting" (Davis 1963, 306). This training was followed by studies in pantomime. As the 1900 school catalog explains, students completed training in harmonic gymnastics and in pantomime because such training was viewed as "necessary for the improvement of the voice and vocal expression" (*Annual Catalogue of the School of Expression* 1900, 15). According to S. S. Curry's "Pantomimic Expression" notes (1897–1899), the objective was "to get the body dominated by thought and emotion" (quoted in Renshaw 1950, 345). Anna Baright Curry also taught the course and referred to it as "Grace and Power" and "harmonic training" (quoted in Renshaw 1950, 343). Training in pantomime included several classes, moving from simple to more complex forms, including representative and elliptical pantomime. S. S. Curry often emphasized the benefits of elliptical or manifestative pantomime, training he felt had been largely ignored in traditional elocutionary approaches. As S. S. Curry explains in *Modes of Pantomimic Expression*, elliptical pantomime "is so named because it reveals or manifests what words refuse to," whereas representative pantomime merely "imitates, indicates or in some way describes an object and its relations" (Delsarte Papers, Range 35, Box 6, Folder 79, p. 1). S. S. Curry continues, "With the imitation of an act is always mingled the spirit which prompts us to do the act. 'I want to hit you' I may say this and describe the act, but the spirit with which I would strike is shown entirely by manifestative pantomime. I may hit you with love, with anger, coquettishly or in a hundred ways. . . . The mere conduct of the individual is shown by representative pantomime, but the feelings, the emotion of the being is shown by manifestative pantomime" (2). The primary distinction between the two forms of pantomime, according to S. S. Curry, is that elliptical pantomime is "spontaneous and unconscious" whereas representative pantomime is "deliberative, conscious, if not imitative" (3). The Curry approach viewed elliptical pantomime as more important because it "manifests the deep emotions and feelings of the heart" (4).

In her discussion of rhythm, Hawhee notes that "as rhythm is achieved, knowledge of fundamentals becomes bodily rather than conscious, and habituation ensues" (Hawhee 2002, 149). This notion of gaining an awareness of fundamentals was also central to the Curry approach for proper habituation but, more significantly, for stimulating the creative and spontaneous, which meant "co-operation and co-ordination of all the faculties": "Essentially it shows an union of all the conscious with the unconscious, the voluntary with the involuntary elements" (Curry 1891, xii). Fundamentals are discussed as "Elementation" or the elemental or primary movements of the body. As S. S. Curry explains in the chapter on "Elementation," from the unpublished manuscript, *Mind and Body Training*, "As in chemistry the vast variety of objects in the world can be traced to a very few elemental substances, so the complex actions we see performed by the human body can all be traced to a few primary movements" (Delsarte Papers, Box 6, Folder 108, p. 3; strikethrough in original). Thus, if the elemental actions are "right," then secondary actions or "accidentals" will be correct; however, if the elementals "are wrong or weak the accidentals will necessarily be perverted" (Curry 1915b, 20). Attributing this understanding of fundamental actions of the body to François Delsarte, S. S. Curry stressed the importance of studying and developing these fundamental movements in order to "secure grace and power of expression" (Curry 1910, 51; 1915b, 21).

S. S. Curry believed that "perversion[s] of nature" were caused by self-conscious or artificial attention to the secondary actions or accidentals. However, training meant the "conscious and deliberative stimulation of nature's own process" (Curry 1907, 18). Not only does "true" expression emerge from within and move outward, but also "many of its activities are subconscious" (152). Mechanical results tend to work from the external to the internal; however, such results "eliminate imagination, feeling, and the higher spontaneous actions of the mind" (152). To maintain the spontaneous, subconscious elements, S. S. Curry asserts that "consciousness and will" should be directed at fundamentals: "When these are right the spontaneous energies awaken of themselves" (153). Developing the fundamentals through practice has the potential to develop right habits, but it also can stimulate imagination and the spontaneous. Effective expression, then, requires both the creative and spontaneous, but they "find their form and outlet" through discipline and proper training (Rahskopf 1968, 278).

S. S. Curry may have developed this emphasis on the importance of training and elementations while studying with Steele MacKay, Delsarte's protégé. In the unpublished manuscript *Nucleus of Delsarte*, S. S. Curry declares that "no one has ever surpassed Delsarte" in making his students train, something ignored by many American practitioners of his ideas:

> He would work a student for three weeks six or eight hours a day on a simple movement. . . . He had a series of movements which he said no one could master in less than three years. . . . His great point was practice, practice, and yet we have people teaching Delsarte by merely giving them notes to copy, by reading lectures to them and never doing a solitary exercise. I have heard that some condemned Mr. McKaye [*sic*] for keeping the

profound secret of Delsarte from the public, and I understand they have done me the honor to include me in the list . . . Mr. McKaye [*sic*] has said again and again that the secret was hard work, that Delsarte enabled a man to work in the right way but that the work must be done. (Delsarte Papers, Range 35, Box 2a, Folder 115, pp. 11–12)

S. S. Curry adds that if a student comes to his school thinking that some such "secret" will be imparted, "we hope he will 'depart in peace' for he certainly will be disappointed" (12). Although he viewed expression as an art, S. S. Curry considered it a teachable skill that required careful and regular practice.

With his focus on the mind, S. S. Curry also emphasized the importance of a positive mental state during training and the need to consciously strive toward an ideal, or the realization of the individual's "own possibilities" (Curry 1915a, 44). In *How to Add Ten Years to Your Life and Double Its Satisfaction*, which links training in expression with better health, S. S. Curry specifically articulates that such practice must be completed "hopefully and joyfully," something not discussed by the Sophists (Curry 1915a, 86). Further, such practice should promote "thought and imagination" but also a "feeling, a normal and ideal emotion": "The realization of the possibility of attaining an ideal, brings joy, hope, courage and confidence" (86). The text, written with *The Smile* to raise an endowment for the School of Expression, urges readers to practice simple morning exercises, which include laughing, deep breathing, expansion of the chest, and stretching. Laughing, according to S. S. Curry, has many benefits: "Exercise in laughter sets free the vital organs and brings all parts into harmonious, normal activity, stimulates the circulation, quickens the metabolism of the cells and causes elimination" (Curry 1915a, 57). In addition, laughing highlights, expresses, and maintains a joyous mental state. Further, like all of the exercises in the book, it benefits the voice, which S. S. Curry believed was integral to all effective exercise: "This is one of the most important tests of an exercise,—does it affect easily, naturally and normally the vocal organs?" (57). The integration of the mind, voice, and body is apparent in this passage. Since the Currys viewed the individual as a complex organism, exercise is needed that addresses, holistically, these different systems.

In terms of practice, S. S. Curry declares that at the start of their morning exercises, students should rid themselves of negative thoughts: "We can and must at once put ourselves in a positive attitude of mind" (Curry 1915a, 38); he later acknowledges, "Effort will be required for a time till the habit is formed" (39). Thus, such practice helped build the discipline to complete further training. However, S. S. Curry saw the process of developing the mind and body not only about practice and physical training but also about the state of the mind and the need to develop a healthy mental outlook and to practice with an ideal in mind: "The feeling that better things are possible inspires all human endeavor" (86). Unlike the Sophists, S. S. Curry considered inspiration to be as important as discipline in promoting further training.

For the Sophists, response was learned through repetition with difference since it was believed that *kairos* could not be taught through a more systematic approach. At the School of Expression, students learned not only response but also self-reliance through regularly scheduled public recitals. In "Suggestions for Recitals," the Currys note that in the past ten years, more than one hundred recitals had been held at the School of Expression (Curry 1895a, 88). As S. S. Curry explains, "The student must be set to doing,—explanation must be subordinate, and only for guidance in the discovery or study of the principles for himself in practice" (Curry 1896a, 1). Thus, the method itself was inductive, stimulating students to make their own discoveries rather than simply regurgitating rules or principles. Under more traditional methods, students were not expected to think for themselves; instead, they were directed to memorize previous conclusions or generalized rules. Knowledge is thus restricted, bound by tradition and existing conclusions. Education means accepting a body of knowledge and passing it on essentially unchanged.

The Currys' emphasis on making students self-reliant was evident throughout the process. For instance, in the selection of a subject, students might be given several books related to the topic, or they might be directed to find other sources at the library: "The student, thus, left free to exercise his own judgment, receives useful training in the proper employment of the rich stores of the Library in his investigations. . . . He must be trained to depend upon himself and to develop his own taste" (Curry 1895a, 88). The aim was to promote a more rigorous thought process, which would be reflected in better vocal and body control. Likewise, the Currys suggest that it is beneficial "to allow students a large share in the management of such recitals" (91). The process, then, could be particularly authorizing to women who made up a significant portion of the school's population. The method challenged the more "mechanical" or prescriptive approaches of the time and instead underscored the role of the reader (not the scholar) in the reading process. It also put the students in a central role by making them responsible agents in the process.

DEPORTMENT AND READING THE BODY

In antiquity, as Hawhee observes, deportment training for young boys started early and was integral to their development of masculinity. This emphasis on "dispositional training" is evident in most aspects of their rhetorical and physical education, with the juncture of this bodily training being particularly apparent in the teaching of rhetorical delivery (Hawhee 2002, 156). More specifically, Hawhee posits that such training was linked to "a kind of bodily reading practice elaborated by Aristotle in his version of the healthy man walking" (158). Further, such training reflected the notion of repetition, with effective deportment being learned through repeated association. In addition, by association "one acquires a habit of 'body reading,' of perceiving desirable qualities and concomitant values" (158). This notion of the importance of deportment and reading the body also is prominent in the Curry Method, as is evident in Anna Baright Curry's observations concerning the walk: "*A good walk always has the elements of grace, precision, decision, and unity.* . . . *First have a desire to go, then have an objective point.* . . . *The mind determines the destination; the eye locates the objective point.* . . . *To cultivate a purposeful walk economize energy, develop proper sequence of action, accentuate levitation, lead from the chest*" (quoted in Harwood and Wagner 1934, 32). The Curry Method was not aimed at developing manhood per se. However, like the Sophists' approach, it aimed at habituation through practice in an effort to create a certain ideal. In her analysis, Hawhee notes the ways Aristotle's remarks about reading the body encourage consideration of Judith Butler's concept of performativity in which Butler defines gender as a "*stylized repetition of acts*" (Butler 1988, 519). As Hawhee asserts, the bodies of Greek athletes and rhetors were "stylized as masculine" (156). Baright Curry's rendition of the walk, in contrast, constituted a more assertive stylization for her female students than typical normative conventions of the period. In Baright Curry's version, the ideal blended poise with decisiveness—a walk, no doubt, that would be empowering to the female students striving to achieve it.

According to Eliza Josephine Harwood, who directed the Department of Physical Training at the School of Expression, the walk is probably an individual's "most revelatory act": "In and through it he reveals his character, disposition, temperament, mental attitudes, habits, thoughts and emotions as much as, if not more so than, through his speech" (Harwood and Wagner 1934, 32). Thus, Harwood concludes that the walk "may well be called 'the barometer of individuality and personality'" (32) and thus demands "careful analysis and practice" by those seeking to develop an "impressive mode and manner of locomotion"

(32). Practice through repetition and study, or students' learning to read carefully their bodies and those of others, was central to the Currys.

Concerns, though, with the reading or *misreading* of the body, particularly women's bodies, is evident in the response of Anna Baright Curry to Genevieve Stebbins's paper on "The Relations of Physical Culture to Expression," printed in *Werner's Magazine* but originally read at the 1897 National Association of Elocution.[11] Stebbins studied the Delsarte method under Steele MacKaye, wrote books about the theory as well as physical culture, provided performances of her adaptation of Delsarte to women from the middle and upper classes, and later founded the New York School of Expression (Ruyter 1999, 48–51).[12] In her presentation, Stebbins summarizes her approach to expression and discusses the benefits of aesthetic gymnastics and "statue-posing," which she clarifies does not "mean tableaux with wigs and whitewash" but instead "is educational, leading on to pantomime and gesture" (Stebbins 1897, 98). In addition, Stebbins responds affirmatively to the question, "Is it true art to put statue-posing on the platform as a number in an entertainment?" (97). Some of the positives Stebbins associates with such practices include that when students pose as Greek statues, for instance, their imagination is stirred to study the "probable emotion or action which preceded the carved one" (98). Further, Stebbins asserts there are physical benefits in "slow motion and held attitudes in forms of beauty and power" (99) and artistic advantages in "familiarizing the students with classical and poetic allusions in a vital, living way" (99).

In her response, also printed in *Werner's Magazine*, Baright Curry strongly objects to such practices on several grounds, including that aesthetic gymnastics "claims to develop grace, but instead develops mannerisms and affectations" and that the beauty of statue-posing is "the physical beauty of woman." Baright Curry declares, "Do not be deceived, it is not beauty in any general abstract sense; it is an excuse for vanity to trade upon the public platform and with conventional sanction in that which should be most sacred to womanhood" (Baright Curry 1897, 103). Further, she contends that such work "leads directly to the variety stage and to the deterioration of true stage art, the destruction of reading as a fine art, and of true and noble platform work" (104). In her lengthy rejoinder, Baright Curry urges women teachers who are using such practices to stop doing so: "Be true to your own womanly instincts, and do not drift with a tide in the support of that which must retard the intellectual and professional liberty of women" (104). Baright Curry's comments suggest the complexities women in the late nineteenth century faced in such public performances, particularly concerning the proper role of the body in such presentations. They also reveal the tension evident in different strands of expression and their contrasting perspectives on reading the body, particularly women's bodies.

CONCLUSION: THE METHOD OF CLUES, MICROHISTORY, AND THE SCHOOL OF EXPRESSION

Depictions of elocution as peculiar, something that doesn't quite fit into the larger history of rhetoric narratives, were what first drew my attention to these private schools of elocution and expression, along with the facts that many of them were run by women and a sizable portion of their students were women. As we have seen, this focus on the marginal or the "normal exception" is a significant aspect of microhistorical research (Peltonen 2001, 351–53). Private institutions like the School of Expression have been doubly marginalized—first in terms of their connection to elocution and second in terms of their association with women.

In addition, I was drawn by the terms associated with the school, such as *harmonic gymnastics, elementations,* and *elliptical pantomime*. These terms and some of the exercises associated with them have also been viewed as somewhat idiosyncratic and apart from traditional historical narratives. However, as Levi asserts, a central concept of microhistorical research "is the belief that microscopic observation will reveal factors previously unobserved" (Levi 2001, 101) and that "completely new meanings" can emerge by reducing the scale of observation (102). After examining the School of Expression, I found that its theories and practices were not merely something that might seem "ludicrous" or "unintelligible" to a contemporary reader (Cohen 1994, 3) but were part of a comprehensive training program aimed at better integrating the mind, body, and voice to achieve effective expression. Seeking the normal exception has enabled me to show the ways expression has been viewed as the exception in traditional narratives and also to reveal a different reality, namely connections between the Curry Method and American Delsartism, both of which "were profoundly committed to embodied knowledge" (Edwards 1999, 65) as well as the Currys' complex, interconnected view of rhetoric, and its popularity, particularly with women.

Hawhee's article on the bodily pedagogies of the early Sophists suggests that parallel training in both physical and rhetorical training was a significant feature of the early rhetorical tradition. Although it might seem more obvious today given the growth of performance studies, the bodily practices and connections to rhetorical training seem to have been largely overlooked in our histories. By investigating the bodily pedagogies of the School of Expression, I hope to draw attention to their significance and to encourage further microhistorical investigation of such practices, of "rhetoric as a *bodily art*: an art learned, practiced, and performed by and with the body as well as the mind" (Hawhee 2002, 144). More important, I hope to underscore the importance of these schools and the pedagogical practices they promoted and to encourage further scholarship on them. As Ginzburg suggests, careful observation of such details can "provide the key to a deeper reality, inaccessible by other methods" (Ginzburg 1983, 87). In a broader sense, as Hawhee and Cory Holding argue, a consideration within rhetorical theory of materiality and bodies may help us "to develop a more expansive conception of what rhetoric is and does" (Hawhee and Holding 2010, 261).

Interestingly enough, the "method of clues" associated with Detective Holmes's skill at noting subtle details, "the apparently trivial," was also central to the School of Expression (Muir 1991, vii). For the Currys, it was the small and subtle gestures and habits that revealed an individual's true character.[13] In discussing, for example, how some view the smile as a "small, insignificant thing," S. S. Curry, a former minister, adamantly counters such notions: "'The Kingdom of God cometh not with observation': No great art work, no great truth, no great deed comes with show. The real significant things are all small. It is the big things, the showy things that are insignificant" (Curry 1915b, 19). This conviction was integral to the school's method, but it was also part of a broader philosophy of life the school was imparting to its largely female students—to observe carefully, to study the subtleties, to see the deeper reality beyond the surface.

In her analysis of American Delsartism, dance historian Nancy Lee Chalfa Ruyter explains that we are unable to perceive or grasp what social scientist Paul Connerton describes as "*incorporating* practice" or "all the messages that a sender or senders impart by means of their own current bodily activity" (quoted in Ruyter 1999, xv). Instead, historians are able to investigate only "the results of what he calls '*inscribing* practice . . . [what remains when] we do something that traps and holds information, long after the human organism has stopped informing'" (xv). Connerton's ideas are helpful in considering the bodily pedagogy that was vital to the Curry Method. In my investigations, I have examined the inscribing practices, which include more obvious sources such as S. S. Curry's books and articles and secondary sources on the School of Expression. However, I have also examined traces in footnotes, drawings, pictures, unpublished and largely forgotten manuscripts, student notebooks and correspondence, and course lecture notes. I have gathered these various serendipitous archival clues in order to understand more fully the incorporating practice of the Curry Method.

Nevertheless, as Ruyter reminds us, we must not draw only on textual data. In addition, we need "to find clues in the data that will help us to understand (in our own bodies) something of the incorporating practices, and to at least suggest to our readers some of the questions or possibilities raised by the data in relation to bodily experience" (Ruyter 1999, xv). Such a suggestion parallels Jacqueline Jones Royster and Gesa E. Kirsch's notion that in feminist rhetorical studies, scholars should use "critical imagination," which they define as "an inquiry tool, a mechanism for seeing the noticed and the unnoticed, rethinking what is there and not there, and speculating what could be there instead" (Royster and Kirsch 2012, 20), which also suggests similarities to microhistory's method of clues. Although Ruyter considers the impact of Delsartism on white middle- and upper-class women, her words also apply to the School of Expression. We must consider the potential consequences of such training on the women who were drawn to the School of Expression and other private schools of elocution—to imagine what the recitals, what the blending of physical and rhetorical training, what the overall bodily experience "might have meant to them" (Ruyter 1999, xv).

Notes

1. In so doing, this analysis extends the work of Paige V. Banaji who recently has argued that in the later decades of the nineteenth century, women involved in expression and physical exercise or physical culture "regender[ed] oratorical education by working to define a new feminine ideal of bodily eloquence that sharply diverge[d] from masculine notions of delivery and the rhetorical body" (Banaji 2013, 155).

2. For a fuller treatment of rhetoric as a bodily art, see Hawhee (2004).

3. See, for instance, Hawhee (2009).

4. According to Jessica Enoch, archival practices that draw on the metaphor of the detective might "make sense" for researchers working in university archives with holdings specifically connected to rhetoric and writing instruction (Enoch 2010, 60). However, as Enoch asserts, in investigating alternate sites of instruction beyond "our" archives (61), we need to recognize that we may have broader responsibilities both to the archives and to the communities we study.

5. I would like to thank David Miller, professor and head of technical services at Curry College's Levin Library, for his wonderful assistance in locating and scanning documents on the Currys. I also would like to thank MaryAnne Curry Schults for providing primary materials on the Currys and for taking the time to address my questions.

6. See footnote 31, page 326.

7. Scholars such as David Gold (2008), Gold and Hobbs (2013, 2014), Lisa Suter (2011, 2013), Paige V. Banaji (2013), Jane Donawerth (2012), Nan Johnson (2002);

Nancy Lee Chalfa Ruyter (1996, 1999), Paul H. Gray (1991), and Edyth Renshaw (1950, 1954) have noted women's significant participation in elocution during the late nineteenth century. Gold currently is completing a broader study of women's involvement in the late nineteenth-century elocutionary movement. More recently, scholars also have begun reconsidering elocution in general. Although this list is not meant to be exhaustive, some relevant examples include Sloane (2014), Harrington (2010), Spoel (1998, 2001), Miller (1997), Ulman (1994).

8.   For connections between the analytical approach of elocution/expression and New Criticism, see Sloane (2014).
9.   See footnote 1.
10. The 1933 edition of the book was titled *How We Train the Body: The Mechanics of Pantomimic Technique.*
11. For more on this discussion and its broader significance to expression/elocution and performance studies, see Edwards (1999, 63–78).
12. For more on Stebbins, see Ruyter (1996, 1999), chapters 4, 7, 8, and 9.
13. See Ginzburg (1983) for more information on this method. The fact that this paradigm is apparent in the Curry Method suggests the depth of this approach in the late nineteenth century.

References

Annual Catalogue of the School of Expression. 1900. Boston: School of Expression.

Bacon, Lenice Ingram. (n.d.). *The Currys of Copley Square.* TS. Box 23 Record Storage Box: Bacon, Lenice Ingram [was Lenice Woods Ingram] Dr. C.C., 1–4. Courtesy of Levin Library, Curry College.

Banaji, Paige V. 2013. "Womanly Eloquence and Rhetorical Bodies: Regendering the Public Speaker through Physical Culture." In *Rhetoric, History, and Women's Oratorical Education,* edited by David Gold and Catherine L. Hobbs, 154–76. New York: Routledge.

Baright Curry, Anna. 1897. Discussion [of Stebbins's "The Relation of Physical Culture to Expression"] *Werner's Magazine* 20 (1): 99–104.

Baright Curry, Anna. 1921. Letter to Haskell B. Curry, May 13. Courtesy of MaryAnne Curry Shults.

Blanchard, Fred C. 1954. "Professional Theatre Schools in the Early Twentieth Century." In *History of Speech Education in America: Background Studies,* edited by Karl Wallace, 617–40. New York: Appleton-Century-Crofts.

Brown, Brenda Gabioud. 1996. "Elocution." In *Encyclopedia of Rhetoric and Composition: Communication from Ancient Times to the Information Age,* edited by Theresa Enos, 211–14. New York: Garland Publishing.

Burke, Kenneth. (1931) 1953. *Counter-Statement.* Los Altos, CA: Hermes.

Butler, Judith. 1988. "Performative Acts and Gender Constitution: An Essay in Phenomenology and Feminist Theory." *Theatre Journal* 40 (4): 519–41. http://dx.doi.org/10.2307/3207893..

Cohen, Herman. 1994. *The History of Speech Communication: The Emergence of a Discipline, 1914–1945.* Annandale, VA: Speech Communication Association.

Conquergood, Dwight. 2006. "Rethinking Elocution: The Trope of the Talking Book and Other Figures of Speech." In *Opening Acts: Performance in/as Communication and Cultural Studies,* edited by Judith Hamera, 141–62. Thousand Oaks, CA: SAGE. http://dx.doi.org/10.4135/9781452233079.n9.

Craigie, Helen [Dean Baright]. 1925. "Baright: - Anna (Curry, Mrs. Samuel Silas)." Box 1 Document Case Box: Archives, Folder 8. Courtesy of Levin Library, Curry College.

Curry, S. S. 1891. *The Province of Expression: A Search for Principles Underlying Adequate Methods of Developing Dramatic and Oratoric Delivery.* Boston, MA: School of Expression.

Curry, S. S. 1895a. "Suggestions for Recitals." *Expression: A Quarterly Review of Art, Literature, and the Spoken Word* 1 (3): 88–94.

Curry, S. S. 1895b. "Where Shall the Teacher Begin to Develop Expression?" *Expression: A Quarterly Review of Art, Literature, and the Spoken Word* 1 (3): 95–105.

Curry, S. S. 1896a. *Imagination and Dramatic Instinct. Some Practical Steps for Their Development.* Boston, MA: Expression Co.

Curry, S. S. 1896b. "Question Box." *Expression: A Quarterly Review of Art, Literature, and the Spoken Word.* [Monroe Number] 2 (3): 264–65.

Curry, S. S. 1907. *Foundations of Expression: Studies and Problems for Developing the Voice, Body, and Mind in Reading and Speaking.* Boston, MA: Expression Co.

Curry, S. S. 1910. *Mind and Voice: Principles and Methods in Vocal Training.* Boston, MA: Expression Co.

Curry, S. S. 1915a. *How to Add Ten Years to Your Life and to Double Its Satisfactions.* Boston, MA: School of Expression.

Curry, S. S. 1915b. *The Smile: If You Can Do Nothing Else You Can Smile.* Boston, MA: School of Expression.

Davis, Katherine Adams. 1959. "The Rise and Fall of Statue-Posing." MA thesis, Louisiana State University and Agricultural and Mechanical College.

Davis, Olive B. 1963. "Samuel Silas Curry—1847–1921." *Speech Teacher* 12 (4): 304–7. Communication & Mass Media Complete, EBSCOhost. http://dx.doi.org/10.1080/03634526309377318.

Delsarte, François. Papers. Hill Memorial Library, Louisiana State University. Baton Rouge, LA.

Donawerth, Jane. 2012. *Conversational Rhetoric: The Rise and Fall of a Women's Tradition, 1600–1900.* Carbondale: Southern Illinois University Press.

Edwards, Paul. 1999. *Unstoried: Teaching Literature in the Age of Performance Studies. Theatre Annual: A Journal of Performance Studies* 52: 1–147.

Enoch, Jessica. 2010. "Changing Research Methods, Changing History: A Reflection on Language, Location, and Archive." *Composition Studies* 38 (2): 47–73.

Fishman, Jenn, Andrea Lunsford, Beth McGregor, and Mark Otuteye. 2005. "Performing Writing Performing Literacy." *College Composition and Communication* 57 (2): 224–52. http://www.jstor.org/stable/30037914.

Freud, Sigmund. 1914. "The Moses of Michelangelo." In *The Standard Edition of the Complete Psychological Works of Sigmund Freud.* Vol. 8. Translated by James Stachey in collaboration with Anna Freud, 211–38. London: Hogarth.

Ginzburg, Carlo. 1983. "Clues: Morelli, Freud, and Sherlock Holmes." ["Morelli, Freud, and Sherlock Holmes: Clues and Scientific Method."] In *The Signs of Three: Dupin, Holmes, Peirce,* edited by Umberto Eco and Thomas A. Sebeok, 81–118. Bloomington: Indiana University Press.

Gold, David. 2008. *Rhetoric at the Margins: Revising the History of Writing Instruction in American Colleges, 1873–1947.* Carbondale: Southern Illinois University Press.

Gold, David, and Catherine L. Hobbs, eds. 2013. *Rhetoric, History, and Women's Oratorical Education: American Women Learn to Speak.* New York: Routledge.

Gold, David, and Catherine L. Hobbs. 2014. *Educating the New Southern Woman: Speech, Writing, and Race at the Public Women's College, 1884.* Carbondale: Southern Illinois University Press.

Gray, Paul H. 1973. "The Evolution of Expression: S. S. Curry's Debt to Elocution." *Speech Teacher* 22 (4): 322–27. Communication & Mass Media Complete. http://dx.doi.org/10.1080/03634527309378039.

Gray, Paul H. 1991. "The Uses of Theory." *Text and Performance Quarterly* 11 (3): 267–77. http://dx.doi.org/10.1080/10462939109366014.

Harrington, Dana. 2010. "Remembering the Body: Eighteenth-Century Elocution and the Oral Tradition." *Rhetorica* 28 (1): 67–95. http://dx.doi.org/10.1525/RH.2010 .28.1.67.

Harwood, Eliza Josephine, and Ralph B. Wagner. (1933) 1934. *How to Train Your Body.* Boston: Walter H. Baker.

Hawhee, Debra. 2002. "Bodily Pedagogies: Rhetoric, Athletics, and the Sophists' Three Rs." *College English* 65 (2): 142–62. http://dx.doi.org/10.2307/3250760.

Hawhee, Debra. 2004. *Bodily Arts: Rhetoric and Athletics in Ancient Greece.* Austin: University of Texas Press.

Hawhee, Debra. 2009. *Moving Bodies: Kenneth Burke at the Edges of Language.* Columbia: University of South Carolina Press.

Hawhee, Debra, and Cory Holding. 2010. "Case Studies in Material Rhetoric: Joseph Priestly and Gilbert Austin." *Rhetorica: A Journal of the History of Rhetoric* 28 (3): 261–89. http://www.jstor.org/stable/10.1525/RH.2010.28.3.261.

Howell, Wilbur Samuel. 1954. "English Backgrounds of Rhetoric." In *History of Speech Education in America: Background Studies,* edited by Karl Wallace, 3–47. New York: Appleton-Century-Crofts.

Johnson, Nan. 2002. *Gender and Rhetorical Space in American Life, 1866–1910.* Carbondale: Southern Illinois University Press.

Levi, Giovanni. 2001. "On Microhistory." In *New Perspectives on Historical Writing.* 2nd ed. Edited by Peter Burke, 97–119.University Park: Pennsylvania State University Press.

Magnússon, Sigurður Gylfi. 2006. "What Is Microhistory?" History News Network. http://historynewsnetwork.org/article/23720.

Magnússon, Sigurður Gylfi, and István M. Szijártó. 2013. *What Is Microhistory? Theory and Practice.* New York: Routledge.

Mather, Kirtley F. 1970. Foreword to *The Currys of Copley Square,* by Lenice Ingram Bacon, May 15. Box 23 Record Storage Box: Bacon, Lenice Ingram [was Lenice Woods Ingram] Dr. C.C., 1–4. Courtesy of Levin Library, Curry College.

Miller, Thomas P. 1997. *The Formation of College English: Rhetoric and Belles Lettres in the British Cultural Provinces.* Pittsburgh, PA: University of Pittsburgh Press.

Muir, Edward. 1991. "Introduction: Observing Trifles." In *Microhistory & the Lost Peoples of Europe,* edited by Muir and Guido Ruggiero, vii–xxviii. Baltimore, MA: Johns Hopkins University Press.

Peltonen, Matti. 2001. "Clues, Margins, and Monads: The Micro-Macro Link in Historical Research." *History and Theory* 40 (3): 347–59. http://dx.doi.org/10.1111/0018-2656 .00172.

Rahskopf, Horace G. 1968. "The Curry Tradition." *Speech Teacher* 17 (4): 273–80. Communication & Mass Media Complete. http://dx.doi.org/10.1080 /03634526809377696.

Renshaw, Edyth. 1950. "Three Schools of Speech: The Emerson College of Oratory; the School of Expression; and the Leland Powers School of the Spoken Word." PhD diss., Columbia University.

Renshaw, Edyth. 1954. "Five Private Schools of Speech." In *History of Speech Education in America: Background Studies,* edited by Karl R. Wallace, 301–25. New York: Appleton-Century-Crofts.

Robb, Mary Margaret. 1968. *Oral Interpretation of Literature in American Colleges and Universities: A Historical Study of Teaching Methods.* Rev. ed. New York: Johnson Reprint.

Royster, Jacqueline Jones, and Gesa E. Kirsch. 2012. *Feminist Rhetorical Practices: New Horizons for Rhetoric, Composition, and Literacy Studies.* Carbondale: Southern Illinois University Press.

Rudnick, Lois. 1991. "The New Woman." In *The Cultural Moment: The New Politics, the New Woman, the New Psychology, the New Art, and the New Theatre in America,* edited by Adele Heller and Lois Rudnick, 69–81. New Brunswick, NJ: Rutgers University Press.

Ruyter, Nancy Lee Chalfa. 1996. "Antique Longings: Genevieve Stebbins and American Delsartean Performance." In *Corporealities: Dancing, Knowledge, Culture and Power*, edited by Susan Leigh Foster, 70–89. London: Routledge.

Ruyter, Nancy Lee Chalfa. 1999. *The Cultivation of Body and Mind in Nineteenth Century Delsartism*. Westport, CT: Greenwood.

Selzer, Jack. 1999. "Habeas Corpus: An Introduction." In *Rhetorical Bodies*, edited by Jack Selzer and Sharon Crowley, 3–15. Madison: University of Wisconsin Press.

Selzer, Jack, and Sharon Crowley, eds. 1999. *Rhetorical Bodies*. Madison: University of Wisconsin Press.

Sloane, Thomas O. 2014. "From Elocution to New Criticism: An Episode in the History of Rhetoric." *Rhetorica* 31 (3): 297–330. http://www.escholarship.org/uc/item/3bd7k0p3.

Spoel, Philippa M. 1998. "The Science of Bodily Rhetoric in Gilbert Austin's *Chironomia*." *Rhetoric Society Quarterly* 28 (4): 5–27. http://dx.doi.org/10.1080/02773949809391128 http://www.jstor.org/stable/3886346.

Spoel, Philippa M. 2001. "Rereading the Elocutionists: The Rhetoric of Thomas Sheridan's A Course of Lectures on Elocution and John Walker's Elements of Elocution." *Rhetorica* 19 (1): 49–91. http://dx.doi.org/10.1525/rh.2001.19.1.49.

Stebbins, Genevieve. 1897. "The Relation of Physical Culture to Expression." *Werner's Magazine* 20 (1): 95–99.

Suter, Lisa. 2011. "Living Pictures, Living Memory: Women's Rhetorical Silence within the American Delsarte Movement." In *Silence and Listening as Rhetorical Arts*, edited by Cheryl Glenn and Krista Ratcliffe, 94–110. Carbondale: Southern Illinois University Press.

Suter, Lisa. 2013. "The Arguments They Wore: The Role of the Neoclassical Toga in American Delsartism." In *Rhetoric, History, and Women's Oratorical Education*, edited by David Gold and Catherine L. Hobbs, 134–53. New York: Routledge.

Ulman, H. Lewis. 1994. *Things, Thoughts, Words & Actions: The Problem of Language in Late Eighteenth-Century British Rhetorical Theory*. Carbondale: Southern Illinois University Press.

6
TEACHING GRAMMAR TO IMPROVE STUDENT WRITING?
Revisiting the Bateman-Zidonis Studies

James T. Zebroski

It is in this manner that one comes to realize that a frozen package of grammatical exercises has no heuristic potential, but is rather a record of the past, to be studied, perhaps, by educational historians eager to plot the course of pedagogical efforts to recover the English class from its medieval preoccupations.

—Donald R. Bateman (1970)

This epigram eerily foreshadows the role I take on in this essay as what Bateman prophetically calls an educational historian "eager to plot the course of pedagogical efforts to recover the English class from its medieval preoccupations," specifically focusing in this case on the work done from about 1959 to 1973 at Ohio State University on grammar and the development of student writing. We, Don and I, did not meet until three years after this epigram was written; in a way it has taken nearly half a century for my path as a scholar to cross Bateman's path as half of the Bateman-Zidonis team that produced research and a curriculum center. The documents and events traced here hardly receive more than a few sentences or a reference or a footnote in the official narratives of rhetoric and composition. Yet they formed a large part of many individuals' lives, including mine. So this essay plots the course of practices—research and pedagogical—in composition in one slice of Columbus, Ohio, and Ohio State University from about 1959 to 1973; but it is also—inevitably—a weaving of my account entering into this conversation as an intellectual and a scholar with this wider composition story.

DOI: 10.7330/9781607324058.c006

1973: BEGINNINGS AND ENDINGS

1973. Winter that year unfolded with two key events in my life—the war in Vietnam came to an end (or at least US ground troops withdrew) in January with a peace treaty, and in February the nation turned its attention to the televised return of American POWs. "Peace with honor," said Richard Nixon—his administration at its highest triumph. I had a draft number of 160, so I had been only marginally likely to go to Vietnam, but now I knew I was not going to be conscripted. I remember hearing from outside my dorm the bells of Orton Hall as they chimed on the Oval at the day and time the treaty went into effect and the war was over. Peace.

Having done some work in the failed McGovern for President campaign in the fall of 1972, I had that winter also noticed a story that began to unfold in the *Washington Post* about one of the Watergate burglars, James McCord, being instructed by Judge John Sirica to tell the truth about that break-in—this was the beginning of the process by which Nixon would a year later be charged with high crimes and misdemeanors and would be the first president in US history to resign.

But also garnering my attention at that time were the more local shifts in life just around the corner. At the margins of the Ohio State campus, a counterculture was burgeoning. Emerging in part as a protest against the Establishment and expanding as the US war in Vietnam took hold in the late 60s, the areas off campus on the other side of North High Street and south on Neil Avenue where the 1970 student riot had begun became home to new enterprises, new ways of living. Pearl Alley, with its record-album stores and incense and candle emporiums. Vegetarian restaurants, including Seva just north of campus on High Street. Long hair. Paisley patterns in shirts. Peasant dresses. Brightly colored babushkas. Jeans. The Gay Liberation Dance under the dome of the stadium. The wall north of campus where gay men met for sex. The smell of pot. Eric Clapton and *Derek and the Dominoes*. Concerts on the Oval or in the quad between the tennis courts and the Towers. Alternative rock on the underground FM radio. Free clinics. Help lines.

I met Donald Bateman during that first week of January. The first thing you must know about Don is that Don made a big deal about everyone's calling him Don and not Dr. Bateman. It seems at first to be a small thing. But it was part of his whole philosophy of teaching—that people taught people and should try to be humane; teachers should call students by name and students should call teachers by name—that we were equals, all students of language, all engaged in and sharing a common enterprise, learning. A sign of those times perhaps.

As a junior at Ohio State, I had started in on my major requirements for English education that term. At the top of the required courses offered that winter term were the two classes on the teaching of English, Humanities Education 561 (four hours) and 612 (three hours). The first course was geared toward teaching composition, while the second focused on teaching grammar. The English-education methods courses in those days were swamped by huge numbers of students. The United States was still riding the crest of the baby boom, and good teaching jobs were still plentiful. In part because Don was dealing with probably fifty students in each of these undergraduate classes, and in part because he was determined to do some innovative things with this limiting situation, Don arranged for us to take both courses as a block. The block course was James Moffett's (1973) *Student Centered Language Arts Curriculum*, which I still have. When I say the course *was* this book, I do not mean we just read it and discussed it and wrote papers on it, the usual stuff Don sometimes called "playing school." I can still remember the first class once he had told us he was going to arrange for us to get credit for both courses; Don said something like "we are going 'to do' Moffett." What that meant was setting up small groups that took up sections of Moffett's curriculum and then did, tried out, the assignments Moffett had created and revised. I can remember doing a sensory description piece of writing with my group across from North High in the McDonald's, which was arrayed in Buckeye football helmet light fixtures. I also remember presenting to the class my own rewrite of *Othello* in an interior monologue form, performing it for the class assembled at the end of the term on a sunny day on the Oval. (I rediscovered this text in the process of doing this research.) Don's class was unlike any other class I had ever taken at university. When I returned to work with Don as a PhD student from 1978 to 1982, it was hardly surprising to me that he had won a prestigious university teaching award.

What I had no idea about, however, is that while all of this was going on—a beginning for me—Don was ending his work on grammar in a fairly dramatic way at the Rochester Curriculum Theory Conference in May of 1973.

In what was his last scholarly presentation, Don read "The Politics of Curriculum" at that curriculum theory conference.[1] In it, there is not a single explicit reference to the Bateman-Zidonis studies or linguistics or composition. There is only, at the very beginning, a strong critique of curriculum developers of the 1960s, of which Bateman was one. In many ways, this presentation foreshadowed the political turn in scholarship in rhetoric and composition that would occur in the late 1980s and early

1990s. Bateman's presentation provided a radical critique of the schools and of reformist and liberal efforts to change the curriculum in incremental ways without doing the preliminary work of changing (or even being aware of) the society that controls the schools and curriculum.

Bateman's 1973 presentation was a thoroughgoing critique, certainly the most radical talk at that conference. Given hindsight, we can see now that this critique takes society, schools, and universities as singular, monolithic, and completely dominated entities. The critique is very deterministic, making little room for individual or collective agency except to commit to revolution and the act of demythologization. Bateman, like the other presenters, takes many ideas and terms from the just-published *Pedagogy of the Oppressed* by Paulo Freire (1970)—it is fascinating how quickly this work affected education and how slowly it came to rhetoric and composition, Ann E. Berthoff (1978) being the earliest compositionist to apply Freire. But, significantly, Bateman also includes other radical critiques from a wide range, including literary criticism available at that time (Louis Kampt, Robert Lauer, Kenneth Kinnamon, Sol Tax). He critiques the Upward Bound and Head Start federal programs as reformist. In a fading echo of his past linguistics projects, Bateman argues that "racism, classism, sexism—those *deeply* internalized social values—are at the *root* of our problems. They are *deep* in our psyches, and they cause our liberal reforms to fail because they treat the *symptoms* and not the *causes*" (Bateman 1974, 64; my emphasis). What we do is not neutral politically, he argues (60). When we shift our attention from the schools to society, we begin to see that the central and primary theme of our age is domination (58). If the pedagogy of domination mythologizes reality, the pedagogy of liberation demythologizes it (60). Bateman was one of the earliest scholars to invoke and appropriate neocolonial critique from the so-called underdeveloped world (including works by Kwame Nkruma) to help us understand our own situation (58). Bateman writes, "Reform is part of the mythology of the pedagogy of domination" and, since schools need reformers to justify themselves, should the reformer commit to liberation, "he would be out of work, and so would a lot of other people" (66).

From this time forward, Don would not even speak of the Bateman-Zidonis projects. There was a complete break in his intellectual project. The Bateman-Zidonis projects ended. There was only silence.

THE METHOD OF THIS INVESTIGATION

The investigation my chapter reports incorporates some of the principles of what has come to be called *microhistory*. McComiskey's introduction to this collection describes in great and helpful detail the reasons microhistory arose and the various arguments for it. This section briefly extends that discussion by considering some of the salient traits of microhistory that relate to my method in this chapter and that contribute to my broader investigation of the Bateman-Zidonis reports, including its relationship to national scholarly discussions.

In his essays "Clues: Roots of an Evidential Paradigm" and "Our Words, and Theirs: A Reflection on the Historian's Craft Today," Carlo Ginzburg constructs a genealogy of microhistory. Ginzburg describes his present historical methodology in relation to past hunting strategies, medical diagnostics, legal practices in Mesopotamia, connoisseurship, the identification of forgeries, and detective stories. Based on all of these past strategies and practices, Ginzburg argues for the microhistorical "analysis of specific cases which could be reconstructed only through traces, symptoms, and clues" (Ginzburg 1989, 104), and cases then lead us back to generalizations (Ginzburg 2012, 113). Ginzburg suggests there is more to microhistory than just the adjustment of scale; there is also an epistemological dimension to it. In fact, the figure of the microscope shows us that once we leave the epic scale of social history and enter the small scale of the individual case, we actually shift our point of view and perceive different things. These different things are fragmentary and come in the form of clues, symptoms, and traces. We observe, analyze, and interpret such clues, symptoms, and traces (for this essay, documentary textual traces) and then patch together a new vision of the larger whole.

Ginzburg (1989, 101) notes that the microhistorical examination of individual cases seeks "marginal facts," instances in which an individual "who was tied to a cultural tradition, relaxed and yielded to purely individual touches" (101). These marginal facts, resulting from individual actions outside of social norms, do not fit the wider cultural pattern and call us to extend and then reconstruct our concepts, ultimately allowing us to see things we did not see before. There is a political dimension to this sort of microhistorical analysis as well. Ginzburg notes, "The same conjectural paradigm employed to develop ever more subtle and capillary forms of control can become a device to dissolve the ideological clouds which increasingly obscure such a complex social structure as fully developed capitalism" (123). And "though reality may seem to be opaque, there are privileged zones—signs, clues—which allow us to penetrate it" (123). Thus, "microhistory has provided an opportunity to subvert pre-existing hierarchies, thanks to the intrinsic evidence . . . of the object under scrutiny" (Ginzburg 2012, 115).

So some of the salient traits I take from Ginzburg's description of microhistory are that microhistory

1. is more than simply small scale;

2. is about seeing the individual case;

3. is about seeing a different set of features than one sees at the macro level because one is looking at the individual case and because point of view has shifted;

4. is about analyzing in great detail these newly seen features;

5. is about looking for and at the lapses, the absences, the gaps, the omissions in these features—that is, the patterns of marginal facts where the discourses relax or break;

6. uses such lapses to reconstitute new patterns;

7. sees its political project to be the reintegration of such capillary detail back into the grand narratives.

Ginzburg (2012) also adds that the categories we use in microhistorical analysis shift in the process of adjusting the scale of analysis. In this discussion, Ginzburg draws heavily on Kenneth Pike, a well-known name in rhetoric and composition, who published with coauthors Richard Young and Alton Becker the classic treatment of heuristics in the important textbook *Rhetoric: Discovery and Change* (Young, Becker, and Pike 1970). Ginzburg, following Pike, argues that one can think of the etic as being the outsider's construction of the traces of the system and its categories while the emic is the insider's perspective, traces, and categories. Ginzburg explains that "historians start from questions using terms that are inevitably anachronistic. The research process modifies the initial questions on the grounds of new evidence, retrieving answers that are articulated in the actors' language and related to categories peculiar to their society, which is utterly different from ours" (2012, 107). According to Ginzburg, "In the total analysis, the initial ETIC description gradually is refined, and ultimately—in principle, but probably never in practice—replaced by one which is totally EMIC" (107). In other words, Ginzburg concludes, "One starts with ETIC questions aiming to get EMIC answers" (108).

So to the above methodological traits of microhistory, one might add one more, which in some respects is the most important—

8. reframing of the research question in terms of the actors.

THE ARGUMENT OF THIS ESSAY

Beginning from the principles at work in microhistory delineated in the section above, I present the basic shape of the argument this chapter develops. An examination of all the available textual evidence from that time, especially of recently available documents on the federal government ERIC website, calls into question the usual disciplinary interpretation of Bateman and Zidonis's work. While the claim of the Bateman-Zidonis projects and reports is in part about teaching grammar and the improvement of student writing, the findings of Bateman-Zidonis are much more complex and interesting than this. This essay, then, will (1) expand the documentary materials available in order to revisit more fully the earlier claims made by Bateman and Zidonis and (2) apply these materials to specify how these terms (*grammar* and *teaching grammar*) were used in the reports and projects in order (3) to argue that the Bateman-Zidonis studies and subsequent curricular works were complex and often at odds with the discipline's later appropriation of Bateman and Zidonis's work.

The grand narratives of composition history have tended to focus on the relationship between grammar and student writing. However, when we shift the scale of our historical analysis down to Columbus, Ohio, from about 1959 to 1970, and to the school of scholars and teachers connected in a loose way with the Bateman-Zidonis projects, we see a different world in which grammar is theory and the question is less about teaching it than it is about inquiring into language—inviting students and teachers to be coinvestigators of language through writing. This chapter argues that Bateman and Zidonis did not make the case for teaching grammar in the usual sense. Instead, the work of these scholars makes a case for teaching inquiry into language for improving student writing. The evidence (some old and some new) supports the paradox that Bateman and Zidonis were neither programmar nor antigrammar but proinquiry.

In a way, the case of the Bateman-Zidonis projects can be understood as the effect of an ongoing tension, present from the start and getting stronger with time, between the local complexity of a developing practice and the more global narratives of our profession. If we see the larger, official narratives as orthodoxy, then the reader is presented in this chapter with what might be considered heresy, an outlier, a case that doesn't fit. As is often the case with such conflicts, their sources lie partly in the documents we include and exclude, in the clues of the absences or the lacunae of these documents. It is perfectly in keeping with the values of microhistory, then, to organize my argument by drawing on the terminology of religious disputes. The essay then is divided into these parts:

1. Orthodoxy: The Disciplinary Construction of Bateman-Zidonis
2. Trajectory 1959–1970: Fragments of Bateman-Zidonis
3. The Canon: Bateman-Zidonis 1966
4. Heresy: Bateman-Zidonis 1970 and the Importance of Inquiry
5. Bateman-Zidonis—Fifty Years Later

ORTHODOXY: THE DISCIPLINARY CONSTRUCTION OF BATEMAN-ZIDONIS

There are, of course, many ways an idea takes root, grows, and becomes the orthodox position within a community. An orthodox position can be said to be the right belief or dogma gauged by a specific community and its leadership.

Recent historical research (Bauer 1996; Crossan 1991, 1998; Mathews 1995; Robinson and Koester 1971; Rubenstein 1999) indicates that, at first, there seems to be neither orthodoxy nor heresy but simply a range of positions, a set of different ideas, indicated by the original meaning of the word *heresy*, *haeresis*, which was "choice." Difference, and a lack of clear distinctions between the various positions, comes first. The questions people have at this early stage are not the questions people later will say they have (see Ginzburg 2012). In the next stage, a debate focuses on one basic question, and sides form around an emerging binary constructed by the most important participants in that debate. Responses in the debate increasingly and explicitly are framed as binary responses to that question, representing either correct belief or incorrect belief. The strongest position takes hold and later is labeled *orthodox* by official leadership and deliberative bodies, and the latter position is labeled *heresy*. Orthodoxy and heresy, then, come as a matched pair. Heresy becomes a way of disciplining. Members of the orthodox community, finally, write histories retrojecting heresy onto the earliest oppositional positions.

What I am suggesting here is that something similar to this process happened with the work of Bateman and Zidonis as it was appropriated by the professional leadership of English. If the work of Bateman and Zidonis cannot be easily pegged and put into our current categories, then that tension can be resolved over fifty years of historical framing by making the questions that generated Bateman and Zidonis's work more about the questions the discipline would later come to see as important, as orthodox. While the Bateman-Zidonis studies do address the teaching of grammar, one can argue that their stress is actually on the *teaching*, not the grammar. To Bateman and Zidonis, the choice of grammar and what is done with it in the classroom and in the Project English Center is a part of the more important point of how to teach it. As someone once said, *how* you teach is *what* you teach. So while the discipline has focused on the *what*, Bateman and Zidonis seem to be more about the *how*.

Partly due to its commitment to English schoolteachers, partly as a response to the public, and partly as a policy response to high-stakes testing at the local and state level, NCTE has felt obliged to deal with the issue, which can be framed as a question: does the teaching of grammar improve student writing? The majority position is: no, the research indicates it does not.

But Bateman and Zidonis, to the extent they engage with that question, seem to answer it by saying, yes, teaching grammar improves student writing. So what is to be done about that? Second, what if, as Ginzburg might suggest, we are framing Bateman-Zidonis with our question, not theirs? When we go back to the original sources, there is strong evidence that has been totally ignored that Bateman and Zidonis had other and larger questions in mind. Thus, we can trace out the discipline and profession's social construction of Bateman-Zidonis fairly easily. Such an account begins with the fact that Bateman never, not even later in life, identified himself as a rhetoric and composition scholar but instead viewed himself as an English-education scholar. So the first source of slippage in the historical accounts of Bateman and Zidonis is that it was, increasingly, rhetoric and composition scholars who cited Bateman and Zidonis's work, and they cited this work as if it were research in rhetoric and composition. Patricia Stock's (2012) book *Composition's Roots in English Education* provides ample evidence that this disciplinary slippage in historical accounts is problematic because of the distinctive contribution English education made to the formation of rhetoric and composition. It is a case of the orthodox community (rhetoric and composition) retrojecting current identities on past debates and characterizing complex historical artifacts as either orthodox or heresy.

It is in the apparatuses of NCTE—its journals, sponsored research, and monographs—that we can trace the orthodoxy as it reconstructs (and thus simplifies) Bateman and Zidonis. The first and perhaps most important major shift in the way Bateman and Zidonis's work is appropriated in subsequent research happens fairly soon—almost immediately—after its publication. John Mellon's (1969) research, reported in the volume *Transformational Sentence Combining: A Method for Enhancing the Development of Syntactic Fluency in English Composition*, is deeply concerned with the intellectual rigor and methodological purity of experimental research, and he critiques Bateman and Zidonis's 1966 NCTE report extensively for its methodological sins. Following a four-page summary of the report, Mellon notes that "the one study which explicitly tests a sentence-structure claim employs questionable design and analytic procedures and rests on a hypothesis which seems altogether unreasonable" (14). Further in the epilogue, Mellon says, "The important thing to note, however, is that I now want to view this experiment as having nothing essentially to do with the teaching of writing styles or grammar. I see it instead as a potentially powerful piece of evidence in support of curriculums based on the idea of enriching the child's language environment, even curriculums which specifically *omit* the teaching of grammar" (84).

Two crucial changes from Bateman and Zidonis's original purpose must be noted here. The first is that Mellon is not concerned with robust classroom practices in the teaching of writing, let alone with curriculum development, as Bateman and Zidonis were. Instead, Mellon is concerned with clean experiments whose methods and results can be trusted. Second, it is Mellon who shifts the focus of the discussion away from the teaching of grammar (which is what Bateman and Zidonis were concerned with) and toward Mellon's own interest, sentence structure and student sentence manipulation, which he believes enhance syntactic fluency. Mellon is the first to use the term *sentence combining*, and in that usage he takes a turn that goes far away from Bateman and Zidonis. Given the Chomskyian foundation in much of Bateman and Zidonis's work, they would have viewed the practice of sentence combining as behaviorist. After Mellon's critique, the work of Bateman and Zidonis is seen less and less as a contribution to the orthodox question of whether we should teach grammar and more as a contribution to the question of what we can replace grammar instruction with, something that wholly contradicts both Bateman and Zidonis's approach and research findings.

In 1973, by publishing a new monograph in its officially sanctioned research reports, NCTE confirms this turn in direction. If we accept that the key question is, should we teach grammar to improve student writing? and if the answer is no, then what? Picking up with Mellon's practice of sentence combining and further stripping the remaining grammatical instructions from student exercises, Frank O'Hare (1973), in his *Sentence Combining: Improving Student Writing without Formal Grammar*

Instruction, provides an answer. We replace grammar with sentence-combining practice. O'Hare is a scrupulous and generous scholar in this monograph, and he revisits Bateman and Zidonis as well as Mellon and others. O'Hare takes Mellon to task (1) for being at times unfairly critical of Bateman-Zidonis and (2) for insisting on the antirhetorical nature of sentence combining (O'Hare 1973, 8, 14). O'Hare calls the work of Bateman and Zidonis a landmark, a pioneering and a significant study (7, 9). O'Hare goes through some of Mellon's criticisms, agreeing with most, but adding, "Although some of Mellon's criticisms are well founded, others are, perhaps, a little too severe" (8). But O'Hare's work then confirms Mellon's remaking of Bateman-Zidonis into a sentence-combining project. While O'Hare cites a good number of relevant texts, including the report in 1964 that Bateman and Zidonis submitted to the federal government, he does not mention Frank Zidonis's *English Journal* essays on the project nor does he mention the final 1970 report, also submitted to the federal government. Without the context provided by these documents, the complex richness of Bateman-Zidonis is reduced to a precursor of sentence combining.

By 1986, the arc of reconstructing Bateman and Zidonis reach completion. George Hillocks's *Research on Written Composition: New Directions for Teaching* comes out. Hillocks does a meta-analysis that calibrated all of the appropriate studies on writing instruction and discovers, among other things, that teaching traditional grammar does not improve student writing, and, in fact, it seems to have a negative effect (Hillocks 1986, 205–6, 225–27). Hillocks reviews Bateman and Zidonis, noting, "Bateman and Zidonis found increases in structural complexity favoring the experimental group, but these were largely due to gains made by four students and were not statistically significant" (136). A few pages later, Bateman and Zidonis are identified with O'Hare and Mellon in the sentence-combining category. Thus, one way to deal with the positive findings of Bateman and Zidonis, making them heresy to later historical orthodoxy, is (1) to deny them as statistically significant but also (2) to affirm them as being precursors to sentence combing.

The consensus of what Bateman-Zidonis signifies has been collectively built, often in NCTE forums and venues. Bateman-Zidonis is rarely cited as evidence that teaching grammar improves student writing, but it is almost always cited as a precursor to sentence combining. In the rest of this essay, I revisit Bateman and Zidonis and their original sources, trying to discover what their questions and words, rather than ours, were.

TRAJECTORY 1959–1970—FRAGMENTS OF BATEMAN-ZIDONIS: IN PLACE OF A HISTORY

The advance which has started with the freshness of sunrise degenerates in a dull accumulation of minor feats of coordination.
    —Alfred Lord Whitehead (quoted in Bateman 1970)

In this section, I give an overview by laying out a wide range of texts, appearing over the years from 1959 to 1970, that track the trajectory of what might collectively be labeled the *Bateman-Zidonis Projects*, the plural indicating a number of related activities (published research and reports about the curriculum center) led by Bateman and Zidonis that are associated with teaching grammar and the improvement of student writing. I briefly describe each text, some published, some unpublished, some only existing now as a reference, and I point out in a sentence or two their relevance to the argument of this chapter. One reason for this section is to draw from the fragments a sketch of the arc or trajectory of the collective projects. Many of these documents are reports of the projects, either written for the federal government or presented to the English profession in *English Journal*. Other documents were written for internal use and were used to explore current issues. Finally, there are some papers presented at national conferences that now—with the exception of "The Politics of Curriculum," published in Pinar's (1974) book—can be found only as lines on a CV that Bateman submitted for an additional federal research grant he and Arewa and Zaharlick authored in 1981 titled *Ethnography of Writing in Nonschool Settings* (Bateman, Arewa, and Zaharlick 1981). (That grant application, by the way, was rejected.)

These texts do two things. First, they broaden the boundaries of what has been thought of as the Bateman-Zidonis projects. To my knowledge, none of these texts, not even the public and still-available articles in *English Journal*, has *ever* been referred to by any of the scholarship that describes or refers to the work of Bateman and Zidonis. Second, while many texts are not published, some of these unpublished reports and manuscripts play an important role in helping us to understand the projects and restore some material regarding the actual practices in the published research and at the Project English Curriculum Center at Ohio State, providing us today with a richer, more detailed sense of the arc of development in the work of the project. One complaint of some critics of the research is that little description of the actual conditions of teaching and curriculum at the University School at Ohio State, or even at the Project English Center, is provided. These documents begin that task of recovery.

What we perhaps have throughout these little-known texts are Ginzburg's "clues." What follows, then, is hypothetical in the sense of an hypothesis—I provide the dots I have discovered, which are totally new as far as I can tell, and I have connected the dots in a tentative way. At this point, these "penciled-in" connections are my best educated guesses based on the evidence and documentary record as to how things went. I can only go with what I have, present new documents, and show my work. The story is still clearly full of gaps. Nonetheless, there are patterns Ginzburg would call "clues" or "symptoms," all of which point to a new sense of what Bateman-Zidonis was all about.

I begin with *Speculations Concerning Symbolism, the Communication Core, and Language.* The Bateman-Zidonis projects might be said to have begun with this case study in 1959. Bateman wrote and published it only locally at Ohio State. We only know about it through several footnotes in the later public material. Mellon apparently had a copy and refers to it and uses it to critique the later work, saying, "The investigators should have confined their attention, as Bateman did in his earlier case study, to embedding transformations only, as well as to factors such as depth of embedding and number of modifications per noun" (Bateman 1959, 12). I have never seen a copy of this document.

But Bateman (1961) refers to *Speculations* (1959) himself in the next available document, his essay "More Mature Writing Through a Better Understanding of Language Structure," published in 1961 in *English Journal.* This article describes the pilot study Bateman conducted that seems to be reported in *Speculations* and which was close to what today we would call *teacher research.* He notes, "The development of a description of the structure of English through modern linguistic procedures would seem to make it possible for students to learn to manage the structures of their language with greater facility. At the same time it seems likely that as their familiarity with the structures of language grow they may be able to express more complex relationships of thought to their writing. These generalizations seem to be borne out in a study undertaken by the writer in working with a group of eighth grade students at the University School, Ohio State University" (457). In the final report of the Project Curriculum Center (*A Grammatico-Semantic Exploration of the Problems of Sentence Formation and Interpretation in the Classroom*), published in 1970, Bateman comments further on this pilot reported in *Speculations* and "More Mature Writing." He notes that "it seemed clear that students had a useful technique for analyzing and talking about style. It also seemed clear to me that students were learning to write sentences that were quite different from the sentences one customarily finds in the eighth grade" (Bateman and Zidonis 1970, 8). At the same time this pilot was being conducted and reported in 1959–1961, Frank Zidonis had in 1961 just completed his dissertation titled *The Role of Linguistics in the High-School Program* (Zidonis 1961). It must have been fairly soon after this that the two joined in collaboration and submitted to the federal government a proposal for funding to complete a research study. Given that the final report on the two-year experiment was sent to the federal government in 1964, it would seem that the actual data was collected in 1963 and 1964 (or perhaps 1962 and 1963).

What is key here is that there were already shifts in the project from the early teacher-research case study described in *Speculations* to this federally funded experiment (1964). In the later documents, Bateman and Zidonis incorporated the most recent linguistic theory, transformational generative grammar, into their experiment rather than the structural linguistics Bateman had used in 1959 and 1961. This first shift in theory foreshadowed a theme throughout all of these documents and across the entire trajectory of the projects—the theory would change as new discoveries became available and new problems emerged. A further shift in the later documents is that the participating students were a year or two older and were followed for a longer time (two years) and carefully tracked in terms of their writing (each sentence of each piece each student wrote, which was quite a lot in the aggregate, a total of seventy thousand words). Finally, the Ohio State Research Foundation was a partner in the projects from about 1962 on and, no doubt, called for the detailed data collection and state-of-the-art (for that time) statistical analysis largely missing from the earlier case study.

Toward the end of 1963, Bateman wrote *The Psychology of Composition: (I) Suitable Conditions for Composing*, which is a discussion of the need for a shift in perspective on composing from product to process and from reader to writer, surely one of the earliest statements of this problem using the very language that, with repetition over decades, became more of a slogan than a thoughtful claim (Bateman 1963). The focus of this document is not linguistics at all, but student writing. The terms *composition* and *composing* are used often. In fact, a sample of one piece of student writing resulting from a shift in perspective on composing is included, surely one of the earliest examples of real student writing in research and scholarship on composition. I elsewhere have argued that such early inclusion of whole student texts "shaped so-called process theory which shaped the subsequent discipline of composition" (Zebroski 2012, 43). This is certainly one of the earliest examples of that use of student-authored texts.

Although most historians of composition assume there is only one Bateman-Zidonis Report of the experiment of 1962–1964, there are, in fact, at least three versions. The first seems to be the 140-page report submitted to the federal government in 1964 titled *The Effect of a Knowledge of Generative Grammar on the Growth of Language Complexity* (Bateman and Zidonis 1964). The second was the 1966 NCTE version of forty pages, which is usually the only account—I call it the *canonical account*—that researchers refer to: *The Effect of a Study of Transformational Grammar on the Writing of Ninth and Tenth Graders* (Bateman and Zidonis 1966). The third, described below, was the final report on the Project English Curriculum Center in 1970 titled *A Grammatico-Semantic Exploration of the Problems of Sentence Formation and Interpretation in the Classroom* (Bateman and Zidonis 1970).

One key observation that results from a view of complex origins is that the projects are dynamic, constantly changing, being updated nearly every year and revised according to evolving changes in linguistic theory and the success or failure for students and teachers in the evolving curriculum. This fluidity questions the standard historical assumption that the projects were about students doing exercises in structural grammar.

From the perspective of 1970, the overall tendencies of Bateman and Zidonis's total work might be described as follows—and here is a lot of connecting of those dots. The first goal was to tie together an analysis of form (syntax) and content (semantics). Second, the projects moved toward tying the form and content in language to the contexts of everyday life. The projects, including the ongoing work of the Project English Center, often used material from students' lives outside of school—the television series *Mannix,* for example, or television advertisements for Head and Shoulders Shampoo or articles in sports magazines about figures like baseball player Harmon Killebrew (see Van Horn 1970, a teacher whose account is part of *A Grammatico-Semantic Exploration of the Problems of Sentence Formation and Interpretation in the Classroom*). Finally, such work always had as its ultimate aim the development of composing processes and improvement of student writing. This purpose has been occulted in later descriptions of Bateman-Zidonis. Of course, one of the key assumptions at work throughout these fourteen years was that doing a rigorous job of understanding sentence production would help researchers, teachers, and students to take the next step to understanding and producing discourse beyond the sentence. The idea was that once syntax was understood, linguistics would go beyond syntax to examine semantics, and then go beyond the syntax and semantics of sentence to text-length discourse. But always style, stylistics, and student composing processes were named as the ultimate point.

According to the NCTE website's "Directory of Rhetoric and Writing Centers 1962–1966," the Ohio State Project English Center came into being in 1965 (College Composition and Communication 2013). This was rather late. Nineteen other curriculum centers had preceded it, the first in Nebraska in 1962. The centers were allotted $250,000 each. As the Project English Center began to take shape and materials were created and circulated to teachers and further research was conducted, Frank Zidonis published two *English Journal* accounts of the Bateman-Zidonis projects, one "Generative Grammar: A Report on Research" in 1965, and the second "Incorporating Transformational Grammar into the English Curriculum" in 1967. These articles, of course, have been publicly available from the start and yet they have never been referred to, even though they provide a crucial description of what were and were not the goals and practices of the projects, a description that does not exist in the 1966 NCTE report (and that report received some criticism for not providing a description of specific goals and practices).

In 1965, Zidonis published an essay in *English Journal*, "Generative Grammar: A Report on Research," which is the best summary of the experiment conducted during the early 1960s. In four double-columned pages, Zidonis gives the details of the study—including a description of what student writing was collected, when, and how it fit into the regular curriculum (Zidonis 1965, 405). In an assumption that seemed obvious to him but which may be in question for us, Zidonis notes that "conscious control of well-formed sentences seems fundamental to the act of writing, and of course what students do not understand they can hardly control" (408). He further argues that previous research on "grammar" and writing are not persuasive since they are bad grammars, inconsistent and illogical: "Even the diligent study of an inconsistent body of materials is no better than the total abandonment of such study" (409). He concludes fairly carefully, arguing that the evidence from the experiment "*suggests*" (his word) that "generative theory currently offers a fruitful *first step* in the teaching of composition" (409; my emphasis).

In 1967, Zidonis published another essay in *English Journal*, "Incorporating Transformational Grammar into the English Curriculum." This article is crucial to seeing the importance inquiry plays in the projects. In arguing for incorporating the insights of linguistics into the curriculum, Zidonis begins by saying, "I think it is a fair judgment to make that the typical school lessons in language are not generally characterized by the spirit of inquiry. Grammatical units—when they are even attempted by the English teacher today—are invested with an aura of certitude that belies the rich complexity of the language they purport to describe" (Zidonis 1967, 1315). Zidonis goes on to argue that, if anything, linguistics in essence offers us a method for inquiry. He states, "The act of discovery, the sense of adventure, the satisfaction of original observation—all these are too often elements missing in our classrooms" (1315). Teachers and students must use the class to make "serious inquiry into the facts of the language we use and into attempts to explain those facts" (1315). Zidonis describes that process, gives an example, and frames it later by correlating it with the inquiry processes described by Jerome Bruner in *The Process of Education* (Bruner 1977, 1317). The essay ends in a rhetorically revealing way by simply describing four strategies schoolteachers use to resist the new English and inquiry, thus maintaining the status quo. These strategies are supported by the beliefs that (1) earlier writers did not study new grammar and wrote well; (2) the new grammar relies too heavily on a complex and new terminology; (3) the evidence for the new grammar is not yet in; and (4) language is beautiful—why pick it to pieces? Such resistance points to the difficulties of transitioning from the experiment and the University School faculty to the wider community of school teachers at which the Project English aims.

In the next two sections, I look more closely at two key documents, the canonical NCTE condensed report of 1966, *The Effect of a Study of Transformational Grammar on the Writing of Ninth and Tenth Graders*, and *A Grammatico-Semantic Exploration of the Problems of Sentence Formation and Interpretation in the Classroom: Vols. 1 and 2*, both authored by Bateman and Zidonis. The monumental final 1970 report of the Project English Center came out in two volumes totaling 681 pages and was their last collaboration.

THE CANON: BATEMAN-ZIDONIS 1966

When one reads *The Effect of a Study of Transformational Grammar on the Writing of Ninth and Tenth Graders*, the 1966 report published by NCTE which was to become the canonical or "official" account of the Bateman-Zidonis studies, several impressions arise. It is an extremely short report—forty regular pages. Those pages are crammed full of tables of numbers—sixteen tables are listed. It is in the standard scientific genre (statement of problem, related research, procedures or method, and presentation and analysis of data). Nearly eleven pages, more than a fourth of the report, are allotted to the presentation of data in tables.

In contrast, the interpretations concerning the data are quite short, often only two or three sentences for the various parts of the study. All of these impressions can be explained by the fact, rarely alluded to in the subsequent research literature, that this report is a condensation (Bateman and Zidonis 1966, vii, x) of the earlier and larger report filed with the US government in 1964. Further, it is critical to note that there are no teaching materials or even references to teaching practices in the report. The authors note this themselves, stating, "The substantive materials that made up the experimental treatment are not reprinted here" (x) but can be found by teachers in the 1964 report; they also end their forward by giving a beginning sense of what might in the future happen in the teaching of grammar by noting that "in the light of recent theoretical discussions in linguistics, the reader is reminded that grammatical materials developed for the experimental study in high schools today might assume a radically different form—even in the transformational-generative tradition" (x).

Beyond this, one is today also struck by the care and precision with which claims are made. Some definitions stipulated in the report are central to understanding the claims made for reading the data and trying to understand the effects of the projects. For example, when the term *grammar* is used, it does not refer to the traditional grammar critiqued early on, nor does it in any way refer to usage (linguistic etiquette), nor to transcription conventions (punctuation, spelling, capitalization). *Grammar*, in Bateman and Zidonis's NCTE report (hereafter BZ66), is a scientific theory of language (6), and that theory is about the structure of English, specifically syntax. Bateman and Zidonis note, "Every composition teacher deals directly with the structure of English. Whether he relegates the role of language to a mere communicative function where it becomes a vehicle or container into which the substance of content and ideas are poured or whether he believes that language can shape ideas as well as convey them, he must nevertheless have some means whereby he can talk about language with his students" (1). For BZ66, grammar is a way for teachers and students both to talk about the ordering of words in a sentence: "Good, acceptable, well-formed sentences are by definition grammatical sentences" (1). Such a grammar accounts for, but perhaps more important, explores "the process of sentence formation" (1). So grammar might be seen as the ordering of a sentence and as an account of that ordering, a crisp definition in agreement with Patrick Hartwell's argument and his description of the grammar in our heads (Grammar 1) and the theory or account of it (Grammar 2) (Hartwell 1985, 109–19). BZ66 provides some evidence against Hartwell's later claim that knowing the rules has nothing to do with producing the sentences. It, of course, comes down to how the words *know* or *consciously know* signify in the context of the classroom. Grammar for BZ66 is restricted, for the moment, always to the sentence. The hope at that time was that someday the principles established at the sentence level might be extended to larger discourse forms.

Further, BZ66 makes clear that in studying grammar, "it is not our aim to make generative grammarians of the students, which would entail them writing generative grammars, but rather to help them become stylists who have expanded their capability of generating varied and well-formed sentences of the language" (ix). So too *error* is precisely used to mean what might be described as syntactic error, sentences that do not derive from the transformational rules (forty-six of them at the time of the study, which accounted for nearly all the possible sentences that can be formed in English, a nearly infinite number) and that are not acceptable to the intuition of the native speaker (in this case, the analysts), both criteria used in linguistics (21). In fact, BZ66 identifies five classes of error, including nonsentences that

1. misapply the transformation rules;
2. use one transformation when another should have been used;
3. use one transformation when none should have been used;
4. omit a required transformation;
5. use mutually exclusive grammatical elements.

Examples from student writing are provided. BZ66 tracks every sentence every student wrote in the sample and describes it as either a sentence or an error in sentence formation given the above definition and criteria. (In the 1970 follow-up report on further research and curricular applications of the Project English Center, this taxonomy of student sentences and nonsentences is reconceptualized and expanded by William Craig [1970].) Further, each student's IQ score is looked at to see if that has any tie to the improvement in writing or to learning the grammar. It doesn't.

These first impressions helpfully frame a description of the experiment. Two classes of ninth graders in the University School at Ohio State, acknowledged as clearly not typical of schools and classes (Bateman and Zidonis 1966, 37), were tracked through the ninth grade and into the tenth grade. This two-year project had the same students with the same teachers through that period. The control class does the regular curriculum, which apparently means no grammar instruction at all (18). The experimental class does the usual curriculum too but also studies transformational generative grammar. Six pieces of writing were collected from each student in the first three months, and six pieces of writing in the last three months of the study. Each piece of the writing done as part of the sample ran from about 1,300 to 1,700 words in length. Both the number of times students wrote and the amount they wrote each time seems quite high compared to what was happening in other high schools at the time. Teachers coordinated assignments in writing, and these samples were part of a flow of assignments and activities that went on regularly before and after collection.

In brief, here is my informal summary of the study's conclusions derived from the analysis of data.

- Students could relatively easily learn transformational generative grammar.
- The structure of the student writing after the students were taught grammar seemed more varied and more complex as defined by embeddings (T-units) than before. Implicitly, the repertoire of grammatical structures seemed to increase in student writing.
- The number of errors as defined above decreased.
- The proportion of well-formed sentences increased to a statistically significant degree.

While careful about its claims, BZ66 notes that "even so, the persistently higher gain scores for the experimental class . . . *strengthens the contention* that the study of a systematic grammar which is a *theoretical* model of the process of sentence production is the logical way to modify the process itself" (37; my emphasis). The notion that studying and becoming more aware of the processes of composing would help writers demystify the processes and help writers to better manage their writing processes is, of course, the motivation behind the writing-process studies of the 1970s and 1980s. It is also one of the earliest claims that composition does have a subject matter.

There are many other potential sidebars, of course. But the fact that all the data show positive results, and that the increase in the quality of student writing as defined by sentence well-formed-ness over two years was significant statistically, remains to this day a hallmark of the study. Such clear and parallel results are rare.

However, the methodology and assumptions of BZ66 were almost immediately called into question. To an outsider to quantitative research, it seems as if in trying to nail down cause and effect, the study tried to do too many things, no doubt in order to both capture the complexity of language instruction and student writing and build multiple sources of evidence for its claim that the study of transformational generative grammar—that is, the study of the structure of the English language—increased the "quality" of student writing (the well-formed-ness of student sentences). Still, despite the critiques, the study was widely distributed and taken up in a variety of ways by other researchers. Considering how badly done (as quantitative research) so much program assessment currently is, and how pervasive such pseudoquantitative research like high-stakes testing is, the BZ66 study is careful, precise, and reasonable. But it is also more interested in robust classroom results than in the purity of method that it is easy to critique.

Even Mellon, who rigorously critiques nearly every aspect of BZ66, acknowledges it is the only experiment at that time to study these aspects of grammar instruction and get results: "Thus it would seem that the transformational grammar unequivocally accomplished what was hypothesized for it, namely, it accelerated the growth of sentence complexity" (Mellon 1969, 11). As Frank O'Hare generously notes in his 1973 monograph, "Although it is at least questionable whether it was a knowledge of generative grammar that led Bateman and Zidonis's students to write more mature sentences, it is not unreasonable to assume that *something* in their experimental treatment must have caused those students to write more maturely" (18; my emphasis). So if it was not the transformational generative grammar, what was it?

HERESY: BATEMAN-ZIDONIS 1970 AND INQUIRY

Frank O'Hare's insight that "something" must have caused those students to write better leads us to the second Bateman-Zidonis report, specifically the introduction authored by Bateman. For decades it wasn't clear that there were many, if any, public copies of the final report submitted in May of 1970 to the US government from the Project English Center (at, it must be noted, the very time the Ohio State campus was closed because of riots against the Cambodian incursion). Formally titled *A Grammatico-Semantic Exploration of the Problems of Sentence Formation and Interpretation in the Classroom* (Project No 2123), the second Bateman-Zidonis study (hereafter BZ70) is not to my knowledge referred to in any of the citations or discussions of research. In the research literature, the references to and short descriptions of the Bateman-Zidonis study have always meant one thing—a description and response to the first BZ66 as the canonical text of the discipline. However we understand that document, researchers and scholars have assumed that they had in BZ66 not simply a rendering of the work of the studies and projects conducted at Ohio State but the official, canonical representation. And the references and descriptions that have reached print in the more than fifty years since BZ66 appeared nearly always to focus on what is seen as that report's primary finding—that teaching transformational grammar improved student writing.

But even in that very short 1966 abbreviation of the work that had been going on at Ohio State (and that was, apparently, a bit more fully represented in the 1964 government report), there were clear indications that BZ66 was *not* simply about having students do transformation grammar exercises and then checking their writing for "improvement." Investigation of the existing public work of Bateman and Zidonis—the *English Journal* pieces, the descriptions and critiques of the Project English Centers published in a variety of disciplinary organs including *English Journal* and *PMLA*—would, at the least, begin to raise questions about the accuracy of this view. These representations were clearly overdetermined by what scholars thought the work was about—or should have been about—rather than by a close reading of what the existing documents say. They were also overdetermined by how research came to be envisioned, how the research apparatus appropriated and still appropriates work, and how research was circulated and rewarded by professional organizations like NCTE and CCCC and by universities.

In any case, the publication of the BZ70 report on ERIC provides the key evidence for rethinking the projects and the findings. A close reading of *A Grammatico-Semantic Exploration of the Problems of Sentence Formation and Interpretation in the Classroom*, especially its introduction (1–48), which was authored by Bateman, is key to contextualizing BZ66 but also the entire trajectory of work from 1959 to 1970. As far as I know, there had always been an ERIC reference and abstract for BZ70. This seems to have been transferred from the earlier systems—mostly microfiche media—to an online version at the ERIC site sometime after the spring of 2013 when I taught a graduate seminar that made use of these documents. At the time of this writing, both volume 1 and volume 2 of that report, including Bateman's introduction, are available, though some pages seem to be missing at the end of volume 2.

Bateman's introduction to BZ70 is his most detailed and, for all practical purposes, final response to the history of these projects. The report includes a deep critique of the project, and that rhetorical gesture allows Bateman also to very briefly and critically respond to some of the criticisms made in John Mellon's work, which was by 1970 available and is cited. For example, earlier discussions of the projects by Bateman and Zidonis were faulted for their methodological unsoundness. However,

BZ70 reframes the goals of the project; it is less experimental and more descriptive (2, 9). Earlier discussions of the Bateman-Zidonis projects did not have examples of what students and teachers did. However, BZ70 includes illustrations, essays composed during the project from its structural linguistics days to the end of the project, and several chapters by teachers themselves, perhaps some of the first teacher research in English (see Barbara Van Horn 1970). Earlier discussions of the projects focused on student improvement defined as increasing variety and complexity of syntactic structures in student writing. However, BZ70 delineates how the theory of these structures evolved over this period both among teachers and students and changed at least six times during this period. Earlier discussions focused on grammar and student writing improvement. However, in the introduction of BZ70, Bateman often makes the point that the study was an attempt to get at *inquiry into language* as a means of improving student writing (7, 8, 9, 11, 12, 36).

BZ70 begins with a strong critique of curriculum and curriculum developers as embodied in Project English Centers but also in the early work of Bateman and Zidonis, aiming to make a sharp distinction between "frozen packages" of exercises—textbooks and a textbook approach to language—and true inquiry that is dynamic, student and teacher centered, open, and part of the stream of life (Bateman and Zidonis 1970, 13). As in Zidonis's 1967 article, Bateman's introduction to the final report on the Project English Curriculum Center at Ohio State stresses the centrality of *inquiry* to their early findings and the later applications and extensions of the work. In Bateman's introduction, there is an explicit critique of linguistics, which is extended in chapters by doctoral students like Thomas Schroyer (1970). As Bateman notes, "One can become so immersed in the study of the model that he forgets that a model must be a model of something and that the whole idea is to understand more fully how 'something' works" (Bateman 1970, 19). The discipline of linguistics is increasingly being formalized and removed from curricular application; it increasingly conceives of grammars as machines and students and teachers as machine operators, which defeats the whole goal of inquiry (1970, 29).

In a short essay contained within the larger introduction, Bateman responds to some critics who charged that BZ66 should have included more about the actual pedagogical materials and approaches. This essay is an account of the six stages of inquiry the project went through from 1959 to 1970 (3–43). The stages are (1) structural linguistics (embeddings of clauses), (2) the First Transformational Period (rules that generate sentences from kernels), (3) the Second Transformation Period (new notations and viewing elements as interactions in grammatical forces), (4) the third Transformation Period (a move to see grammars as machines that produce sentences), (5) a period of Generative Semantics (Fillmore's case grammar), and, finally, (6) an attempt to tie analysis of sentence form to sentence content via Grammatico-Semantic Structure. So the curriculum changes as the discipline changes. There are also illustrations of class activities like the coloring of passages in a seventh-grade class after a study of embeddings in the prose of professional writers (8). It is noted that there was a daily examination of prose in the class (7) and that the grammar study was also accompanied by regular writing assignments (9). Then an extensive report of one schoolteacher (Barbara Van Horn) and how her class took up theory is presented. Finally, there is a good deal of humor and irony (9, 39–40) in the document and a serious attempt to think about what it would mean to illustrate in this report the fourteen-year-old process in a way in which the content of the process fits the form of this essay (2–3), what one might see as an incipient genre of teacher research or action research.

I will briefly focus now on the theme of authentic inquiry, which is repeated throughout the report. Even from the title, one already gets a hint of the pervasiveness of true inquiry with the stress on exploration, problems, and interpretation. In his introduction to BZ70, Bateman notes that "language curriculum development is the continuing exploration of the heuristic possibilities of evolving linguistic structures. A meaningful report of these varied activities and changing perspectives must illustratively describe the exploratory process *one must engage in with children* if he is to be a curriculum developer rather than a producer and distributor of frozen packages" (2; my emphasis). A curriculum guided by inquiry is the opposite of one driven by textbooks and frozen packages of materials (let alone testing). Bateman argues that curriculum must be "invented out of the stream of new knowledge by *particular teachers and classes.* . . . Inquiry is invention, not reconstruction; its rewards are mainly uncertain conclusions and the need to continue, rarely the clever discovery of the hidden fact" (2; my emphasis). What follow are just a few examples of Bateman in this short introduction driving home the point that inquiry is not about frozen packages but about collective, dynamic study. I have italicized this point in each passage.

In a comment about the pilot study that can be applied to the entire set of curricular innovations that characterize the Bateman-Zidonis projects, Bateman says, "The important thing about this . . . investigation of style was . . . that its content was *invented by a teacher and a class*" (9). He notes that this is a "process of never-ending visions and revisions, of successes and failures, of trials and errors, that characterize the investigative enterprise" (12). He repeats, "This process of formulation, investigation, evaluation, and reformulation may be called *inquiry as long as a teacher and his students can continue meaningful revisions*" (17). And, "When models yield innovative pedagogical adaptations, though such innovative activity might cause a linguist to shudder, *teachers and students, once again, are engaging in inquiry*, and new insights into language structure are acquired" (26). Further, "Language study can become exciting when syntactic irregularity is investigated. When *teacher, and the student, who should both be investigators, try to explain how sentences mean*" (34). In speaking of the teachers' and students' analysis of their own writing, this final sentence concludes the introduction: "Hopefully, this set will be expanded and amended by *teachers and students exploring together the sentences they write*" (43). The "something" O'Hare (1973) noted has improved student writing is not exercises or textbooks, but *inquiry*. Both students and teachers are students of language.

BATEMAN-ZIDONIS—FIFTY YEARS LATER

Reviewing the materials available, we can return to some basic questions.

What did *grammar* signify in these documents? It meant sentence-level syntactic theory, but it was obvious in BZ70 that such theory would and did change from structural to transformational to semantic theory. It seems important that the BZ70 project report ends with studies on literature, aesthetics, and pop culture, which also implies that theories were chosen because they were new and interesting. But what if other theories of language emerged and were more interesting? It would seem logical to take up those more appropriate forms of theory and not do linguistics. Grammar was a *theory* of language, one that was revised along the way by the students and teachers. The goal was never to turn students into grammarians or linguists—or to teach grammar for its own sake—but to help students and teachers become more aware *writers* and more active *stylists* who bring new strategies to their writing to manage their own processes of sentence formation more successfully.

What did *error* signify in these documents? Error was never about usage or literacy conventions but rather about sentences that went wrong. The finding that half of the sentences of the ninth and tenth graders did go wrong is a critical finding never taken up by researchers. This does not mean we have to police such errors, but quite the opposite—young writers must write through such moments in their development. It suggests that the study of language and composition are needed and are ongoing well into maturity (even into college), a finding that compares well with what Lev Vygotsky (1986, 180–84) discovered. Writing ability comes late, has its own slow development, and continues to develop across the lifespan, and that development can be aided, according to Bateman and Zidonis, by continued study and frequent reflection.

What did it signify to say that *students were taught and learned grammar?* It meant that students and teachers studied language, explored it together, and looked at it as something complex and open to inspection. Students and teachers collaborated in theorizing language. Transformational grammar was simply one tool to do this, one that changed several times from 1959 to 1970 for Bateman and Zidonis.

What did it signify to say that *inquiry* was the means by which this study took place? Perhaps the most important claim I am making is that the Bateman-Zidonis Projects were centered on inquiry into language rather than workbook or textbook exercises in grammar, as the histories suggest about them. A careful reading of BZ70 indicates that inquiry meant (1) teachers and students worked as a team exploring language together rather than filling in workbooks, doing exercises, or taking tests; (2) they were using the advances and current explorations of a discipline to frame this work; (3) they related this collaborative disciplinary work to writing; (4) they related writing to everyday life; (5) they frequently reflected and theorized (both in discussions and in written pieces) on how this process was going and what needed to be done next.

The Bateman-Zidonis studies show that when teachers and students systematically investigate and theorize language, in an authentic way (which means there is no preformed answer), drawing on work in the disciplines but also work that is local and lively, and then connect it to writing, there is a marked improvement in the quality of writing. We can also see that the discipline took little notice of this finding and increasingly appropriated this work for its own narrow purposes, whether to make arguments about sentence combining or about grammar. Finally, we are able to draw contrary conclusions because of the witness of existing documentary evidence, including the federal government's ERIC online archival project.

Appendix 6.1

A CHRONOLOGY OF DOCUMENTS RELATED TO
THE BATEMAN-ZIDONIS REPORTS, 1959–1973

1959   Bateman, Donald R. *Speculations Concerning Symbolism, the Communication Core, and Language.* Columbus: Center for School Experimentation. Ms. 39 pg. mimeo.

1961   Zidonis, Frank J. "The Role of Linguistics in the High-School Program." Diss., Ohio State University.

1961   Bateman, Donald R. "More Mature Writing Through a Better Understanding of Language Structure." *English Journal* 50 (7): 457–60, 468.

1963   Bateman, Donald R. "The Psychology of Composition: (I) Suitable Conditions for Composing." Columbus: Center for School Experimentation. Ms. 15 pg. mimeo.*

1964   Bateman, Donald R., and Frank J. Zidonis. "The Effect of a Knowledge of Generative Grammar on the Growth of Language Complexity." Final Report to US Office of Education. Cooperative Research Project 1746. 120 pp. ERIC. http://eric.ed.gov/?q=bateman+and+zidonis&id=ED001241.#

1964   Bateman, Donald R., and Frank J. Zidonis. *How Grammatical Sentences Are Formed: A Manual for Studying a Generative Grammar of English.* Columbus: Ohio State University Research Foundation. Ms. 141 pg. mimeo.#

1964   Zidonis, Frank. J. "Generative Grammar: A Report on Research." *English Journal* 54 (5): 405–9.

1966   Bateman, Donald R., and Frank J. Zidonis. *The Effect of a Study of Transformational Grammar on the Writing of Ninth and Tenth Graders.* No. 6 Research Reports. Urbana, IL: NCTE.

1967   Zidonis, Frank J. "Incorporating Transformational Grammar into the English Curriculum." *English Journal* 50 (9): 1315–1320.

1970   Bateman, Donald R., and Frank J. Zidonis. "A Grammatico-Semantic Exploration of the Problems of Sentence Formation and Interpretation in the Classroom: Vol. I and II." Final Report 2133. US Department of Health, Education, and Welfare. ERIC. http://eric.ed.gov/?q=bateman+and+zidonis&id=ED048244.

1970   Bateman, Donald R. "Generative Semantics for the Classroom." Unpublished ms.#

1973   Bateman, Donald R. "The Politics of Curriculum." Paper presented at Rochester Curriculum Conference, Rochester, NY, May 3–5. Published in 1974 in *Heightened Consciousness, Cultural Revolution, and Curriculum Theory*, edited by William Pinar, 54–68. Berkeley: McCutcheon.

1975   Bateman, Donald R. "Since Feeling is First, Who Cares about the Syntax of Things . . ." Paper Presented at National Middle School Conference, Columbus, OH, March.#

1980   Bateman, Donald R. "Dialectical Reflections on the Process of Writing." Unpublished ms. 11 pp.*

1980   Bateman, Donald R. "Characteristics of the Dialectic: Part I." Unpublished ms. 4 pp.*

1981   Bateman, Donald R., E. Ojo Arewa, and Amy Zaharlick. "Ethnography of Writing in Nonschool Settings." Technical Proposal in Response to NIE-R-81-0004. US National Institute of Education. Unpublished ms. 90+ pp.*

Note

1.   This 1973 conference presentation was published the following year in William Pinar's (1974) edited collection, *Heightened Consciousness, Cultural Revolution, and Curriculum Theory*. Quotes of this presentation come from the text printed in Pinar and so are listed as 1974.

References

Bateman, Donald R. 1959. *Speculations Concerning Symbolism, the Communication Core, and Language*. Columbus: Center for School Experimentation.

Bateman, Donald R. 1961. "More Mature Writing through a Better Understanding of Language Structure." *English Journal* 50 (7): 457–60, 468. http://dx.doi.org/10.2307/811199.

Bateman, Donald R. 1963. "The Psychology of Composition: (I) Suitable Conditions for Composing." Columbus: Center for School Experimentation. Manuscript mimeograph.

Bateman, Donald R. 1970. "Generative Semantics for the Classroom." Unpublished manuscript.

Bateman, Donald R. 1974. "The Politics of Curriculum." In *Heightened Consciousness, Cultural Revolution, and Curriculum Theory*, edited by William Pinar, 54–68. Berkeley: McCutcheon.

Bateman, Donald R., E. Ojo Arewa, and Amy Zaharlick. 1981. *Ethnography of Writing in Nonschool Settings*. Technical Proposal in Response to NIE-R–81–0004. US National Institute of Education. Unpublished manuscript.

Bateman, Donald R., and Frank J. Zidonis. 1964. "The Effect of a Knowledge of Generative Grammar on the Growth of Language Complexity." ERIC Document No. ED002141. http://eric.ed.gov/?q=bateman+and+zidonis&id=ED001241.

Bateman, Donald R., and Frank J. Zidonis. 1966. *The Effect of a Study of Transformational Grammar on the Writing of Ninth and Tenth Graders*. Urbana, IL: NCTE.

Bateman, Donald R., and Frank J. Zidonis. 1970. *A Grammatico-Semantic Exploration of the Problems of Sentence Formation and Interpretation in the Classroom, Volume 2. Final Report* ERIC Document No. 048244. http://eric.ed.gov/?q=bateman+and+zidonis&id=ED048244.

Bauer, Walter. 1996. *Orthodoxy and Heresy in Earliest Christianity*. Mifflintown, PA: Sigler.

Berthoff, Ann E. 1978. "Tolstoy, Vygotsky, and the Making of Meaning." *College Composition and Communication* 29 (3): 249–55. http://dx.doi.org/10.2307/356939.

Bruner, Jerome. (1960) 1977. *The Process of Education*. Cambridge, MA: Harvard University Press.

Conference on College Composition and Communication. 2013. "A Directory of Rhetoric and Writing Research Centers, 1962–1966." NCTE. www.ncte.org/cccc /research/appendix1960.

Craig, William. 1970. "Investigation of Syntactic-Semantic Relationships in the Selected Writing of Students in Grades 4–12." In *A Grammatico-Semantic Exploration of the Problems of Sentence Formation and Interpretation in the Classroom, Volume 2. Final Report,* edited by Donald Bateman and Frank Zidonis, 67–293. ERIC Document No. 048244. http://eric.ed.gov/?q=bateman+and+zidonis&id=ED048244.

Crossan, John Dominic. 1991. *The Historical Jesus: The Life of a Mediterranean Peasant.* San Francisco, CA: Harpers.

Crossan, John Dominic. 1998. *The Birth of Christianity.* San Francisco, CA: Harpers.

Freire, Paulo. 1970. *Pedagogy of the Oppressed.* New York: Herder and Herder.

Ginzburg, Carlo. 1989. *Clues, Myths, and the Historical Method.* Baltimore, MD: Johns Hopkins University Press.

Ginzburg, Carlo. 2012. "Our Words, and Theirs: A Reflection on the Historian's Craft, Today." In *Historical Knowledge: In Quest of Theory, Method, and Evidence,* edited by Susanna Fellman and Marjatta Rahikainen, 97–120. Newcastle upon Tyne: Cambridge Scholars.

Hartwell, Patrick. 1985. "Grammar, Grammars, and the Teaching of Grammar." *College English* 47 (2): 105–27. http://dx.doi.org/10.2307/376562.

Hillocks, George. 1986. *Research on Written Composition: New Directions for Teaching.* Urbana, IL: ERIC Clearinghouse on Reading and Communication Skills.

Mathews, Thomas. 1995. *The Clash of Gods.* Princeton, NJ: Princeton University Press.

Mellon, John. 1969. *Transformational Sentence Combining: A Method for Enhancing the Development of Syntactic Fluency in English Composition.* Urbana, IL: NCTE.

Moffett, James. 1973. *A Student-Centered Language Arts Curriculum, Grades K–13: A Handbook for Teachers.* Boston: Houghton Mifflin.

O'Hare, Frank. 1973. *Sentence Combining: Improving Student Writing Without Formal Grammar Instruction.* Urbana, IL: NCTE.

Pinar, William, ed. 1974. *Heightened Consciousness, Cultural Revolution, and Curriculum Theory.* Berkeley, CA: McCutcheon.

Robinson, James M., and Helmut Koester. 1971. *Trajectories through Early Christianity.* Eugene, OR: Wipf and Stock.

Rubenstein, Richard. 1999. *When Jesus Became God.* New York: Harcourt Brace.

Schroyer, Thomas. 1970. "An Investigation of the Semantics of English Sentences as a Proposed Basis for Language Curriculum Material." In *A Grammatico-Semantic Exploration of the Problems of Sentence Formation and Interpretation in the Classroom, Volume 2. Final Report,* edited by Donald Bateman and Frank Zidonis, 49–298. ERIC Document No. 048244. http://eric.ed.gov/?q=bateman+and+zidonis&id=ED048244.

Stock, Patricia. 2012. *Composition's Roots in English Education.* Portsmouth, NH: Heinemann.

Van Horn, Barbara. 1970. "An Anecdotal Account of a Classroom Investigation of the Semantics of English Sentences." In *A Grammatico-Semantic Exploration of the Problems of Sentence Formation and Interpretation in the Classroom, Volume 2. Final Report,* edited by Donald Bateman and Frank Zidonis, 299–380. ERIC Document No. 048244. http:// eric.ed.gov/?q=bateman+and+zidonis&id=ED048244.

Vygotsky, Lev. (1962) 1986. *Thought and Language.* Cambridge, MA: MIT Press.

Young, Richard, Alton Becker, and Kenneth Pike. 1970. *Rhetoric: Discovery and Change.* New York: Harcourt Brace Jovanovich.

Zebroski, James T. 2012. "Hidden from History: English Education and the Multiple Origins of Contemporary Composition Studies, 1960–2000." In *Composition's Roots in English Education,* edited by. Patricia Lambert Stock, 26–50. Portsmouth, NH: Heinemann.

Zidonis, Frank J. 1961. *The Role of Linguistics in the High-School Program.* PhD diss., Ohio State University.

Zidonis, Frank J. 1965. "Generative Grammar: A Report on Research." *English Journal* 54 (5): 405–9. http://dx.doi.org/10.2307/811232.

Zidonis, Frank J. 1967. "Incorporating Transformational Grammar into the English Curriculum." *English Journal* 56 (9): 1315–20. http://dx.doi.org/10.2307/812429.

7
WHO WAS WARREN TAYLOR?
A Microhistorical Footnote to
James A. Berlin's Rhetoric and Reality

David Stock

In the opening chapter of *Rhetoric and Reality: Writing Instruction in American Colleges, 1900–1985,* James Berlin describes the purpose of his sweeping history as "vindicat[ing] the position of writing instruction in the college curriculum—particularly the freshman course" (Berlin 1987, 1). *Rhetoric and Reality* was one of several notable histories from the 1980s and 1990s seeking to legitimize composition instruction as a scholarly practice by documenting and narrating its origin stories and deriving from them a meaningful identity (Brereton 1995, xi). While exclusive treatment of the college composition course in these histories strikes many as reductive and myopic, it is worth remembering that such emphasis was instrumental in legitimizing the emerging discipline of composition studies and in making possible subsequent criticism of the centrality of first-year writing to that discipline. It is also worth remembering that longstanding conflicts between composition and English departments became especially pronounced while Berlin was writing his history, as illustrated in Maxine Hairston's 1985 call at the Conference on College Composition and Communication for composition to break its bonds with literature. This antagonism is apparent in Berlin's praise for transactional rhetorics and blame for subjective rhetorics and in his alignment of each with composition and English, respectively. Indeed, Berlin's history constitutes a kind of metonymic, Marxist allegory in which the composition proletariat, under the banner of social-epistemic rhetoric, is cast as the revolutionary vanguard poised to liberate students and faculty by exposing the false consciousness of current-traditional rhetoric on its way to overthrowing the hegemony of literature as manifest in the belletristic rhetoric of liberal culture.

DOI: 10.7330/9781607324058.c007

Berlin's seminal history was informed by cultural, political, theoretical, institutional, and disciplinary developments of the 1980s; in short, it was a product of his time. This point merits emphasis because the historical exigencies and influences on Berlin's work are often overlooked, and his history and taxonomies are often treated as historical facts rather than as social constructions. Although only one of several histories of composition to emerge during the period, Berlin's work has had an enduring and disproportionate influence on the field's perception of its history and pedagogies. Multiple generations of scholars and practitioners have been introduced and initiated into the field of composition studies through Berlin's work and continue to struggle with the normative legacy of his reified taxonomies. It is difficult to imagine designing an introductory course or seminar on the history of composition without assigning Berlin's work in part or in whole. David Gold's observation, paraphrasing Alfred North Whitehead's claim about philosophy since Plato, is illustrative: "Rhetoric and composition historiography might be considered a series of footnotes to Berlin" (Gold 2012, 19–20). Recognizing the historical context informing Berlin's work is necessary for scholars and practitioners to contest its "normative effect" on composition history and pedagogy and thereby "write [Berlin] into the historical narrative he helped create" (Gold 2012, 20). Fortunately, as Gold and Bruce McComiskey (this volume) illustrate, a growing number of historians in composition and rhetoric have produced increasingly complex, varied, and localized accounts of rhetoric and writing instruction that challenge and ultimately enrich Berlin's and other early histories of composition. The emphasis of such work signals a new norm, moving beyond mere recovery of marginalized figures or simple contestation of dominant narratives toward advancing larger scholarly conversations that transcend local or particular accounts. As Gold illustrates, microhistory—methodologically, epistemologically, and ideologically—has been particularly useful in advancing historiography in rhetoric and composition (Gold 2012, 25–26).

In this chapter, I draw on the methods of microhistory to recuperate an individual who makes a brief but notable appearance in Berlin's *Rhetoric and Reality*: Warren Taylor (1903–1991), a professor of English who taught composition, literature, and humanities courses at Oberlin College for nearly forty years. Berlin praises Warren Taylor's article "Rhetoric in a Democracy," published in the 1938 college edition of *English Journal*, as "perhaps the most eloquent plea for a freshman course based on a rhetoric of public discourse" to have emerged in the 1930s (Berlin 1987, 86). Berlin spends two pages summarizing, contextualizing, and moderately critiquing but clearly endorsing Taylor's view of composition's central role in the college curriculum (88). However, Berlin mistakenly attributes the article to Warner Taylor, a professor of English and director of the freshman English program at the University of Wisconsin-Madison during the 1920s and 1930s. Warner Taylor's nationwide survey of freshman English, published in 1929, is cited in most early histories of composition, including Berlin's (Taylor 1929). This misattribution leads Berlin to make inaccurate inferences about institutional influences on Warren Taylor's argument; it has also prevented scholars from identifying and studying Warren Taylor's prolific work: poems published in southern avant-garde periodicals; a dissertation on Tudor figures of rhetoric; essays, articles, and talks on topics ranging from composition and Shakespeare to propaganda, humanities, and higher education; textbooks for teaching composition and poetry; innovative teaching in composition and literature courses; the development of an interdisciplinary humanities program at Oberlin College; and professional service to the National Council of Teachers of English and the American Association of University Professors. The volume of publications and archived materials, along with Berlin's misattribution, raises several questions: Who was Warren Taylor? What were his contributions to rhetoric and composition and higher education in the twentieth century? How does Berlin's interpretation of a single article compare with a broader examination of Taylor's work? What does Taylor's overlooked work and life contribute to rhetoric and composition today?

A microhistorical approach is particularly fitting in addressing these questions. Microhistories promote engagement with "small units of analysis" to gain "insight into a lost world which would otherwise have remained closed" (Magnússon and Szijártó 2013, 158). In microhistorical terms, I aim to recuperate, analyze, and situate Warren Taylor "in the context of [his] particularity" (Levi 2012, 125) and trace the impact of his life experiences on his world-view and professional work. This approach reinforces the limitations of "broad-brush approach[es]" to social history, which provide general accounts that often minimize or efface actual people's lives and experiences (Magnússon and Szijártó 2013, 124). Identifying and humanizing Warren Taylor reinforces the related microhistorical practices of according historical agency to individuals, avoiding labels based on preconceived norms, and rendering, in Jorma Kalela's words, "a plausible and fair description" of individual historical actors (quoted in Magnússon and Szijártó 2013, 153). Microhistory helps avoid the "simplifications, dualistic hypotheses, polarizations, rigid typologies and the search for typical characteristics"

(Levi 2001, 110) evident in Berlin's narrative. In contrast to Berlin's superficial, single-source approach, my analysis draws on an extensive review of Taylor's published scholarship and a variety of archived materials, including syllabi, course materials, and annual reports written by Taylor to the president of Oberlin—all of which provide a more detailed account of Taylor's conception of the democratic potential of higher education. My extensive examination confirms Berlin's claim that Taylor viewed composition as central to preparing students for democratic society, but it also complicates that claim by demonstrating that Taylor eventually came to view interdisciplinary humanistic education, not composition instruction, as serving a vital democratic function. This shift reflects Taylor's professional development: whereas his early teaching was primarily in composition, his subsequent academic training and teaching were exclusively in literature and the humanities. While Taylor remained committed to the belief that a college education must train students for life in a democratic society, his understanding of the pedagogical mechanism for such training shifted as his own teaching, training, and identity shifted throughout his career.

Cautioning against increased fragmentation in rhetoric and composition historiography, Gold invites scholars to frame their research as "additive, rather than oppositional" and to adopt an attitude of "scholarly synthesis, rather than antithesis" (Gold 2012, 24). Consequently, I aim to expand rather than contradict Berlin's treatment of Warren Taylor's early work. After documenting Berlin's misattribution of Warren Taylor's "Rhetoric in a Democracy" to Warner Taylor and briefly qualifying Berlin's interpretation of Warren Taylor's article, I document Taylor's experience teaching composition at Oberlin College, summarizing annual reports in which Taylor outlines his beliefs about and approaches to the course. These materials affirm Berlin's interpretation of Taylor's belief in the democratic potential of composition instruction, but they also reveal how the same democratic orientation informs Taylor's arguments for the importance of liberal education and interdisciplinary humanities as mechanisms for preparing students for democratic life. I then review two interdisciplinary humanities courses Taylor developed and coordinated later in his career: The Humanistic Tradition (at Oberlin College) and The Twentieth Century (at Hiram College). These courses highlight how, despite his continued emphasis on preparation for democratic society, Taylor grounded such preparation primarily in exposure to the humanistic arts as opposed to explicit composition instruction he had advocated earlier in his career. Rather than label this shift as good or bad, I draw from it implications for the disciplinary development of composition and rhetoric.

As Bruce McComiskey notes (this volume), methodological self-consciousness is a common feature of microhistorical research because it helps to minimize the distance between readers and researchers that results from a traditionally impersonal, objective stance. Thus, in this spirit of methodological self-consciousness, I will briefly explain my interest in Warren Taylor and my discovery of Berlin's misattribution. I first read *Rhetoric and Reality* while working on an MA thesis that explored the relationship between rhetoric and general education. Warren Taylor's argument in "Rhetoric in a Democracy," as summarized by Berlin, resonated with my own interest in the democratic potential of rhetorical education, and Taylor's assumptions, filtered through Berlin, found a prominent place in my thesis. Several years later, while conducting dissertation research on the history of rhetoric and writing instruction at the University of Wisconsin-Madison, I recalled Berlin's argument that Wisconsin's progressive history influenced Warren Taylor's work, so I requested Taylor's faculty file from the University of Wisconsin-Madison archives. The university archivist indicated that no file for Warren Taylor existed but provided instead a record for Warner Taylor, who taught at the university from 1911 to 1941 and who directed the freshman English program. Confused, I revisited Berlin's discussion of Taylor in *Rhetoric and Reality* and found both Warren Taylor's article and Warner Taylor's survey in the list of references. A Google search revealed Warren Taylor's affiliation with Oberlin College, not the University of Wisconsin-Madison, so I began corresponding with Oberlin's archivists to identify background and bibliographic information. An extensive but partial publication list included book titles such as *Tudor Figures of Rhetoric* and *Models for Thinking and Writing* as well as articles such as "What is Propaganda?" "The Moral Obligations of American Colleges" and "Educational Myopia: Eight Causes and Treatments" published in such journals as *College English, School and Society*, and the *Journal of Higher Education*. The focus of my dissertation required that I postpone additional research on Warren Taylor, although I included a footnote in the introduction of my dissertation about Berlin's misattribution as indicative of potential limitations of general histories of composition. Now, having been able to review the majority of Warren Taylor's publications, consult Taylor's papers in the Oberlin College archive, and speak with a few individuals who knew and worked with Taylor, I can expand that footnote into a substantial examination.

BERLIN ON WARREN TAYLOR'S "RHETORIC IN A DEMOCRACY"

Writing about the influence of progressive education on writing instruction in the early twentieth century, Berlin argues that composition moved from an "inherently creative" activity to "a social act with public consequences," especially in the economic, social, and political upheaval following the Great Depression (Berlin 1987, 60). Berlin finds several examples of pedagogies during this period that move away from expressionism and current-traditional rhetorics and toward a "rhetoric of public discourse" (82, 84), but he is especially impressed with Warren Taylor's 1938 *English Journal* article "Rhetoric in a Democracy." Berlin provides a lengthy summary of Taylor's argument about the role of composition instruction in preparing students for life in a democracy. Berlin's interpretation is generally accurate: Taylor does criticize traditional approaches to writing instruction that emphasize rules and form; he does advocate an approach to teaching writing attuned to individuals' political roles in democratic societies; and he does advocate "a remarkably expanded role for the place of composition in the college curriculum" (Berlin 1987, 88). However, using "Rhetoric in a Democracy" as a harbinger of social-epistemic rhetoric, Berlin minimizes the significance of Taylor's distinction between a rhetoric of persuasion and a rhetoric of elucidation. Taylor argues that the art of persuasion, "the power of speech to lead men to the conclusion the speaker desires them to have," is the art of the dictator, who conceals his motives from view and usurps decision-making ability from his audience (Taylor 1938, 856). In contrast, Taylor argues that democracy requires "an art of elucidation," or "a practical art of communication," which is speech that clearly demarcates all "possible lines of action and their respective consequences" and thereby facilitates citizens' ability to "evaluate public utterances rationally" (856). By facilitating critical-rational deliberation and collective decision making, the art of elucidation enables individuals in a democracy to participate in and assume responsibility for actions that shape society (856). While this characterization of elucidation leads Berlin to criticize Taylor's "innocent faith in rational discourse" and lack of confidence in public dialogue to shape collective action, Berlin nonetheless characterizes Taylor's argument as "an enlightened conception of the role of a social rhetoric of public discourse in a democratic state" (Berlin 1987, 88).

Berlin's laudatory treatment of Warren Taylor's "Rhetoric in a Democracy" stems in part from Taylor's claim that "formulating the principles of a rhetoric for a democracy and stating the criteria for the evaluation of the use of those principles in public utterances is rightly the job of teachers of composition" (Taylor 1938, 857). However, Taylor's distinction between persuasion and elucidation underscores a less radical conception of composition than Berlin suggests. Taylor argues that because colleges and universities are "the banking houses . . . of understanding and of reason," they have an obligation "to circulate their intellectual currency" by communicating knowledge in a way that allows the body politic to benefit from "the rewards of learning" (855). Taylor characterizes the role of teachers as imparting knowledge without promoting action, as moving students enough to make them "genuinely interested in the subject under discussion" but without persuading them to act (857). For Taylor, what's true of classroom instruction is also true of democratic deliberation: "Rhetoric should not attempt to offer means of moving to action; it should trust a body politic, enlightened by education, to make its own decisions" (857). This perspective suggests that Taylor was more concerned about the role of composition in promoting the critical reception of political discourse needed to shape public discourse into rational deliberation—an interpretation that differs, however slightly, from Berlin's characterization. Yes, Taylor argues that composition ought to advance a rhetoric of public discourse, but probably not in the way Berlin images or advocates.

More significant is Berlin's erroneous interpretation of institutional influences on Warren Taylor's argument in "Rhetoric in a Democracy." There are two places in *Rhetoric and Reality* where Berlin makes this mistake. First, Berlin describes Warren Taylor's argument as "especially compelling" given that "he was one of the few instructors of professorial rank teaching the freshman course at Wisconsin" (Berlin 1987, 86). Second, Berlin attempts to account for how such an "enlightened" argument was possible at the time by identifying "the influence of progressive politics in defining the service mission of the University of Wisconsin" (88). While Oberlin and the University of Wisconsin operate in relatively close proximity and in a region that was heavily influenced by progressivism, their institutional differences—a private liberal-arts college versus a public research university—suggest different missions and trajectories in their respective adaptations of progressivism for educational reform. While progressivism clearly influenced Oberlin, it was more profoundly influential and visible in Wisconsin because of the strong partnership between the state government and the state university. Consequently, understanding the institutional history of Oberlin and the influence of progressivism there provides a more accurate picture of the institutional influences on Warren Taylor's development as a scholar and teacher, including the evolution of his democratic orientation toward teaching composition and the humanities.

INSTITUTIONAL AND DEPARTMENTAL
INFLUENCES: OBERLIN COLLEGE

In *From Evangelicalism to Progressivism at Oberlin College, 1866–1917,* historian John Barnard (1969) identifies in Oberlin's nineteenth-century evangelical origins ripe conditions for the transition into twentieth-century progressivism. Already in its infancy, the college developed a reputation for supporting "a variety of religious and reform causes" along with several "unusual" practices including admitting African Americans, strongly supporting abolitionism, practicing coeducation, and promoting similar "moral and social-reform causes" (3). Under the leadership of Henry Churchill King, who taught for eighteen years at Oberlin before presiding from 1902 to 1927, the college managed to transition from an evangelical faith grounded in individual salvation and moral development to a social-gospel ethos that linked individual salvation with social redemption (115). In his talks, publications, and teaching, King "reinterpreted the social dimension of Oberlin's theological tradition" with an emphasis on a new view of humanity: "The sacredness of the person was both a description of an actual tendency in human relations and a fundamental ethical principle. . . . It led to the recognition of the whole man and to a quickening of social conscience," which was represented by a "confidence in the value and sacredness of each person" (Barnard 1969, 115, 117). Barnard describes King's 1911 publication of *The Moral and Religious Challenges of Our Times* as a prime example of how Oberlin's social-gospel impulses informed its adaptation of political and social progressivism (Barnard 1969, 124).

Warren Taylor strongly admired King and, in his lectures and addresses, frequently referred to King's discussion of the "primacy" of the individual as a distinctive value of Oberlin. For instance, "Democracy and the Oberlin Idea," a lecture Taylor delivered to Oberlin alumni in 1950, aptly illustrates how Taylor interprets in Oberlin's institutional history the integration of humanistic and democratic projects. Taylor describes the Oberlin Idea as comprising "four strands of conviction": "the primacy of the person; the democratic spirit; the breadth and thoroughness of work; and the obligation of all to be socially useful" (Taylor, Box 5, Talks). Although Oberlin was founded during the evangelical reform movement, Taylor claims the college was free of religious dogma and open to supporting social reforms because its early leaders made a deep respect for individual personality and agency central to religious practice. Taylor sees Oberlin's humanism as central to democratic living because it facilitates individual responsibility and self-governance necessary to sustain human progress. Quoting King, Taylor explains that the social and political work of a college is to help bring "rational and ethical democracy" (quoted in Taylor, Box 5, Talks). As evidence of Oberlin's commitment to this idea, Taylor notes its century-long history of faculty governance, which had been earned by faculty who had developed "character through the discipline of scholarship" (Taylor, Box 5, Talks). Disciplined work in a democratic atmosphere promotes the growth of individuals, and colleges fulfill their institutional and social obligations when they create conditions that allow for the emergence of "the whole self."

Just as Oberlin's institutional context influenced Warren Taylor's conception of education and training for democracy, the history and culture of the English department also shaped Taylor's professional work and identity. In his brief history of the English department at Oberlin College, *English at Oberlin: 1880–1960*, Robert Longsworth notes that shortly after the creation of the department in the late 1880s, teaching English composition became the department's mainstay. This prompted complaints about the course and efforts to relegate it to the margins of the department; hence, like most colleges at the time, "lament[ing] the drudgery of reading and correcting student compositions" and "inflict[ing] that drudgery disproportionately" on junior faculty existed almost from the inception of the department (Longsworth n.d., 20). In 1900, Charles Henry Adams Wager was hired to chair the English department. An Arnoldian humanist trained at Yale, Wager was an exceptional teacher, but he held a strong bias toward composition and a strong preference for hierarchy. Serving as chair until mandatory retirement in 1935, Wager was instrumental in creating a department culture that eschewed scholarship and maintained a hierarchical division between literature and composition. Between 1900 and 1910, student enrollment in the department increased because of growing demand for English composition instruction, due in part to the college's requirement that students complete two years of English composition (Longsworth n.d., 26, 37). Wager and his small staff begrudgingly bore the brunt of composition, but only temporarily. By 1910, Wager's request to be relieved from teaching composition was granted when an associate professor was assigned responsibility for administering freshmen composition with a staff of nine young instructors, only two of whom held MAs. Four instructors staffed fifteen sections of freshman composition, and five instructors staffed eleven sections of sophomore composition. Some staff taught an introductory literature course and the introductory English-language course, which was required for the major. Wager assumed responsibility for all advanced work (Longsworth n.d., 27–28).

Despite the development of the major through the 1920s, "the heaviest pedagogic investment of the department was in the teaching of English composition" (Longsworth n.d., 40). The consistent demand for composition instruction prompted Wager to institute a practice of hiring new faculty into "rotating instructorships" in which they were assigned to teach four sections of English composition per semester. Instructors who received permanent appointment status were promoted to assistant professor and permitted to teach one or two advanced courses. Only full professors taught advanced courses exclusively. Securing a permanent appointment was mostly a case of endurance and seniority, and guidelines for promotion were never explicit. Unsurprisingly, turnover among new staff was high.

This was the context in which Warren Taylor was hired in 1930 after completing an MA in English at Vanderbilt in 1926 and teaching at the University of Tennessee through 1929. As a rotating instructor at Oberlin, Taylor taught four sections of freshman composition per semester. However, rather than wither under such a load, Taylor flourished. During this time, Oberlin required all faculty to submit annual reports directly to the president, the first section of which asked faculty to report on "significant developments or problems in teaching." These annual reports provide extensive evidence of Taylor's ideals and practices in the composition classroom. Initially, Taylor was deeply committed to composition, and he invested substantial energy in teaching it effectively and in imagining alternatives to current pedagogy. Signs of innovation include eschewing lectures and textbooks in favor of discussion- and problem-based learning; encouraging students to write about topics of genuine interest; and replacing theme correction with instructor-student conferences to determine grades. These early reports confirm Berlin's characterization of Taylor as a champion of innovative composition instruction attuned to the needs of democratic living. However, Taylor's later reports reflect a shift toward literature and humanistic education more generally as mechanisms for such instruction, thereby highlighting the limitation of Berlin's characterization of Taylor as well as Berlin's implicit argument that preparing students for democratic living is the exclusive province of composition.

WARREN TAYLOR ON TEACHING COMPOSITION

In his 1931 annual report, Taylor describes a successful composition course as one that moves beyond "routine obligations, the study of words, the parsing of sentences, the development of paragraphs" and instead helps students develop an abiding respect for "good form in thinking and in writing" (Taylor, Box 12). Conveying the value of clear communication and developing "a critical point of view" can help students distinguish truth from error in writing and speech in its myriad forms, from newspapers and magazines to plays and conversations. For Taylor, the composition course "should be centered quite simply in extensive reading and constant writing rather than in unapplied theory or in a slavish devotion to textbooks." In terms of actual instructional practices, Taylor required "two short papers each week" on subjects that reflected students' "genuine concerns" and "honest opinions rather than conventional responses" in order to help students identify topics "worth thinking, writing, and reading about." All of Taylor's students wrote on the same subject to facilitate "intelligent discussion of the students' papers in class," and they were also trained in writing a source-based term paper. Taylor stressed substantial revision, asking students not simply to "correct in red ink the errors in the original drafts of their papers, but to completely re-organize and re-write" them. Taylor graded original and revised compositions to help students see the rationale behind the grades he assigned.

Resisting such instructional methods as lecture, recitation, or meandering discussion, Taylor describes implementing a "forum method" in his composition classroom. This method entailed the instructor's or student's presenting a problem or set of problems related to some aspect of composition as manifested in an assigned reading, in students' papers, or in students' oral summaries of their peers' papers. Following this presentation, the instructor would facilitate a focused discussion of the problem aimed at helping students "substantiate their opinions" by identifying specific criteria to aid in critical evaluation and then aligning their opinions with the collectively generated criteria (Taylor, Box 12). Taylor also applied this approach to his introductory literature course with similar results: in helping students "discover" literature, its types, its creators, its audiences, and its uses, the forum method developed in students "an enduring curiosity, a desire to discover and to know, and an ability to judge and to appreciate intelligently" literary works of art.

Midway through his second year of teaching composition, Taylor suggested a radical change to the traditional approach of theme correction. Questioning the validity and desirability of "reading and marking papers in private and returning them to the students, who correct them when they are alone," Taylor proposed a "Conference Plan" which would replace the private reading of papers with student conferences (Taylor, Box 12). According to Taylor's calculations, the usual procedures for composition instruction required six hours of preparation, nine hours of classroom teaching, fifteen hours of reading papers, and six hours of conferencing with students. In Taylor's proposed plan, both preparation and classroom teaching would be reduced to three hours each, time spent reading papers privately would be eliminated, and thirty hours would be allotted to conferencing with students. Both plans require thirty-six hours, but Taylor's conference plan would capitalize on the "advantages of individual instruction." It would also demand a significant amount of interaction between students and instructor: "Five hours are provided every day for conferences of thirty minutes each. During that time, two papers could be read and corrected by the student and instructor, and further work could be assigned." And it would require lowering class size and finding adequate space for conferences. Given Taylor's appointment as a rotating instructor, it is unlikely that he was able to implement this proposed method. But both his conference plan and his forum method illustrate innovative approaches to composition instruction. As further evidence of innovation, Taylor describes integrating writing and speaking instruction into the composition course by requiring that each student deliver an oral summary of a book, to which all students and the instructor wrote a critical response. The instructor then conferenced with the student in private to discuss both the summary and the responses with the intent of strengthening the student's oral and written skills.

Warren Taylor was keenly aware of the limitations of composition instruction as traditionally imagined and implemented. His 1933 annual report consists of a lengthy discussion of acknowledged problems, including the contentless nature of the course, which left it subject to instructors' preferences, whether surveying topics of general interest, or developing taste and culture, or emphasizing mechanical correctness. (Taylor, Box 12). Taylor faulted these approaches for interfering with the course's central focus, speaking and writing, and its purpose, helping students improve these skills. Taylor believed that if students and faculty understood that speaking and writing are central to "human existence" because they deal with "sharing and exchanging states of mind," then the reputation of the course might improve. Reiterating that effective writing instruction depends on instructors giving "far more attention to the work of each student" than is currently possible with large class sizes and high teaching loads, and reminiscent of his conference-plan proposal, Taylor advocates seeing students as apprentices who need to discuss their work in depth with the instructor on a weekly basis.

In a notable shift, Warren Taylor turns his attention in his 1934 annual report toward the relationship between the status of the English department faculty and the quality of student writing campus wide. Taylor criticizes the department as drifting and not "defining and realizing its purposes . . . for its members and for its students" (Taylor, Box 12). Taylor argues that the uneven writing in the college's student publications is indicative of the failure on behalf of English department faculty in modeling the processes of scholarly production. In other words, if faculty aren't publishing or are publishing poorly, students' efforts will follow suit. Taylor offers several recommendations, some of which stem from his own experience as well as from his opinion of composition. In addition to making individual scholarship a higher priority, Taylor argues that the department should collaborate on a scholarly project, and he references the Fugitive group at Vanderbilt, which was highly influential for Taylor when he was a student there. Further, teaching assignments need more equal distribution among professors and instructors, who operate in "two distinct worlds": the professors neglect composition, "the most important course the department offers to the college group as a whole," while the instructors "turn the theme mill." Taylor also advocates creating opportunities for interested students to develop their writing, whether through more consultations with faculty or through creative clubs where students share and discuss and possibly even publish their writing. On this point, he again recalls his experience at Vanderbilt publishing with fellow students "a book of very bad poems we had written," but the experience was invigorating and was inspired, in part, by their faculty who "were publishing a magazine of literary significance, nationally, not locally." The magazine was undoubtedly *The Fugitive*, a literary magazine of poetry and criticism published from 1922 to 1925.

By 1934, facing the prospect of a reduced teaching appointment and reduced salary, Warren Taylor was granted a leave of absence to complete his PhD at the University of Chicago, which he had started in 1930 just prior to being hired at Oberlin. Returning to Oberlin in 1937 with PhD in hand, Taylor resumed the heavy English-composition load he had taught as an instructor, but with some courses in literature. As evidence of his continued commitment to composition, he describes working on a college textbook, which he had begun drafting in 1932. In his 1938 report, Taylor describes *A New Rhetoric for College Students* as intended for "a new type of English Composition course" that would "enable students to make reasoned evaluations of what they write, say, hear, and read" (Taylor, Box 12). The new dimension of the textbook was perhaps an intention to address "the parts that modern logic and psychology play in

communication" as well as an emphasis on "problems in American life."
Echoing a theme that would appear in his forthcoming article "Rhetoric
in a Democracy," Taylor explained that the textbook was "designed as a
rhetoric for a democracy whose citizens should be able to detect motives
and values beneath all public utterances." Equally important, the textbook focused on deriving an understanding of rhetoric based on how
society uses language as opposed to, presumably, the typical emphasis
on forms or modes of writing. By 1940, Taylor had changed the title to
Thinking, Reading, and Writing. By 1941, it was under contract with D. C.
Heath and Company and was 661 pages complete. By 1942, the title had
changed back to *A New Rhetoric for College Students,* and by 1943 Taylor
had completed over 900 pages of the estimated 1,250. The last annual
report available, from 1944, mentions that the textbook was still in preparation. Apparently, it never reached completion.

Warren Taylor eventually published a composition textbook in 1966,
but it seems notably different from the version he spent a decade writing and preparing. The premise of *Models for Thinking and Writing* is
that "thinking and writing are inseparable and deeply personal" (xi).
The 331-page book consists of two parts: the first, titled "Models," consists of twenty-six essays to facilitate broad education in the humanities accompanied by study questions to help develop "close, analytical
reading for both substance and method" (Taylor 1966, xii); the second,
titled "On Developing Ideas," includes ten chapters that address modes
of discourse and methods of argument. Each chapter includes multiple
excerpts from sample sources that model the various methods discussed,
and some have brief commentary or material added by Taylor. Excerpts
are frequently from sources students would typically read, namely textbooks and periodicals. However, the inclusion of essays and the emphasis on modes of discourse suggests a more literary approach to composition than the more socially oriented linguistic training evident in
Taylor's earlier characterization of the textbook he never finished.

I see in these two textbooks different trajectories in Warren Taylor's
career, and the completion of *Models for Thinking and Writing* at the
expense of *A New Rhetoric for College Students* as marking an intellectual
and professional shift toward literature and, eventually, the humanities
in place of composition. And I see Taylor's completion of his PhD at
Chicago as a significant moment in this shift. Under the direction of
literary critic Ronald Salmon (R. S.) Crane, Taylor examined William
Shakespeare's use of rhetorical figures. Although his dissertation, titled
Tudor Figures of Rhetoric, suggests scholarly interests that exceed the borders of traditional literary studies, Taylor's subsequent scholarship and

professional activities signal clear commitment to literature and the humanities and less interest in composition. This shift is apparent in Taylor's annual reports and publications during the 1940s. For instance, in his 1942 annual report, Taylor describes how introductory literature instruction should focus on a few major works, provide a comparative analysis of "past and present literary and social problems," and offer solutions to help students to "develop perspective, to view cultural traditions and innovations in terms of their own lives, to respect not only the acquisition of knowledge but also the use of it in shaping both our national and our separate being" (Taylor, Box 12). In this description, the study of literature is poised to perform the social function Taylor had previously ascribed to composition. In the last available report, written in 1944, Taylor conveys his belief in the need for colleges to help students "feel deeply their obligations and responsibilities in the civilizing processes of their society and of the world. Colleges must emphasize civic accountability as well as specialized work." This kind of "deep social conscience" aids in the development of a "critical and a creative intelligence to be directed toward the achievement of social ends. As evident in publications and teaching during his remaining career at Oberlin, Taylor remained committed to the ideal of colleges preparing students to live in a democratic society. But composition and rhetoric became ancillary to that ideal.

WARREN TAYLOR'S TRANSITION TO HUMANITIES

The appearance of the term "critical and creative intelligence" is indicative of Warren Taylor's shift away from composition and toward humanism, and this term becomes a theme in Taylor's many publications on the role of the humanities in higher education. What began as a description of the nature and role of criticism and judgment regarding knowledge, action, and values (Taylor 1942) and expanded into an explanation of the influence of intelligence on human relations (Taylor 1943) evolved into a clear theme of critical, creative intelligence as the central purpose of a humanistic education in a liberal arts institution (Taylor 1945a). In "Dogma, Drift, or Humanism?" Warren Taylor (1945a) writes that liberal education must help students develop the creativity and compassion needed to become free along with a critical-creative intelligence to engage in productive social relations. In "The Emerging College," Taylor claims that the post-war college must "prepare students to live intelligently and creatively in a society of interacting, cross-connected problems and interests" (Taylor 1945b, 114). In "Literature and General

Education," Taylor (1946) points to liberal education as freeing one's mind to be both critical and creative, which makes liberal education highly valuable in a democracy. But rather than point to rhetoric as the means for ensuring freedom, as he did in 1938, throughout these later publications Taylor argues that literature can fulfill the mandate for general education in the post-war college to "undertake anew to aid its students in becoming free, mature citizens, capable of leadership in a free, democratic society" (245). The study of literature furthers the outcomes of general education by helping students see their interdependence with others, experience imaginative and creative processes, and acquire perspective for judgment and action. The processes of discovery and creation are central to life and, hence, education; they are likewise central to literature (245). In his conclusion, which is worth quoting at length, Taylor argues that literature

> exercises man's consciousness, his habits of mind, in both its lyrical responsiveness and in its dramatic comprehensiveness. Through literature flow motives, events, and their consequences; through literature flow human purposiveness and actions. Those attitudes, events, and values, in their great variety, supply a common core of experience which enables men to communicate with and to understand one another. The study of literature, as an exercise in perception and in judgment, adds both depth and perspective to the training of men and women who must, as informed, independently minded, sympathetic, and judicious citizens, assume the task of maintaining and enlarging our democratic civilization. (Taylor 1946, 248)

While a democratic orientation toward higher education remained a constant emphasis throughout his career, Taylor increasingly relied on literature and interdisciplinary humanities instruction as the primary mechanisms for training in democratic living.

In addition to Taylor's successful completion of the PhD at the University of Chicago, with such specialization deepening his investment in literature, the departmental culture at Oberlin continued to direct Taylor's career development away from composition. As mentioned earlier, the English department at Oberlin was stagnant under Wager, who as chair for thirty-five years perpetuated the division between professors and instructors Taylor had criticized. While the department curriculum and culture through the 1930s remained "largely impervious" to change, staffing changes through the late 1940s, namely the departure of Wager and other full professors who had reached the age of mandatory retirement, prompted an insurrection among the remaining senior faculty who drafted a constitution for shared governance of the department. The constitution stipulated that a council of tenured professors would make decisions about curriculum, appointments, and budget, and the department chair would serve on a three-year rotating basis. These faculty, including Taylor, sought to prevent the chair from having disproportionate influence on the department and to create a more equitable distribution of power. In *English at Oberlin: 1880–1960*, Longworth writes that unfortunately, this arrangement merely distributed the decision-making power from the chair to a council that maintained the previous administration's hierarchical approach to literature and composition by continuing the practice of rotating instructorships in which junior faculty taught composition and senior faculty taught literature (Longsworth n.d., 59). Consequently, turnover of new staff, who now were PhD candidates or holders, was especially "jolting" to the department, and its reputation in the college continued to suffer for the next fifteen years (Longsworth n.d., 61). Eventually, this issue was addressed by the next generation of English-department faculty, who managed to convince college faculty in 1967 to vote to eliminate English composition as a requirement for graduation at Oberlin (Longsworth n.d., 65). According to Longsworth, the argument for abolishing the requirement was that students were increasingly well prepared in high school, making the requirement redundant. The course became an elective for all students except those who failed an entrance exam. By 1970, when Taylor reached the age of mandatory retirement, the same faculty member who directed the effort to abolish the first-year requirement became chair of the department and restored conditions for improved collegiality by having junior and senior staff share the teaching load of introductory and advanced courses (Longsworth n.d., 65).

As Robert Longsworth told me in a phone interview on July 18, 2014, Warren Taylor vehemently opposed the decision to abolish freshman English, but he had long since left the composition classroom and, in fact, had refused to teach it. It seems strange that Taylor would publish a composition textbook, *Models for Thinking and Writing*, at a time when he was no longer involved, or even interested, in teaching composition. However baffling, this oddity ought not to diminish the significance or value of the initial thinking and teaching Taylor devoted to composition instruction at Oberlin. There is much to admire in the content of Taylor's early composition instruction and in his conviction of composition's importance. But looking beyond a single article or a specific period in an individual's career reveals how institutional cultures and practices shape an individual's ongoing scholarly development and professional work. Taylor's interests shifted from composition to the humanities, but his commitment to democratic education remained constant, a point illustrated by examining Taylor's leading role in creating an interdisciplinary humanities course at Oberlin (the Humanistic Tradition) and, later, at Hiram College (The Twentieth Century).

WARREN TAYLOR ON TEACHING HUMANITIES

The Humanistic Tradition, which Warren Taylor often called a capstone course, was a two-semester, interdisciplinary upper-division humanities seminar with concentrations in art, literature, religion, and philosophy. In "The Purpose of the Divisional Course, 'The Humanist Tradition,'" Taylor writes that the course, first offered in 1947, aimed to synthesize students' education in the College of Arts and Science at Oberlin and to prepare them for life after college (Taylor, Box 7). The course consisted of weekly readings, large lectures, and small discussion groups, and it was very popular among students for nearly two decades. Documentation about the course, produced by the divisional committee Taylor chaired, clearly bears Taylor's imprint. Indeed, Taylor was very defensive about the value of the course which, incidentally, was discontinued soon after his retirement (Longsworth, pers. comm., 2014). Hence, although the course was committee generated and had widespread participation from faculty at Oberlin and beyond, it can be read as representing Taylor's particular beliefs about how an integrated humanistic educational program can accomplish democratic ends.

In "Purpose of the Divisional Course," Taylor writes that The Humanistic Tradition had two primary objectives: first, to enable juniors and seniors to broaden their perspective and understanding of "multiple and divergent interpretations and values which human beings, across centuries, have assigned to their attitudes, their ideas, and their actions"; and second, to help these students develop and exercise "their faculties of choice, their powers of informed discrimination and judgment, in accepting or rejecting attitudes, ideas, and actions which will make up their own lives and which may give constructive meaning and value to the life of their society" (Taylor, Box 7). The interdisciplinary nature of the course promoted students' synthesis of various branches of humanistic knowledge with a developing sense of their own interests, values, and purposes for living and an increased capacity to contribute to society. Students were encouraged to "add their own inquiries into interdisciplinary and interdepartmental problems." In this way, they developed a critical and creative intelligence—the same kind of capacity that appeared with increasing frequency in Taylor's publications that appeared during this period.

The underlying motivation for this course was to maintain the role of college education in preserving democratic society: "One prime purpose of college education in a democratic society is to afford young men and women, as self-governing and social-minded individuals, ample surroundings, occasions, and obligations for the disciplining and the unfolding of their perceptions and their choices." In "Purpose of the Divisional Course," Taylor writes that the increase in "mechanization, depersonalization," propaganda, and "stratification of responsibility," along with the encroaching influence of indoctrination on education, threatened to undermine the "intelligence and responsibility of individuals and thus the fundamental tenets of democracy" (Taylor, Box 7). Though less ominous a threat, specialization at the university level was nonetheless inadequate in providing for "the intellectual and emotional growth of maturing men and women" because it privileged the treatment of subjects in isolation, thus promoting superficial and narrow learning. According to Taylor and other committee members, "The supreme end of a college education in a democracy is to release within students a competence for self-development" and self-government. But to do this, colleges need "a clearly understood and shared sense of what college education in a democracy is for." For Taylor, this purpose was to help students develop awareness of the interests and welfare of humankind. Colleges best addressed this purpose by developing "interdepartmental, cross-fertilizing courses and programs" to facilitate the kind of learning and living necessary for democracy.

As outlined on the syllabus for The Humanistic Tradition, the first-semester lectures focused on antiquity through the Middle Ages; the second-semester lectures covered the Renaissance through the present. The course included a list of readings that was grouped topically and spanned the various humanities disciplines the course meant to bring together: visual arts, music, philosophy, religion, and literature. Interestingly, work by Kenneth Burke, John Dewey, and I. A. Richards appear on the list, but the variety of texts and topics addressed cannot be interpreted as an effort to advance a specific discipline or theory. For each weekly lecture, students completed a required reading assignment related to the lecture topic and selections from an extensive list of readings grouped according to topic. Some readings were accompanied by questions for study and discussion. Taylor delivered one to three lectures per semester on topics such as criticism in humanities, romanticism and realism, democracy and religious liberty, and transcendentalism and evolution. In subsequent versions of the course, certain faculty lectures became panel discussions on topics such as the merits and limitations of science, totalitarianism and liberalism, and cultural relativism and cultural ideals.

Taylor offered a similar version of this course at Hiram College, where he taught for four years after reaching mandatory retirement age at Oberlin in 1970. The course, The Twentieth Century, was modified slightly but remained similar in content, purpose, and structure: according to Taylor, in "The Twentieth Century: The Future of man," written in 1973, it introduced students to "some representative major concerns of the twentieth century and of the arts and sciences" in order to cultivate "awareness of the intellectual, aesthetic, and ethical responsibilities of educated men and women—because a genuinely educated free citizen in a free society sees the whole of life and himself as a responsible and creative individual in it" (Taylor, Box 10). The first quarter, called "The Growth and Freedom of Human Beings," focused on "the ethical, artistic, and intellectual dimensions within the personalities of each human being" and addressed psychology, religion, art, science and history. The second quarter, "The Future of Man," focused on "man's responsibilities in sustaining and enlarging life today and tomorrow, by analysis, comparisons, and evaluation of major concepts and achievements" in economics, politics, governments, art, architecture, and music. The third quarter, called "The Future of America," focused on "ideals and actualities in both foreign and domestic policies" in foreign relations, use of technology, the economy, and democratic sustainability. Overall, the course balanced delivery of much "factual knowledge for mastery and reflection" with "occasions for students to enlarge and enrich their awareness by directly experiencing excellence in the expressive disciplines: art, music, literature."

As in The Humanistic Tradition, students in The Twentieth Century completed reading assignments before attending a Monday briefing session; they attended a lecture on Wednesday morning and a film or concert on Wednesday evening; and they used the materials they had gathered from these events to prepare short papers or outlines for use in their small-group discussion sessions on Thursday or Friday. In "The Twentieth Century: Class Procedures," written in 1973, Taylor writes that grades were determined by "the quality of the papers, the evaluative comments on lectures and films, and participation in briefing sessions and group discussions" (Taylor, Box 10). In addition, each student was expected to identify and complete an "independent achievement" project that was "personally meaningful," whether it was writing a research paper, making a film, or creating a reading list on a topic of personal interest. In "The Twentieth Century: The Future of Man," Taylor writes that the underlying aim of both courses was to help students broaden their outlook and develop critical judgment necessary to make informed decisions that benefit society.

As with The Humanistic Tradition, Warren Taylor made preparation for democratic society a central feature of The Twentieth Century. The course included a booklet, *The Future of Man* (Taylor, Box 10) with the syllabus, calendar, handouts, and copies of certain lectures, including one of Taylor's entitled "The Responsibility of Man for the Future of Man." This was an opening lecture for the course, and it describes the purpose of a college education as preparing individuals for the responsibility of developing a quality of life that serves themselves and society. Such responsibilities include cultivating "the moral sensibility and the fully informed and tested choices, decisions, and judgments of responsible citizens. Here Taylor reiterates his longstanding position on the relationship between democratic ability and higher education, the latter of which is responsible for "prepar[ing] citizens to earn their freedom by making informed and responsible decisions within wide perspectives and by conserving and enriching, not mechanizing and destroying, human personalities. An interdisciplinary approach to the humanities was central to such cultivation because it allowed students to develop a broad perspective, to detach themselves from absolutes, and to subordinate emotion to reason as they encountered and discussed art and culture. According to Taylor, the experience of a humanities education mirrored the socialization process in democratic societies, where individuals learn to live with others in a diverse society by developing capacities for judging fairly and determining right and wrong independently.

Warren Taylor did not disregard composition instruction completely in his interdisciplinary humanities courses, but his approach was heavily informed by literature. For instance, in the course booklet titled *The Growth and Freedom of Human Beings,* Taylor included supplemental materials to help students practice critical reading. These materials illustrate how Taylor aimed to help students develop critical intelligence. An untitled handout includes generally applicable questions that invite students to test the factual and logical nature of the argument in a given text, identifying definitions of terms and use of fact, logic, premise, and conclusion to make an argument; other questions address the comprehensiveness, coherence, judiciousness, utility, and originality (Taylor, Box 10). There are other materials, designed to help students critically analyze and evaluate information, that resemble the kinds of questions common in composition or literature textbooks that focus on logical or rhetorical analysis (e.g., consider the author's background, the selection of materials, the reliability of the information, the significance of the work; identify errors in logic or reasoning). One handout, titled "Evaluation of Organization and Expression," includes three categories for evaluating written work: paragraphs, sentences, and words. Each category has a series of questions that, again, resemble questions in current textbooks. For instance, questions under paragraphs and sentences tend to converge around questions of unity, coherence, and emphasis. But such materials were meant to help students develop critical reading and reasoning skills; while Taylor continued to conference with students and critique students' writing, his pedagogic materials and scholarly publications do not indicate more than superficial interest in composition.

In evaluations for both courses, students nearly unanimously praise Taylor for inspiring them to learn and express admiration for his conviction, although many acknowledge his occasionally overbearing nature. One student found discussions with Taylor to be difficult; another said the lecture content was over his head but he liked it that way because it motivated him to learn the material. One student complained that Taylor didn't bring sufficient controversy into group discussion because she found herself "agreeing with most things he said" (Taylor, Box 10). Another student wrote, Taylor "often aggrivated [sic] me with his broad generalizations and statements of what he believes to be fact. Yet I agree with most of what he says and am motivated to continue study in certain areas. One student said, "[I appreciated being] "forced to look at myself objectively and stand up for my own opinion" and learning "about being a person." Another chose to evaluate the course by reflecting on her own development. She describes the course with Taylor as "the greatest 10-week period in [her] life" in terms of development in world-view and in understanding relations among disciplines, what it means to be educated, and what she wants out of life. Here we see Taylor's outcome of a humanities education dramatized in the intellectual transformation of a single student. Equally revealing comments are from those students who note that other faculty did not exude Taylor's energy and enthusiasm for the course, which students regretted. One student doubts that he would have had a similarly influential experience had he been assigned to another faculty member's section; the same student wonders whether other faculty members' attitudes about the course can realistically be changed to mirror Taylor's.

Ultimately, the success and eventual decline of Warren Taylor's interdisciplinary courses at Oberlin and Hiram stemmed from the force of his presence and, later, absence. As Longsworth (1991) notes in "A Memorial Minute for Warrant Taylor," Taylor was charismatic teacher, a dynamic lecturer, and students flocked to his courses; he earned the title of one of the institution's "most memorable and influential teachers" (Taylor, Faculty File). While some scoffed at Taylor's over-the-top performance, many tended to recognize the implications of his very dramatic presence as both provocative and informative (Longsworth, pers. comm., 2014). In a personal letter to William V. Mayer written in 1961, Donald Love writes that Taylor had a reputation as "a man of deep philosophic conviction" who "believe[d] in the liberal arts tradition with an almost religious fervor" and whose convictions would lead to "stubborn adherence to a particular point of view," however unsound it was (Taylor, Faculty File). By the same token, according to Love, Taylor was considered "fair, judicious, and considerate," and Longsworth wrote in "A Memorial Minute for Warren Taylor" that he thought of Taylor as "Oberlin's most prominent humanist" (Longsworth 1991, 1) Taylor was described as a "formidable looking man: tall and heavy; large, craggy face; white hair; very intense eyes" (Feldman 1970, 9). Longsworth (2014, pers. comm.) described him in his later years as "a rather didactic human being" and "rather prickly." Students' comments confirm this, as does the tone of a note Taylor wrote in 1920 to the department chair, Chester Shaver, to protest a retirement party in his honor: "I want neither party nor gift. . . . I have talked with [others] about this and have told them that, for me, the matter is beyond reconsideration. If there is a party, I shall not attend. If there is a gift, I shall refuse to accept it" (Taylor, Box 18). Over time, Taylor grew increasingly intolerant of perspectives different from his own. He opposed in principle anything associated with authoritarianism. He was a passionate, even intolerant, Democrat. Despite the eventual demise of the interdisciplinary courses Taylor developed and sustained over the course of several decades, Taylor had a salutary influence on the many students he taught and on Oberlin College (Longsworth, pers. comm., 2014). In light of such a complex and contradictory character, one wonders whether the content of his courses—whether composition, literature, or humanities—or the presence of his personality was ultimately more meaningful for his students and more influential for the institutions than his initial investment in composition or his eventual commitment to literature and the humanities.

CONCLUSION

Despite having devoted a chapter to recuperating Warren Taylor's scholarship and professional activities, I have accounted for only a portion of the available materials, published and archived, that shed light on Taylor's life, work, and contributions to higher education. By recovering a historical figure previously hidden by Berlin's misattribution in *Rhetoric and Reality*, I hope to have illustrated that general histories of composition can continue to be generative sites for local historical work, and that the insights gleaned from even the slightest errors can result in research that is additive to the field's understanding of composition history. This study also illustrates how institutional and departmental histories and influences can have a profound impact on the scholarly and professional development of individuals. When Oberlin hired Warren Taylor to teach composition, he engaged in the project with energy and creativity. Educational advancement (earning a PhD at Chicago), departmental culture (working and becoming tenured in a place that valued literature over composition), and institutional influences (having the opportunity to create an interdisciplinary course) each played a significant role in shaping Taylor's intellectual interests and professional practices. Such influences must be taken into account as scholars continue to recuperate and integrate past figures into current conversations.

But perhaps more significantly, this study points to limitations in scholarship or attitudes that make democratic training the exclusive province of a course or discipline, as Berlin did with composition, and as many in composition and rhetoric are prone to do today. Writing disciplinary histories of composition or rhetoric can cause historians to laud or vilify pedagogies or persons of the past depending on whether those pedagogies or persons align with current disciplinary values and practices. Rather than read Taylor's shift from composition to literature and the humanities as abandoning the field of composition as we (or others, like Berlin) understand it, I see Taylor moving along the continuum of liberal education, which encompasses all language arts—speaking, writing, reading, listening—and which is the underlying mechanism that, in Taylor's view, sustains democratic vitality. Rather than use Taylor to recommend a specific approach to composition or literature or to endorse a normative view of the discipline of composition, I see in Taylor's work an argument for the potential of interdisciplinary humanities programs to revitalize higher education by providing a compelling alternative to specialization. Taking cues from Taylor, scholars in the inherently interdisciplinary field of composition and rhetoric ought to consider how their work and professions position them to promote interdisciplinary programs that address social issues as opposed to engaging in work that reinforces, if not deepens, disciplinary boundaries. If interdisciplinary, publicly oriented liberal-arts programs such as Taylor's become increasingly common as colleges and universities seek to sustain not only liberal education but also their own professions and institutions, then composition and rhetoric's perennial concern with its own disciplinary identity may need adjustment. Rhetoric and composition historiography can help in this regard by prompting more interdisciplinary thinking through historical work that situates composition and rhetoric more purposefully alongside neighboring language arts and their associated fields and disciplines. Historical projects that highlight shared histories and practices rather than reinforce discrete disciplinary identities may prompt alliances and collaborations that could revitalize academic and public culture.

References

Barnard, John. 1969. *From Evangelicalism to Progressivism at Oberlin College, 1866–1917.* Columbus: Ohio State University Press.

Berlin, James. 1987. *Rhetoric and Reality: Writing Instruction in American Colleges, 1900–1985.* Carbondale: Southern Illinois University Press.

Brereton, John, ed. 1995. *The Origins of Composition Studies in the American College, 1875–1925: A Documentary History.* Pittsburgh, PA: University of Pittsburg Press.

Feldman, Paul. 1970. "My Job is Not to Measure You: Two Pages and Some Photographs on Warren Taylor." *Oberlin Alumni Magazine,* May 8–9.

Gold, David. 2012. "Remapping Revisionist Historiography." *College Composition and Communication* 64 (1): 15–34.

Hairston, Maxine. 1985. "Breaking Our Bonds and Reaffirming Our Connections." *College Composition and Communication* 36 (3): 272–82. http://dx.doi.org/10.2307/357971.

Levi, Giovanni. 2001. "On Microhistory." In *New Perspectives on Historical Writing.* 2nd ed. Edited by Peter Burke, 97–119. University Park: Pennsylvania State University Press.

Levi, Giovanni. 2012. "Microhistory and the Recovery of Complexity." In *Historical Knowledge: In Quest of Theory, Method, and Evidence,* edited by Susanna Fellman and Marjatta Rahikainen, 121–32. Newcastle upon Tyne: Cambridge Scholars.

Longsworth, Robert. 1991. "A Memorial Minute for Warren Taylor, Presented at a Meeting of the General Faculty." April 16, 1991. Oberlin College Archives.

Longsworth, Robert. n.d. "English at Oberlin: 1880–1960." Oberlin College Archives.

Magnússon, Sigurður Gylfi, and István M. Szijártó. 2013. *What Is Microhistory? Theory and Practice.* London: Routledge.

Taylor, Warner. 1929. "A National Survey of Conditions in Freshman English." *Bureau of Educational Research Bulletin* 11. Madison: University of Wisconsin.

Taylor, Warren. Papers. Oberlin College Archives. Oberlin, Ohio.

Taylor, Warren. 1938. "Rhetoric in a Democracy." *English Journal* 27 (10): 851–8.

Taylor, Warren. 1942. "Education and Criticism of Life." *Educational Record* 23 (2): 219–34.

Taylor, Warren. 1943. "What Colleges Learn from War." *School and Society* 57 (1479): 487–92.

Taylor, Warren. 1945a. "Dogma, Drift, or Humanism?" *Humanist* 5 (1): 21–3.

Taylor, Warren. 1945b. "The Emerging College." *School and Society* 62: 113–15.

Taylor, Warren. 1946. "Literature and General Education." *Bulletin of the American Association of University Professors* 32 (2): 235–48. http://dx.doi.org/10.2307/40220147.

Taylor, Warren. 1966. *Models for Thinking and Writing.* Cleveland, OH: World Publishing.

8
REMEMBERING ROGER GARRISON
Composition Studies and the Star-Making Machine

Neal Lerner

THE NAMETAG GAME

We can't help but play the nametag game at professional conferences: look at the face, look at the name tag, look back at the face. Or skip the first step and just focus on the nametag. Sometimes it happens in elevators. Sometimes at the book exhibit. Sometimes in a quick glance when passing in a hallway. Is that a recognizable name? Someone I've read? Someone well known? Someone I should know? Then, we tell others whom we've seen, a collaborative collection of star sightings. It seems a benign practice, not nearly to the level of star stalking, but simply a reminder that like any field, we have our stars in composition studies, both present and past, the ones whose nametags might as well be printed in forty-point font.

Here's a variation that's happened to me a couple of times during an elevator ride: person looks at my name tag and asks, "Should I know who you are?"

Star making is an odd cultural practice, in my view, and not just because of the awkward moments such as the one above. The academic conference itself is an assemblage of stars, after all, featured sessions and room appropriations based on star power or lack thereof. It feels like an uneasy caste system, ill fitting for the field of composition studies with its egalitarian leanings and common critique of seemingly elitist literature colleagues. By no means do I claim that our perceived stars are not worthy of special attention, larger audiences, nametag gawking, and leadership positions. I am asking if the star-making process chokes off possibilities as much as it elevates a select few.

Identifying those worthy of stardom is not simply a practice occurring at conferences, of course. It can happen historically, a kind of deliberate remembering and forgetting of the figures who came before, the

DOI: 10.7330/9781607324058.c008

creation of disciplinary origin stories and the attempt to build a genealogy. In composition studies, which one might argue is a relatively young
discipline with a handful of early "grand narratives" (e.g., Berlin 1987;
Connors 1997; Kitzhaber 1990) and a growing number of "small" stories
(e.g., Fleming 2011; Gold 2008; Ritter 2009; Varnum 1996), attempts
to construct history are also attempts to assert identity. Wolf Lepenies
and Peter Weingart write that disciplinary histories "serve the function
of legitimation" (Lepenies and Weingart 1983, xv), and that "histories
of disciplines are being written and rewritten, to extend the present (or
what is to become the future) as far as possible into the past, thereby
constructing an image of continuity, consistency and determinacy"
(xvii). However, these histories run the risk of normalizing certain stories and excluding others. As Sidney I. Dobrin describes,

> the drive to historically locate what We do is certainly a form of self-vali-
> dation, and it works hand-in-hand with a push toward standardization in
> order to more easily confer what we do upon a population under the com-
> monality of discipline or, more accurately, the discipline of commonality.
> One can easily argue that standardization is a crucial step in discipline
> formation, in validation of a field's boundaries, of the place that a given
> field occupies. Standardization operates as a mechanism specifically of
> boundary formation. This is what We do; everything else falls outside our
> governance. Standardization makes validation easier, but standardization
> is always a reduction, not an elevation. (Dobrin 2011, 103)

Microhistorians caution us to be wary of such reductions or of totalizing histories with a focus on those easily recognizable as major players or influences. Instead, as Giovanni Levi describes, "the excluded,
the little people, the far-off" (Levi 2012, 125) are often the subject of
microhistories in that the stories of these players can reveal complexities and nuance often missing from accounts of the recognizable. Still,
a focus on individuals in the tradition of microhistory is not meant to
simply highlight one individual's overlooked contribution to a field.
Rather, the value of that focus, in Jill Lepore's words, "lies not in its
uniqueness, but in its exemplariness, in how that individual's life
serves as an allegory for broader issues affecting the culture as a whole"
(Lepore 2001, 133). Microhistory's concept of the "exceptional normal" is key here (Magnússon and Szijártó 2013, 20), particularly for historical research on the non-elite or, in composition studies, for examining those historical figures from institutions outside of the mainstream.
As Sigurður Magnússon and István Szijártó describe, "A marginal case
can reveal a hidden reality, when the sources are silent about the lower
social strata" (20).

Normalcy is a construct, after all, and totalizing histories offer that normalcy as the master narrative. For example, the story of freshman composition originating at Harvard University with English A in the late nineteenth century and then spreading to most other postsecondary institutions has long dominated. Correctives such as the collection *Local Histories: Reading the Archives of Composition* (Donahue and Flesher Moon 2007) stress exceptions to that normalizing narrative with accounts of institutions and their creation of first-year writing programs independent of (and often predating) the events at Harvard. These exceptions create a new normal, a reminder that individual accounts or microscale analyses challenge the power dynamic inherent in the politics of constructing disciplinary history or the remembering and forgetting that shape the constructed narrative. As described by Carlo Ginzburg and Carlo Poni, the "normal exceptions" are "the marginal cases that bring the old paradigm back into the arena of discussion, thus helping to create a new paradigm, richer and better articulated. These marginal cases function, that is, as clues or traces of a hidden reality, which is not usually apparent in the [historical] documentation" (Ginzburg and Poni 1991, 8).

In what follows, I offer an account of a figure in composition's history, a normal exception who has been largely forgotten or is, in Dobrin's terms, the product of a reduced narrative. However, my attempt to jog our cultural memory is not merely an attempt to recover a lost figure but instead to draw attention to our processes of remembering and forgetting. What I wonder is whom else we might have forgotten in our past, what else has been reduced, and who might share credit for the work we do now as well as provide guidance for the uncertain future. Who has no chance at all of being written into future histories of composition studies?

THREE OUT OF FOUR

In his 1994 account of the transformation of the first-year writing program at UMass Amherst from "current traditional" to "process-oriented," Charles Moran cites four key scholars as responsible for that shift. I will bet that most, if not all, compositionists have heard of the first three: Peter Elbow, Janet Emig, and Donald Murray. But how many have heard of the fourth, Roger Garrison?

Moran reports that he never met Garrison but that his influence came from Garrison's publication in 1974 of the article "One-to-One: Tutorial Instruction in Freshman Composition." Moran also speculates as to why

Garrison faded from view in contrast to Murray, telling his readers that "Garrison was a self-styled outsider and iconoclast, a person who deliberately remained outside the growing community of scholars in the field; Murray was, and is, a generous and sociable man who moves comfortably in the world of professional conferences" (Moran 1994, 137).

Moran also attributes the Garrison-Murray contrast to the difference in their instructional contexts: Murray spent his academic career at the University of New Hampshire, a four-year PhD-granting institution. Garrison's career was spent at two-year colleges, ending at Westbrook College in Portland, Maine. According to Moran, "Garrison and Murray were working in different cultures. Two-year college English teachers have easy access to the published work of their colleagues who teach in four-year research institutions; their own knowledge, not often cast in the form of the published research article, circulates, most often oral and embodied, within their two-year college community—except in the extraordinary circumstances that brought Garrison's work to our attention in 1973" (Moran 1994, 173).

Murray and Garrison are two historical figures in composition studies, then, one who had a tremendous influence on notions of teaching writing as a process and who achieved exalted status in the field, the other more of a footnote in the historical archive, an "outsider," "iconoclast," someone perhaps known in writing center circles for his advocacy of one-to-one methods of teaching writing and thus perhaps most closely aligned with a subfield, writing centers, that similarly struggles with outsider or iconoclastic status.

My intent in this chapter is not to knock the reputation of Murray. Indeed, I count *A Writer Teaches Writing* as one of the most influential texts on my own development as a writing teacher, and I cannot imagine having survived my first several years in the classroom without it. But what I wonder now is why it is Murray we know well and Garrison who is relatively obscure and what this difference says about composition's relationship to its history and to those who get to count as major figures.

COLLECTING HISTORICAL FIGURES

In describing the methods of microhistory, Levi notes that one aim is to "attempt to narrate without concealing the rules of the game that the historian is following. And by this I mean more than simply referencing one's source material . . . but by openly declaring the process by means of which the history is being constructed: by showing both the fruitful paths and the dead-ends, the manner in which questions were formulated and answers sought" (Levi 2012, 125). In that spirit, let me tell you about my quest to know more about Garrison.

I have been involved with writing centers—as a tutor, director, or researcher—pretty much continuously since 1986 when I was hired as an MA student to tutor in the San Jose State University Writing Center. At the time, we were working with students in basic writing classes who were assigned to the writing center for an extra instructional hour each week, a fairly common model in place then and now. Those basic writing students—a mix of San Jose-area Latinos, what later came to be labeled Generation 1.5 students, and international students largely recruited for the basketball team—were assigned grammar-and-usage worksheets from *The Least You Should Know about English* (currently in print in its eleventh edition) as well as a writing prompt to which they needed to write a paragraph each week. I was never quite sure of the connection between this work and what was happening in their classrooms, and I never asked. We usually split that hour in two: thirty minutes on the language-level exercises, thirty minutes responding to students' paragraphs. I saw quite a few students develop mastery of those exercises, but then the language-level errors they seemingly mastered would show up in their paragraphs. And I saw the opposite: students whose paragraphs were relatively error free struggled to complete the exercises. I learned then of the futility of decontextualized language-level exercise and of their ubiquity in the teaching of English, particularly for basic writing students. It was one of several contradictions that would complicate my understanding of the enterprise of teaching writing.

Some years later, I was enrolled in a doctorate-in-education program, taking a course on the history of urban schooling. That faculty member, a sociologist, offered the advice that to understand a reform one needs to go back to the start, to the original reformers and try to understand what their intent might have been. In education in particular, the force of the status quo powerfully blunts reform, often altering it into an unrecognizable version over time. I view the efforts to champion a one-to-one method of teaching writing, whether in a student-teacher conference, in a classroom, or in a writing center (or lab or clinic or whatever the appellation might have been) as one such reform, particularly in reaction to the lecture-recitation pedagogy that dominated rhetoric/composition classrooms into the late nineteenth century (Kitzhaber 1990). As I have somewhat obsessively looked into the history of writing centers, tracing them to "laboratory methods" of writing instruction that were part of a larger movement toward one-to-one instruction starting in the 1890s (Lerner 2009), I have found a history much more complex and much more nuanced than that often told in contemporary publications. Thus, rather than a dark past of drill-and-kill exercises followed by a bright present of liberatory pedagogy and alternative spaces for learning, writing center history is filled with figures who believed in both—or neither—another contradiction to complicate matters.

I suppose I collect historical figures in writing center studies, the normal exceptions, ones that come up in the occasional publication or reference but about whom we know little. One such figure was Robert H. Moore (1950), a graduate student at the University of Illinois who directed its writing clinic in the late 1940s and published "The Writing Clinic and the Writing Laboratory" in *College English* in 1950, an article that has often been cited by contemporary writing center scholars as a key indicator of those bad old days (e.g., Murphy and Law 1995). After some initial correspondence with the archivist at Illinois, I learned enough to be hopeful that material on Moore and his writing clinic existed and to make it worth my while to travel to those archives, where I spent two full days reading through committee notes, annual reports, and college catalogs and directories and retracing Moore's steps in Champagne/Urbana in the 1940s. The story I told from that research (Lerner 2001) was of a writing clinic that existed from 1940 until the mid 1980s, one that filled a comfortable niche in the English department, largely a one-person operation that long outlasted Moore and offered students the interaction and support familiar to contemporary writing centers. The bad old days, then, weren't necessarily so bad.

Garrison is another figure, but unlike Moore, Garrison seemed to be venerated in writing center studies. His 1974 article, "Teaching One-to-One," came up repeatedly as I explored writing center history, and I also knew he had been one of the ten writers Thomas J. Reigstad described in his 1980 dissertation on writing-conference pedagogies. But I knew little more. Thus, on a bright June day, I made my way from Boston to the University of New England in Portland, Maine, where I had made previous e-mail contact with the archivist confirming that they did, indeed, have two boxes of material on Garrison from when the campus was Westbrook College (Westbrook and UNE merged in 1996). For several hours, I went through correspondence, brochures, announcements, and newspaper clippings documenting Garrison's career at Westbrook. The library staff served me lunch. They gave me a signed copy of a pictorial history of the college (Bibber 2009). And then I looked at materials some more.

WHAT I KNOW ABOUT ROGER GARRISON

Let me tell you what I learned about Garrison from my archival research and from his published works. He was born in 1918 and was an undergraduate at Oberlin College, a World War II veteran, and a journalist for *Life Magazine* before starting his academic career in 1947 as English department chair at Briarcliff College in Briarcliff Manor, New York. In 1967, Garrison joined the English faculty at Westbrook, where he would teach until his death during coronary bypass surgery in 1984.

I also learned that Garrison did not always toil in obscurity; his work was not merely "oral and embodied," as Moran had described. He published his first textbook, *A Creative Approach to Writing*, in 1951 and then offered guidance to new college students with *The Adventure of Learning in College: An Undergraduate Guide to Productive Study* in 1959 (Garrison 1951, 1959). His 1981 textbook for college writers, *How a Writer Works*, was reviewed by former 4Cs conference chair Chris Anson in *Indiana English* that year. A revised edition of *How a Writer Works* was published shortly after Garrison's death in 1985, and the book was reprinted in 1997 under Longman and is still available on Amazon.com. As Amazon reviewer Dennis P. Quinn reports, "Garrison's is a fine book for students or more experienced writers, one of the very best."

In the early 1980s, there was much talk in the professional literature of the Garrison method of composition instruction, a conferencing approach adopted at many institutions after Garrison's description of that method published in his 1974 monograph and again in his 1981 textbook. Perhaps most visible was Jo An McGuire Simmons's 1984 *College Composition and Communication* article, "The One-to-One Method of Teaching Composition," in which she writes that "after a semester of using Garrison's method, most teachers find that holding regular conferences is creative and enjoyable" (229). And Garrison himself did occupy some status within composition studies at the time; he was included, as I noted previously, as one of the ten professional writers whose process was analyzed in Reigstad's 1980 dissertation *Conferencing Practices of Professional Writers*, and he was asked to contribute to Coles and Vopat's (1985) *What Makes Writing Good*, a collection of student essays framed by the instructor's assignment and a brief analysis of why the instructor chose that essay. Garrison's contribution to that 1985 volume sits among many luminaries of the field, including Nell Ann Pickett, Toby Fulwiler, James Britton, Edward Corbett, Erika Lindemann, James Sledd, Andrea Lunsford, and, of course, Murray. Here's what Garrison says in his piece about "good writing": "Good writing is inevitably honest writing. Every writer, beginner or not, needs what Hemingway called 'a built-in crap detector.' All of us, like it or not, are daily immersed in tides of phony, posturing, pretentious, tired, imprecise, slovenly language, which both suffocate and corrupt the mind. . . . Academics haven't helped honest writing much either. If I read 'outcome,' 'cognitive,' 'interact,' 'heuristic,' or 'viable' many more times, I shall throw up" (Garrison 1985, 273).

In many of his publications, Garrison calls for a kind of clear, honest writing he sees as the hallmark of how he was trained as a journalist; his extolling of conferencing methods is simply how he believes journalists learn to write in the presence of a managing editor. As Garrison describes in "One-to-One," "The *most* effective teaching method is one-to-one: tutorial, or editor-to-writer. The student brings his work-in-progress to the face-to-face session; and you, the teacher-editor, bring analytical reading, judgment, diagnosis, and suggestions for further action by the student" (Garrison 1974, 69). Or as he offers in *How a Writer Works*: "This is a short book—deliberately. There is just so much to be said about writing: the rest is elaboration and fancywork. If you want to learn to write, *do it*" (Garrison 1981, 1).

In Garrison's scheme, the classroom is like a bustling newsroom, with each student writer busily drafting and redrafting and coming up to the teacher for quick, focused conferences or feedback. In this setup, Garrison imagined up to thirty-five students at a time could productively learn to write under the tutelage of the teacher-editor. In an unpublished manuscript titled "Why Can't Our Students Write?" Garrison elaborated on the teacher's classroom responsibilities: "Your role: read quickly, respond verbally, as your students struggle to say what they mean. You do not need to take endless stacks of papers home to comment on, grade, and return 'sometime later.' You are teaching a process, not a subject. The feedback loop should be kept close, immediate, person-to-person. You can do this once you recognize that what your students need is an audience, not a judge" (Garrison n.d., 9).

These ideas of teaching writing as a process were central to Garrison's approach, easily woven into the fabric of the process movement of the late 1970s and early 1980s. Garrison, however, was not taking a research interest in students as writers nor a theoretical approach to understand the relationship between writing and knowledge making. Instead, Garrison offered a pragmatic, from-the-newsroom approach, roll up your sleeves and get to work, stop your complaining. In Garrison's words, "Writing is a process: it is not a product to be studied, analyzed, and imitated. We learn to express ourselves on paper by trying to say what we mean; by revising what we have tried; revising again, working to be clear—again and again. Revising (*re*-vision–seeing again) is the basic tool for learning to write. Thus, writing is largely self-taught" (Garrison n.d., 6).

There's a powerful appeal to this approach, one that many writing teachers might identify in their histories as writers, a seductive simplicity that echoes Elbow's (1973) *Writing without Teachers*. But perhaps 1984, the year of Garrison's death, was also a turning point for our trusting students to have something to say. In a *CCC* review of Garrison's book *How a Writer Works*, Katherine H. Adams noted that "[Garrison's] assumption that students begin with something to say and require no aid with invention or motivation does not suit the reality of our freshman sections. Thus Garrison's manual and method may prove of more value to the teacher than his book to the student" (Adams 1984, 248).

THE GARRISON ONE-ON-ONE METHOD

While Garrison's approach was extolled in the late 1970s and early 1980s for its benefits to student learning and teacher creativity, it was not necessarily a model of student-centered learning. Lad Tobin characterizes the Garrison method as "first generation" writing conferences with the teacher clearly in control of agenda setting, timing, and content, while he describes Murray's approach as "second generation," which "focused more on questions than on answers, more on structural issues than superficial problems" (Tobin 1990, 98).[1]

Reigstad provides direct evidence of Garrison's technique based on observations of four conferences as well as on postconference interviews with Garrison and his students. Here's how Reigstad described what he saw: "[Garrison] maintained a teacher-to-student relationship with students, although the climate was not particularly formal. The predominant teacher-student (rather than conversant-conversant) pose can be seen in the various types of tutor roles that Garrison adopted during the conferences: initiator, rule giver, expert, evaluator, interested reader, and partner in writing. . . . Perhaps the most common role adopted by Garrison was that of expert. As expert, he would identify a writing problem and either prescribe a solution or correct it himself" (Reigstad 1980, 84–85). Reigstad also found that Garrison focused primarily on students' syntactical issues in their papers rather than on larger rhetorical concerns. In interviews following conferences, "Garrison's students mentioned how during conferences he would usually tell them when they had committed errors, correct them by writing on their papers, and explain 'how to fix it'" (89). This largely language-level and teacher-centered approach is not quite state of the art when it comes to that recommended in writing center literature, where higher-order concerns (versus lower-order concerns, both terms coined by Reigstad and McAndrew 1984) and a student-centered approach are recommended.

Thus, as I pointed out earlier, my intention in this chapter is not to recover Garrison for what he might contribute to the ways we teach writing in classrooms, writing centers, our offices, or cafes. While elements of his approach certainly are useful, particularly the intensity and focus of brief conferences (Geller et al. 2007, 35), other aspects born of a newsroom editor-cub reporter model clearly would not work for a great number of students, and there's an overall narrowness to the genres he offers in *How Writing Works*, with an overall emphasis on essayist prose. Many of these same charges, however, might be leveled against Murray's contributions to the one-to-one teaching of writing, despite Tobin's (1990) placement of Murray's method as more highly evolved. Still, based on the citation record, Garrison did hit an evolutionary dead end of sorts.

MURRAY VERSUS GARRISON

After 1984, Garrison largely faded from view in composition's literature, whether referenced in contemporary accounts or in historical ones. Here is a checklist of the historical studies:

TABLE 8.1

SOURCE	# OF REFERENCES TO GARRISON
Berlin (1987), *Rhetoric and Reality: Writing Instruction in American Colleges, 1900–1985*	0
Connors (1997), *Composition-Rhetoric: Backgrounds, Theory, and Pedagogy*	0
Crowley (1998), *Composition in the University: Historical and Polemical Essays*	0
Goggin (2000), *Authoring a Discipline: Scholarly Journals and the Post-World War II Emergence of Rhetoric and Composition*	0
North (1987), *The Making of Knowledge in Composition: Portrait of an Emerging Field*	0

In the collection *Taking Stock: The Writing Process Movement in the '90s* in which Moran's description of Garrison's influence on the UMass Amherst Writing Program appears, only one other contributor makes reference to Garrison: Thomas Newkirk, a UNH faculty member, notes that the in-class conferencing Barrett Wendell designed at Harvard in the 1890s was similar to that "popularized by Roger Garrison eighty years later" (Newkirk 1994, 125).

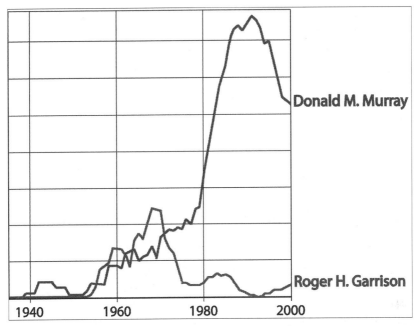

Figure 8.1. Google Ngram results for "Donald M. Murray" and "Roger H. Garrison."

In writing-center-related publications from the 1970s and 1980s, Garrison fares somewhat better, getting referenced in Muriel Harris's (1982, 1986) *Tutoring Writing: A Sourcebook for Writing Labs* and *Teaching One-to-One: The Writing Conference,* Steward and Croft's (1982) *The Writing Laboratory: Organization, Management and Methods;* Laque and Sherwood's (1977) *A Laboratory Approach to Writing;* and Reigstad and McAndrew's (1984) *Training Tutors for Writing Conferences.* However, my check of comppile.org produced only three references to Garrison since 1984 while I found eighteen references to Murray since that time. A search in Google books via the ngram viewer (https://books.google.com/ngrams) for "Donald M. Murray" and "Roger H. Garrison" offers a visual depiction of one figure rising to great heights, the other falling after a brief intersection at around 1974, the year Garrison's "One-to-One" article appeared.

Amazon.com currently reports that Murray's 1985 edition of *A Writer Teaches Writing* ranks 794,227 among the bestsellers while Garrison's *How a Writer Works,* revised edition, ranks 1,463,309. The marketplace has spoken, I suppose.

In composition studies, then, citing Murray and not Garrison is a common pattern. However, when one looks beyond the world of composition studies for the relative influence of these two figures, a different picture emerges. After all, composition scholarship is only one slice of our professional worlds, albeit one with visibility and star-making potential not always possible in other kinds of work. Garrison ardently pursued those other kinds of work.

GARRISON AND THE MASTER-TEACHER SEMINAR

Starting in 1973, Garrison teamed up with two University of New Hampshire faculty to offer a summer workshop for community college English teachers. The initial announcement from the Westbrook College *Alumnae News* reads as follows:

> The University of New Hampshire and Westbrook College will initiate a cooperative "first" this summer when the two institutions combine to offer a four-week institute for English instructors in community and junior colleges throughout the country. Co-directors of the institute are Professor Terence Logan, Assistant Provost of the University of New Hampshire and Roger Garrison of the Westbrook faculty. The project has been financed by the U.S. Office of Education in a grant given jointly to the University and Westbrook.
>
> Dates for the institute are June 17th through July 10th, with the week of June 17th being spent on the Westbrook campus, followed by three weeks on the University campus in Durham. About 35 participants are expected to attend representing colleges from a cross-section of the United States.
>
> Four weeks of intensive study will be concentrated upon two major concerns of English instructors at colleges generally: effective teaching of composition and the teaching of literature in basic college English courses.
>
> It is hoped that a successful first summer institute will lead to more cooperative efforts between the University of New Hampshire and Westbrook.

Four years later, the workshop was reduced to two weeks, but the number of participants more than doubled as seen in the June 6, 1977, announcement from Westbrook College News Service, Office of College Relations: "Teachers of English from community colleges throughout the country will attend a two-week institute on "How to Teach Writing—Better," hosted by Westbrook College, June 16–29. Now in its fifth year, this special institute is sponsored by Westbrook College and the University of New Hampshire and draws some 80 participants from both the US and Canada." In a letter Garrison sent to community college English department chairs around the country that year to recruit participants, he stressed the focus on Garrison methods: "The Institute emphasizes the *process* of teaching writing; the development of the instructor's skill in diagnosis, prescription, and guidance, especially for marginal students more than he typically can using traditional methods. For example, teachers will learn how to manage the instruction-learning situation so that they will *never again* have to take home papers to be corrected. And their students' writing productivity should be almost double what is usual." According to Mary Sue Koeppel (2005), who had participated in and then co-led a Garrison summer workshop, these workshops ran for eleven years under Garrison's leadership. After his death in 1984, they were continued by teachers who had worked under Garrison and ran until 1994. These summer workshops, begun the year before James Gray formed what would become the National Writing Project's summer institutes to K–12 teachers (http://www.nwp.org/cs/public/print/doc/about/history.csp), exposed hundreds of community college English teachers to the Garrison methods of teaching writing.

Garrison's work with community college colleagues was not limited to supporting writing teachers. In 1969, Garrison founded a more general master teaching seminar, which has run continuously since then and has now branched out to multiple seminars run each summer in several states. In 2014, eight Great Teacher Seminars were offered in six US locations and two in Canada (http://ngtm.net/2014-events/). The 2014 Arizona Master Teacher Seminar offers in its description the links back to Garrison.

> The sole aim of the seminar is the practical exploration of ways to improve teaching. Roger Garrison founded the original seminar on the beliefs that:
>
> - Much excellent teaching takes place in American higher education
> - Teachers who are striving toward mastery of their craft have much to share with others
> - Bringing teachers together in a relaxed, informal atmosphere to share their successes and their problems will enhance the skills of all. (http://mcli.maricopa.edu/masterteacher)

Garrison's reach, then, is monumental when one considers the number of teachers who either participated in a summer seminar, learned from another teacher participant, or were influenced by reading an account from those participants. Koeppel, writing over twenty years after Garrison's death, describes this impact: "Garrison affected, directly or indirectly, thousands of community-college faculty. They in turn, affected tens of thousands of community-college students. Thus,

Garrison reaches us still" (Koeppel 2005, 95). In composition studies, of course, that reach is largely invisible.[2]

REMEMBERING, FORGETTING, AND GENEALOGY

My speculation on the reasons for composition studies' collective forgetting of Garrison leads to at least three questions.

1. Did conferencing methods of teaching writing fall out of favor after the mid 1980s? Garrison's consistent attention to the one-to-one practices of teaching—the interactions between teachers and student writers and the interactions between students and their texts—perhaps slipped out of the mainstream after 1984. However, this explanation seems doubtful given Murray's popularity and the fact that Murray similarly extolled the virtues of teacher-student conferences. Perhaps if Garrison had been more Murray-like, more of us would have heard of him, hold him in high regard, and return to his ideas for inspiration and guidance. But perhaps being more Murray-like would not have been enough. In a remembrance published in *College English* after Murray's death in 2007, his former UNH student Bruce Ballenger (2008) recalls that as early as 1991, Murray found it difficult to publish his "Murrayesque" essays in mainstream composition journals, being told that his writing lacked the "generalizations and theoretical moves" mainstream composition scholarship seemingly required (297). Ballenger offers a "reconsideration" of Murray in that article, a caution not to reject the "pedagogy of surprise" but instead to follow Murray's urgings for writers to learn by writing and to share that writing with others. There's no mention of Garrison in Ballenger's reflection, but that, at least, is not a surprise.

2. Was Garrison's personality off-putting? At the start of this chapter, I offered one of Moran's contrasts between Garrison and Murray: "Garrison was a self-styled outsider and iconoclast, a person who deliberately remained outside the growing community of scholars in the field; Murray was, and is, a generous and sociable man who moves comfortably in the world of professional conferences" (Moran 1994, 137). Moran admits, however, that he never met Garrison. Koeppel, who worked with Garrison on his Master Teacher Seminars for several years, opens her chapter with this description: "Picture a gray-bearded, curly-haired man in lumberjack-plaid shirt sitting at a baby grand piano pounding out Beethoven's 'Apassionata,' tears streaming down his cheeks, foot stamping on the soft pedal. That was Roger H. Garrison to hundreds and hundreds of community-college faculty" (Koeppel 2005, 90). One person's "outsider" is another person's (or, more accurately, thousands of people's) mentor.

3. Does composition studies' genealogical reconstruction narrow blood-
   lines and limit possibilities? One likely explanation for the differences between Murray and Garrison is genealogical—as I noted earlier,
   Murray taught for many years at the University of New Hampshire, a
   PhD-granting institution, and thus Murray was in a position to be a
   strong genealogical influence on UNH-trained compositionists (and,
   subsequently, on their graduate students). Garrison spent his entire
   career at two-year colleges and could only have offered that influence through his publications. Still, his lack of "impact factor" is an
   all-too-common phenomenon in composition studies when it comes
   to forgetting to include the contributions of our two-year college colleagues (Tinberg 2006).

Genealogical explanations, however, don't quite get at the processes
of remembering and forgetting (or not knowing in the first place) that
seems to govern our knowledge of composition's history. Ginzburg
reminds us that "all phases through which research unfolds are constructed and not given: the identification of the object and its importance; the elaboration of the categories through which it is analyzed; the
criteria for proof; the stylistic and narrative forms by which the results
are transmitted to the reader" (Ginzburg 1993, 32). Constructing genealogies are one example of this social process. Sid Dobrin (2011) is
particularly critical of the essential conservative mechanisms of genealogical projects. In referring to a Writing Program Administrator listserv
discussion of genealogical roots (likely referring to the CUNY Graduate
Center's Writing Studies Tree project http://writingstudiestree.org),
Dobrin writes that "the conversation smacked of elitism, of lineage, of
royalty, of dynasty. More to the point, the conversation was an attempt
to validate through bloodline. . . . This desire to seek identity in the
traceable lineage of 'golden' compositionists is precisely the kind of
conversation that hampers any sort of move beyond composition studies' limit-situation by refusing to align the work of administration with
potential in favor of aligning with historical narrative, looking aft instead
of fore. Yet this attempt to validate through ancestry lacked any real critical attention to the homogenizing effect of the conversation" (Dobrin
2011, 101–2).

However, genealogical projects do not necessarily have to equal a
purification process. Instead, they can represent an attempt to expand
our knowledge of influences, both direct and indirect. I am reminded of
two of my influences from my MA in English program in the late 1980s
at San Jose State University. One was Hans Guth, a relative "star" in composition in the 1960s, perhaps best known for copresenting at Humor

Night at the annual CCCC convention for many years and cofounder of the annual Young Rhetoricians' Conference (http://youngrhetoriciansconference.com/). Another was Gabrielle Rico (1983), author of *Writing the Natural Way*, an influential text in the 1980s in its emphasis on brain research and creativity as essential to writing, and cofounder of the YRC with Guth. Neither Guth nor Rico figures prominently in the citation history of our field (Comppile.org shows no entries for Guth after 1985; Rico has six entries in that time, including one for a revised edition of *Writing the Natural Way*). Nevertheless, their influence on me is unmistakable and one I have not mentioned in print until this very moment.

The narrowing of perspective is very difficult to resist in the overall processes of memory and forgetting, particularly in the need to construct a coherent narrative of our past. Coherency, of course, potentially works against the project of microhistory and a focus on what has been forgotten or on the exceptional normal. Judith Halberstam writes about the necessity of resisting normalizing historical narratives: "Generational logic underpins our investments in the dialectic of memory and forgetting; we tend to organize the chaotic process of historical change by anchoring it to an idea of generational shifts (from father to son), and we obscure questions about the arbitrariness of memory and the necessity of forgetting by falling back on some notion of the inevitable force of progression and succession" (Halberstam 2011, 69). Certainly, composition studies is replete with efforts to begin again, to break from past practices, whether those are current-traditional paradigms of teaching or sectioning of students into "hospital English." However, this rejection of the past can be far too broad, taking up in its sweep influences such as Garrison. Further, when this remembering and forgetting seems strongly correlated to privilege—we remember our colleagues from four-year and PhD-granting institutions but forget contributors from two-year institutions—we seem ripe for charges of elitism and for creating a troubling star-making apparatus that rewards just a few.

What I am calling for, then, is a process of critically remembering. We should remember, acknowledge, and think critically about our forebears, understanding how their efforts might help us better understand what we do. But, perhaps more important, we need to expand our notions of who is included in our discipline, whom we should remember, who are the exceptional normal, whose stories, practices, theories, and research could help us navigate the uncertain future. Who has influenced us individually and how might we acknowledge those influences? What could we learn from the thousands of community college teachers affected by Garrison's summer seminars? What might our disciplinary identity look like if we focus less on the star players and more on those who contribute in a wide variety of ways in a wide variety of contexts?

Ultimately, whom we choose to remember is a reflection of our disciplinary values. We can we see our work as represented only by our stars or by the great many who have contributed. We can represent our discipline as primarily focused on first-year writing classes in four-year colleges and universities or we can turn our attention to two-year institutions and writing in classrooms outside of writing programs as well as in nonclassroom and community contexts, such as writing centers or wherever student writers go for instruction and feedback, whether physical or virtual locations. That few in composition studies have heard of Garrison might say more about us than what it says about him. We can find many more Garrisons if we choose to look.[3]

Notes

1. Tobin's (1990) timeline of Garrison as representative of first-generation student-teacher writing conferences is not quite accurate given the long history of writing teachers extolling the benefits of one-to-one conferencing (see Lerner 2005).

2. This invisibility might also be a consequence of the relative lack of structure of the Great Teacher Seminars. As described on their website (http://ngtm.net/about-the-ngtm/),

> the National Great Teachers Movement is called a "movement" because it is not associated with, nor does it constitute a corporation or an organization of any kind. Thus, it serves no institutional or commercial interests. There is no headquarters or address, and there are no officials, owners, employees or politics. There are no manuals or handbooks, only a few simple guidelines.
>
> Everything is passed on by oral tradition in order to prevent the development of any form of true-believership or fixed procedure which might come to be followed to the letter and of which the educational profession would soon tire. The many annual Great Teachers Seminars throughout North America, and now in several foreign countries, exist and persist only because of the initiative and selfless ambition of people who want to share the experience with teachers in their own geographic area. (Gottshall 2014)

3. Many thanks to Roberta Gray of the University of New England for her gracious hosting of me during my time in the Westbrook College archives, as well as to the rest of the library staff for their hospitality. Also, I am grateful to Andrea Scott, Michele Eodice, Steve Price, Kerri Jordan, and Bruce McComiskey for feedback on earlier versions of this chapter. Finally, thanks to *The Writing Center Journal* 2014 Virtual Writing Retreat participants for their support and encouragement.

References

Adams, Katherine H. 1984. "Review of *How a Writer Works*." *College Composition and Communication* 35 (2): 247–48. http://dx.doi.org/10.2307/358106.

Ballenger, Bruce. 2008. "Reconsiderations: Donald Murray and the Pedagogy of Surprise." *College English* 70 (3): 209–303.

Berlin, James. 1987. *Rhetoric and Reality: Writing Instruction in American Colleges, 1900–1985*. Carbondale: Southern Illinois University Press.

Bibber, Joyce K. 2009. *The Campus History Series: Westbrook College Campus*. Charleston, SC: Arcadia.

Coles, William E. Jr., and James Vopat. 1985. *What Makes Writing Good*. Lexington, MA: D.C. Heath.

Connors, Robert J. 1997. *Composition-Rhetoric: Backgrounds, Theory, and Pedagogy*. Pittsburgh, PA: University of Pittsburgh Press.

Crowley, Sharon. 1998. *Composition in the University: Historical and Polemical Essays*. Pittsburgh, PA: University of Pittsburgh Press.

Dobrin, Sidney I. 2011. *Postcomposition*. Carbondale: Southern Illinois University Press.

Donahue, Patricia, and Gretchen Flesher Moon, eds. 2007. *Local Histories: Reading the Archives of Composition*. Pittsburgh, PA: University of Pittsburgh Press.

Elbow, Peter. 1973. *Writing Without Teachers*. New York: Oxford University Press.

Fleming, David. 2011. *From Form to Meaning: Freshman Composition and the Long Sixties, 1957–1974*. Pittsburgh, PA: Pittsburgh University Press.

Garrison, Roger H. 1951. *A Creative Approach to Writing*. New York: Holt.

Garrison, Roger H. 1959. *The Adventure of Learning in College*. New York: Harper.

Garrison, Roger H. 1974. "One-to-One: Tutorial Instruction in Freshman Composition." *New Directions for Community Colleges: Implementing Innovative Instruction* 5 (5): 55–84. http://dx.doi.org/10.1002/cc.36819740509.

Garrison, Roger H. 1981. *How a Writer Works*. New York: Harper & Row.

Garrison, Roger H. 1985. *How a Writer Works*. Rev. ed. New York: Addison, Wesley, Longman.

Garrison, Roger H. n.d. "Why Can't Our Students Write?" Westbrook College Archives. Portland, ME.

Geller, Anne Ellen, Michele Eodice, Frankie Condon, Meg Carroll, and Elizabeth H. Boquet. 2007. *The Everyday Writing Center: A Community of Practice*. Logan: Utah State University Press.

Ginzburg, Carlo, and Carlo Poni. 1991. "The Name and the Game: Unequal Exchange and the Historiographic Marketplace." In *Microhistory and the Lost Peoples of Europe*, edited by Edward Muir and Guido Ruggiero, 1–10. Baltimore, MD: Johns Hopkins University Press.

Ginzburg, Carlo. 1993. Trans. John Tedeschi and Anne C. Tedeschi. "Microhistory: Two or Three Things That I Know about It." *Critical Inquiry* 20 (1): 10–35. http://dx.doi.org/10.1086/448699.

Goggin, Maureen Daly. 2000. *Authoring a Discipline: Scholarly Journals and the Post-World War II Emergence of Rhetoric and Composition*. Mahwah, NJ: Lawrence Erlbaum.

Gold, David. 2008. *Rhetoric at the Margins: Revising the History of Writing Instruction in American Colleges, 1873–1947*. Carbondale: Southern Illinois University Press.

Gottshall, David B. 2014. "About the NGTM." Official Web Niche of the National Great Teachers Movement. http://ngtm.net/about-the-ngtm/.

Halberstam, Judith. 2011. *The Queer Art of Failure*. Durham, NC: Duke University Press. http://dx.doi.org/10.1215/9780822394358.

Harris, Muriel. 1982. *Tutoring Writing: A Sourcebook for Writing Labs*. Glenview, IL: Scott, Foresman.

Harris, Muriel. 1986. *Teaching One-to-One: The Writing Conference*. Urbana, IL: NCTE.

Kitzhaber, Albert R. 1990. *Rhetoric in American Colleges, 1850–1900.* Dallas: Southern Methodist University Press.

Koeppel, Mary Sue. 2005. "Roger Garrison (1918–1984): Teacher of Teachers." In *The Profession of English in the 2-Year College,* edited by Mark Reynolds and Sylvia Holladay-Hicks, 90–97. Portsmouth, NH: Heinemann.

Laque, Carol Feiser, and Phyllis A. Sherwood. 1977. *A Laboratory Approach to Writing.* Urbana, IL: NCTE.

Lepenies, Wolf, and Peter Weingart. 1983. Introduction to *Functions and Uses of Disciplinary Histories.* Vol. 7. Edited by Loren Graham, Wolf Lepenies, and Peter Weingart, ix–xx. Dordrecht, Holland: D. Reidel.

Lepore, Jill. 2001. "Historians Who Love Too Much: Reflections on Microhistory and Biography." *Journal of American History* 88 (1): 129–44. http://dx.doi.org/10.2307 /2674921.

Lerner, Neal. 2001. "Searching for Robert Moore." *Writing Center Journal* 22 (1): 9–32.

Lerner, Neal. 2005. "The Teacher-Student Writing Conference and the Desire for Intimacy." *College English* 68 (2): 186–208. http://dx.doi.org/10.2307/30044673.

Lerner, Neal. 2009. *The Idea of a Writing Laboratory.* Urbana: Southern Illinois University Press.

Levi, Giovanni. 2012. "Microhistory and the Recovery of Complexity." In *Historical Knowledge: In Quest of Theory, Method, and Evidence,* edited by Susanna Fellman and Marjatta Rahikainen, 121–32. London: Cambridge Scholars.

Magnússon, Sigurður Gylfi, and István Szijártó. 2013. *What Is Microhistory? Theory and Practice.* New York: Routledge.

Moore, Robert H. 1950. "The Writing Clinic and the Writing Laboratory." *College English* 11 (7): 388–93. http://dx.doi.org/10.2307/586024.

Moran, Charles. 1994. "How the Writing Process Came to UMass/Amherst: Roger Garrison, Donald Murray, and Institutional Change." In *Taking Stock: The Writing Process Movement in the '90s,* edited by Lad Tobin and Thomas Newkirk, 133–52. Portsmouth, NH: Heinemann.

Murphy, Christina, and Joe Law, eds. 1995. *Landmark Essays on Writing Centers.* Davis, CA: Hermagoras.

Murray, Donald M. 1985. *A Writer Teaches Writing.* 2nd ed. Boston, MA: Houghton Mifflin Harcourt.

Newkirk, Thomas. 1994. "The Politics of Intimacy: The Defeat of Barrett Wendell at Harvard." In *Taking Stock: The Writing Process Movement in the '90s,* edited by Lad Tobin and Thomas Newkirk, 115–32. Portsmouth, NH: Heinemann.

North, Stephen M. 1987. *The Making of Knowledge in Composition: Portrait of an Emerging Field.* Upper Montclair, NJ: Boynton/Cook.

Reigstad, Thomas J. 1980. *Conferencing Practices of Professional Writers: Ten Case Studies.* PhD diss., SUNY Buffalo.

Reigstad, Thomas J., and Donald A. McAndrew. 1984. *Training Tutors for Writing Conferences.* Urbana, IL: NCTE.

Rico, Gabrielle. 1983. *Writing the Natural Way.* Los Angeles: J. P. Tarcher.

Ritter, Kelly. 2009. *Before Shaughnessy: Basic Writing at Yale and Harvard, 1920–1960.* Carbondale: Southern Illinois University Press.

Simmons, Jo An McGuire. 1984. "The One-to-One Method of Teaching Composition." *College Composition and Communication* 35 (2): 222–29. http://dx.doi.org/10.2307 /358099.

Steward, Joyce S., and Mary K. Croft. 1982. *The Writing Laboratory: Organization, Management and Methods.* Glenview, IL: Scott Foresman.

Tinberg, Howard. 2006. "In the Land of the Cited." *Pedagogy* 6 (3): 397–403. http:// dx.doi.org/10.1215/15314200-2006-002.

Tobin, Lad. 1990. "Productive Tension in the Writing Conference: Studying Our Students and Ourselves." In *To Compose: Teaching Writing in High School and College.* 2nd ed. Edited by Thomas Newkirk, 95–112. Portsmouth, NH: Heinemann.

Varnum, Robin. 1996. *Fencing with Words: A History of Writing Instruction at Amherst College During the Era of Theodore Baird, 1938–1966.* Urbana, IL: NCTE.

9
ELIZABETH ERVIN AND THE CHALLENGE OF CIVIC ENGAGEMENT
A Composition and Rhetoric Teacher's
Struggle to Make Writing Matter

David Gold

In 1997, Elizabeth Ervin, a young composition scholar at the University of North Carolina Wilmington (UNCW), published an enthusiastic call in *Rhetoric Review* for teaching citizenship through writing. In that article, "Encouraging Civic Participation among First-Year Writing Students," Ervin optimistically engages with the then-emergent public turn in composition studies by detailing her efforts at having her composition students "take a public stand" (384) on issues that matter. This work would eventually lead to a 2000 textbook, *Public Literacy* (Ervin 2000b), aimed at helping students write in various public genres for the purpose of "getting things done in the world" (v).

Roughly a decade later, in a 2006 *College English* essay, "Teaching Public Literacy: The Partisanship Problem," Ervin sounds a more cautious note. Having found students resistant to politically charged discourse, she now advocates for teaching what she terms a "publicist rhetorical orientation" in which the "particular content of . . . issues is largely immaterial" (Ervin 2006b, 412). In the following year's "Composition and the Gentrification of 'Public Literacy'" for the volume *The Locations of Composition*, she questions whether our field's interest in public discourse emerged less out of a genuine commitment to civic engagement than out of "disciplinary ennui" (Ervin 2007, 38).

What would make this dedicated and theoretically well-grounded teacher-scholar step back from her earlier claims? How do we get from public writing to publicist writing? And what does such a shift signal for our field? In this essay, I seek to address these questions through a microhistorical examination of Ervin's scholarship over the arc of her career, from one of her first scholarly publications in 1991 to her last in

DOI: 10.7330/9781607324058.c009

2007. Though Ervin is not as well known as she might be—she spent her career at a teaching college without an English PhD program and she died young, at the age of forty-three in 2008—she grappled with some of the most compelling pedagogical issues of her day, and she demonstrates the larger struggle of how individual instructors come to terms with emerging rhetoric and composition theory as well as how that theory evolves in the crucible of classroom practice.

As a microhistorical examination, this work rests on two key theoretical foundations. Foremost is the assumption of Ervin's agency as a historical actor and, by extension, that of other classroom teachers, past and present, wrestling with the pedagogical issues of their day. Within rhetoric and composition historiography, we have had a tendency to occasionally treat teachers as victims of ideology and historical circumstance and students as passive victims of their contemporary culture, a legacy of the influence on our field of cultural studies and critical theory in the 1980s and 1990s (see Gold 2012). Microhistorians, in contrast, tend to be suspicious of the deterministic force of ideologies and social structures. For Giovanni Levi, "A more realistic description" of human behavior recognizes "a normative reality which, though pervasive, nevertheless offers many possibilities for personal interpretations and freedoms" (Levi 2001, 98–99). Or, as István M. Szijártó bluntly puts it, individuals "are not merely puppets on the hands of great underlying forces of history" but "conscious actors" (Szijártó 2013, 5). Though Ervin was certainly influenced by and even subject to the pedagogical trends of her day, her scholarship evidences a self-aware individual continually reflecting on her own subjectivity and ideological position.

Second is the assumption that small-scale observation, at the level of the individual or small group, location, or event, can yield insights into larger historical questions. This does not mean that the objects of microhistorical study are necessarily representative figures yielding coherent, systematic narratives. But central to microhistorical approaches is the attempt to capture the lived experiences of individuals. Writes Edward Muir, "The purpose of microhistory is to elucidate historical causation on the level . . . where most of real life takes place and to open history to peoples who would be left out by other methods" (Muir 1991, xxi).[1] This is also the level at which "the complexity of the past" can best "be represented for readers," as it is the level "where both the actors and these readers live their lives" (Szijártó 2013, 7). Over the course of her career, Ervin produced a remarkable body of work, largely in the form of self-reflective teacher narratives; documenting in steady chronological detail the lived experience of her pedagogical journey, these documents lend themselves particularly well to microhistorical examination.[2]

As Ervin came to understand, the (re)discovery of rhetoric has not solved the problem of the subject of the composition classroom, and as a field we continue to struggle with the teaching of public argument. Indeed, Amy Wan has recently charged our field with fostering sometimes shallow articulations of the link between "writing instruction" and "the preparation of good citizens" (Wan 2011, 28). Far from participating in a mere "rote invocation of citizenship," however, Ervin continually reflected on the meaning and limits of citizenship education, anticipating Wan's call to "create a space where our own citizen-making through the teaching of literacy is a more deliberate activity" (46). By examining how one instructor wrestled with and reconciled these issues over the arc of her own career, we might find lessons for our own.

LOCATING ELIZABETH ERVIN

For many readers of this volume, Ervin may not be household name. Though she was a prolific writer, she is not as widely read as she might be, in part, perhaps, because she never published a research monograph and certainly because of her untimely death.[3] Nonetheless, she participated in and, I argue, contributed to critical conversations still relevant to the field of rhetoric and composition studies, particularly one that has long served as a key exigence for much of our teaching and scholarship: how to teach writing *in* the classroom that engages with the world *outside* the classroom.

I did not become consciously aware of Ervin's work myself until 2010 when I was preparing to teach upcoming graduate courses in composition pedagogy and the history of rhetoric and actively looking for materials on civic engagement and public writing, hoping that someone, somehow, somewhere was finding answers to those exigent questions. Reading Wendy Sharer's bibliographic essay "Civic Participation and the Undergraduate Curriculum" (Sharer 2009) for the recently published *SAGE Handbook of Rhetorical Studies*, I first discovered Ervin's 2006 "Teaching Public Literacy: The Partisanship Problem," which led me to her 1997 "Encouraging Civic Participation." The two essays could not have been more different in tone, yet they were the work of the same author.

Around this time, I was working with Catherine Hobbs on an update to the chapter on the twentieth century for the third edition of *A Short History of Writing Instruction* (Gold, Hobbs, and Berlin 2012),[4] which was now to encompass the first decade of the twenty-first. One of our themes for the new millennium, we decided, had to be civic engagement, and it struck us that Ervin's essays perfectly encapsulated the struggles of our field to bridge the gap between the classroom and the public sphere. As we wrote, "While the public or social turn of the late twentieth century . . . stressed the importance of teaching writing as public argument and encouraging civic participation, publicly engaged instruction in the new century has begun to explore and appreciate just how complicated that directive is." Ervin, we suggested, understood this, her two essays "nearly a decade apart illustrat[ing] the field's growing sense of the challenge" (Gold, Hobbs, and Berlin 2012, 264). What we did not say in this bibliographic essay, and what I have since come to appreciate more, was how brave and forthcoming Ervin was in acknowledging these challenges and her own perceived failures in meeting them.

Thinking I might invite Ervin to Skype in on a class, I decided to look her up; one of the first returns was an obituary—Ervin had died just a few years previously, in 2008, at the age of forty-three.[5] Later I would learn she had died of breast cancer, diagnosed at the age of forty-one; she left behind a young daughter, about the same age as I had been when my own father died of cancer. I found myself profoundly moved by the death of this scholar I had never met.

I often tell students there are many ways to have a satisfying career in academia beyond seeking a tenure-line job at a Research I school, and Ervin evidenced that. Teaching at UNCW her entire career alongside her husband, fellow rhetoric and composition scholar Donald Bushman, she enjoyed "satisfying work" in a field she loved and, until she became ill, "a wonderful, healthy life filled with friendship and travel and a loving family" (Ervin, *Star-News Online*, March 28, 2008). Ervin also demonstrates, as I also try to persuade my students, that good work will out, that good scholarship will get read and matter, and that, like teaching, we never know what its impact will be. Had I not received the call for papers for this volume, I would not likely have written an essay about Ervin, but I would have continued to quietly teach her work and engage with her scholarship.

This study is based on Ervin's published scholarship and public writing in regional and national publications as well as a selection of her course materials contained in her papers (Elizabeth Ervin Papers, 1994–2001) at the UNCW archives.[6] As a historical work, this examination is necessarily incomplete. This essay does not engage with the entirety of her scholarship, teaching, or service—she was also concerned with collaboration, mentoring, feminist political action, classical rhetoric, and teacher education—nor does it dwell on the details of her personal life. Rather, it traces her professional interest in the area of inquiry to which she devoted the bulk of her scholarly energy: public writing and civic engagement.

A PUBLICLY MINDED SCHOLAR

Born in 1965 in the rural community of Grand Island, Nebraska, Elizabeth "Betsy" Ervin earned her BA from the University of Nebraska at Kearney in 1987, her MA from Texas Christian University (TCU) in 1990, and her PhD from the University of Arizona in 1994 ("Elizabeth E. Ervin," *Star-News*, August 24, 2008). Though she once described TCU as a "small private university" that "hardly anybody [at her PhD program] had even heard of" (Ervin 1994a, 10), she studied there with at least two pioneering faculty in rhetoric and composition who influenced her later career track, Winifred Bryan Horner, for whom she served as a graduate assistant, and Jim Corder, whom, as her husband Donald Bushman told me in an e-mail message on July 3, 2014, she "loved as a teacher and a person" (see also Ervin 1999b). At Arizona, she worked with John Warnock, who chaired her dissertation, Theresa Enos, Dana Fox, and Thomas Miller, all scholars with a strong interest in civic literacy and the public outcomes of rhetoric and composition instruction. Upon graduating, she took a position as an assistant professor of English at UNCW along with Bushman, whom she had married in 1991.[7]

Ervin's earliest work evidences a lively and assertive voice and an engagement with a broad range of scholarly concerns. In one of her first publications, a 1991 review of Gregory Clark's *Dialogue, Dialectic, and Conversation: A Social Perspective on the Function of Writing*, she pulls no punches, finding his argument provocative but less than clear: "We go around in circles but don't seem to make any progress; we read the same words over and over, but we're not always sure where one idea leaves off and another starts—or if it matters" (Ervin 1991, 365). In a 1995 essay for *Women's Studies*, she opens with the assertion, "In my five years of graduate school in English, I have not been mentored well" (Ervin 1995a, 447). Her 1994 dissertation, "Mentoring Recomposed: A Study of Gender, History, and the Discourses of Education," is in part a response to this experience and that of other women students and faculty, an activist, feminist intervention that examines academic mentoring practices that reproduce conventional "constructions of masculinity and femininity" (Ervin 1994a, 8).

In one of her first full-length research articles, the 1993 "Interdisciplinarity or 'An Elaborate Edifice Built on Sand'? Rethinking Rhetoric's Place" for *Rhetoric Review*, Ervin (1993) argues that rhetorical historiographers need to pay more attention to the methods of historiography.

Rhetoric, she argues, claims interdisciplinarity, yet "strategically neglect[s] scholarship" in other disciplines, whose members, in turn, "don't even know that an organized study of rhetoric exists, and seldom engage with our scholarship if they do" (98). She concludes that "if we are serious about having more influence in other disciplines . . . then we must admit that it matters what those disciplines think of us" (100).

I do not wish to make too much of these early essays in laying the groundwork for her later scholarship or to craft a seamless narrative of professional development. But looking back from the perspective of that later scholarship, three features in particular seem notable. First, as perhaps might be expected from one influenced by postmodern and feminist theory, Ervin carefully delineates her subjectivity; she is candid about the relationship between her life experiences and her scholarship in a way that enhances the latter. Second, like many of her colleagues, she wants scholarship in rhetoric and composition to matter in contexts beyond the scholarly. Finally, and perhaps more uncommonly, she is cognizant of the need to engage an audience on its own terms; in short, she understands the power of *doxa*. This latter trope in particular will emerge as an important theme in her later work as she encounters publics resistant to scholarly persuasion and students resistant to engaging in public discourse.

Beginning in 1995, Ervin's scholarly trajectory began to take a more definitive turn. For perhaps the majority of humanities scholars, their dissertations serve as the foundation for the first part of their career, ideally leading to a monograph or a series of research articles that will form the basis for tenure. Though Ervin would produce work originating in her dissertation and remained interested in mentoring and feminist activism, the bulk of her scholarship engaged in pedagogical questions of how to promote what she termed "public discursive interventions" (Ervin 1998, 38) or, more simply, "public literacy" (Ervin 2000b). By her own account, she was "led . . . back to scholarship in composition studies" (Clifford and Ervin 1999, 195) after engaging in her own first attempts at public writing in the summer of 1995, a letter to the editor and then a coauthored Op-Ed (Ervin and Bushman, *Morning Star*, July 26, 1995) in response to an attack by syndicated columnist George Will (*Washington Post*, July 2, 1995) on college writing instruction. Challenging Will's assertion that "more and more schools refuse, on the basis of various political and ethical and intellectual theories, to teach writing," Ervin and Bushman wrote, "It is clear [Will] hasn't been in a college writing classroom in decades," and invited residents to visit their classes to "find out what really happens there" (Ervin and Bushman, *Morning Star*, July 26, 1995).

As a microhistorian sensitive to recognizing the agency of historical subjects, I am reluctant to attribute too much causality to any one historical moment or event. Yet it does not require much application of critical imagination (see Royster and Kirsch 2012) to appreciate how important Ervin saw this moment to her own personal and professional development, as she referenced it on at least four occasions (Clifford and Ervin 1999, 194–95; Ervin 1997, 382, 397; 1998, 49; 1999a, 448), consistently describing the experience as germinal. Though she had always longed to take a more active part in public life, she was also hesitant to "engage in any activity that might be perceived as boat rocking" (Clifford and Ervin 1999, 194), particularly as a young scholar. Finally, frustrated by her own silence and fearful of becoming "one of those . . . ineffectual professors who bemoans her students' indifference from the comfort of her academic office" (195), she took the plunge into public discourse, following up the letter and Op-Ed with her first community-based writing assignments that fall, leading in 1997 to arguably her best-known and certainly most cited essay, "Encouraging Civic Participation among First-Year Writing Students; or, Why Composition Class Should Be More Like a Bowling Team."[8]

I do not recall reading the essay at the time of publication, but I do remember the widespread excitement in the field that attended the possibility of transforming composition instruction through attention to rhetoric and public discourse. In "Encouraging Civic Participation," Ervin raises a troubling question about the efficacy of such writing instruction: does having students write about public issues in class lead to their acting on issues outside of class? Given the enthusiasm for public-oriented writing at the time, this question was not necessarily obvious. Examining several issues-oriented textbooks, such as Robert Atwan's 1994 *America Now: Short Readings from Recent Periodicals*, as well as her own classroom practice, Ervin concludes that having students simply discuss and write about issues in the classroom "do[es] not particularly encourage students' participation in the world beyond the classroom, and may unwittingly repress it" (Ervin 1997, 382), as students come to see classroom talk as the equivalent of action, their civic duties discharged simply by becoming more informed about issues without having to do anything about them. With disarming candor, she describes her own previous pedagogy as passive and her modeling of civic behavior as poor. Hence her drafting of a letter to the editor and then a full-blown Op-Ed responding to George Will, in this context, is indeed a "big deal" (382), a first step toward being the sort of citizen-scholar she is trying to foster.

To help students move "from class participation to civic participation," Ervin (1997, 389) offers three suggestions: "reimagining students as citizens . . . reinventing the classroom as a 'secondary association' . . . and creating structured opportunities for students to engage in public discourses" (393). These guidelines are inspiring, but somewhat vague—what will such practice look like? Although she closes with a largely positive illustrative example, a brief account of a service-learning project in which students helped contribute to a local history of the nearby community of Sunset Beach, she does not offer many details, and, as she would acknowledge in a few years, she left out many of the challenges she encountered.

Closely following on "Encouraging Civic Participation," Ervin offers a much more detailed account of what such a publicly oriented course might look like in a 1998 "Course Designs" article for *Composition Studies*, "English 496: Senior Seminar in Writing" (Ervin 1998). With the theme of Writing for Diverse Publics, the course both introduces students to public-sphere theory and asks them to engage in public discourse; students weekly identify sites of potential "public discursive interventions"—rhetorical situations they might productively address—which ideally form the basis for four major public-writing assignments (38). While students are not required to submit their work for public consideration, Ervin hopes they will; both she and her students condemn the "hollowness" of assignments such as "fake" letters to the editor (50).

The course evidences her engagement with public-sphere theory and emerging scholarship on service learning, community literacy, and public writing—readings include work by Lloyd Bitzer, Nancy Fraser, Walter Fisher, Michael Warner, and Susan Wells—and she is deeply informed by work in rhetoric and composition that resists portrayals of the teacher as interventionist expert or hero, including that of Wells, Ellen Cushman, and Linda Flower. She assumes students "[do] indeed have interests and convictions" but need "explicit instruction . . . in constructing meaningful writing projects" to make them explicit (Ervin 1998, 47). She is also motivated by the transformative experience of writing that first letter to the editor: "This experience so liberated me that I actually live in the world differently now, with the assumption that I will participate in my community's ongoing, public conversations" (49). Her hope is to engender that same feeling in her students, to encourage students to see themselves as "agents" in a world brimming with "rhetorical situations" ready for discursive intervention (46–47).[9]

Her efforts as she describes them are only somewhat successful. Students need more assistance in imagining potential discursive interventions or public-writing genres than she had hoped and have difficulty in productively addressing audiences. She and her students seem unable to reconcile the tension between the expectations of school writing, which, for all its seemingly artificial rules, is an understood genre, and the somewhat more inchoate rhetorical structures of public writing. But she remains heartened that while most of her students didn't take their writing public, some did; messy as these interventions may have been, she writes, "at least they were out there *doing* something—which is more than I can say for all those literary analyses in the recycling bin" (Ervin 1998, 56).

Ervin continued to interrogate her practice, and in the following year's "Academics and the Negotiation of Local Knowledge" (Ervin 1999a) in *College English*, the optimism that marked her earliest incursions into public discourse is somewhat tempered. Where previously she described her letter to the editor and coauthored response to George Will as a "big deal" (Ervin 1997, 382), she now acknowledges that such endeavors are not without risk; indeed, what she considered a "rather bland response" (Ervin 1999a, 448) to Will generated surprisingly hostile letters to the editor and even a subsequent counter Op-Ed by a local resident that accused her of being "obviously ignorant of the necessity of basic writing skills" (Moore, *Morning Star*, August 5, 1995).

Troubled by these reactions, as well as by the tenor of other public debates in Wilmington between local academics and nonacademics that devolve into what she terms "discursive entrenchment," wherein parties on both sides "rhetorically dig in their heels" (Ervin 1999a, 449), she examines discursive patterns in recent debates over the teaching of evolution. Perhaps not surprisingly, she finds academic responses woefully inadequate, concluding that if "academics really want authentic public discourse," that is, "debate in which all participants risk being persuaded" rather than "simply to own and dispense knowledge in a public forum" (467), they must give up their privileged "expert" status and learn to speak the language of the publics they wish to persuade as equal citizens of those publics.

In 2000's "Learning to Write with a Civic Tongue," Ervin critiques the sometimes overly optimistic teaching narratives such "civic-minded" pedagogies engender and calls for "more honest narratives, full of inconvenient and even troubling detail about the challenges new pedagogies pose and the incongruities that exist between our practices and our ideologies" (Ervin 2000a, 144–45). Turning to her own practice, she acknowledges that the Sunset Beach service-learning project she described in 1997 was not as seamless and democratic as she had presented it, nor was its counterpart project, which she had not written about, a sourcebook on African American history written for a local public-housing community group. Students required constant pep talks and cheerleading to sustain interest; logistical problems continually threatened to derail the project; the democratic classroom she envisioned was undermined by exigencies requiring her to make unilateral decisions; assignment designs seemed to reify the kind of "do-goodism" (Ervin 2000a, 154) and paternalism scholars such as Ellen Cushman (1996) had warned against; and the final project, while substantial, did not get the traction Ervin and her students had hoped with the audiences for whom it had ostensibly been produced.[10] But Ervin does come away with some practical lessons. Perhaps most important for the purposes of this essay is her recognition that her "very talented, very motivated" students were "ill-equipped to devise their own assignment[s]" (Ervin 2000a, 150). For Ervin, this lack is not the fault of her students but a teachable moment of critical self-reflection, one that will lead to her most public and comprehensive attempt at public-writing pedagogy, her 2000 textbook, *Public Literacy*.

FROM PUBLIC WRITING TO *PUBLIC LITERACY*

The first edition of *Public Literacy* is a small, slim volume, roughly six-by-nine inches and 101 pages, divided into ten brief chapters.[11] The book is designed to guide students through the process of doing public writing in the public interest by helping them to (1) identify rhetorical situations demanding a written response and (2) find appropriate rhetorical genres for doing so. Chapters 1–4 introduce students to the concept of public literacy and publics theory; Ervin notes that there exists a multiplicity of public spheres and publics (national, local, everyday), each with its own literacy practices, rhetorical genres, audiences, and rhetorical norms, and offers various exercises to help students identify issues worth writing about. She emphasizes that what may seem at first like a private concern may indeed be a public one urging a rhetorical intervention in the public interest. Chapters 5–8 form the pragmatic heart of the book, introducing various public rhetorical genres—research in the public interest; letters (including letters to the editor, letters of concern, mass appeals, and open letters); press releases, press conferences, and press kits; and grant proposals—with examples taken both from the popular press and student experiences. The final two chapters suggest further public roles for students by describing various opportunities in community service and activism and careers in public literacy.

The text throughout is easily digestible—the first four chapters could be covered in two class sessions—the emphasis on getting students writing as quickly as possible. In developing the volume, Ervin has clearly drawn on her own classroom challenges. While still encouraging students to brainstorm possible discursive interventions, she no longer expects them to invent their own. Rather, she explicitly outlines various public-writing genres they might participate in, and she is particularly careful to note various examples of "everyday" or vernacular rhetorical gestures such as satirical flyers students might not otherwise see as legitimate or academically robust. Mindful also of what can happen if students take on projects that are more than they can reasonably handle or do not take into account their audiences, she explicitly asks students to think about constraints, which she presents as less of a rhetorical concern than a pragmatic one: "Do I have the time, commitment, and resources to create an appropriate public literacy document?" (Ervin 2000b, 31). She also asks students to consider whether their projects are truly "rhetorical" (i.e., changeable through writing), "urgent," and "in the public interest" (22–23).[12]

Public Literacy does not appear to have found a large audience. I have found no published reviews of the work and only a few syllabi online making use of it, and as of 2014 it exists in a scant fourteen WorldCat libraries. It did, however, sell well enough to justify a second edition (Ervin 2003), still in print, which Ervin revised extensively, writing a new chapter on petitions and ballot initiatives, fleshing out previous material—for example, adding sections on the challenges of the rise of global publics and digitization's effects on the public domain—and including more powerful examples of student discursive interventions.

EVOLVING PEDAGOGIES

During this time, Ervin's personal and professional commitments expanded. She obtained tenure in 2000, her daughter Willa was born in 2001, and she became the founding director of the Women's Studies and Resources Center (WSRC) at UNCW in 2002, serving a two-year term. She continued to refine her pedagogy, publishing various teaching narratives and book reviews between 2001 and 2005 reflecting her evolving interest in rhetoric and composition's public turn.

In her 2001 review of Rosa Eberly's *Citizen Critics: Literary Public Spheres*, Ervin keys in on the tensions Eberly explores between the discourses of ordinary citizens and academic experts over controversial literary works. Eberly argues that "citizen critics" have often raised significant topoi about the social meaning and purpose of texts which, though sometimes at variance with the aesthetic considerations of academic experts, constitute legitimate "public acts of interpretation" (Eberly 2000, 2). Ervin, perhaps thinking of the rhetorical failures of the Wilmington evolution debates, writes that Eberly's analysis suggests a "central tension" in contemporary public discourse: while "citizen critics can play a subversive role in discussing matters of shared concern . . . public intellectuals can actually constrain the very forms of participation that they think they're advocating" (Ervin 2001, 474).

In her 2005 review of Barbara Couture and Thomas Kent's edited collection *The Private, the Public, and the Published: Reconciling Private Lives and Public Rhetoric*, Ervin (2005) notes that recent discussions of public writing and civic engagement within composition studies, while invigorating the field, have sometimes depended on somewhat reductive definitions of public and private. Thus, while welcoming the volume, she is somewhat troubled by the willingness of some of its contributors to equate the "personal" with the "private" and thus dismiss expressivist-oriented rhetorics as having little to offer compositionists interested in public writing and public spheres (479). While Ervin has never been an advocate of expressivist pedagogy, she has long recognized, from both her own teaching experience and exposure to feminist theory, how the personal may indeed be public, and she calls for "increased critical interrogation of how, why, and to what effect textual conventions associated with the personal and the public are strategically employed" (480).

Ervin was a firm believer that "becoming a teacher depends not on a fixed philosophy but on the constant reexamination of our practices" (Huntley-Johnston and Ervin 1999, 102). In a coauthored 1999 essay on the importance of fostering an attitude of self-reflection among pre-service teachers, Ervin, in a personal reflection, describes a paradox likely experienced by many composition instructors: "'Being a learner' is a risky role for teachers. For a lot of students and administrators, modeling learning looks a lot like modeling incompetence" (Huntley-Johnston and Ervin 1999, 118).

Despite this risk, Ervin, perhaps following her own advice in *Public Literacy* that the "worst" that can happen in going public is that people "disagree with you . . . or prove you wrong" (Ervin 2000b, 25), continued to practice what she preached, crafting ambitious teaching projects that modeled learning for her students and demonstrated her commitment to public writing, even as these experiments revealed new pedagogical challenges. It is a telling mark of her commitment to self-reflection as a means of pedagogical growth that in the 2003 coauthored "Writing against Time: Students Composing 'Legacies' in a History Conscious City" (Ervin and Collins 2003), Ervin offers one of her *own* sections of English 103 as an example of what not to do. In 1997, inspired by UNCW's fiftieth-anniversary celebrations, as well as public-memory efforts in Wilmington and on campus that seemed to flatten local history, Ervin developed what she hoped would be a robust class project to help students understand and take part in the process by which history is made: an institutional history of UNCW. Despite student enthusiasm and a carefully scaffolded assignment sequence of "oral history, archival research, scholarly research, and public presentation" (Ervin 2003, 48), she found the project undermined by the attempts of institutional stakeholders to control the history students were trying to uncover: "Because we proceeded without any understanding of the local rhetorical ecosystem, we found ourselves working from a generically academic model of historiography rather than a rhetorically localized one, and the result was a history that did not fit—could not be written or read, spoken or heard—in the available discourse" (50).

In "Rhetorical Situations and the Straits of Inappropriateness: Teaching Feminist Activism," Ervin (2006a) describes an introduction to women's studies class in which she introduced the concept, borrowed from the French situationists, of *détournement,* by which cultural signifiers are reappropriated for subversive purposes or to expose the ideologies they represent. By introducing students to a strategic understanding of "rhetorical inappropriateness," Ervin hoped to "offer students the tools" to decide when to accept and when to reject rhetorical constraints in any given rhetorical situation (331). Students, for example, examined the activist artwork of the Guerrilla Girls, creatively reworked Barbie greeting cards and teen-romance comics, and discussed the power of various rhetorical strategies to advance feminist activism.[13]

Though students found these activities provocative, they were largely reluctant to "embrac[e] inappropriateness as a governing principle of feminist activism" (Ervin 2006a, 330), a concern Ervin regards as legitimate. Following Randy Bomer, she insists students are "free moral agents" (331) with the right to reject our pedagogy. If we truly wish to embrace a radical or democratic critical pedagogy, she concludes, "we must face the difficult truth that we will be fair game for students' critiques" (331).

QUESTIONING PRIOR COMMITMENTS

Around this time, Ervin began to evidence a growing "uneas[e] with the growth of public writing within composition studies" (Ervin 2007,

37), questioning the efficacy and even the premises of public-writing pedagogy and scholarship. Unlike her initial entrée into public writing, there appears to have been no one singular event that inspired this shift. Rather, it appears to have been a gradual one, motivated by her cumulative experiences as a scholar, teacher, and citizen.

In the 2006 "Teaching Public Literacy: The Partisanship Problem," Ervin describes an emerging political climate in which the very notion of the public good is questioned. Though she rejects Stanley Fish's argument that academics, including writing teachers, should not be in the business of inculcating citizenship, she recognizes that the broad constituencies universities serve often view civically engaged initiatives such as public intellectualism, service learning, and community writing with suspicion. Indeed, in an era of hyperpartisanship and the ascent of neoliberal economic ideologies, "English classrooms organized around public literacy are likely to be regarded by a significant number of our students as part of an ongoing liberal effort 'hostile' to their own academic and professional goals" (Ervin 2006b, 412).

In response, Ervin argues that we should shift away from the treatment of public issues in favor of teaching "publicist rhetorical strategies"—for example, branding, framing, coalition building, and agitation—students can use to advance personal, even self-serving, interests, such as promoting one's band, "unencumbered by specifically civic intentions" (Ervin 2006b, 415–16). Such rhetorical strategies, she argues, have the same power to evoke publics and inspire rhetorical awareness as writing about public issues but without the messy complications the latter often entails: "When we introduce our students to a kind of publicist orientation that does not carry counterproductive partisan connotations, we prepare them to practice and reflect upon publicism in more significant and sophisticated ways" (419).

In the 2007 "Composition and the Gentrification of 'Public Literacy,'" Ervin takes her critique one step further, suggesting that there is "something vaguely imperialistic about this attempt to expand the disciplinary boundaries of composition's influence and representation beyond its accepted sphere" of the classroom (38). She even comes close to disavowing her own 1997 article in which she "wrote buoyantly" (42) about the possibility of inspiring civic participation: "But the fact of the matter is that there is no clear evidence to support the notion that public-spirited arrangements in the writing classroom . . . have a lasting effect on political conditions outside the classroom" (43).

Moreover, she suggests, such pedagogies may actually help promulgate a commodified and less democratic public sphere, reifying inequities even as we imagine ourselves as agents of emancipatory power. For example, if we attend only to "the most resourceful, efficacious examples of public literacy," then who will teach basic literacy? If we focus on public literacies, then who will teach academic writing? The responsibility, she writes, will fall on under-prepared, under-resourced instructors in other locations. Thus, our "gentrification" of public literacy may have very real consequences for ourselves and our constituencies. Ervin calls for more "self-reflective academic engagement with public literacy" (Ervin 2007, 48), including a reconsideration of the ways professional success is rewarded. In the last sentence she would publish for an academic audience, she concludes, "We must regard our adventures in public discourse less as fodder for our scholarship, or as performances of our expertise, or quests for representativeness than as the simple—though, of course, not so simple—exercise of citizenship" (50).

ETHICAL PEDAGOGY

In the concluding chapter of *What Is Microhistory*, Sigurður Magnússon takes issue with the desire of microhistorians to "contextualiz[e] their findings," warning that this creates the risk of replicating the "grand narrative" tradition such histories ostensibly work against (Magnússon 2013, 158). I do not wish to suggest that Ervin's career development represents an untroubled—or untroubling—narrative arc. Her final essays are not easy documents to read. When I have taught "Teaching Public Literacy," students have found her schema of "publicist" rhetorical strategies potentially generative but have worried about the seeming promotion of self-interest its application might entail: "What are the democratic ramifications of teaching the partisan 'I' rather than the public 'we'?" one student asked. Another presciently saw the question Ervin was working toward and would soon explicitly address: "Is it possible that we use civic participation in the comp classroom as a way to legitimate, if you will, the curriculum of a writing class?"

Ervin's break with some of her previously professed pedagogical commitments is a reminder that no pedagogy is self-evident, no initiative a cure-all for the persistent question of the subject of the composition classroom. And despite its seeming contradictions, her work, I believe, also evidences a consistency of purpose throughout her career. In her last scholarly essay, Ervin takes note of "formerly ubiquitous" terms within composition studies such as "communities" and "contact zones" that had "a relatively short shelf life . . . because they backfired in the classroom" (Ervin 2007, 42). Ervin never broke faith with civically engaged pedagogies, but she did not want them to become another tried-and-forgotten conceptual trend or an empty vehicle for professional advancement. For her, the testing ground of any pedagogy was the classroom, and the test of any rhetorical theory was its rhetorical effectiveness, not necessarily in persuading an audience but in joining in authentic conversation with one.

At the heart of Ervin's practice was an essential trust in and commitment to the moral agency of her students. "Ethics," she wrote, "is the ultimate arbiter of rhetorical action" (Ervin 2006a, 332), and she constantly sought not only to offer students the means to make ethical rhetorical choices but to also engage in ethical teaching, by which students must be free to make their own rhetorical choices. Here she prefigures John Duffy's recent call to understand the teaching of writing as the teaching of "ethical communication," of argumentative virtues as ethical virtues; by offering evidence, we "acknowledge the rationality" of an audience; in addressing counterarguments, we "expose [our]selves to the doubts and contradictions that adhere to every worthwhile question"; in making a claim, we "propose a relationship between others and ourselves" (Duffy 2012; see also Duffy 2014).

For Ervin, the relationship between rhetor and audience was central. Throughout her work, Ervin also recognizes, to a degree not always explicitly treated in our field, that the opinions of the publics we serve matter, be they academics in other fields, administrators, students, parents, or community members. Ervin's work suggests that if we wish to continue to pursue civic-minded pedagogies, to take writing public, both our own and that of our students, we must make the case beyond our scholarly enclaves. As would-be public intellectuals engaging with citizen critics or as teachers professing deeply held ideological and pedagogical convictions, we cannot assume our expertise will be welcomed or even acknowledged; rather, we must meet our audiences on their own terms—and take a chance on being persuaded ourselves.

Notes

1.   It is telling, as Muir (1991, xiii–xiv) observes, that microhistorians tend not to cite Foucault: "No matter how aware they are of the ways in which texts influence their own meanings, they assume that there is a reality external to those texts . . . that can be known."

2.   Ervin was early inspired by Ruth E. Ray's advocacy of teacher research, writing a laudatory review of her 1993 *The Practice of Theory: Teacher Research in Composition* for the *North Carolina English Teacher* in 1994 (Ervin 1994b) and interviewing Ray the following year for the same publication (Ervin 1995b). She also appears to have taken to heart Ray's declaration that "a teacher is always a work in progress" (18).

3. In an e-mail message to the author on March 23, 2014, Bruce McComiskey described her as "a rising star who was connecting in complicated ways with difficult issues in composition." He said, "Her death . . . still haunts me, both in the sense of tragic loss and anticipation of what she could have done for the field if she were still here."

4. James Berlin wrote the chapter for the first edition in 1990, and Catherine Hobbs, who had studied with Berlin at Purdue, updated it for the second in 2001 following Berlin's death in 1994. I am grateful to Catherine for inviting me to work with her on the update for the third edition.

5. Had I been paying closer attention, I might have known this; she's listed in the 2009 CCCC program's "In Memoriam" section as Betsy Ervin, and the 2010 program contained a panel dedicated to her life and work, "Following a Leader: The Inimitable Elizabeth (Betsy) Ervin."

6. I am grateful to UNCW archivist Adina Riggins for her assistance in providing archival materials.

7. The couple met at CCCC in 1990.

8. The title references Robert D. Putnam's 1995 article "Bowling Alone: America's Declining Social Capital," later developed into the 2000 book *Bowling Alone: The Collapse and Revival of American Community* (Putnam 2000).

9. Through at least 1999, her English 103 class assignments include an "agency essay" in which students "articulate [an] agenda" they care about and discuss "concrete actions" they might take (Ervin 1994–2001, Box 1, Folder 9).

10. In a long, reflective letter to the class that begins "Dear Citizen-Writers," written late in the term, Ervin acknowledges many of these concerns, urging students to keep in mind that, despite the project's challenges, they are "constructing an original manuscript, the likes of which has never been done before" (Ervin 1994–2001, Box 1, Folder 2).

11. The volume was originally published as part of Longman's three-part Literacy Library series, which also included entries on workplace and academic literacy.

12. See pages 40–41 and 32–33 in the second edition (2003).

13. Though Ervin does not explicitly say so here, it is likely the class was at least partly inspired by events on campus in 2003. In response to the school's sponsoring a concert by the rapper Ludacris, widely criticized for his misogynistic lyrics, the WSRC engaged in "talking back" (see Ervin 2006a, 323) by distributing "poster-size comics" featuring "empowered women responding with condescending comebacks . . . to characters spewing lines" (Rouch, *Morning Star*, March 25, 2003) from his songs.

References

Clifford, John, and Elizabeth Ervin. 1999. "The Ethics of Process." In *Post-Process Theory: Beyond the Writing-Process Paradigm*, edited by Thomas Kent, 179–97. Carbondale: Southern Illinois University Press.

Cushman, Ellen. 1996. "The Rhetorician as an Agent of Social Change." *College Composition and Communication* 47 (1): 7–28. http://dx.doi.org/10.2307/358271.

Duffy, John. 2012. "Virtuous Arguments." *Inside Higher Ed*, March 16. https://www.insidehighered.com/views/2012/03/16/essay-value-first-year-writing-courses.

Duffy, John. 2014. "Ethical Dispositions: A Discourse for Rhetoric and Composition." *JAC* 34 (1–2): 209–37.

Eberly, Rosa A. 2000. *Citizen Critics: Literary Public Spheres*. Urbana: University of Illinois Press.

Elizabeth Ervin Papers. 1994–2001. University of North Carolina, Wilmington Archives. W. M. Randall Library.

Ervin, Elizabeth. 1991. "Review of *Dialogue, Dialectic, and Conversation: A Social Perspective on the Function of Writing*, by Gregory Clark." *Rhetoric Review* 9 (2): 365–68.

Ervin, Elizabeth. 1993. "Interdisciplinarity or 'An Elaborate Edifice Built on Sand'? Rethinking Rhetoric's Place." *Rhetoric Review* 12 (1): 84–105. http://dx.doi.org /10.1080/07350199309389028.

Ervin, Elizabeth. 1994a. "Mentoring Recomposed: A Study of Gender, History, and the Discourses of Education." PhD diss., University of Arizona.

Ervin, Elizabeth. 1994b. "Review of *The Practice of Theory: Teacher Research in Composition*, by Ruth E. Ray." *North Carolina English Teacher* 52 (1): 30–31.

Ervin, Elizabeth. 1995a. "Power, Frustration, and 'Fierce Negotiation' in Mentoring Relationships: Four Women Tell Their Stories." *Women's Studies* 24 (5): 447–81. http://dx.doi.org/10.1080/00497878.1995.9979072.

Ervin, Elizabeth. 1995b. "A Teacher Is Always a Work in Progress (A Conversation with . . . Ruth Ray)." *North Carolina English Teacher* 53 (1): 16–23.

Ervin, Elizabeth. 1997. "Encouraging Civic Participation among First-Year Writing Students; or, Why Composition Class Should Be More Like a Bowling Team." *Rhetoric Review* 15 (2): 382–99. http://dx.doi.org/10.1080/07350199709359225.

Ervin, Elizabeth. 1998. "English 496: Senior Seminar in Writing." *Composition Studies* 26 (1): 37–57.

Ervin, Elizabeth. 1999a. "Academics and the Negotiation of Local Knowledge." *College English* 61 (4): 448–70. http://dx.doi.org/10.2307/378922.

Ervin, Elizabeth. 1999b. "Love Composes Us (In Memory of Jim Corder)." *Rhetoric Review* 17 (2): 322–30. http://dx.doi.org/10.1080/07350199909359248.

Ervin, Elizabeth. 2000a. "Learning to Write with a Civic Tongue." In *Blundering for a Change: Errors and Expectations in Critical Pedagogy*, edited by John Paul Tassoni and William H. Thelin, 144–57. Portsmouth, NH: Boynton/Cook.

Ervin, Elizabeth. 2000b. *Public Literacy*. New York: Longman.

Ervin, Elizabeth. 2001. "Review of *Citizen Critics: Literary Public Spheres*, by Rosa A. Eberly." *JAC* 21 (2): 472–77.

Ervin, Elizabeth. 2003. *Public Literacy*. 2nd ed. New York: Longman.

Ervin, Elizabeth. 2005. "Review of *The Private, the Public, and the Published: Reconciling Private Lives and Public Rhetoric*, edited by Barbara Couture and Thomas Kent." *Rhetoric Review* 24 (4): 477–80.

Ervin, Elizabeth. 2006a. "Rhetorical Situations and the Straits of Inappropriateness: Teaching Feminist Activism." *Rhetoric Review* 25 (3): 316–33. http://dx.doi.org /10.1207/s15327981rr2503_5.

Ervin, Elizabeth. 2006b. "Teaching Public Literacy: The Partisanship Problem." *College English* 68 (4): 407–21. http://dx.doi.org/10.2307/25472161.

Ervin, Elizabeth. 2007. "Composition and the Gentrification of 'Public Literacy.'" In *The Locations of Composition*, edited by Christopher J. Keller and Christian R. Weisser, 37–54. Albany: SUNY Press.

Ervin, Elizabeth, and Dan Collins. 2003. "Writing against Time: Students Composing 'Legacies' in a History Conscious City." In *City Comp: Identities, Spaces, Practices*, edited by Bruce McComiskey and Cynthia Ryan, 38–56. Albany: SUNY Press.

Gold, David. 2012. "Remapping Revisionist Historiography." *College Composition and Communication* 64 (1): 15–34.

Gold, David, Catherine L. Hobbs, and James A. Berlin. 2012. "Writing Instruction in School and College English: The Twentieth Century and the New Millennium." In *A Short History of Writing Instruction: From Ancient Greece to Contemporary America*. 3rd ed. Edited by James J. Murphy, 232–72. New York: Routledge.

Huntley-Johnston, Lu, and Elizabeth Ervin. 1999. "A Change of Course: Creating a Context for Reforming Literacy Education." In *The Literacy Connection*, edited by Ronald A. Sudol and Alice S. Horning, 97–119. Creskill, NJ: Hampton.

Levi, Giovanni. 2001. "On Microhistory." In *New Perspectives on Historical Writing*. 2nd ed. Edited by Peter Burke, 97–119. University Park: Pennsylvania State University Press.

Magnússon, Sigurður Gylfi. 2013. "Postscript: To Step into the Same Stream Twice." In *What Is Microhistory? Theory and Practice*, edited by Sigurður Gylfi Magnússon and István M. Szijártó, 147–59. New York: Routledge.

Muir, Edward. 1991. "Introduction: Observing Trifles." In *Microhistory and the Lost Peoples of Europe*, edited by Edward Muir and Guido Ruggiero, vii–xxviii. Baltimore, MD: Johns Hopkins University Press.

Putnam, Robert D. 1995. "Bowling Alone: America's Declining Social Capital." *Journal of Democracy* 6 (1): 65–78. http://dx.doi.org/10.1353/jod.1995.0002.

Putnam, Robert D. 2000. *Bowling Alone: The Collapse and Revival of American Community*. New York: Simon & Schuster. http://dx.doi.org/10.1145/358916.361990.

Royster, Jacqueline Jones, and Gesa E. Kirsch. 2012. *Feminist Rhetorical Practices: New Horizons for Rhetoric, Composition, and Literacy Studies*. Carbondale: Southern Illinois University Press.

Sharer, Wendy B. 2009. "Civic Participation and the Undergraduate Curriculum." In *The SAGE Handbook of Rhetorical Studies*, edited by Andrea A. Lunsford, Kirt H. Wilson, and Rosa A. Eberly, 373–90. Los Angeles: SAGE. http://dx.doi.org/10.4135/9781412982795.d24.

Szijártó, István M. 2013. "Introduction: Against Simple Truths." In *What Is Microhistory? Theory and Practice*, edited by Sigurður Gylfi Magnússon and István M. Szijártó, 1–11. New York: Routledge.

Wan, Amy J. 2011. "In the Name of Citizenship: The Writing Classroom and the Promise of Citizenship." *College English* 74 (1): 28–49.

10
GOING PUBLIC WITH KEN MACRORIE

Brian Gogan

Concepts today more than ever require further explanation and verification through concrete events into which the abstracted individual must be reinserted, where he or she belongs to a particular, specific form of society, whose concrete circumstances allow us to evaluate the success or otherwise of his or her efforts to change it.

—Giovanni Levi, "Microhistory and
the Recovery of Complexity"

Disciplinary concepts, as the above remark from microhistorian Giovanni Levi suggests, often require recalibration. According to Levi, the "conceptual instruments of our profession" are susceptible to deterioration: "Rendered shabby with long use, worn and torn by allusion and metaphor, they are coated with a rust of ambiguity" (Levi 2012, 125). Microhistorians and the microhistories they compose target this deterioration, aiming to knock the rust off of corroded concepts and categories by reconsidering the historical particulars and by reinserting the individual into history. One of the ways microhistorians combat conceptual and categorical corrosion is by reducing the scale of their inquiry. Levi, in fact, argues that a reduction in the scale of inquiry constitutes the "unifying principle of all microhistorical research," as microhistorians are united in "the belief that microscopic observation will reveal factors previously unobserved" (Levi 2001, 101).[1] To put this belief differently, microhistories are revealing, and concomitant with this belief—at least from Levi's perspective—is the microhistorian's rigorous practice of embracing complexity and "retrieving uncertainty, inconsistency, [and] nonlinearity" (Levi 2012, 129).

Microhistorical inquiries—the present one included—often begin with some uncertainty about an inconsistent source that does not neatly line up with other sources, established histories, or disciplinary concepts. Microhistorian Sigurður Gylfi Magnússon refers to these inconsistent sources as "outliers" (Magnússon and Szijártó 2013, 152). Magnússon recognizes that, while certain types of historians and statisticians work

DOI: 10.7330/9781607324058.c010

around outlying research material, "microhistorians approach this research material differently: they specifically search out the outliers" (152). For the microhistorian, outlying source material provides an opportunity to investigate particulars otherwise lost to corrosion—that is, an opportunity to ask "new questions from an unexpected perspective" (Magnússon and Szijártó 2013, 153). Important to note is that the unexpected perspective from which the microhistorian views source material foregrounds the microhistorian's own position—as scholar and interpreter—with respect to the source material. Although Magnússon suggests that the initial positioning of the microhistorian with respect to the outlying source material is deliberate—that microhistorians "specifically search out" this material (152)—my own experience suggests that microhistorical inquiry can begin when a scholar accidentally or inadvertently finds outlying source material that challenges disciplinary histories and concepts.

While researching approaches to the teaching of public rhetoric and writing in college composition classrooms, I stumbled upon a 1963 *College Composition and Communication* (*CCC*) article by Ken Macrorie that seemed to challenge established histories and concepts within the discipline of composition studies. I'll offer a more detailed discussion of this particular article, "Spitting on the Campus Newspaper," later in this microhistory, but suffice it to say that, initially, I found the article interesting for three reasons. First, this article was somewhat of an outlier with respect to the history of public rhetoric and writing pedagogy in composition studies. The history of teaching public rhetoric and writing to college composition students, or what has been called the *public turn* in composition studies, is regularly charted as gaining momentum in the 1990s.[2] However, this 1963 article vociferously endorses one of our discipline's oldest public rhetoric and writing assignments—writing a letter to the editor of a newspaper—and, consequently, it can be read as expanding this history by decades. Second, and relatedly, the arguments Macrorie forwards in this article struck me as outliers for the fact that these arguments supporting a publicly oriented pedagogy were issued by Macrorie. Among histories of the composition studies discipline, Macrorie is often listed first among a group of scholar-teachers known as "expressionists" (Berlin 1982, 771). The label of "expressionist" gained disciplinary traction in the work of James A. Berlin (1982, 1987, 1988; Elbow 2004, 18), and the pedagogy associated with this category has been viewed by scholars such as Christian R. Weisser as being inconsistent with the aims of public rhetoric and writing pedagogy (Weisser 2002, 16–20). Third and finally, Macrorie's 1963 article interested me because Macrorie wrote the article while he served as a member of the Department of English at Western Michigan University—the same department in which and the same institution at which I hold an appointment. Thus, the article spoke to institutional history, and in order to explore the inconsistency between the histories of composition studies and Macrorie's relationship to public rhetoric and writing pedagogy further, I turned to this institutional history and entered the Western Michigan University Archives and Regional History Collections.

I approached the archives guided by one overarching question: in what sense, if any, could Macrorie be seen as *going public*? Central to this question is the phrase *going public*, a phrase popularized within the composition studies discipline by Peter Mortensen's 1998 argument that scholars should "grant access to audiences outside the profession, beyond the academy" and "accommodate their writing about college composition to broader, nonacademic audiences" (182, 198). Since then, the phrase has been taken up for various purposes by a number of composition studies scholars, among them Sidney I. Dobrin, Shirley K. Rose, and Irwin Weiser. Dobrin uses the phrase *going public* throughout an essay premised upon the point that writing is always already public (Dobrin 2004, 220–21). *Going public*, for Dobrin, is therefore an ironic phrase. Rose and Weiser use the phrase to hold together a collection of essays about civic and community engagement from the perspective of writing teachers and leaders (Rose and Weiser 2010, 5). For Rose and Weiser, the phrase is descriptive of academic work in composition studies.

For me, the phrase *going public* served as a heuristic for my microhistorical inquiry. The multiple purposes for which the phrase has been used within our discipline opened my research to any evidence that would further explain Macrorie's positioning as a writer, teacher, researcher, and leader with respect to variously mediated publics. To be sure, at the beginning of my work in the archives, as much uncertainty surrounded my use of the phrase *going public* as it did the whole research project: the meaning of the phrase and the meaning of the microhistory would both emerge from my work with the archival sources. I was, at this point in my inquiry, deliberately looking for the outlying source materials Magnússon describes as unveiling "diverse strands of connection" within a particular community (Magnússon and Szijártó 2013, 152). The connections I sought to trace pertained to Macrorie's orientation with respect to various publics, and besides ferreting through boxes of committee meeting minutes and decades-old curricular materials, my search for these public particulars led, somewhat ironically, to Macrorie's personnel file.[3]

JANUARY 1964

Toward the front of Macrorie's personnel file, I found two documents. Composed only one day apart in January 1964, the documents outlined the kinds of concrete situations and the kinds of curious inconsistencies that enable and invite a microhistorical reevaluation of an individual like Macrorie. When read in succession, these two documents, as I detail below, seem to reveal a good number of connections between disciplinary histories of composition studies and Macrorie's relation to various publics.

The first of these two documents is a typewritten letter Macrorie wrote to Frederick J. Rogers, the head of the Department of English at Western Michigan University, on January 6, 1964. This letter notifies Rogers that Macrorie is "not taking up the offer of Jim Squire, Executive Secretary of the National Council of Teachers of English, to take another 3-year appointment as editor" of the Conference on College Composition and Communication's journal *CCC*. Although Macrorie indicates that he "enjoyed and learned from this editorship, corresponding with leading scholars and thinkers all over the country," his letter explains that he wants "to turn to other projects and interests." Macrorie's letter, however, fails to describe these "other projects and interests" in any further detail, leaving them open to the kind of interpretation characteristic of microhistorical inquiry—that is, interpretation concerned with the individual, the concrete, and the particular. One plausible reading of Macrorie's reference to "other projects and interests" might view the phrase as a nondescript rationale that sacrifices specificity in order to maintain politeness and professionalism. But such an explanation is inconsistent with many of Macrorie's other letters to Rogers—letters both polite and professional but often quite forthright and specific, too. Another plausible reading of Macrorie's reference—one offered earlier in this collection by Kelly Ritter—is that Macrorie's "other projects and interests" were projects and interests related to his own writing. But perhaps the best indication of what Macrorie's "other projects and interests" might have been is revealed by a document Macrorie composed the next day.

On January 7, 1964, Macrorie composed responses to thirteen prompts that solicited information about his research, teaching, and service contributions to Western Michigan University. These responses comprise his Departmental Information Sheet, or DIS, and Macrorie's responses to a good number of these prompts reflect, as might be expected, his deep professional engagement with the discipline of composition studies. Since Macrorie had only recently announced that 1964 would be his final year editing *CCC*, his typewritten DIS explicitly acknowledges the influence of this editorial work on his research and service. Macrorie, for example, includes his role as editor under the professional recognition section of the DIS, and he also notes his editorship when discussing his service to the university. Although Macrorie served as sponsor for a student publication and coproposed a university writing institute, he qualifies this service, writing: "I have turned down two all-University committee jobs because I feel while I'm editor of *CCC* I can't extend myself further." Admittedly, there's good evidence to suggest Macrorie might have actually viewed this reduction in committee work as a benefit to editing *CCC*.[4] However, the point remains that Macrorie's DIS quite prominently mentions the impact of his editorial work on his research and service.

By way of contrast, Macrorie's responses to teaching-related prompts contain no explicit mention of the way the editorship impacted his teaching even though Macrorie's work editing *CCC* did take him away from the classroom. Macrorie received a one-course reduction for each of the six semesters during which he edited the journal. These six semesters were, coincidentally, six of Macrorie's first seven semesters at Western Michigan University, as he began his editorship and his appointment at Western Michigan University during the same academic year, 1961–1962.[5] As Macrorie explains in a letter dated June 19, 1961, his editorship was actually contingent upon Western Michigan University's providing him with some release from his teaching duties. In a letter sent some months later on January 10, 1962, to a Western Michigan University comptroller, Macrorie explains "that the organization always demands the university where the desired editor works release him from some of his teaching before it confers the job." Macrorie further requested that his course assignments be made in a way that would reduce his course preparations and leave him time for morning editorial work.[6]

Macrorie's failure to mention the impact of his editorial work on his teaching is a revealing omission for it draws attention to the information he actually includes about his teaching at Western Michigan University. In these teaching-related responses, there is a marked difference between Macrorie's description of past teaching assignments and his description of future teaching assignments. When prompted to describe the courses he previously taught at Western Michigan University, Macrorie simply lists four course-catalog titles: Literary Interpretation, Communication, Senior Studies, and Advanced Writing. In contrast, when prompted to list the courses he felt "best qualified to teach, in some order of preference," Macrorie offers a substantially more detailed response. In this response, Macrorie lists four course-catalog titles—Literary Interpretation, Communication, Mass Communication, and Understanding of Film—and states that his preference for teaching one course over another cannot be rated meaningfully, suggesting that he would have liked to teach all of these courses equally. But beyond listing these four courses, he previews the topics of these courses by detailing a few course titles, including the title found at the end of this note: "I teach all my classes at times in a seminar fashion so think I'm equipped to handle seminar-type courses, for example, a Senior Studies course in 'The Public Language and Literature.'"

Here, then, in the DIS Macrorie composed on January 7, 1964, is what I find to be an indication of the "other projects and interests" to which he referred in the letter sent to Rogers the day before. The detail with which Macrorie describes his future teaching assignments suggests that, as his editorial duties ceased, Macrorie was turning enthusiastically toward teaching-related projects and interests. Maybe Macrorie's increased interest in teaching stemmed from recent successes he had experienced in the classroom.[7] Maybe he saw an affinity between teaching and the university writing institute he was busy proposing. Or, maybe he really wanted the opportunity to pilot his ideas for courses, such as his Public Language and Literature course. Whatever the case might have been, the DIS suggests that, in January 1964, Macrorie was busy conceiving of courses he might teach, among them a course titled Public Language and Literature.

The prominence that Macrorie's title for this senior-studies course, Public Language and Literature, gives to the word *public* challenges disciplinary histories that expressly distance Macrorie and his pedagogy from publics and public-writing pedagogy. But in this commonplace 1964 form, Macrorie makes special note of his qualifications to teach a course titled Public Language and Literature. Macrorie was, in other words, closely associating himself with public writing. I, for one, cannot help but wonder about Macrorie's interest in this particular course. What might have been Macrorie's goals for this public language and literature course? How might Macrorie have structured this course? What might public rhetoric and writing pedagogy look like in Macrorie's classroom?[8] Again, what might going public with Ken Macrorie entail?

GETTING WITH THE COLLEGE PAPER AS GOING PUBLIC

In February 1963—nearly one year before he would suggest he was qualified to teach a course in public language and literature—Macrorie published the *CCC* article "Spitting on the Campus Newspaper." This article sparked my initial interest in Macrorie's relation to publics and public writing; it raised questions that eventually led me into the archives; and, it is suggestive, in part, of what going public with Macrorie might have entailed. In the article, Macrorie challenges English professors to reserve their criticism of campus newspapers and instead "get with the good writing in the college paper" (Macrorie 1963b, 31). As Macrorie explains, "getting with" the campus newspaper means not only encouraging strong writers to contribute their writing to the paper but also assigning "an occasional paper in class that is to be a letter to the editor commenting on a campus matter that matters to the student" (31). In the piece, Macrorie exhibits a number of student-written editorials and letters to editors from campus papers—papers including San Francisco State College's *Daily Gater*, Northwestern University's *Daily Northwestern*, Ohio State University's *Lantern*, the University of Southern California's *Daily Trojan*, the University of Michigan's *Michigan Daily*, and Western Michigan University's *Western Herald*—as examples to illustrate the use of satire, humor, critique, attitude, and the ability "of the student to relate what he studies in the classroom to his [*sic*] own world" (29).

As Macrorie saw it, the college paper of the 1960s offered a venue in which students could go public, and this venue suggested a means by which an assignment, unit, or entire composition course might also go public. Macrorie reinforces this perspective in a speech he delivered at Western Michigan University's 1965 Annual General Studies Staff Meeting. A typescript copy of this 1965 speech is included in Macrorie's personnel file and, like his 1963 article, the speech echoes the sentiment that writing teachers can go public by "getting with" campus newspapers. Macrorie's 1965 speech discusses "how a good teacher can invite and demand and encourage his students *outside* the classroom" (Macrorie 1965a) by outlining eight strategies for general-studies staff who wish to extend learning beyond the classroom. Among these eight strategies, the second strategy concerns the faculty's interaction with Western Michigan University's campus newspaper. Macrorie writes, "Another way to encourage students is to read their letters to the editor in their newspaper, the *Western Herald*, and when we find one that impresses us, to write a card or letter of congratulations and encouragement to the writer. I have known many English teachers in the country who have written condescending or vicious *public* letters attacking student's [*sic*] letters, but few who have written serious and encouraging *private* letters complimenting students on their letters." These remarks constitute another instance of Macrorie's suggesting that students "get with" the campus newspaper. The suggestion Macrorie offers here—namely, that faculty should encourage the student writers of particularly good letters to the editor published in the student newspaper—speaks to a broad notion of encouragement that becomes more prevalent in his later work.[9] The encouragement for which Macrorie advocates is notably predicated upon a student writer's decision to submit a letter to the editor of the *Western Herald*. Thus, in the context of this the second strategy, encouragement of learning outside the classroom seems to also function as an endorsement of public writing. Macrorie suggests that teachers support students who engage in activities that aim to achieve publicity for their writing.

It is important to note, though, that Macrorie's endorsement is complex, as it backs *private* letter writing as an effective way to support *public* letter writing. On the one hand, Macrorie positions public letters written by faculty in response to letters written by students as a familiar kind of response as well as a vehicle of attack. On the other hand, he positions private letters as a much rarer and much more encouraging response to the same situation. Macrorie's endorsement relies upon a distinction between public writing and private writing, and two important points emerge, I think, from this distinction. First, Macrorie's distinction relies upon a dichotomy between public and private that, in the past two decades, has been challenged by many scholars, including many composition studies scholars.[10] Although Macrorie staked much of his career on disabling dichotomies, especially the dichotomy of objectivity and subjectivity,[11] and although Macrorie would challenge the division between public and private later in his career,[12] the dichotomy between public and private seems to proceed unchallenged in this instance. Indeed, the letters to which Macrorie refers could better be described as more or less private and more or less public—that is, private or public to a degree. Second and related, Macrorie's distinction depends upon his knowledge of letters written by faculty and sent to student letter writers. It follows that Macrorie would have better knowledge of letters that were more public—for instance, letters published in a campus newspaper—than he would have of letters that were less public—for instance, letters exchanged between one faculty member and one student. But since the possibility remains that faculty might have been writing private attack letters (of which Macrorie would not have had any knowledge), I would guess that knowledge is not Macrorie's central point: he seems more interested in guiding pedagogy than he does in preserving the dichotomy between public letters and private letters. Put differently, Macrorie's point is to criticize condescending and vicious public attacks of student writers by teachers.[13]

As he urges writing teachers to "get with" the campus newspaper and criticizes faculty attacks on student writers who go public in those same newspapers, Macrorie can be understood as articulating a pedagogical stance in which the writing teacher encourages public writing. The writing teacher, Macrorie tells us, should be encouraging student writers to write for the campus newspaper and, in effect, go public: "The teacher should encourage his best students to try their hand at revising, or to criticize the critics in letters to the editor" (Macrorie 1963b, 30). Indeed, this measuredly optimistic stance proves to be one Macrorie would occupy throughout his career.[14] Macrorie also signals that, concomitant with this stance, pedagogues must be aware that their highest aspirations for students' public writing might need to be tempered. Macrorie writes that "we must remember that these students on the campus newspaper are taking their first swing at writing for the press," and he challenges us to recall what our first writings were like (30). Viewed in terms of these remarks about writing for the college paper in the early 1960s, Macrorie can be understood as articulating a writing pedagogy that vigorously and supportively encourages public participation.

GETTING PUBLISHED AS GOING PUBLIC

In his work and in his writing, Macrorie emboldens teachers to find ways to publish student work—that is, over and above the letters section of the college newspaper. Publication, of course, constitutes a way of going public, and it is an important aspect of what I might venture to describe as Macrorie's *public writing pedagogy*.[15] The most lucid and succinct description of publication's place in Macrorie's pedagogy occurs at the end of the revised edition of *Telling Writing* in the section "Suggestions for Teachers." In this section, Macrorie enumerates thirteen points that "make up the core of a writing program" (Macrorie 1976, 265). The thirteenth point reads, "Promise publication of the best writing: The dittoed two-column handout is itself a kind of publication. My students have frequently said, 'When I saw my paper *printed* [it was actually only dittoed] in the handout, I could spot faults immediately.' Thumbtack good writing on bulletin boards in the halls. Try to find resources for publishing a magazine or handout to be distributed beyond the classroom. As writers, the wider our readership, the more we feel pressure and desire to tell truths that count" (Macrorie 1976, 265). Interestingly, the material Macrorie uses to elaborate on this point about publication is material that appeared in his 1965 speech to the general-studies staff at Western Michigan University. Among the eight suggestions Macrorie presents in his 1965 speech are

the suggestions that faculty (1) "get hold of and read student publications"; (2) share exciting student work with administrators or even leg-
islators; and (3) "set up a bulletin board which beguiles students into
running argument with each other about matters worth arguing about"
(Macrorie 1965a, 4–6). Since there is evidence that these three suggestions significantly influenced his practices more generally, the very strong
possibility remains that these three strategies would have been implemented in Macrorie's course on public language and literature.

Macrorie enacted his first suggestion—that faculty familiarize themselves with student publication—almost immediately upon joining the faculty at Western Michigan University, which was some four years before he
would include this strategy in his speech. Macrorie's 1964 DIS acknowledges his sponsorship of *Calliope*, a "student literary magazine." Not only
did Macrorie sponsor the *Calliope* publication, he also served as faculty
advisor for "the literary and philosophical supplement" to the campus
newspaper titled the *Western Review*,[16] and he founded and coedited a
magazine featuring college and high-school writing named *Undressed*.
As department minutes and correspondence confirm, Macrorie's support of this last publication far exceeded dedicating time and energy
to the publication, as Macrorie personally financed the printing of
Undressed (Department of English Collection; Schroeder and Boe 2004,
6–7). Macrorie's efforts behind no fewer than five publications that featured student writing indicate that establishing and sustaining opportunities for student writing to reach or perhaps constitute a wider readership was, indeed, a significant part of his work. But since Macrorie was
very much interested in and counted himself among the readership and
leadership of these student publications, his support of student publication cannot be viewed merely as an effort to maintain venues for student expression. In a March 25, 1965, letter to the director of Western
Michigan University's honors program, Macrorie outlines a pedagogical
and institutional rationale for publishing student writing. According to
Macrorie, publication helps students learn to write better and enhances
the reputation of the university. In this letter, Macrorie writes that a
"great many" students "have appeared in print in *Calliope*, the literary
magazine and the *Western Review*, the supplement to the *Western Herald*."
But, Macrorie contends that more publication is needed: "The best
encouragement they [i.e., students] can get is publication, we think,
in campus publications and in organizational and general magazines
throughout the country."

The second suggestion—that faculty share student work with
administrators—speaks to Macrorie's understanding of the potent

and potentially dangerous effects of public writing. In *Telling Writing*, Macrorie's rationale for encouraging students to publish their writing seems to be an intrinsic rationale he attributes to students. Macrorie explains that students "feel the pressure of possible publication," and he clearly views this pressure as a good thing for students to feel (Macrorie 1976, 266). But publication has effects beyond individual feelings. The effects of writing, when writing goes public, are infinite—but not always good, and not always pertaining to feelings. Macrorie acknowledges as much in *Uptaught* when he recounts an experience with one student's writing gone public—an experience he dates as occurring on April 22, 1966, less than a year after he presented his speech to the general-studies staff (Macrorie 1970, 26–27). According to Macrorie, a story written in one of his freshman classes was published in an eleven thousand-copy press run of the *Western Review*. The story, which was written by a student named Millie, identified a number of patients in a medical facility without maintaining their confidentiality. Within three hours of the story's being distributed, the director of the medical facility had contacted the university president, who contacted Macrorie, admonishing him that "things are said about individuals and about the home that shouldn't be publicized with real names" (26). Publicity, as Macrorie recalls, was at issue here, and Macrorie makes special note of the potency, vitality, honesty, and even danger student writing can have when it achieves publicity (27). That Macrorie understood the effects of public writing as more than just a feeling is further substantiated by a number of letters he exchanged with various campus administrators regarding student writing that achieved publicity. These letters keep administrators abreast of potentially volatile student work. For instance, a letter written by Macrorie on December 18, 1968, and sent to the chair of the English department and to the president of Western Michigan University alerts them to forthcoming articles in *Undressed* that address generational differences, race relations, and drug use. After explaining his editorial decisions about these pieces, Macrorie reminds his readers that "the university loves to talk about being the inviolable place for the free exchange of ideas, but it has done damned little to encourage the students to exchange freely their ideas with others." Macrorie's comments here not only defend the freedom of the student writer to exchange ideas through publication but also emphasize the responsibility of the teacher to encourage the exchange of ideas through publication. Ostensibly, the teacher who encourages student writers to seek publicity for their compositions, whether through publication or another means, also feels pressure and confronts risk. Communicating with administrators not only helps the public-writing teacher lessen this pressure and mitigate risk but also makes it possible for the teacher to reap the rewards of encouraging students to go public. Case in point: Western Michigan University president James Miller funded a portion of the publication *Undwessed* using his discretionary funds.[17]

The third suggestion mentioned above—that teachers create bulletin boards on which they might publicize student writing—emphasizes Macrorie's expansive definition of publication. This particular suggestion appears twice during Macrorie's 1965 speech—first as an introductory anecdote and second as one of the eight strategies Macrorie recommends for encouraging learning outside the classroom. Macrorie begins the speech by describing a "bulletin board for *Good Writing by Western Students*" (Macrorie 1965a, 1). Macrorie then reads a short essay from that bulletin board along with the sixteen comments written in response to that essay. Macrorie notes his "delight" in the responses, and he recommends that more teachers use the bulletin-board strategy—one he had seen used on at least three college campuses—to publish student work and invite further commentary (3–4). Later in his speech, when he enumerates this strategy for publishing student writing among seven other strategies, he likens these bulletin-board exchanges to "an instant letter to the editor column, which is full of attack and defense, students versus administration, faculty, and students" (4). As his comparison between a piece of student writing thumbtacked to a bulletin board and a piece of student writing printed in a student newspaper implies, publication, for Macrorie, is not merely the end result of a production process involving writers, editors, and designers and yielding a mass-distributed piece of writing. Rather, Macrorie's use of the word *publication* seems more akin to the contemporary usage of the word *publicity* in that it involves degrees of condition and of action. Publicity is, as I have argued, the central characteristic of public-writing pedagogy, and it manifests both as a condition met by a written product and as an action that constitutes a public (Gogan 2014, 538–39). It seems that the importance of this bulletin-board strategy was in the readership the piece he read drew through publicity as well as in the participatory exchange that publicity facilitated.[18] The sixteen comments, each of which were written on the "blank pieces of paper" that were posted on the bulletin board alongside the student essay, are not that much different than those comments that might appear in a contemporary online comment forum: the comments are, as Macrorie notes, "serious, but lightly rather than heavily serious, not ponderous, like a professor's lecture" (Macrorie 1965a, 1, 3).

Across all of these strategies, the point remains that Macrorie was thinking hard about the concept of publicity—that is, publication—at the same time he was proposing to teach a course titled Public Language and Literature. Macrorie's pedagogy valued publicity highly and took its effects seriously, and I suspect that Public Language and Literature would have, too. Macrorie sought to encourage students to seize opportunities through which their writing might meet the condition of publicity and actively attract a wider reading public. Likewise, Macrorie prodded teachers to support, if not create, opportunities for student writing to go public—all with the goal of encouraging exchange between writers and participating readers.

GETTING WITH MASS COMMUNICATION AS GOING PUBLIC

Macrorie maintained a keen personal and professional interest in mass communication. During an interview with Eric Schroeder and John Boe, Macrorie recalls that, as a child, he regularly accompanied his uncle, who ran a thirty-minute broadcast radio news program in Toledo, Ohio, to work (Schroeder and Boe 2004, 5). Macrorie also notes that shadowing his uncle allowed him "to make some associations between speaking and writing" and to observe one person's process of collecting, organizing, and cutting words (Schroeder and Boe 2004, 5). Later, in 1955, as part of his dissertation work, Macrorie shadowed two newspaper reporters—Ken Zwicker of the Ridgewood, New Jersey, *Sunday News* and Peter Khiss of the *New York Times*—observing their reportorial and writing processes. Macrorie's dissertation project charted an evolving notion of objectivity and responsibility in news reporting and, as Maureen Daly Goggin notes, the topic of Macrorie's dissertation was exceptional among his generation of editor peers in composition studies because it did not focus "on a literary topic" (Goggin 2000, 153).

Indeed, Macrorie's interest in mass communication does seem exceptional, especially around the time he edited *CCC*. Just prior to assuming his post as editor, Macrorie referred to mass communication as "A Literature without Criticism" in a 1961 *College English* article of the same name.[19] In this article, he calls upon English departments to offer at least "one upper-class course in the criticism of mass communication" (Macrorie 1961a, 577). Macrorie supports his call for a new course with a largely civic rationale: he wants to transform citizens into citizen-critics who spread across the country, sift through a vast quantity of messages, write thoughtful critiques about these messages, and submit these critiques as letters to the local newspaper (577).[20] Macrorie quips, "What a shocking thought—a continuing critical response to mass communication by the people!" (577). After his stint as editor of *CCC* ended, Macrorie published another argument in favor of offering a course in the criticism of mass communication. His 1965 "What Freshmen Communication Courses Left Behind" appeared in the *California English Journal* and, once again, argues that English professors should encourage students to study mass communication, "as the newspaper report, the recipe, the expository essay, the magazine article of fact moves toward the best of its kind, it moves toward literature" (Macrorie 1965b, 22).

In these two articles, Macrorie strikes me as suggesting that the everyday and very public messages that comprise mass communication are concomitantly the public literature that occupies half of his proposed course's title. As such, Macrorie's proposed course Public Language and Literature might very well have asked students to analyze mass communication, stressing the civic nature of the critical act. But Macrorie's proposed course would probably not have been restricted to the analysis of public writing, as Macrorie was resolute in his view that analysis should be accompanied by production—that "writing papers" and attending to "the realities of communication" prove crucial to the student of public language and literature (Macrorie 1965b, 27). Macrorie's courses coupled criticism and craft, and his course in public language and literature would have most likely done so as well.

Macrorie's pedagogical approach to mass communication—that is, public language and literature—was a novel one in that it departed from an old approach that "branded all news reporters as dishonest and dissembling" (Macrorie 1965b, 21). Macrorie's new approach grew out of his dissertation work, work explicitly and primarily addressed to "teachers of college English and communication" and work framed by a survey of twelve schools, members of which were also members of the Conference on College Composition and Communication (Macrorie 1955, v, 6–10). Macrorie's survey revealed that the study of newspapers in college composition and communication courses "followed the lead of content analysts of propaganda" by "looking for tricks and misrepresentations of language" (10). Macrorie—as a member of the communication skills department at Michigan State College (now Michigan State University) and the English department at San Francisco State College (now San Francisco State University), as well as the author of *The Perceptive Writer, Reader, and Speaker* (Macrorie 1959b, a textbook that includes a section on understanding mass communication)—would hone his approach to teaching mass communication before arriving at Western Michigan University and assuming the editorship of *CCC*. Indeed, Macrorie's work in mass communication provides some context for Diana George and John Trimbur's observation that "from the time Ken Macrorie took over as *CCC* editor in 1962, articles on the 'communication approach,' on mass media, propaganda analysis, and general semantics virtually disappeared from the journal" (George and Trimbur 1999, 685). Macrorie's own remarks in 1961 confirm this point: "A course emphasizing the old propaganda approach to communication confirms or enforces prejudices; a course attempting to describe the characteristics inherent in the process of each medium sharpens perceptions and sometimes opens the eye and the ear to totally new experience" (Macrorie 1961a, 576). Macrorie's purpose was, in other words, to abandon the old, widespread, and prejudiced approach to teaching publicly oriented college composition and communication courses, and it seems he used his editorial position to do so on a national level.[21]

On a more local level, Macrorie took steps toward enacting this same shift at Western Michigan University even before he arrived on campus. Teaching a course in the criticism of mass communication actually became a central point in Macrorie's spring 1961 negotiations with Western Michigan University. At the same time he negotiated his salary and his rank, he also, in a letter written on April 3, 1961, asked for "assurance that [he] could soon teach one upper-class course in the criticism of mass communication." During these negotiations, as a matter of fact, Macrorie gave up his rank as associate professor sooner than he gave up mention of teaching a course in the criticism of mass communication.[22] While Macrorie's April 3, 1961, letter indicates his willingness "to help shape the freshman courses in composition and com[munication]"— albeit not in any administrative capacity—the letter suggests Macrorie preferred involvement with the communication course over and above the composition course. "I think I can do more," Macrorie writes, "by continuing a scholarly investigation of the problems involved in the criticism of mass communication."

Committee meeting minutes seem to substantiate Macrorie's preference for the communication course, as he appears to have been less active at college writing-staff meetings and more active at the communication-staff meetings. Macrorie attended writing-staff meetings less frequently than he did communication-staff meeting. At times, he offered his thoughts on writing to the writing staff, the department, and the university. For instance, on October 7, 1965, he led a college writing-staff seminar that outlined his pedagogy and also included a discussion of writing for publication (John R. Phillips Collection). However,

Macrorie never assumed a leadership role on the college writing committee, which was charged with administering the composition course. Maintaining his aversion to administering such courses, Macrorie declined a nomination to that committee on December 8, 1965 (John R. Phillips Collection).

By comparison, Macrorie regularly attended communication-staff meetings, contributing to the discussions and working to develop new course proposals—largely in an attempt to shift the pedagogical approach with which teachers approached such courses. The local dimensions of this shift were perhaps best articulated by Macrorie at a December 3, 1965, communication-staff meeting (Department of English Collection). The meeting minutes reflect that, during this meeting, Macrorie advised his colleagues to abandon "the mechanical, mathematical approach to a description of the communication process because it tends to make the process seem manipulative" and instead urged them "to emphasize the craft of creating communication, not a self-obsession with analyzing communication."

GETTING PERSONAL AS GOING PUBLIC

In *Uptaught*, Macrorie recounts an experience he had speaking at "a national conference" to "an audience of college teachers" in Louisville, Kentucky (Macrorie 1970, 136). This particular conference was the 1967 Conference on College Composition and Communication convention, as indicated by a November 14, 1966, correspondence between Macrorie and program chairman Dudley Bailey. Bailey invited Richard Larson, Hans Guth, and Macrorie to present talks "on current practices in the teaching of rhetoric." Macrorie's talk, as he recalls it in *Uptaught*, featured his reading of a short piece written by a high-school student named Louise Freyburger. The piece, which was titled "Reed," elicited a response from an audience member, who claimed that the piece of writing was "too personal" and that writing "teachers need to teach our students *public* writing, which they must employ throughout college and in graduate school" (137). This comment serves as the opening anecdote to the "Graduate School" section of *Uptaught*. Macrorie titles the anecdote "Public Writing" and refers to the audience member's comments as he ruminates on two relationships—the first, between the personal and the public, and the second, between school and society—both of which inform his public-writing pedagogy.

In the first place, the audience member's comments position personal writing and public writing as a pair of antithetical terms in which the public or social is valued more than the private or personal. By labeling the writing that emerges from Macrorie's pedagogy as "too personal," the audience member critiques the value of Macrorie's approach to teaching writing (Macrorie 1970, 137). These comments reflect a conventional view in composition studies and, since Macrorie is often associated with the personal or the private, Macrorie's pedagogy is typically devalued. For instance, the environment created by Macrorie's pedagogy has been described by Weisser as aiming to "cultivate the individual development of students, not through direct political or social confrontation, but through greater attention to the individual's private version of reality" (Weisser 2002, 19). Weisser bases his synopsis of Macrorie's pedagogy on Macrorie's later work, but, as I have been attempting to demonstrate in this piece, Macrorie's later work echoes aspects of his earlier work—work that made space for public writing.

The dichotomy between the public (or social) and the private (or personal), which is captured by the anecdote from the 1967 convention, is one that has been challenged by composition studies scholars over the past twenty years. As I noted earlier in this piece, Macrorie appeared to reinforce this dichotomy in his 1965 speech to the general-studies staff by recommending that professors send private letters to students who publish work in the campus newspaper. Later, he would assert that "the line between writing privately and writing publicly is difficult to draw" (Macrorie 1968, 39). Nonetheless, in Macrorie's case, the dichotomy between the personal and the public need not be a bad one, for Macrorie's personal history arguably provides some of the best evidence of his engagement with public-writing pedagogy. The personal correspondence included in the archives at Western Michigan University have, of course, furnished a great deal of the evidence that suggests what going public with Macrorie would have entailed, but the importance of the eight-page "Graduate School" section of *Uptaught* to my argument must not be overlooked either. In this section, Macrorie details his experiences taking two graduate courses: one, Public Opinion, at Columbia University and one in writing for publics at Teachers College. In the first class, Macrorie was assigned Walter Lippmann's *Public Opinion*, a text he had already read by a thinker who has since been invoked by composition studies scholars in discussions about public-writing pedagogy (Macrorie 1970, 139–40).[23] In the second class, Macrorie was excited to be working with two well-known professors, and he thought he would be writing for readers other than the teacher (140). Macrorie documents his deep dissatisfaction with each course and, in doing so, demonstrates that, sometime during his graduate work between 1952 and 1954, his personal experience with two disappointing courses allowed him to begin formulating a view of effective public-writing pedagogy.

The opening anecdote to the "Graduate School" section of *Uptaught* is surprising, in the second place, because the audience member suggests that public writing is taught in school so that public writing can serve school. Here, the audience member's comments stumble upon another dichotomy that pervades composition studies scholarship on public writing: the dichotomy between school and society, or academic writing and public writing. As David Fleming notes, composition studies scholars who study and teach public writing often operate according to a binary logic that pits school against society, impugning the writing that occurs in the classroom and lauding the writing that occurs in society (Fleming 2010, 212). The audience member's comments contest this logic by collapsing the distinction in a way that makes school both the ends and the means of public-writing pedagogy. Macrorie, like his readers, probably appreciated the irony in this comment, as the suggestion that public writing should only serve academic purposes is an argumentative backing rarely invoked in discussions about public writing. Yet, the binary logic that pits school against society has been challenged on different grounds—namely, that any division between school and society is less clear than it may initially seem. Fleming and others, myself included, have made this argument, and it seems that Macrorie makes it too (Fleming 2010, 215–20, 225; Gogan 2014, 543–47).

Macrorie dissolves the distinction between the public and the academic by arguing that publics can be created in school, that one can go public in a classroom. In *Uptaught*, Macrorie makes this point clear when he observes, "English professors customarily bridle at a social gathering when they hear the remark, 'Oh, an English teacher! I'll have to watch my grammar!' The professors are insulted. They would never correct anyone's grammar in public. They forget the classroom is public" (Macrorie 1970, 66). Macrorie reinforces this view that the classroom is public when he describes his disappointing graduate courses. In the class Public Opinion, the professor talked in a way Macrorie categorizes as "seldom entertaining or instructive" (140). However, the professor persisted in giving these lectures because, as Macrorie recognizes, the professor "had a small public in front of him" (140).[24] In the other graduate course, Macrorie expected he "would be writing for the other mature students around the table, a public, and our writing would take on a liveliness and dignity that it could not possess when students wrote only for Teacher" (140). Since Macrorie sees the classroom as a public, his comments anticipate the work of a good number of public-writing pedagogues who admit the possibility of a classroom functioning as or like a public. Susan Wells, for instance, finds a potentially public exigency in the cultural studies classroom (Wells 1996, 338), while Rosa A. Eberly (1999, 166–67; 2000, 169–70) and Nathaniel A. Rivers and Ryan P. Weber (Rivers and Weber 2011, 206–7) favor viewing the classroom as a protopublic—that is, as sort of practice ground for going public. Whereas the views forwarded by Wells, Eberly, and Rivers and Weber all hinge upon the authenticity of the classroom experience as a public experience, Macrorie's perspective in *Uptaught* makes no such distinction. For Macrorie, the distinction between a classroom and a public seems to be one of degree or scale; small or large, classrooms are publics.

Macrorie's view of the classroom as a public is often overshadowed by his comments about truth telling and honesty—comments that lead scholars such as Barbara Couture to contend that Macrorie's pedagogy "presupposes that public environments for rhetorical expression, particularly the public school setting, actively work against one's telling the truth because they suppress self-identity" (Couture 1998, 49). Couture's characterization of Macrorie focuses on only one of thirty components Macrorie, in 1968, listed as comprising his pedagogical program. The characterization occurs in the context of a larger argument that attempts to delineate rhetorical dimensions of narcissism, and, therefore, the characterization is meant to emphasize the individual, personal, and expressive dimensions of Macrorie's pedagogy. Couture is right to note that Macrorie rails against stifled expression— personal, public, or both—but it should be noted that Macrorie views stifled expression more as a function of bad or ineffective teaching than as a function of going public. Indeed, Macrorie's personal experience with publicly oriented courses seems to suppose the opposite: public environments help encourage rhetorical expression and help make writing better.

BEYOND CORRODED CATEGORIES

More than getting with the college paper, getting published, or getting with mass communication, getting to know a more publicly oriented Macrorie might, in fact, be the best way to conceptualize what going public with Macrorie and his course Public Language and Literature might have entailed. Reinserting Macrorie into our disciplinary histories—by way of small-scale, concrete, microhistorical inquiry—qualifies abstract categorizations of an individual who, in many ways, encouraged public writing. Put simply, Macrorie's relationship to publics and public-writing pedagogy proves much more complex than some of our discipline's worn and rusted categories would admit.

The primary category to which I refer is that of the *expressionist* or *expressivist* label used to classify Macrorie. Over three decades ago, Berlin's "Contemporary Composition: The Major Pedagogical Theories" listed Macrorie first among a group of individuals Berlin associated with what he described as "expressionist" theories of composition instruction or "expressionist" rhetoric (Berlin 1982, 772). Berlin traces this rhetoric back to Plato but also notes its consonance with American transcendentalism (Berlin 1982, 771). As he explains in "Rhetoric and Ideology in the Writing Class," Berlin sees expressionistic writing pedagogies as responding to "current economic, political, and social arrangements" through "a resistance that is always construed in individual terms" (Berlin 1988, 487). The expressionist, expressionistic, or, as it would later be called, expressivist category was not a static one, as Berlin eventually dissected it into the two subcategories of anarchical expressionists and individual expressionists (Berlin 1987, 145–46), but the category was a compelling one: commenting on the success of Berlin's taxonomy, Peter Elbow once remarked that the labels forged by Berlin, labels including the expressivist label, "set like concrete in our profession" (Elbow 2004, 19; cf. Stock, this collection). The category has, as Elbow suggests, widely influenced composition studies scholarship, including scholarship on public writing. Most often, the category of expressivist rhetoric or writing pedagogy acts as a foil to public rhetoric. Perhaps the most pronounced example of this category's acting as a foil to public rhetoric is found in *Moving beyond Academic Discourse*, in which Weisser claims that Macrorie and other expressivists "inadvertently invalidated collective political, social, and public writing practices" (Weisser 2002, 20). Weisser's claim is simply too sweeping to reflect the complexities of any one individual writer, teacher, researcher, or leader—especially Macrorie.

Abstracted into large-scale claims that depart from concrete evidence, the expressivist category requires recalibration with historical evidence. Such a recalibration qualifies the kind of historical project Berlin undertook as well as the kind of historical evidence he used to support his study. Berlin outlines both in *Rhetoric and Reality*, where he explains that his taxonomy "is simply an attempt to make manageable the discussion of major rhetorics" (Berlin 1987, 6). In order to manage the discussion, Berlin offers macrolevel conclusions indicative of a cultural history. The evidence Berlin uses to arrive at these conclusions and the categories that capture them are largely the academic texts published by composition scholars. In the opening to *Rhetoric and Reality*, Berlin writes, "I will thus be as concerned with what the authors of articles and textbooks say they are attempting as with their pedagogical strategies for achieving their aims" (5). Of Macrorie's articles and textbooks, Berlin only consults two—Macrorie's (1976) *Telling Writing* and the short 1964 *CCC* piece "Composition as Art" (Macrorie 1964a)—as the evidence upon which he draws his conclusions about Macrorie's place in the history of composition.[25]

By shifting the scale of historical inquiry and the kinds of historical evidence examined, this microhistory responds to the categorization of Macrorie as an expressivist, underscoring and verifying previous observations about Macrorie issued by Elbow and Gerald Nelms. In "Ken Macrorie's Commitment and the Need for What's Wild," Elbow repudiates Berlin's category and also Macrorie's characterization within "that little box labeled 'expressivist'" (Elbow 2004, 18). Elbow explains that, contrary to the expressivist label, "Ken was a sophisticated, complicated character" (18). In a brief entry about Macrorie for the *Encyclopedia of Rhetoric and Composition*, Nelms writes, "Macrorie has often been labeled a 'Romantic' or 'Expressivist' (see James Berlin's *Rhetoric and Reality*), but on closer examination, he problematizes easy classification" (Nelms 1996, 420). To support this claim, Nelms draws upon Macrorie's published articles and books. Microhistorical inquiry and a small-scale dig into the archives reveals even more support. The correspondence, curricular materials, committee-meeting minutes, typescripts, and other miscellanea all work to reveal that Macrorie's complex character is not easily categorized.

To be clear: the revelation that Macrorie went public, and went public regularly, should not be read as an attempt to replace Berlin's expressionist category with another more appropriate category.[26] Microhistorical inquiry does not seek to substitute one grand narrative for another and, in Macrorie's case, some historical evidence does support Berlin's perspective that Macrorie carried on in the American transcendental tradition. After all, Macrorie regularly taught a course in Thoreau at Western Michigan University, and he peppered his publications with references to Thoreau.[27] Furthermore, the 1965 speech Macrorie delivered to the general-studies staff received its title, "An Immense Frivolity," from Thoreau's 1863 essay "Life without Principle" (Macrorie 1965a, 3). And, perhaps most strikingly, Macrorie twice turned down extraordinary professional opportunities with lines that all but mentioned Walden Pond and all but positioned Macrorie as a reincarnated Henry David Thoreau. On October 29, 1965, Macrorie rejected an offer of a permanent faculty position from Western Washington State College, explaining, "My wife and I are in love with a pond we live on in the country—not a house in sight." Again, on January 18, 1966, he declined a summer teaching appointment at Loretto Heights College because of a previous engagement before noting, "I am not at all sure that if you were to ask me for another summer that I would accept; for I am always busy at a writing project and I love my country home in the woods by a pond."

Rather than replace the expressivist category, this microhistory has attempted to retune this dominant historical category in composition studies by recalibrating it with particular pieces of archival evidence. Put differently, the goal of this microhistory has been to knock the rust off of the corroded expressivist category and to simultaneously render a more nuanced representation of Macrorie in composition studies by reducing the scale of the historical inquiry. This microhistory demonstrates that composition studies scholars should become more familiar with a more publicly oriented Macrorie: the Macrorie who went public as a writer, teacher, researcher, and leader; the Macrorie who wrote his own letters to the editor of the *Kalamazoo Gazette* addressing topics from traffic safety to race riots, from fallout shelters to the Vietnam War;[28] the Macrorie who was not only a member of the National Council of Teachers of English and the Michigan Council of Teachers of English but who was also a member of the American Association of University Professors, the American Civil Liberties Union, and the National Association for the Advancement of Colored People;[29] the Macrorie who notes on his 1964 DIS that he "was on a small committee that produced an advertisement in the *Kalamazoo Gazette* against the government program of spending money for air raid shelters, signed by 262 citizens"; and, the Macrorie who, on that same 1964 DIS, suggested that he was qualified to teach a course titled Public Language and Literature.

Notes

1. Levi's argument finds support in the work of microhistorian Carlo Ginzburg (1989, 101) even though Ginzburg's version of microhistory differs from Levi's version (cf. Magnússon and Szijártó 2013, 16).

2. While it can be argued that rhetoric is ever public and that the history of public rhetoric spans millennia, two detailed histories of the public turn within composition studies can be found in Farmer (2013, 1–11) and Mathieu (2005, 1–14). For a discussion of the challenges related to this turn, see also David Gold's contribution to this volume.

3. Unless otherwise noted in the text, all archival materials, including personal correspondences, departmental communications, presentations, and publications are from Ken Macrorie's personnel file, which is kept by the Western Michigan University Archives and Regional History Collections.

4. While Macrorie was quite active on a number of committees, he also excused himself from a good number, especially when he did not believe in the committee's charge or when he felt his time was better spent elsewhere. For instance, in a letter dated January 8, 1973, Macrorie laments that "at Michigan State and here [Western Michigan University] I seemed to be on all the committees, and I did little for the cause of teaching and learning," which leads Macrorie to remark, "I have found ways of making my words persuade other teachers and they are not committee ways." For more examples, see letters dated October 18, 1965; October 10, 1966; and, May 19, 1972, and compare with Macrorie's 1966 "A Letter."

5. There was some confusion as to when Macrorie's editorial duties would commence and as to whether he would need a course release in fall of 1961, his first semester at Western Michigan University. A July 13, 1961, letter makes it appear that the course reduction commenced with Macrorie's editorial duties in the spring of 1962.

6. See the letter from Macrorie to Rogers dated February 6, 1962.

7. Macrorie's 1964 DIS reveals his enthusiasm for the course Objectivity and Subjectivity in Writing that had recently concluded. Macrorie writes, "I thought this an unusually successful class, but can't be sure whether it was the subject and design or the students, who happened to be one of the most brilliant groups I've ever taught anywhere—and I've taught all honors classes at Michigan State and Graduate seminars at San Francisco State."

8. Information that Macrorie offers in *A Vulnerable Teacher* suggests he might actually have taught a version of his course Public Language and Literature, but under a different name. In *A Vulnerable Teacher*, Macrorie includes a description of a senior seminar course New Ways of Responding to Literature, and the description has students "commenting on a piece of writing or a film so as to show what the work means to the reader as an individual as well as to the larger public" (Macrorie 1974, 44).

9. Later in his speech Macrorie explains that he has "been talking about encouraging students" and bluntly asserts, "That is my point" (Macrorie 1965a, 7). The point of encouragement is threaded throughout Macrorie's writing, including *Uptaught* (Macrorie 1970), *Telling Writing* (Macrorie 1976), and *A Vulnerable Teacher*, where Macrorie writes, "Encourage, encourage. One of my fundamentals in teaching" (Macrorie 1974, 132).

10. Dobrin (2004, 217) argues that "public discourse is as much private discourse as private discourse is public." Dobrin's position is, in fact, shared by a good number of composition studies scholars, among them postprocess theorists who follow Thomas Kent (1999, 1) in viewing all writing as public. These pedagogues acknowledge, as Couture and Kent (2004) note in their collection *The Private, the Public, and the Published: Reconciling Private Lives and Public Rhetoric*, that there has been a significant blurring of and "confusion over the boundaries of the public and the private" (Couture 2004, 2–3; Kent 2004, ix).

11. See, for example, Macrorie 1955, 1956a, 1956b, 1959a, 1961b; 1964b.

12. Three years after delivering his address, Macrorie (1968, 39) would write that "the line between writing privately and publicly is difficult to draw."

13. Macrorie reinforces this point when he issues his forceful critique of Albert Kitzhaber's *Themes, Theories, and Therapy*, stating, "At many schools where English teachers care about writing, a literary magazine really flourishes and teachers point to the powerful letters to the editor written by students for the campus newspaper" (Macrorie 1963a, 269).

14. For more on Macrorie's stance of encouragement, see Ritter's discussion of Macrorie's 1964 *CCC* editor's report in this collection.

15. In "Macrorie's Gifts," Ed Darling contends that Macrorie "did not require publication but invited it, and in his own teaching he provided publications in which

student writing could appear" (Darling 2004, 27). Darling's assertion is based upon his familiarity with Macrorie's *Writing to Be Read*, and it is largely corroborated by my research.

16. In an October 10, 1966, letter sent to the head of the Department of English, Macrorie notes that he is "still serving as advisor" to the *Western Review*, indicating that his service began well before 1966.

17. See the "Publisher's Note" in the April 14, 1969, issue of *Unduressed* in Macrorie's personnel file, as well as Schroeder and Boe (2004, 6–7).

18. This point can be traced back to Macrorie's 1952 piece "'Two-Campism' in Education," in which he draws upon George Herbert Mead to define communication as "an exchange of responses" (Macrorie 1952b, 299).

19. This article was written and published, as its "author note" mentions, while Macrorie was a member of the faculty at San Francisco State College. However, Macrorie sent the manuscript version of this article to Western Michigan University as part of his application for a faculty position. In a February 18, 1961, follow-up correspondence with Western Michigan University's Department of English, Macrorie notes the article's acceptance by *College English* and expresses his "hope that its eventual publication in a magazine more and more devoted to the study of literature will help to attract good minds to the study of mass communication and to dignify the pursuit in English departments." (See also Macrorie 1952a and 1952b as well as Panel and Workshop Reports [1958, 1959] that were published in *CCC*.)

20. My use of the construction *citizen-critic* is meant to suggest the connection between Macrorie's argument in this particular *College English* article and Eberly's argument in *Citizen Critics*. Neither Macrorie nor Eberly use the hyphenated construction *citizen–critic*, but both envision a public role for criticism and both use the words *citizen* and *critic* to expound upon this vision.

21. In a June 19, 1961, letter to the head of the Department of English at Western Michigan University, Macrorie discloses that he has been encouraged to shift aspects of the *CCC* journal in order "to make it a stronger and livelier publication." He further acknowledges the role he will play in these changes as editor, referencing his own "revolutionary plans" for *CCC*. For more on this shift, see Goggin (2000, 60–65).

22. After serving as an associate professor at San Francisco State College, Macrorie was hired as an assistant professor at Western Michigan University. During these negotiations, the question of rank seems to have been finalized in a letter from Rogers to Macrorie dated April 19, 1961. However, the question of teaching a criticism of mass communication course was not put to rest until late May, as indicated by a letter sent from Macrorie to Rogers on May 24, 1961. Macrorie, as it turns out, would be promoted to associate professor the following year, elevated to full professor by 1965, and granted tenure in 1966. As a letter from Macrorie to Rogers, dated January 6, 1964, documents, this unusual situation often forced Macrorie to have to advocate for his own advancement within the department.

23. Indeed, Eberly (1999, 167), Ryder (2011, 34–37), and Farmer (2013, 23) all acknowledge Lippmann's work on the public and, at the same time, mention Dewey. When considering the qualifications Macrorie might have had to teach a course titled Public Language and Literature, it is important to realize that Macrorie was familiar with Lippmann as well as Dewey—so much so, in the case of the latter, Chris Burnham (2004, 42) recognizes Macrorie "as clearly working from Dewey and his experiential school."

24. Lindemann's review essay captures the scene quite well: "And, once again, he encountered teachers who lectured for hours about communicating with the public

but seemed insensitive to the small public attending class every day" (Lindemann 1982, 360).

25.   Berlin's treatment of Macrorie, as described in this piece, is quite similar to his treatment of Warren Taylor, as described by David Stock earlier in this collection.

26.   If the purpose of this microhistory were to merely replace the expressivist category with another more appropriate category, then Macrorie's category of "personal-public" writing (Macrorie 1984, 207) might be a strong contender. Macrorie forges this hyphenated construction in the third edition of *Writing to Be Read*, using it to capture an approach to writing Darling summarizes as allowing "a writer to choose personal topics that matter and, at the same time, produce writing aimed at a public audience" (Darling 2004, 27). Not only does this personal-public construct seem to encapsulate the goal of much of Macrorie's work, but it also approximates the work of contemporary composition scholars such as Linda K. Shamoon and Eileen Medeiros, who work to draw students "into expressing themselves publicly on an issue" (Shamoon and Medeiros 2010, 184).

27.   For a detailed description of one iteration of his Thoreau class, see "A Thoreau Course" in *A Vulnerable Teacher* (Macrorie 1974, 55–82). Note, also, references to Thoreau in Macrorie's other work (Macrorie 1959a, 1965b, 1968, 1970, 1976, 1980).

28.   Macrorie's letters to the editor of the *Kalamazoo Gazette* number seven: December 3, 1965; "Gull Road Speed Limit Cut Asked; Long-Range Disposal Plan Sought," June 8, 1966; "Ky and Wife Batman Stars?" March 24, 1967; August 8, 1967; "Fallout Shelter Poll Criticized," November 3, 1967; "Cites Dangers in High-Speed Chases," June 25, 1969; and, "Stop Our Killing," May 25, 1972.

29.   Macrorie's memberships in these organizations are documented on forms in his personnel file at the Western Michigan University Archives and Regional History Collections as well in as his biographical file at the Michigan State University Archives and Historical Collections.

References

Berlin, James A. 1982. "Contemporary Composition: The Major Pedagogical Theories." *College English* 44 (8): 765–77. http://dx.doi.org/10.2307/377329.

Berlin, James A. 1987. *Rhetoric and Reality: Writing Instruction in American Colleges, 1900–1985*. Carbondale: Southern Illinois University Press.

Berlin, James A. 1988. "Rhetoric and Ideology in the Writing Class." *College English* 50 (5): 477–94. http://dx.doi.org/10.2307/377477.

Burnham, Chris. 2004. "Still *Uptaught* after All These Years." *Writing on the Edge* 15 (1): 35–43.

Couture, Barbara. 1998. *Toward a Phenomenological Rhetoric: Writing, Professionalism, and Altruism*. Carbondale: Southern Illinois University Press.

Couture, Barbara. 2004. "Reconciling Private Lives and Public Rhetoric: What's at Stake?" In *The Private, the Public, and the Published: Reconciling Private Lives and Public Rhetoric*, edited by Barbara Couture and Thomas Kent, 1–16. Logan: Utah State University Press.

Couture, Barbara, and Thomas Kent, eds. 2004. *The Private, the Public, and the Published: Reconciling Private Lives and Public Rhetoric*. Logan: Utah State University Press.

Darling, Ed. 2004. "Macrorie's Gifts." *Writing on the Edge* 15 (1): 27–32.

Department of English Collection. Western Michigan University Archives and Regional History Collections, Kalamazoo. Record Group 22/8.

Dobrin, Sidney I. 2004. "Going Public: Locating Public/Private Discourse." In *The Private, the Public, and the Published: Reconciling Private Lives and Public Rhetoric*, edited by Barbara Couture and Thomas Kent, 216–30. Logan: Utah State University Press.

Eberly, Rosa A. 1999. "From Writers, Audience, and Communities to Publics: Writing Classrooms as Protopublic Spaces." *Rhetoric Review* 18 (1): 165–78. http://dx.doi.org /10.1080/07350199909359262.

Eberly, Rosa A. 2000. *Citizen Critics: Literary Public Spheres.* Chicago: University of Illinois Press.

Elbow, Peter. 2004. "Ken Macrorie's Commitment and the Need for What's Wild." *Writing on the Edge* 15 (1): 18–23.

Farmer, Frank. 2013. *After the Public Turn: Composition, Counterpublics, and the Citizen Bricoleur.* Logan: Utah State University Press.

Fleming, David. 2010. "Finding a Place for School in Rhetoric's Public Turn." In *The Public Work of Rhetoric: Citizen-Scholars and Civic Engagement*, edited by John M. Ackerman and David J. Coogan, 211–28. Columbia: University of South Carolina Press.

George, Diana, and John Trimbur. 1999. "The 'Communication Battle,' or Whatever Happened to the 4th C?" *College Composition and Communication* 50 (4): 682–98. http://dx.doi.org/10.2307/358487.

Ginzburg, Carlo. (1986) 1989. *Clues, Myths, and the Historical Method.* Translated by John Tedeschi and Anne C. Tedeschi. Baltimore, MD: Johns Hopkins University Press.

Gogan, Brian. 2014. "Expanding the Aims of Public Rhetoric and Writing Pedagogy: Writing Letters to Editors." *College Composition and Communication* 65 (4): 534–59.

Goggin, Maureen Daly. 2000. *Authoring a Discipline: Scholarly Journals and the Post-World War II Emergence of Rhetoric and Composition.* Mahwah, NJ: Lawrence Earlbaum.

John R. Phillips Collection. Western Michigan University Archives and Regional History Collections, Kalamazoo. Record Group 22/8.

Kent, Thomas. 1999. Introduction to *Post-Process Theory: Beyond the Writing-Process Paradigm*, edited by Thomas Kent, 1–6. Carbondale: Southern Illinois University Press.

Kent, Thomas. 2004. Preface to *The Private, the Public, and the Published: Reconciling Private Lives and Public Rhetoric*, edited by Barbara Couture and Thomas Kent, ix–xiii. Logan: Utah State University Press.

Levi, Giovanni. (1991) 2001. "On Microhistory." In *New Perspectives on Historical Writing.* 2nd ed. Edited by Peter Burke, 97–119. University Park: Pennsylvania State University Press.

Levi, Giovanni. 2012. "Microhistory and the Recovery of Complexity." In *Historical Knowledge: In Quest of Theory, Method, and Evidence*, edited by Susanna Fellman and Marjatta Rahikainen, 121–32. London: Cambridge Scholars.

Lindemann, Erika. 1982. "Ken Macrorie: A Review Essay." *College English* 44 (4): 358–67. http://dx.doi.org/10.2307/376597.

Macrorie, Ken. 1952a. "Examining the Newspaper." *College English* 14 (2): 112–13. http:// dx.doi.org/10.2307/371774.

Macrorie, Ken. 1952b. "Two-Campism in Education." *Bulletin of the American Association of University Professors* 38 (2): 296–303. http://dx.doi.org/10.2307/40220895.

Macrorie, Ken. 1955. "Objectivity and Responsibility in Newspaper Reporting." PhD diss., Columbia University. Ann Arbor, MI: Doctoral Dissertation Series (12064).

Macrorie, Ken. 1956a. "The Objective Reporter." *Antioch Review* 16 (3): 385–91. http:// dx.doi.org/10.2307/4609893.

Macrorie, Ken. 1956b. "The Process of News Reporting." *Etc.; a Review of General Semantics* 13 (4): 254–64.

Macrorie, Ken. 1959a. "Objectivity: Dead or Alive?" *Journalism Quarterly* 36 (2): 145–50. http://dx.doi.org/10.1177/107769905903600201.

Macrorie, Ken. 1959b. *The Perceptive Writer, Reader, and Speaker.* New York: Harcourt, Brace, and Company.

Macrorie, Ken. 1961a. "A Literature without Criticism." *College English* 22 (8): 565–56, 575–68. http://dx.doi.org/10.2307/373500.

Macrorie, Ken. 1961b. "Re-Enactment of Reality." *Nieman Reports* 15 (April): 35–7.

Macrorie, Ken. 1963a. "Review of *Themes, Theories, and Therapy: The Teaching of Writing in College*, by Albert Kitzhaber." *College Composition and Communication* 14 (4): 267–70. http://dx.doi.org/10.2307/355643.

Macrorie, Ken. 1963b. "Spitting on the Campus Newspaper." *College Composition and Communication* 14 (1): 28–31. http://dx.doi.org/10.2307/355295.

Macrorie, Ken. 1964a. "Composition as Art." *College Composition and Communication* 15 (1): back matter.

Macrorie, Ken. 1964b. "The Objectivity-Subjectivity Trap." *Antioch Review* 24 (4): 479–88. http://dx.doi.org/10.2307/4610636.

Macrorie, Ken. 1965a. "An Immense Frivolity." Speech delivered at the Annual General Studies Staff Meeting, Kalamazoo, MI. In Ken Macrorie, Personnel File, Western Michigan University Archives and Regional History Collections, Kalamazoo. Record Group 22/8. Reprinted in *Western Michigan University Magazine* 24 (Winter): 4–8. Page references are to the speech manuscript.

Macrorie, Ken. 1965b. "What Freshman Communication Courses Left Behind." *California English Journal* 1 (1): 20–28.

Macrorie, Ken. 1966. "A Letter to One More Newly-Elected Committee Set up to Plan and Administer a Course in Freshman Composition." *College English* 27 (8): 629–30. http://dx.doi.org/10.2307/374703.

Macrorie, Ken. 1968. *Writing to Be Read.* New York: Hayden Book.

Macrorie, Ken. 1970. *Uptaught.* New York: Hayden Book.

Macrorie, Ken. 1974. *A Vulnerable Teacher.* Rochelle Park, NJ: Hayden Book.

Macrorie, Ken. (1970) 1976. *Telling Writing.* Rev. 2nd ed. Rochelle Park, NJ: Hayden Book.

Macrorie, Ken. 1980. *Searching Writing.* Rochelle Park, NJ: Hayden Book Company.

Macrorie, Ken. 1984. *Writing to Be Read.* Rev. 3rd ed. Portsmouth, NH: Boynton/Cook.

Macrorie, Ken. Biographical File. Michigan State University Archives and Historical Collections, East Lansing.

Macrorie, Ken. Personnel File. Western Michigan University Archives and Regional History Collections, Kalamazoo. Record Group 22/8.

Magnússon, Sigurður Gylfi, and István M. Szijártó. 2013. *What Is Microhistory? Theory and Practice.* New York: Routledge.

Mathieu, Paula. 2005. *Tactics of Hope: The Public Turn in English Composition.* Portsmouth, NH: Boynton/Cook.

Mortensen, Peter. 1998. "Going Public." *College Composition and Communication* 50 (2): 182–205. http://dx.doi.org/10.2307/358513.

Nelms, Gerald. 1996. "Macrorie, Ken." In *Encyclopedia of Rhetoric and Composition: Communication from Ancient Times to the Information Age*, edited by Theresa Enos, 420. New York: Garland.

Panel and Workshop Reports. 1958. "How Do We Form Attitudes Toward News Reporting?" *College Composition and Communication* 9 (3): 139–41. http://dx.doi.org/10.2307/354713.

Panel and Workshop Reports. 1959. "New Techniques in Teaching Composition Communication Courses." *College Composition and Communication* 10 (3): 137–9. http://dx.doi.org/10.2307/354351.

Rivers, Nathaniel A., and Ryan P. Weber. 2011. "Ecological, Pedagogical, Public Rhetoric." *College Composition and Communication* 63 (2): 187–218.

Rose, Shirley, and Irwin Weiser, eds. 2010. *Going Public: What Writing Programs Learn from Engagement.* Logan: Utah State University Press.

Ryder, Phyllis Mentzell. 2011. *Rhetorics for Community Action: Public Writing and Writing Publics.* Lanham, MD: Lexington Books.

Schroeder, Eric, and John Boe. 2004. "An Interview with Ken Macrorie: 'Arrangements for Truthtelling.'" *Writing on the Edge* 15 (1): 5–17.

Shamoon, Linda K., and Eileen Medeiros. 2010. "Not Politics as Usual: Public Writing as Writing for Engagement." In *Going Public: What Writing Programs Learn from Engagement*, edited by Shirley Rose and Irwin Weiser, 177–92. Logan: Utah State University Press.

Weisser, Christian R. 2002. *Moving beyond Academic Discourse: Composition Studies and the Public Sphere*. Carbondale: Southern Illinois University Press.

Wells, Susan. 1996. "Rogue Cops and Health Care: What Do We Want from Public Writing?" *College Composition and Communication* 47 (3): 325–41. http://dx.doi.org/10.2307/358292.

11
AGAINST THE RHETORIC AND COMPOSITION GRAIN
A Microhistorical View

Jacob Craig, Matthew Davis, Christine Martorana, Josh Mehler, Kendra Mitchell, Antony N. Ricks, Bret Zawilski, and Kathleen Blake Yancey

Like other disciplines, rhetoric and composition finds its origin stories located in competing grand narratives, most of them situated in a given philosophy or ideology. But as historians more generally are discovering (e.g., Martyn Lyons 2012), lived experience plays an underappreciated but equally significant role in any field's founding, and so too for rhetoric and composition. Accounts of such lived experience are provided in a set of interviews of leaders in the field—many of whom were participants in the field's founding—conducted by Florida State University graduate students: taken together, these interviews provide a rich corpus of source material for developing several microhistories of rhetoric and composition. Here, we draw on our interview with Charles Bazerman (2011), who in recounting his own experience pursuing a lifelong career in rhetoric and composition speaks explicitly to his relationship with, and resistance to, the normative academic structures of the time, among them the structures of literature in English departments; of rhetoric in the forming field of rhetoric and composition; of the early writing across the curriculum's "missionary" efforts to infuse writing studies' nascent knowledge about writing practices and knowledge into disciplinary sites of writing; and, in some interesting ways, of the emerging field, now discipline, of rhetoric and composition itself.

As the work of Giovanni Levi suggests, Bazerman navigated his way through a field he participated in founding through "constant negation, manipulation, choices, and decisions in the face of normative reality which, though pervasive, nevertheless offers many possibilities for personal interpretations and freedoms" (Levi 2001, 98–99). The continuing

DOI: 10.7330/9781607324058.c011

query for Bazerman (2011), as he explains throughout the interview, focuses on disciplinarity—not so much the disciplinarity of the field identified by some as an end (e.g., Hairston), nor the interdisciplinarity lauded by others (e.g., Bartholomae), but rather the role of disciplinarity in writing itself and the primary significance of research in its formation, both then and now.

Before beginning this analysis, however, it is helpful to highlight some working assumptions of microhistory and provide a rationale for Bazerman as our choice for a human lens into the history of rhetoric and composition. As other chapters in this volume attest, one value of a microhistorical approach is its doubled perspective, its emphasis on both the structures situating individuals and the individuals themselves as actors in the history. Thus, as Sigurður Gylfi Magnússon and István M. Szijártó explain, "Microhistory still seems the best means to point to the fact that structures—at a given moment those unalterable conditions that limit the historical actors' freedom of action—are to a large extent the product of individual decisions that point to the responsibility of the actor" (Magnússon and Szijártó 2013, 69). Moreover, as Magnússon and Szijártó point out, individuals do more than make decisions within or contributing to structures: "Structures of history are built, upheld and demolished by the actions of individuals" (75).

If microhistory is committed to locating the effects of both structures and individuals, a key question for us was, which individual's history might be employed for this purpose? As indicated, we have interviewed several leaders of writing studies contemporaneous with Bazerman—among them Lester Faigley, Amy Devitt, and Shirley Wilson Logan—and several of them, like Bazerman, speak to finding what we might call a *peripheral way into the field*, via linguistics for Devitt, for example, and African American history for Logan, which makes sense given that the field itself wasn't fully established when they began studying rhetoric and composition; and it is worth noting that these ancillary or peripheral areas of interest providing a way in continue to contribute to the field today. But in reviewing Bazerman's (2011) interview, we began to understand his specific history as involving more than finding a way in; rather, he was interested in changing the field both before it was fully established—Bazerman being interested in redirecting its course-in-process, as it were, to reflect better his own values and actions—and after. In this sense, we see Bazerman as an "exceptional normal," as defined by, Magnússon and Szijártó.

> How to choose then, the relevant and significant cases? The answer of the microhistorian to this theoretical challenge is the concept of the "exceptional normal" (eccezionalmente normale) or "normal exceptions."

According to this in preindustrial societies, breaking certain rules was in fact the norm. But it also means, and this is its more important meaning, that a really exceptional document, a marginal case can reveal a hidden reality, when the sources are silent about the lower social strata, or when they systematically distort their social reality (Ginzburg and Poni 1991: 7–8, cf. Ginzburg 1993: 21, Grendi 1996: 238). Hans Medick argues that the meaning of this opaque term, opposed to statistical representativity, has broadened to denote the capacity of deep and contextualizing analyses of individual cases to go beneath the surface and reveal what was possible and what was not (Medick 1994: 46). (Magnússon and Szijártó 2013, 19)

As an exceptional normal, Bazerman speaks eloquently to the structures, both formed and emerging, that he found inhospitable and that thus motivated him to seek other paths, other ways of being. Furthermore, his narrative works more generally to reveal how social structures of the time—in English departments, in the field, and in WAC programs—both have and have not prevailed.

Not least, however, microhistory also represents a way to make abstract narratives of general history more complex and to show what they occlude and thus make invisible. By analyzing the experiences of Bazerman in the spirit of Levi, we seek to add both crosscurrents and complexity to our understanding of composition's established historical narratives. As Levi observes, microhistory arises from a necessity to abandon "schematic and general interpretations in order to properly identify the real origins of forms of behavior, choice and solidarity" (Levi 2012, 123). Microhistory, for Levi, aims at reconstructing particular moments, events, and persons not simply as examples in the absence of any general explanations but instead "as physical correlatives to the complexity of the contexts within which men and women live and move" (125). That's not to say that grand narratives of history are rejected; rather, microhistory shows historical actors' complex experiences in the contexts of historical structures. For Magnússon and Szijártó, microhistory seeks to analyze how actors viewed their past as well as "meanings they attributed to the things that happened to them on one hand and on the other give explanations with references to historical structures, long-lived mentalities and global processes using a retrospective analysis, all of which were absent from the actors' own horizons of interpretation." This complexity can only be presented without oversimplifying it by focusing on "a very narrowly defined object" (Magnússon and Szijártó 2013, 75). What is also interesting here, however, is that while Bazerman necessarily speaks retrospectively in the interview, his memory is that at the time he is recalling, the late 1960s and early 1970s, he *was* aware of structures encouraging if not enforcing a given behavior and set of approaches, found those at odds with his own values and experiences, and so deliberately sought out other opportunities and pathways. In this sense, given an individual's awareness not only in retrospect but also *at the time*, our analysis provides more nuance and flexibility to Magnússon and Szijártó's theory; it suggests that individuals may understand the power of structures both during a given period of time and later on and also be motivated by them.

Our analysis is, however, principally interested in the history of rhetoric and composition: by making the experiences of Bazerman the narrowly defined object of our analysis, we aim to deepen our understanding of the uncertainty, inconsistency, and nonlinearity of one scholar's experience within the history of composition as well as to make more complex our understanding of composition's past. As Levi notes, microhistory highlights the inconsistencies of reality and the "necessary partiality" of our knowledge—and it is this acknowledgment that points to "the possibility of further discussion and other possible interpretations" (Levi 2012, 129). It is our hope that this microhistory of composition elicits such continuing discussion of composition's history.

In this context, we next provide background for the Bazerman interview, identifying the circumstances of the interview and outlining our interview process. Then, turning to Bazerman's account of the field in terms of his lived experience, we mark four themes emerging from the interview and important for Bazerman's formation as a scholar, his account of the field, and our own understanding of the field's origins.

THE BAZERMAN INTERVIEW

Since 2006, the rhetoric and composition program housed in the English department at Florida State University has played host to an ever-growing list of scholars from across the field. As part of the Visiting Speakers Series, the visiting scholar typically provides a talk to the department about his or her research, meets informally with graduate students and faculty, and participates in an interview conducted by a team of graduate students. These interviews provide a unique and valuable opportunity to explore the personal and professional practices of members of the field and of scholars working at the field's periphery in connected disciplines (such as social semiotics and education). Each interview is conducted by a team of two to six graduate students. The interview team and visiting scholar typically gather in the Rhet/Comp Suite in the Williams Building on FSU's campus or in the FSU Digital Studio, both spaces that provide an intimate setting for the interview, one that encourages an informal conversation with the visiting scholar and invites students and scholar to interact as mentees/mentor. In other words, the interviews are designed to provide an outlet through which experienced scholars within the field can offer guidance, advice, and reflections to individuals preparing to enter the same field.

A set of seven questions act as a heuristic structuring the interviews.

1. How did you get into the field?

2. Which scholars in the field have most influenced your thinking?

3. How about life experiences: how have they shaped your thinking?

4. What classes do you teach, which are your favorite, and why?

5. What's on your nightstand?

6. What do you think is the most important question that students in R/C should be considering today?

7. And where do you see the field of literacy studies/rhetoric and composition going?

Although these questions guide the general flow of the interviews, as with any conversation, there are often follow-up questions and comments combined with tangential stories and anecdotes that emerge as the interview progresses. Once the interview session is completed, we distribute the audio recordings among the interview participants who then set about transcribing the occasion, and in this case, we invited Charles Bazerman to review the interview; he has edited it for factual errors.

THEME ONE: A SOCIAL SELF FORMED THROUGH WRITING

In reviewing the transcript of Bazerman's interview (2011), we were struck by the parallel chronology of Bazerman and the field. Our first theme, then, begins where Bazerman did, as a graduate student and teacher in the late 1960s at the beginning of his shift from literature to writing, a shift motivated by the profound influence of three experiences—alienation from literature, teaching in an elementary school, and psychotherapy—through which Bazerman began to understand himself as a social self formed through writing. It's also worth noting that this shift occurred at a certain larger moment in the United States, what we might call its Zeitgeist. The early 1960s, a time then and now referred to as *Camelot*, had first been replaced by Lyndon Johnson's era of civil-rights legislation, then later by increasing escalation in Vietnam, by urban riots, and by antiwar demonstrations, all these setting the stage for a turn to the right. As Rick Perlstein explains, "In 1964, the Democratic presidential candidate Lyndon B. Johnson won practically the biggest landslide in American history, with 61.05 percent of the popular vote and 486 of 538 electoral college votes. In 1972, the Republican presidential candidate Richard M. Nixon won a strikingly similar landslide—60.67 percent and 520 electoral college votes. In the eight years in between, the lines that define our culture and politics were forged in blood and fire" (Perlstein 2008, xi). During this time, particularly in the context of the Vietnam War, the enthusiasm of the Camelot young had given way to cynicism, as suggested in Crosby, Stills, Nash, and Young's "Ohio" memorializing both the students murdered at Kent State University and the larger generation of college-aged students: "Tin soldiers and Nixon coming/We're finally on our own." And in the midst of this tectonic shift in national politics and identity, there was attention to college composition and, ironically, to the attention it was not receiving: "Too many college instructors, their graduate study devoted almost entirely to literature, have made no advanced study of composition, display little more than average competence in their own writing, and see their professional advancement associated with literary or linguistic scholarship. It is no wonder that study and research in the deeper aspects of composing have not traditionally received the sustained attention of our best minds" (Conference on College Composition and Communication 1968, 81).

Sociologically, the decade of the 1960s in the United States, for the country and the field, celebrated the individual, at least in contrast to the conformity of the 1950s. Students especially located their individuality in various causes, some serious and some less so, from civil rights and protests of the Vietnam War to the celebration of LSD's power to raise consciousness. This focus on the individual was echoed by the field, which located its early studies of writing process within the individual writer. Donald Murray (1982), for example, conceptualized writers even as their own first readers; likewise, our studies of writing process are memorable precisely because of their focus on individual writers like Sondra Perl's (1979) Tony. Charles Bazerman, who found himself working against this grain in conceptualizing the self, saw the self not as individual node apart but rather as a connected node on a highly structured and interactive network; moreover, he accounts in his oral interview for his developing sense of the self as culminating through three seemingly unrelated concurrent events: his "re-orientation" away from literature; his teaching in an elementary school; and his experience with psychotherapy. As Bazerman puts it, "That's probably the most important series of events, cluster of events that really re-oriented me and gave me direction." Together, these events exercised foundational influences on his view of writing as a human-affirming practice located in structured social systems, a view at odds with the more popular view of English and literature as hospitable sites for writing and of writing as an individual process. In other words, even before he entered the field of rhetoric and composition, Bazerman was an exceptional normal. In this sense, of course, in recounting his recollections, Bazerman isn't responding to the histories we read now since they didn't exist at the time; he is responding to what he perceived as the historical trajectories of the day. Other narratives of the time give emphasis to other themes— New Criticism for literature, for example, and a kind of nonconformist's conformity of the 1960s. But for Bazerman as an exceptional normal, what stand out are his reactions to what he saw as an overemphasis on individualism and an absence of methodology, reactions that became foundational for his way of seeing composition.

Bazerman's first step in this direction is what he calls a "re-orientation" pivoting him away from literature and toward literacy and writing in particular. Pursuing a graduate degree in literature in the late 1960s, Bazerman, by his own account a student with many interests, didn't view a prospective career in literature with enthusiasm: "In '67 and '68 I wasn't particularly happy with being a lit[erature] grad student; I was doing some Renaissance drama and poetry. I had tried a lot of undergraduate majors and had wound up doing literature, and although there were certain aspects of literature I liked, I wasn't happy with where it was leading me for a career." In fact, after a brief stint teaching in an elementary school, described below, Bazerman returned to complete his PhD in literature, not because of a passion for or commitment to literature but principally because he could not think of other viable options: "I went back and finished up Literature, because of my own limitations and lack of imagination of alternatives. I finished up very quickly, and when I got my first real job after that, it was to teach composition." This experience, however, contributed to Bazerman's relationship to literature and to English departments more generally. He cites Maxine Hairston, for example, in talking about how the field should define itself. When reflecting on how he planned his CCCC Chair's Address, he notes that he thought in terms of Hairston's (1985) admonition that the field "break" with literature: "I also had messages of, kind of a next step after Maxine Hairston, in her call to break from literary studies, is that we needed to keep on defining ourselves in our own lights and not by the lights of the field we happen to come out of."

Likewise, as opposed to many who claim their relationship to English departments with pride and see literature as sibling or parent to composition—David Bartholomae is perhaps the preeminent example—Bazerman sees literature as only one among many disciplines, and as important, one not defined, as most disciplines are, by its methods. Instead, literature is without methodological definition: "We [compositionists] come out of the US, out of literary studies and humanities that, in fact, almost consider themselves anti-methodological. And I have had the experience—and maybe you have—of asking literary scholars, so, what's our methodology? [And] they often say we don't have methodology. It's individual." In other words, Bazerman understands that compared to other disciplines, literature is methodologically anomalous; implied in his response is that Bazerman views this as a problem. As important, linking himself to Hairston—whose CCCC Chair's observation about literature colleagues' neglect of composition, "THEY'RE NOT LISTENING," still resonates—Bazerman casts literature institutionally as a site that, if we let it, will cast its shadow over and define composition. Put in terms of sponsorship, Bazerman rejects English departments as sponsors of composition, seeing composition instead as a self-sponsored field with multiple disciplinary relations. Not least, Bazerman rejects what he perceives as the individualism characterizing literary studies, in which a scholar's individually distinctive account of a text or its composer substitutes for a shared methodology that could locate and bring together a social field and its researchers, which is the kind of field Bazerman seeks.

Like others during this time, Bazerman sought a way to avoid fighting in Vietnam; in his case, between beginning and completing his doctorate, Bazerman began teaching elementary school, a second factor in his foundational cluster. He began this teaching opportunistically: "They took the graduate deferment away and the only way I could not go kill people was to—the last job they were going to give a deferment for was inner city teaching, which I did." He found himself teaching first and third grades in conditions that were "tough," a task for which he was neither prepared nor trained. Still, what struck him was twofold: how important the job was and how important literacy is. "Teaching literacy really seemed to transform lives, and you could see the effect of literacy or the effect on the child of not taking to literacy. The trajectories of these kids were taking shape, even by third grade. So, that teaching was the transformative event." Bazerman's use of the word *transformative* twice in this brief passage underscores how important this teaching was for him and how purposeful, how in contrast to his anemic interest in literature.

Interestingly and ironically, unlike others in our field for whom teaching composition is the centerpiece (a point made well in Joseph Harris's [1996] *A Teaching Subject*), Bazerman finds his interest in literacy less in teaching and more in the power and wonder of writing itself.

Finally, during this period, Bazerman engaged in psychotherapy, the final factor within this foundational cluster of lived experiences. The therapy, conducted by "somebody who was highly influenced by Sullivan," provided Bazerman with his "first introduction to that intellectual world. I came to reframe myself in a much more social sense, and to understand the power of social science and the pragmatist orientation." Someone with a self-labeled "very troubled family life," Bazerman found in therapy an intellectual home allowing him to bring separate elements—school and the rest of social life—together into a coherent philosophy, one keyed to structures and relationships. "I didn't have much of a social place and not much of a social support system, except for school . . . I didn't like my family—I liked school." School, as it turns out, provided a powerful framework for Bazerman—to see himself "in relations to others," to see how school provides a context and structure for human relationships, to see the relationship of practice to theory, and to see writing itself as social interaction.

> I liked school. Then I started to develop an understanding which gave me relations to others, and my place in them, which gave me also a way to sort of monitor my behavior and see who I was in social circumstances. This perspective gave me the practical consequences of theories, and then, that then also provided some of my orientation to writing, as I started to see writing as social interaction, and as creating identity and social positioning, writing as engaged within social systems rather than as the product of the individual. That all really came out of my psychotherapy.

School provided a context for living and understanding the social and relationships, while psychotherapy provided the space and intellectual material to articulate observations based on this experience, observations directly connected to what Bazerman recognizes as literacy's power in social settings: how it impacts the children and their lives—both present and future—in material ways. Bazerman, as an exceptional normal, remembers "start[ing] to see writing as social interaction," a very different way of conceptualizing writing, one almost canonical now but very much at odds with a then-current Murrayesque, Elbowian notion of the individual writer making meaning not so much with others but rather with the self and on the page. And here, too, we see a hint of another theme to come: Bazerman's interest in learning to write as an activity with a future, as a lifelong activity.

In sum, in this foundational moment, Bazerman's approach to life, writing, and research spun away from an understanding of the self as individual, one reified in literature study, and toward seeing the self in "relations"—engaging in composing as a social interaction and participating in society.

THEME TWO: TEACHING AT CUNY AND A NEW EXIGENCE

Although the United States, with the election in 1968 of Richard Nixon, had turned to the right, a new social experiment was taking place under the leadership of Mayor John Lindsay in New York City. More specifically, in 1970, the "giant City University of New York" became even bigger and more diverse as it moved to open admissions in the service of students whose discourses were very different than those faculty typically encountered: "With its 16 campuses and over-all enrollment of 190,000, [CUNY] last week became the first municipal institution to open its doors to all high school graduates in the most extensive urban test of open admission. It embraced a freshman class of 35,035, compared with 19,559 last year and 26,000 who would have entered this month in the normal pre-open enrollment course" (*New York Times*, September 20, 1970). Moreover, what was happening at CUNY was happening elsewhere as more community colleges opened their doors and as basic writing became a new college subject, all of which meant that teachers needed to find new ways to help students learn. "As college entrance requirements are being lowered or completely disregarded in favor of a neglected segment of our population, college teachers find that they cannot rely on traditional methods of teaching. In particular, freshman composition teachers cannot depend on the time-worn method: assign the reading material, discuss and analyze it, assign the composition, then hand back the composition with corrections" (Griffin 1969, 360). For many in composition, as for Bazerman, it was a watershed moment in higher education; these new students, attending college as composition's process movement began to take center stage in the profession, prompted considerable research-based pedagogical work, some of which occurred at CUNY. Based on her work with these new CUNY students, for example, Mina Shaughnessy began the theorizing about student language that would be published in her award-winning *Errors and Expectations* just as the new field of basic writing began forming. Also teaching basic writing at CUNY during this time, Charles Bazerman became convinced that what we needed was independent research on writing informed by a research agenda that doesn't necessarily attend to pedagogy; in conducting such research, he argued, we would become the experts of our own field. At the same time, again as an exceptional normal, what he labels an "outlier," Bazerman saw his passion for and definition of research composition as peripheral to the larger field, which focused on teaching—then and now.

According to Bazerman's account, he was one of several teaching at CUNY during this period, what he calls "the Mina Shaughnessy period": "There was a large group of people who were committed to writing, which became called Basic Writing." His interest in writing, however, was different than that of his colleagues; they, like teachers in the field nationally, focused on the incoming students and what they needed during that first year, while Bazerman attended to the larger social scene these students were entering and the kinds of writing they would do *after* FYC as they progressed into college and even after they left—as Bazerman put it, "writing all the way up": "To me it wasn't just the beginning points—Basic Writing kind of orients the students at the beginning points—But what does it take to succeed in higher education and beyond, into writing in the professional world, writing all the way up? That leads to another type of question. For many years I was an outlier, or at least I think of myself as an outlier because of the interest in the higher end of writing, writing outside the freshman classroom." Given this interest, this other "type of question," Bazerman began learning about that "higher ed of writing . . . outside the freshman classroom": "So I started to investigate what academic writing was. I didn't phrase it quite that same way, but what kind of writing would they need to do at the university? I started to collect information about writing in other disciplines. First, I started to think about what we now call intertextuality, that the writing was heavily in the context of their readings." This experience, teaching basic writing in a community of colleagues to diverse students at CUNY, provided a new purpose for Bazerman, one located in the idea that learning to write within a social context is a lifelong process, making writing not "knowable" in one classroom or in a single semester: instead, one needs to learn about writing elsewhere and everywhere.

Linked to this experience is another fundamental observation for Bazerman, that practitioners and researchers play important but different roles in advancing writing, that the field requires both, and that the field should support both—and ultimately, that teaching well is built on a foundation of research about writing. We need, he says, to take our research much more seriously. We view ourselves as practitioners. Even assuming we knew what writing was and kind of—let me find the right way to say this, it's not flowing so easily—but well there is this thing we kind of know what it is and we'll just teach people how to do it. Some people have a hard time getting it but not that we have a really—we also assume that to some degree we all know what it is to write. And that we have the sense of what the full competence is, whereas at the same time everyone still feels insecure about their writing. But we don't have the courage to go and find out what's the full extent and variety of writing, how complex it is. We are very much at the surface of understanding what writing is, so we have a responsibility to investigate it deeply.

The gaps in our knowledge about writing, echoing what Bazerman didn't know when he began teaching basic writing, motivate his view of what we need to do: although we "view ourselves as practitioners," and even though "we also assume that to some degree we all know what it is to write," we don't yet know "the full extent and variety of writing." To investigate writing more deeply is our responsibility, but one that also requires courage—to learn about writing elsewhere, to understand writing on a deeper, more encompassing level than is possible by remaining within the safety of the writing classroom.

This problem—that we haven't learned enough about writing—has been exacerbated, according to Bazerman, by the leading professional and scholarly organization in the field, the Conference on College Composition and Communication (CCCC, or Cs), the organization that he himself chaired in 2009. Bazerman "and other people have had . . . a kind of frustration with the C's . . . C's is very much a practice-based organization." Bazerman understands why: "Most of the people spend most of their time teaching in the class as I did for many years. And they don't have the time, the perspective, the reward system to pursue other lines of work. But, as a result of that, the convention has had a great weighting towards classroom presentations. And there has been no real venue to present hardcore research papers." Without the "hardcore research papers," we don't know what we need to know, a point Bazerman makes by referring to his experience teaching third grade: "So how can writing instruction in third grade and the goals of writing be the same as high school or higher ed? It just, it does not make sense. So we need a really fundamental research field to start to understand many, many things. And we can't do our work well if we don't understand these things."

Perhaps to help us understand that other fields have experienced the same issue, Bazerman points to medicine as a field analogous to writing studies in the ways both fields have developed.[1]

So in a way we are like clinical doctors. I am not here suggesting teaching of writing as repairing the wounded and curing pathology. Think of a health-oriented medical system. Here I am just talking about the knowledge needed to provide effective guidance. If you have doctors who are simply treating patients and have no pharmacological knowledge, no biological knowledge, no knowledge of people's lives and the relationship of nature and nurture, they won't be very good doctors, right? And that was the position of doctors up until the beginning of the 20th Century. Ok, that is the position we are mostly in. When I say we have a shallow view of the field, we see our students and we respond on a kind of surface level. Of course, there are better choices and worse choices to be made at that level. But until we get a much deeper understanding of what writing is, what writing development is, what it is that we want and they want to accomplish, how you go about doing those things, then our capacities will be very limited.

To meet this need, Bazerman suggests that a research group should be formed, but as important is that the researchers need to be in dialogue with practitioners. "I would say research—there needs to be some group, whether it's us—whoever that is—or some other group, who takes writing seriously as—who tries to understand writing. There is also a need of people who will teach it—or support the development of individuals and communities at various parts of their writing development." According to Bazerman, neither practice nor research can or should stand alone; it is to the benefit of the field if we engage the two in a reciprocal relationship, to its detriment if we do not. Teaching at CUNY, then, Bazerman saw students entering the university and wanted to know about writing beyond FYC and "all the way up"; in taking up this query, "collect[ing] information about writing in other disciplines," he sees the need to learn more about the practices we are fostering, and not surprisingly given his understanding of structures, also sees the need for a research group to organize this research.

THEME THREE: THE IDENTIFICATION OF AN ANTECEDENT AND INTELLECTUAL BACKGROUND

As the field formed, it looked for intellectual antecedents, most prominent among them rhetoric. The strongest claims about our intellectual heritage position rhetoric as the ur-discipline; for example, Robert Connors has argued that "we need at the beginning to understand that 'history of composition' is not a *sui generis* subfield of composition studies. Like composition studies itself, history of composition is a branch of the larger field of rhetorical studies, which has existed for over 2000 years" (Connors 1991, 50). Others like Jason Thompson and

Theresa Enos recall a deliberate linking of rhetoric and composition, again with rhetoric acting as frame and substance for the composition course: "In the heady revolutionary days of the 1970s and throughout most of the 1980s, rhetoric in its vigorous revival not only marched hand in hand with the process movement but also ensconced itself as the very core of the college writing course" (Thompson and Enos 2012, 162). And it is not surprising that many in the field remember it this way; after all, the flagship journal of the field, *College Composition and Communication*, offered as its third special issue the October 1965 issue "Further toward a New Rhetoric" following issues dedicated to composition as art and polemics, with articles like Francis Christensen's (1965) "A Generative Rhetoric of the Paragraph," which employs rhetoric as an inventional device for discourse, and Richard Hughes's (1965) "The Contemporaneity of Classical Rhetoric," which seeks to establish classical rhetoric as the heart of composition. Interestingly, at least some of this scholarship, like Edward Corbett's (1969) edited *Rhetorical Analyses of Literary Works* and Wayne Booth's (1961) *The Rhetoric of Fiction*, was keyed to literature rather than to writing, probably because the authors were situated in English departments and had literary backgrounds themselves. In sum, as Gerald Mulderig points out, "One can readily understand how . . . the 2,500-year history of rhetorical theory and practice seemed to promise an intellectual foundation upon which a new conception of writing instruction might be built" (Mulderig 1999, 164).

It is thus a truism that in the modern iteration of composition studies, the early scholars and teachers looked for intellectual antecedents and found them in Greece; ancient rhetoric provided a distinguished history for the field as well as intellectual materials for members of a field and for college writers (e.g., Corbett's [1971] *Classical Rhetoric for the Modern Student*) to think with. When Charles Bazerman looked for intellectual antecedents for the field, however, he rejected classical rhetoric in favor of figures like Adam Smith, whom we might think of as a rhetor working in the world; theorists like Lev Vygotsky, who is known for his emphasis on the relationship between social interactions, thought, and language; and American pragmatists such as John Dewey. Central to all of these figures is what we might call their *world relationship* and the way writing enacts their theories and structures our relationships.

In thinking about the role of classical rhetoric in providing a background and possible intellectual ballast for writing studies, Bazerman finds it too constrained by its own origins to be very helpful to *writers*: "I found a couple of concepts from classical rhetoric very useful, but classical rhetoric as a whole I found too constrained by the socio-historical circumstances in which it was created and the purpose it was created for. It wasn't created for literacy, for writing—it was created for high-stakes oral presentation within the social structure of Greece and Rome, and the replications of that, after that." At the same time, he is interested in what we might call *the rhetoric of*, that is, the ways we come to a set of questions, the structures we use, and the enactments writing makes possible: "In terms of sociologists, when I got interested in rhetoric of science I was directed to Robert Merton—who's like the founder of the sociology of science. . . . Merton was very influential, and I think you can see that in my work in that I try to understand how larger structures arise, and people orient towards larger structures in their writing, and how they orient to activity systems, for example." Moreover, Bazerman is interested in rhetoricians—or given their role in the world, what we might call *rhetors*—but as he concedes, they are not the ones we in the field typically reference.

> In terms of rhetoricians, I would say the ones that influenced me most deeply, and I've written on them, are Adam Smith and Joseph Priestly. They represent eighteenth century attempts to remake rhetoric. They're not even viewed as the major eighteenth century rhetoricians, but in my mind, I think they were much more interesting in what they were attempting to do than the ones that are more commonly cited. I think Adam Smith in particular was very, very deep . . . in his rhetoric. . . . What was he doing rhetorically in *The Wealth of Nations*—and you have to reconstruct how he came to conceive of language and the role of communication—it then becomes evident that the early work is interesting. It's interesting; it opens a couple of issues, and you can see him trying to cope with writing, and you can see him trying to cope with a more complex and more modern psychology and with social and political problems that were outside of the assumptions of Greek and Roman politics.

What interests Bazerman in Adam Smith is, in part, that he, much like Bazerman himself, is more learner than teacher: for example, Smith, as described by Bazerman, tries "to cope with writing," modeling for us the kind of "attempting" we also engage in today. What also interests Bazerman is that Smith is taking up the issues of his own time, "social and political problems . . . outside of the assumptions of Greek and Roman politics," which again speaks to his sense that to be valuable, writing and rhetoric must engage with the issues of the time in a framework also of the time.

Bazerman cites another set of intellectual antecedents as influential, these focused on cognition and the individual, especially "within the social situation."

> I also was very influenced by the Russian psychologists, Vygotsky, and all those that came after, in the way they understood cognition, and

cognitive development in relationship to, not just social situation, but the individual's activities within the social situation—and how they came to understand that. That, and also, the third pole of influence was American pragmatists: Dewey, George Herbert Mead, Harry Stack Sullivan—and actually he's not as often thought of in that group—but he clearly grew out of that group. He was a psychiatrist, but with a very social-biographical orientation towards how people come to learn to live in their world and solve problems about living in their world.

For Bazerman, theorists such as Vygotsky and Dewey highlight "how people come to learn to live in their world and solve problems about living in their world."

It is worth noting, of course, that Bazerman is not the only scholar of his time looking to Vygotsky and Dewey as intellectual forbears: in that sense, he is not alone in being an exceptional normal. But he is exceptional in the combination of (1) citing Vygotsky and (2) moving beyond literature and reifying the individual, as a quick comparison with the scholar Janet Emig demonstrates. Emig, author of the 1971 ground-breaking study of writing process, *The Composing Processes of 12th graders*, also looked beyond rhetoric to Vygotsky as a helpful theorist, but she did so, perhaps unintentionally, in the context of literature and the individual. Emig's (1971) case, in other words, is instructive in terms of how normalized and naturalized literature and the genius individual were as a default context at this time, even for someone intentionally looking to Vygotsky. As Steven Schreiner explains,

At the root of Emig's study is an author whose composing process has less to do with students' composing practices than with a notion of literary authorship based on a modernist aesthetic prevalent in an academy shaped by new critical methods. Valéry, Eliot, Yeats, Hardy, Rilke, and Woolf figure prominently in Emig's bibliography, which includes over ninety items on artistic composition by authors and their critics. Her conviction that the processes of established writers—principally poets—reveal how good writing works in general underlies her observations of the composing processes of twelfth graders. Stephen North has noted that, as a clinician, Emig used a case-study model to find traits in the individual that would hold true for the larger population: Just as her case-studies of eight students helped her construct a typical twelfth-grade writer, her investigation of literary authors helped her construct a model of good composing practices. In all fairness, Emig looked to literature because the most readily available data on the writing process came from discussions by and about literary authors, most notably in *The Paris Review Interviews*. But even though she dismisses such data as idiosyncratic, it clearly informs her idea of a model writer and writing process. Emig's case-study of well-trained subjects, and particularly of her chief subject, Lynn, paved the way for investigations of the writing process of diversely skilled and prepared students. But despite the liberating potential of Emig's work, it was never-theless modeled on a type of composition that required a privileged level of preparedness and instruction in English. (Schreiner 1997, 88)

In this sense, then, Bazerman, in moving beyond the trifecta of lit-erature, the individual, and rhetoric, is an exceptional normal of a most pronounced variety.

Nor does he identify with the "language people." In closing this sec-tion of the interview, Bazerman (2011) again refers to his antecedents as a way of explaining his own stance—"You'll notice none of them are lan-guage people"—again drawing attention to the idea that we have much to learn from disciplines not our own. For Bazerman, one of the main benefits of looking to theorists beyond our field is that they allow us to attend to the choices we make as writers and the social structures that result from and inform these choices: "I think you can see that in my work in that I try to understand how larger structures arise, and people orient towards larger structures in their writing, and how they orient to activity systems." Not least, he brings this point home by invoking the interview itself as such a structured situation: "You're treating me very nicely here and with a lot of respect as a senior professor, that makes this an event between senior professor and graduate students. We're making it that way. If we'd come with a different orientation to each other—with beers, right, and there was a television screen up here and we were watching the game, it would be a different event and our set of relations would be different and the social structures that would be engaged would be different. That's structurational."

THEME FOUR: THE FUNCTION AND FORM OF WAC
Several master narratives account for the beginning of the WAC move-ment, with at least three schools contending for the honor of originating WAC—Carleton College, Beaver College, and Michigan Technological University. Central to the narrative for all the WAC pioneers is the lead-ing role of English faculty: helping their (benighted) colleagues learn how to teach writing in their classes, typically through writing-to-learn activities like journaling. Barbara Walvoord, for example, identifying WAC as a kind of movement, claims that "like any movement, [it] was influenced by societal factors. It may be seen in part as a move by writing faculty to extend their power and influence, helped by wide-spread per-ception that student writing was inadequate" (Walvoord 1996, 61). Chris Anson takes this argument even further: "So important [for WAC lead-ers] was the need to sell the idea that writing is . . . 'a powerful tool for

learning,' and so focused was the call to support it in all subject areas, that proponents theorized little about possible differences in emphasis, programmatic orientation, or intellectual activity in diverse settings" (Anson 2006, 101). Because of several motivations—chief among them an interest in being helpful—faculty in composition studies working in WAC did not attend to the differences across diverse writing contexts. And in the case of Carleton College specifically, we see the continuation of an earlier theme. At Carleton, there was neither sufficient faculty in English nor sufficient interest on the part of faculty in working with WAC colleagues, so another approach was implemented, but it too was grounded in classical rhetoric: put simply, the administration brought together faculty from across the curriculum to read in rhetoric. In this small institutional narrative, we're reminded again of the identity of rhetoric as the intellectual foundation for writing efforts led by English and writing faculty—here, even outside of English departments as well.

In contrast to this rhetoric/composition-dominated approach to WAC, Charles Bazerman saw the emergence of writing across the curriculum as exigence: not to teach others about how to write based on his expertise as a compositionist but rather to *learn*, in this case about writing across the curriculum in its multiple contexts and disciplines so as to develop expertise in writing defined capaciously. As he noted, "The WAC [writing across the curriculum] movement sort of started . . . —and my first reaction is that we're trying to go across the curriculum but we don't know what kind of writing they do. We need to go out and find out."

When Bazerman taught elementary school, he was impressed by the dramatic change just two years, here between first and third grades, makes in our development as writers; when he taught at CUNY, he looked to the places his students would write in the future as both locus of activity and site of research. Bazerman's response to early WAC approaches, consistent with this trajectory, was that we needed to learn *before* we could share, much less lead. He understood that "first generation WAC was sort of the exporting process models and journaling across the curriculum," but, he said, "I had this different view—that we needed to go out and actually find out what was out there and what the needs were." For Bazerman, the origin narrative of WAC is a reversal of the one typically circulated; rather than a narrative that presents composition instructors as experts reaching out to share their invaluable expertise, writing faculty, in Bazerman's account, should research the multiple practices of writing located in WAC.

In fact, Bazerman's teaching at CUNY motivated his interest in WAC, which provided a starting point for his research into sites of writing other than FYC. He saw that to help students succeed as college writers, he had to "get [them] interested in writing" because "this is what I could get them interested in writing for": "I understood that the reason why students were required to take our courses was so they could succeed at the university, and it wasn't any of the other wonderful uses of writing that was important, or the other aspects—to help the students succeed in the university was why we were being paid. So, if I could get students interested in writing, this is what I could get them interested in writing for. So I started to investigate what academic writing was." Bazerman's exploration began with the role of reading in writing. Driven by two questions—"How do you write after you've read something? How do you write after you've read *two* things?"—this research led to *The Informed Writer*, a textbook helping students write their own research. In addition, that research led to "follow-up research on the history of the scientific paper. How did it get that way? And how did it work within the society of scientists?" This, in a nutshell, is "how [his] trajectory started."

When Bazerman was teaching at CUNY and writing *The Informed Writer*, some few compositionists were also tapping the insights of other disciplines in our explorations into composing processes; perhaps the most celebrated researchers, Linda Flower from composition and John Hayes from cognitive psychology, modeled for Bazerman what was possible, a kind of interdisciplinary approach to the disciplinary questions of writing. But that approach was subjected to considerable critique (e.g., Bizzell 1982), and by the time Bazerman began to publish on his research into scientific writing, such interdisciplinary efforts were fading: "There were engagements with certain branches of psychology around Flower and Hayes but that vanished. We were phobic about that. I think there were real limits with the way they were approaching it. But there is something beyond that response, that critique—there was a real phobic reaction against that." Bazerman didn't lose his enthusiasm for the role of interdisciplinary research into writing, however. He noted, for example, that psychology wasn't the only discipline that could inform writing: what Bazerman saw, instead, was that each discipline would have something to contribute to what ultimately is an uber study of writing limited only to "writing's role in society, and the forms that writing took": "I was saying well, it's good we have psychology, we also need a sociology. Also, writing—from sociology then I got to a history, which is different from the history of writing instruction, or the history of rhetorics. There's the history of writing practices, and the emergence of writing practices, and writing's role in society, and the forms that writing took." Today, of course, some of the leading WAC programs in the country do exactly what he advocated, and they do so programmatically, working with faculty to articulate how writing works, specifically in terms of the kinds of problems a discipline poses, the kinds of evidence that count, and the genres in which they are shared (Flash, forthcoming). In this example, if twenty-five years later, we see Bazerman's approach and the field's beginning to align.

CONCLUSION

More generally, in this interview with Charles Bazerman and thus through the eyes of what we have identified as an exceptional normal, we see a different kind of founding narrative of rhetoric and composition take shape. A founding narrative suggests that people come together and agree upon goals/aims/purposes they then seek to achieve. In the case of rhetoric and composition, two founding narratives have held center stage: (1) a devotion to teaching, and the teaching of first-year composition especially (e.g., Harris 1996); and (2) a grounding of composition in rhetoric (e.g., Berlin 1987). As the discussion above demonstrates, however, through this interview with Charles Bazerman we see a different founding narrative of rhetoric and composition emerge, one testifying to a richer history of the discipline than has previously been acknowledged. This microhistory—highlighting Bazerman's attention to writing as a researchable disciplinary social practice—shows us how other factors played a role in the founding of the field, in his case beginning with teaching elementary school, shifting out of literature as focus of study and default context, and undergoing psychotherapy. Likewise, in these threefold processes, he became committed to a notion of the self that is social, that is supported and constrained by activities and structures; this construct of the self then systematically informs his research activity, an activity Bazerman understands as central to the discipline.

As a researcher, Bazerman reverses the commonplace dynamic of the field: rather than focusing on teaching students, Bazerman focuses on teachers learning. In addition, beginning to conduct research in the 1980s, he focused on what this moment in history—given the field's interest *in* writing but our little knowledge *about* writing—can mean: he sees a different future than his contemporaries, one untethered from the classroom, one oriented to a writing that is lifewide and life-long.[2] Likewise, he rejects the conventional intellectual rhetorical heritage so valued by early scholars in the field (and of course still valued), finding other intellectual antecedents whose approach to writing in the world and cognition seem to him more congruent with his definition of writing and his aspirations for the discipline. So too his interest in disciplines that have their own writing practices and knowledge: in learning from them, Bazerman claims, we contribute to a writing studies unbound from rhetoric. Not least, he sees the field's need for an organized research effort; even now, he says, current influential structures like the CCCC annual conference privilege practice at the cost of theory. He thus argues for a writing studies organization that will focus on research, and it is likely no coincidence that he is the founder of the Writing Research across Borders conferences and the related International Society for the Advancement of Writing Research. Bazerman's interdisciplinary approach to writing, then, differed considerably from the more common approach in the field, which was to see writing as a rhetorically influenced individual activity anchored in FYC and more field than discipline. Interested in a writing that goes "all the way up," Bazerman sees interdisciplinary research as a critical means of developing writing studies as its own discipline.

At the same time, this narrative we have woven could be seen as seamless as the one Bazerman disrupts, but within it are both seams and incongruities. Put more specifically, Bazerman is at odds with the field in some ways, as we see in his interest in the social, in systems, and in structures, and in his founding of an international forum focused on writing research. Even as Bazerman chronicles this microhistory, however, he points to what we might think of as overlaps within narratives, points of important intersections. In recounting his resistance to English departmental institutional sponsorship of composition, for example, Bazerman makes it clear that he is not alone in his view: Bazerman cites Hairston's (1985) similar aversion to such sponsorship, and it's worth noting that Hairston, as Chair of the CCCC in the early 1980s, wasn't an outlier. Likewise, Bazerman points to Mina Shaughnessy as perhaps inadvertently providing a "license" for the work he wanted to undertake: "In some ways, just because of her influence in sponsorship, Mina Shaughnessy was important, and in taking student writing seriously—I think there were one or two sentences she made in passing in *Errors and Expectations* which I saw as providing a kind of license for what I was doing, even though I was going in a different direction." These overlaps, of course, attest to ways narratives intersect and speak to each other as well as to the complexity of the field's founding.

As Bazerman himself says, he "was an outlier," and in very specific ways. But as this volume demonstrates, none of our master narratives is seamless; and microhistories, like this one located in an interview, help us see how variegated the experience of any field's founding necessarily is.

Including ours.

Notes

1.   It is worth noting that in this comparison, Bazerman is arguing as well that medicine and composition are serving different but equally significant human needs.
2.   The expression *lifewide and lifelong* is frequently applied to electronic portfolios, but here it seems an apt descriptor for Bazerman's approach.

References

Anson, Chris. 2006. "Assessing Writing in Cross-curricular Programs: Determining the Locus of Activity." *Assessing Writing* 11 (2): 100–12. http://dx.doi.org/10.1016/j.asw .2006.07.001.

Bazerman, Charles. 2011. Florida State University Rhetoric and Composition Speakers' Series Interview, February 11.

Berlin, James. 1987. *Rhetoric and Reality: Writing Instruction in American Colleges, 1900–1985*. Carbondale: Southern Illinois University Press.

Bizzell, Patricia. 1982. "Cognition, Convention, and Certainty: What We Need to Know About Writing." *Pre/Text* 3 (3): 213–43.

Booth, Wayne. 1961. *The Rhetoric of Fiction*. Chicago, IL: University of Chicago Press.

Christensen, Francis. 1965. "A Generative Rhetoric of the Paragraph." *College Composition and Communication* 16 (3): 144–56. http://dx.doi.org/10.2307/355728.

Conference on College Composition and Communication. 1968. "The Status of Freshman Composition." *College Composition and Communication* 19 (1): 81. http:// dx.doi.org/10.2307/355252.

Connors, Robert. 1991. "Writing the History of our Discipline." In *Introduction to Composition Studies*, edited by Gary Tate and Erika Lindemann, 49–71. New York: Oxford University Press.

Corbett, Edward P. J., ed. 1969. *Rhetorical Analyses of Literary Works*. New York: Oxford University Press.

Corbett, Edward P. J., ed. 1971. *Classical Rhetoric for the Modern Student*. London: Oxford University Press.

Emig, Janet. 1971. *The Composing Processes of 12th Graders*. Urbana, IL: NCTE.

Flash, Pamela. Forthcoming. "From Apprised to Revised: Faculty in the Disciplines Change What They Never Knew They Knew." In *A Rhetoric of Reflection*, edited by Kathleen Blake Yancey. Logan: Utah State University Press.

Griffin, Jacqueline. 1969. "Remedial Composition at an Open-Door College." *College Composition and Communication* 20 (5): 360–63. http://dx.doi.org/10.2307/355042.

Hairston, Maxine. 1985. "Breaking Our Bonds and Reaffirming Our Connections." *College Composition and Communication* 36 (3): 272–82. http://dx.doi.org/10.2307 /357971.

Harris, Joseph. 1996. *A Teaching Subject: Composition since 1966*. New York: Prentice Hall.

Hughes, Richard. 1965. "The Contemporaneity of Classical Rhetoric." *College Composition and Communication* 16 (3): 157–59. http://dx.doi.org/10.2307/355729.

Levi, Giovanni. 2001. "On Microhistory." In *New Perspectives on Historical Writing*, 2nd ed. Edited by Peter Burke, 97–119. University Park: Pennsylvania State University Press.

Levi, Giovanni. 2012. "Microhistory and the Recovery of Complexity." In *Historical Knowledge: In Quest of Theory, Method, and Evidence*, edited by Susanna Fellman and Marjatta Rahikainen, 121–32. London: Cambridge Scholars.

Lyons, Martyn. 2012. *The Writing Culture of Ordinary People in Europe*. Cambridge: Cambridge University Press. http://dx.doi.org/10.1017/CBO9781139093538.

Magnússon, Sigurður Gylfi, and István M. Szijártó. 2013. *What Is Microhistory? Theory and Practice*. London: Routledge.

Mulderig, Gerald. 1999. "Is There Still a Place for Rhetorical History in Composition Studies?" In *History, Reflection, and Narrative: The Professionalization of Composition, 1963–1983*, edited by Mary Rosner, Beth Boehm, and Debra Journet, 163–77. Stanford: Ablex.

Murray, Donald. 1982. "Teaching the Other Self: The Writer's First Reader." *College Composition and Communication* 33 (2): 140–47. http://dx.doi.org/10.2307/357621.

Perl, Sondra. 1979. "The Composing Processes of Unskilled College Writers." *Research in the Teaching of English* 13 (4): 317–36.

Perlstein, Rich. 2008. *Nixonland*. New York: Scribner.

Schreiner, Steven. 1997. "A Portrait of the Student as a Young Writer: Re-evaluating Emig and the Process Movement." *College Composition and Communication* 48 (1): 86–104. http://dx.doi.org/10.2307/358772.

Thompson, Jason, and Theresa Enos. 2012. "The Rhetoric of Obfuscation and Technologies of Hidden Writing: Poets and Palimpsests, Painters and Purposes." In *On the Blunt Edge: Technology in Composition's History and Pedagogy*, edited by Shane Borrowman, 152–73. Anderson, SC: Parlor.

Walvoord, Barbara. 1996. "The Future of WAC." *College English* 58 (1): 58–79. http://dx.doi.org/10.2307/378534.

ABOUT THE AUTHORS

BRUCE McCOMISKEY is a professor of rhetoric and composition and director of professional writing in the English department at the University of Alabama at Birmingham. He is the author of *Dialectical Rhetoric, Gorgias and the New Sophistic Rhetoric,* and *Teaching Composition as a Social Process.* He is also the editor of *English Studies: An Introduction to the Discipline(s)* and the coeditor of *City Comp: Identities, Spaces, Practices.* His most recent work applies rhetorical methodologies to the Dead Sea Scrolls.

* * *

CHERYL E. BALL is an associate professor of digital publishing studies at West Virginia University and editor of *Kairos: A Journal of Rhetoric, Technology, and Pedagogy.* She teaches classes in editing, multimedia authoring, and digital publishing. Ball has published numerous articles and webtexts on multimodal composition and digital publishing and several books, including *The New Work of Composing* (coedited with Debra Journet and Ryan Trauman); *RAW: Reading and Writing New Media* (coedited with Jim Kalmbach); and *Writer/ Designer: A Guide to Making Multimodal Projects* (coauthored with Kristin Arola and Jenny Sheppard). She is co-PI on a $1 million Andrew W. Mellon Foundation grant to build an open-access, multimedia, academic publishing platform, Vega.

SUZANNE BORDELON is a professor in the Department of Rhetoric and Writing Studies at San Diego State University. Her research interests include women's rhetorical practices and pedagogies, rhetorical education, archival studies and historiography, and literacy studies. She is the author of *A Feminist Legacy: The Rhetoric and Pedagogy of Gertrude Buck.* In addition, her writing has appeared in *Advances in the History of Rhetoric, College Composition and Communication, Rhetoric Society Quarterly, Rhetoric Review, JAC: A Journal of Rhetoric, Culture & Politics,* the *Journal of Teaching Writing,* and *Nineteenth-Century Prose.*

JACOB CRAIG is a doctoral candidate in rhetoric and composition at Florida State University. His research investigates the relationships between composing practices, writing technologies, and material spaces with special attention to the formation of composing practices over time. He has taught courses in FSU's Editing, Writing, and Media program and has served as the coordinator for the English department's computer writing classrooms.

MATTHEW DAVIS is an assistant professor of English at the University of Massachusetts Boston, where he teaches graduate and undergraduate courses in literacy, composition, and new media. He also directs the professional writing and freshman composition tutoring programs. His research interests include literacy studies, multimodal studies, and writing pedagogy. His work has appeared in *enculturation* and *Computers and Composition* and in the *South Atlantic Review.* He also has book chapters in *Teaching with Student Texts* and *Undergraduate Writing Majors: Eighteen Program Profiles.*

DOUGLAS EYMAN teaches courses in digital rhetoric and professional writing at George Mason University. Eyman is the senior editor of *Kairos: A Journal of Rhetoric, Technology, and Pedagogy,* an online journal that has been publishing peer-reviewed scholarship on computers and writing since 1996. In addition to *Digital Rhetoric: Theory, Method, Practice,* his scholarly work has appeared in *enculturation, Computers and Composition,* and the *South Atlantic Review.* His current research interests include digital rhetoric, new media scholarship, electronic publication, information design, teaching in digital environments, and massive multiplayer online role-playing games as sites for digital rhetoric research.

BRIAN GOGAN is an assistant professor in the Department of English at Western Michigan University. He teaches courses in public and professional writing as well as in rhetorical theory and criticism for the rhetoric and writing studies program. In 2014, the positive impact his work in the classroom has on local publics was recognized with the Timothy Ryan Hurttgam Memorial Faculty Award. He studies writing pedagogy, Baudrillardian rhetoric, and rhetorics of altruism, reciprocity, and exchange. His writing has appeared in *Across the Disciplines*, *Rhetoric Review*, and *College Composition and Communication*.

DAVID GOLD, associate professor of English at the University of Michigan, is the author of *Rhetoric at the Margins: Revising the History of Writing Instruction in American Colleges, 1873–1947*, winner of the 2010 CCCC Outstanding Book Award; and coauthor of *Educating the New Southern Woman: Speech, Writing, and Race at the Public Women's Colleges, 1884–1945* with Catherine Hobbs, with whom he collaborated on the edited collection *Rhetoric, History, and Women's Oratorical Education: American Women Learn to Speak*. He is currently studying women's participation in the elocution movement and the rhetoric of bobbed hair in 1920s America.

NEAL LERNER is an associate professor of English and writing program director at Northeastern University in Boston, Massachusetts. He is the author of *The Idea of a Writing Laboratory*, which won the 2011 NCTE David H. Russell Award for Distinguished Research in the Teaching of English; coauthor of *Learning to Communicate as a Scientist and Engineer: Case Studies from MIT*; winner of the 2012 CCCC Advancement of Knowledge Award; and coauthor of *The Longman Guide to Peer Tutoring*. He writes about the history, theory, administration, and practice of teaching writing in classrooms, laboratories, and writing centers.

CHRISTINE MARTORANA is an assistant professor at the College of Staten Island, CUNY. Her research centers upon the intersections among feminist activism, feminist agency, and composition. Specifically, her research explores the potential reciprocity between public, nonacademic acts of composing and those acts that occur within the writing classroom. Christine grew up near Dayton, Ohio, and received a master's degree from the University of Dayton.

JOSH MEHLER is a lecturer in the writing program at the University of California, Santa Barbara and an assistant editor for *Kairos: Rhetoric, Technology, and Pedagogy*. He teaches classes in writing, rhetoric, and multimodal composition. His current research explores how portable technologies have historically played a formative role in the development of everyday writing communities. He received his PhD from Florida State University's rhetoric and composition program.

ANNIE S. MENDENHALL is an assistant professor of English at Armstrong State University in Savannah, Georgia, where she teaches courses in writing, rhetoric, and composition theory. She received her PhD from Ohio State University in rhetoric, composition, and literacy studies. Her research interests include institutional histories of rhetoric and composition, archival research methods, disciplinary identity, and composition pedagogy. Her scholarship has appeared in *College English* and *Composition Studies*. She is currently working on a local history of desegregation at two state universities, exploring the impact of that history on institutional rhetorics, disciplinary identity, and the development of writing programs.

KENDRA MITCHELL is a Fulbright Fellow in South Africa. A Kingsbury Award recipient, Mitchell has interests in race, literacy, and historically black universities, as evident in her chapter "Reconstructing Reconstruction: A Sociohistorical Perspective on a Digital

Curriculum Initiative within a Southern Historically Black College or University (HBCU)" and her dissertation, *Language in the Center: A Case Study of Multilingualism in a Historically Black University*, which describes the tutor-tutee language interaction within an ethnic-specific writing center. She also serves as the board president for the local community literacy organization.

LOUISE WETHERBEE PHELPS is Emeritus Professor of Writing and Rhetoric at Syracuse University and, currently, adjunct professor of rhetoric and writing at Old Dominion University, where she teaches in the English department's interdisciplinary PhD program. Phelps has published *Composition as a Human Science*, two coedited volumes, and more than fifty-five essays on rhetoric, composition, and writing studies. She has been studying writing studies in Canada since visiting the University of Winnipeg as a Fulbright Specialist scholar and consultant in 2011. Her latest project is a coauthored book with Canadian and American colleagues on cross-border interdependencies in Canadian writing studies.

ANTONY N. RICKS is an assistant professor of English at Alabama Agricultural and Mechanical University, where he works with the composition program and teaches courses in composition and literature. His professional research interests include composition pedagogies, writing center theory and practice, and writing program administration.

KELLY RITTER is a professor of English and director of undergraduate rhetoric at the University of Illinois at Urbana-Champaign. Her work investigates the history of basic writing at elite institutions (*Before Shaughnessy: Basic Writing at Yale and Harvard, 1920–1960*), writing instruction at a public woman's college (*To Know Her Own History: Writing at the Woman's College, 1943–1963*), and midcentury lay-reader programs ("'Ladies Who Don't Know Us Correct Our Papers': Postwar Lay Reader Programs and Twenty-First Century Contingent Labor in First-Year Writing"). Her most recent book, *Sometimes We Expect Great Things: Postwar Instructional Film and the Legacy of Class-Conscious Mass Literacies*, is forthcoming from the University of Pittsburgh press. Ritter is the current editor of *College English*.

DAVID STOCK is an assistant professor of English and coordinator of the writing center at Brigham Young University. He earned his PhD in composition and rhetoric from the University of Wisconsin-Madison. His research interests include histories and pedagogies of rhetorical education, writing studies, and writing centers. His work has appeared in *Rhetoric Society Quarterly, Praxis: A Writing Center Journal, WPA: Writing Program Administration*, and other venues. At BYU, David cofounded and co-coordinates the research and writing center, a collaborative service where undergraduate research consultants and writing tutors work side by side to provide students with research and writing assistance.

KATHLEEN BLAKE YANCEY is Kellogg W. Hunt Professor of English and Distinguished Research Professor at Florida State University. A (past) president of CCCC, NCTE, CWPA, and SAMLA, she cofounded and coedited *Assessing Writing* for seven years; she was the editor of *College Composition and Communication* from 2010 to 2014. Author of over ninety articles and book chapters, she has authored, coauthored, edited, or coedited twelve books—including *Delivering College Composition: The Fifth Canon* and *Writing across Contexts: Composition, Transfer, and Sites of Writing*. She is the recipient of several awards, including the FSU Graduate Mentor Award, the CWPA Best Book Award, and the CCCC Research Impact Award.

BRET ZAWILSKI is an assistant professor at Appalachian State University. He served at Florida State University as a teaching assistant in the Editing, Writing, and Media program, assistant director of the FSU Digital Studio, and coordinator for the English department's computer writing classrooms. Currently he is also serving as an assistant editor for *Kairos: A Journal of Rhetoric, Technology, and Pedagogy*. His main academic interests revolve around new media composition, multimodality, and the role of material awareness in knowledge transfer. Outside the academy, he dabbles in writing science fiction, sketching, and playing the saxophone.

JAMES T. ZEBROSKI is the senior composition faculty person at the University of Houston. The focus of his scholarship over the last thirty-five years has been critical theory and writing. This work has centered on unauthorized writing. In nearly fifty published essays, he has widely explored a variety of related topics including Vygotsky, social class, histories of rhetoric and composition, ethnographic writing, and post-Stonewall gay literature. His book, *Thinking Through Theory: Vygotskian Perspectives on the Teaching of Writing*, published in 1994, is still in print. It is the first and only book-length treatment of the work of Lev Vygotsky in rhetoric and composition.

INDEX